TEACHER RESOURCE BOOK

Ready® Common Core

1 Reading INSTRUCTION

Teacher Resource Book

Advisors

Crystal Bailey, Math Impact Teacher, Eastern Guilford Middle School, Guilford County Schools, Gibsonville, NC

Leslie Blauman, Classroom Teacher, Cherry Hills Village Elementary, Cherry Creek School District, Cherry Hills Village, CO

Max Brand, Reading Specialist, Indian Run Elementary, Dublin City School District, Dublin, OH

Kathy Briguet, Retired Curriculum Coordinator for K–12 Literacy, Forest Lake Area Schools, Forest Lake, MN; Adjunct Instructor, Reading Instruction in the Elementary Grades, University of Minnesota, Minneapolis, MN

Helen Comba, Supervisor of Basic Skills & Language Arts, School District of the Chathams, Chatham, NJ

Cindy Dean, Classroom Teacher, Mt. Diablo Unified School District, Concord, CA

Randall E. Groth, Ph.D., Associate Professor of Mathematics Education, Salisbury University, Salisbury, MD

Jennifer Geaber, Kingston Hill Academy Charter School, South Kingstown, RI

Bill Laraway, Classroom Teacher, Silver Oak Elementary, Evergreen School District, San Jose, CA

Susie Legg, Elementary Curriculum Coordinator, Kansas City Public Schools, Kansas City, KS

Sarah Levine, Classroom Teacher, Springhurst Elementary School, Dobbs Ferry School District, Dobbs Ferry, NY

Nicole Peirce, Classroom Teacher, Eleanor Roosevelt Elementary, Pennsbury School District, Morrisville, PA

Donna Phillips, Classroom Teacher, Farmington R-7 School District, Farmington, MO

Kari Ross, Reading Specialist, MN

Sunita Sangari, Math Coach, PS/MS 29, New York City Public Schools, New York, NY

Shannon Tsuruda, Classroom Teacher, Mt. Diablo Unified School District, Concord, CA

Mark Hoover Thames, Research Scientist, University of Michigan, Ann Arbor, MI

Acknowledgments

Project Managers: Claudia Herman & Maura Wolk
Cover Designer & Illustrator: Julia Bourque
Book Designer: Mark Nodland
Executive Editor: Sarah Moore
Director–Product Development: Daniel J. Smith
Vice President–Product Development: Adam Berkin

ISBN 978-0-7609-8717-9

North Billerica, MA 01862

30 29 28 27 26 25 24 23 22 21

BTS19

Table of Contents

Ready® Common Core Program Overview A6

Supporting the Implementation of the Common Core A7

Answering the Demands of the Common Core with *Ready* A8
The Importance of Complex Read Aloud Text A9
Close-Up on Close Reading A10
Trade Books and Projectables in *Ready* A11

Using *Ready Common Core* A12

Teaching with *Ready Common Core* A14
Connecting with the *Ready* Teacher Toolbox A16
Using *i-Ready® Diagnostic* with *Ready Common Core* A18
Features of *Ready Common Core* A20
Supporting Research A34

Correlation Charts

Common Core State Standards Coverage by *Ready* A38

Lesson Plans (with Answers)

Unit 1: Key Ideas and Details in Literature 1

Read Aloud Lesson A: *The Empty Pot* 3
CCSS Focus - RL.1.2 *Additional Standards - RL.1.1, 3; RF.1.1a, 2a; W.1.3; SL.1.1, 2, 4, 5; L.1.1e, 5c, d*

Read Aloud Lesson B: *The Polar Bear Son: An Inuit Tale* 9
CCSS Focus - RL.1.2 *Additional Standards - RL.1.1, 3, 7; RF.1.2b, c; W.1.7; SL.1.1, 2, 4, 5; L.1.1g, 5c*

Lesson 1: Asking Questions 15
CCSS Focus - RL.1.1 *Additional Standards - RL.1.2, 7; SL.1.1, 2, 4; L.1.1, 2*

Read Aloud Lesson C: *My Rotten Redheaded Older Brother* 21
CCSS Focus - RL.1.2 *Additional Standards - RL.1.1, 3, 7; RF.1.2d, 3a; W.1.8; SL.1.1a, b, 2, 4, 5, 6; L.1f, j, 2a, b, 4a, b, 5a, c*

Lesson 2: Describing Characters 27
CCSS Focus - RL.1.3 *Additional Standards - RL.1.1, 2, 7; SL.1.1, 3, 4; L.1.1, 2*

Read Aloud Lesson D: *Mice and Beans* 33
CCSS Focus - RL.1.2 *Additional Standards - RL.1.1, 3, 7; RF.1.3b, c; W.1.1; SL.1.1, 2, 4, 5, 6; L.1.1f, j, 4a, 5c*

Lesson 3: Describing Setting 39
CCSS Focus - RL.1.3 *Additional Standards - RL.1.1, 2, 7; SL.1.1, 4; L.1.1, 2*

Lesson 4: Describing Events 45
CCSS Focus - RL.1.3 *Additional Standards - RL.1.1, 2, 7; SL.1.1, 2, 4; L.1.1, 2*

Lesson 5: Central Message 51
CCSS Focus - RL.1.2 *Additional Standards - RL.1.1, 2, 3; SL.1.1, 2, 4; L.1.1, 2*

Unit 1 Check 57

Unit 2: Key Ideas and Details in Informational Text 59

Read Aloud Lesson E: *Who Eats What? Food Chains and Food Webs* 61
CCSS Focus - RI.1.2 Additional Standards - RI.1.1, 3, 7; RF.1.3d, e; W.1.8; SL.1.1, 2, 3, 4, 5; L.1.1, 2a, b, 4a, 5c

Read Aloud Lesson F: *Nic Bishop: Butterflies and Moths* 67
CCSS Focus - RI.1.2 Additional Standards - RI.1.1, 3; RF.1.2b, 3a; W.1.2; SL.1.1, 2, 4, 5; L.1.1f, 2, 4a, 5b, c

Lesson 6: Asking Questions 73
CCSS Focus - RI.1.1 Additional Standards - RI.1.2, 7; SL.1.1, 2, 4; L.1.1, 2

Lesson 7: Main Topic 79
CCSS Focus - RI.1.2 Additional Standards - RI.1.1; SL.1.1, 2, 4; L.1.1, 2

Read Aloud Lesson G: *Elizabeth Leads the Way: Elizabeth Cady Stanton and the Right to Vote* 85
CCSS Focus - RI.1.2 Additional Standards - RI.1.1, 3, 7; RF.1.3f, g; W.1.3; SL.1.1, 2, 4, 5; L.1.1h, 2, 4a, 5c

Lesson 8: Describing Connections 91
CCSS Focus - RI.1.3 Additional Standards - RI.1.1, 2, 7; SL.1.1, 2; L.1.1, 2

Unit 2 Check 97

Unit 3: Craft and Structure in Literature 99

Lesson 9: Feeling Words 101
CCSS Focus - RL.1.4 Additional Standards - RL.1.2; SL.1.1, 4; L.1.1, 2, 5

Read Aloud Lesson H: *Mike Mulligan and His Steam Shovel* 107
CCSS Focus - RL.1.2 Additional Standards - RL.1.1, 3, 7; RF.1.2a, d, 3f; W.1.1; SL.1.1, 2, 4, 5; L.1.1b, 2a, 4a

Lesson 10: Sensory Words 113
CCSS Focus - RL.1.4 Additional Standards - RL.1.2; W.1.5; SL.1.1, 4; L.1.1, 2, 5

Lesson 11: Types of Books 119
CCSS Focus - RL.1.5 Additional Standards - RL.1.2, 7; RI.1.2, 7; SL.1.1, 2, 5

Lesson 12: Who Is Telling the Story? 125
CCSS Focus - RL.1.6 Additional Standards - RL.1.2, 7; SL.1.1, 2, 4, 5; L.1.1, 2

Unit 3 Check 131

Unit 4: Craft and Structure in Informational Text 133

Read Aloud Lesson I: *Earthworms* 135
CCSS Focus - RI.1.2 Additional Standards - RI.1.1; RF.1.3a, c, g; W.1.2; SL.1.1a, b, 2, 3, 5; L.1.1f, 2, 4a

Lesson 13: Finding Word Meanings 141
CCSS Focus - RI.1.4 Additional Standards - RI.1.1, 2, 7; SL.1.1, 4; L.1.1, 2, 4, 5

Lesson 14: Text Features 147
CCSS Focus - RI.1.5 Additional Standards - RI.1.2; SL.1.1, 3; L.1.1, 2

Lesson 15: More Text Features 153
CCSS Focus - RI.1.5 Additional Standards - SL.1.1, 5; L.1.1, 2

Unit 4: Craft and Structure in Informational Text *(continued)*

Lesson 16: Words and Pictures 159

CCSS Focus - RI.1.6 *Additional Standards - RI.1.1, 2; SL.1.1, 2, 4; L.1.1, 2*

Unit 4 Check 165

Unit 5: Integration of Knowledge and Ideas in Literature **167**

Lesson 17: Story Words and Pictures 169

CCSS Focus - RL.1.7 *Additional Standards - RL.1.1, 2, 3, 4; SL.1.1, 2, 4; L.1.1, 2*

Lesson 18: Comparing Characters 175

CCSS Focus - RL.1.9 *Additional Standards - RL.1.1, 2, 3, 7; SL.1.1, 4; L.1.1, 2*

Unit 5 Check 181

Unit 6: Integration of Knowledge and Ideas in Informational Text **183**

Lesson 19: Words with Pictures 185

CCSS Focus - RI.1.7 *Additional Standards - RI.1.2, 6; SL.1.1, 4; L.1.1, 2*

Lesson 20: Identifying Reasons 191

CCSS Focus - RI.1.8 *Additional Standards - RI.1.2; SL.1.1, 2; L.1.1, 2*

Lesson 21: Comparing Two Texts 197

CCSS Focus - RI.1.9 *Additional Standards - RI.1.2; SL.1.1, 2; L.1.1, 2*

Unit 6 Check 203

Projectables

Projectable 1: *Happy Birthday Surprise!* 205

Projectable 2: *Sometimes* 207

Projectable 3: *I'm Staying Home From School Today* 209

Projectable 4: *Famous Women: Susan B. Anthony* 211

Projectable 5: *Upsetting the Balance* 215

Ready® *Common Core* Program Overview

Ready*® *Common Core is an interactive read-aloud program built to teach the Common Core State Standards (CCSS) for Reading. The main focus of the program is the CCSS Reading Literature and Informational Text strands. Other Reading and ELA standards are integrated throughout the lessons. The components of the program are described below.

Built for the Common Core. Not just aligned.

Student Instruction

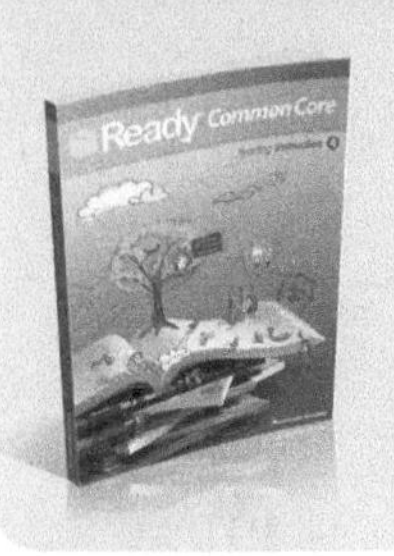

Ready Common Core Student Book includes thoughtful, text-based activities that encourage students to apply and practice the CCSS. Lessons follow a repetitive, predictable structure that supports emergent readers and scaffolds student learning. Each time students complete a lesson, they have independently applied a new skill.

Teacher Resource Book, Trade Book Collection, and Teacher Toolbox

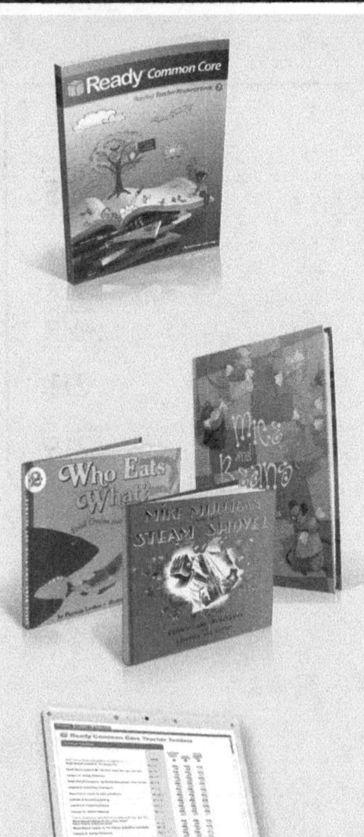

Ready Common Core Teacher Resource Book supports teachers with strong professional development, step-by-step lesson plans, and developmentally appropriate best practices for implementing the CCSS.

Ready Common Core Trade Book Collection includes nine high-quality literature and informational texts from a variety of genres. These rich, complex texts are the vehicle for teaching and modeling the standards. See page A11 for a listing of the trade books and Projectables.

The online ***Ready*** Teacher Toolbox (Toolbox sold separately) gives teachers access to a host of multilevel resources, such as PDFs of the Student Book and Teacher Resource Book lessons, instructional support, online lessons, and lessons for prerequisite skills. (See pages A16–A17 for more.)

Features

- Built with brand-new content

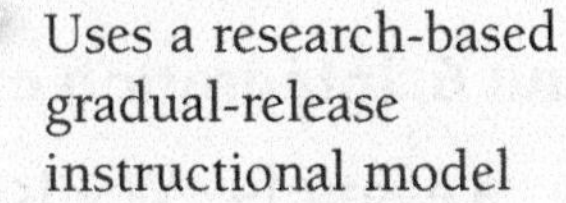

- Uses a research-based gradual-release instructional model

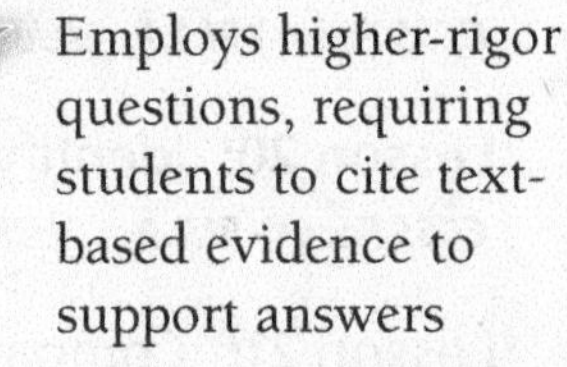

- Employs higher-rigor questions, requiring students to cite text-based evidence to support answers

- Includes award-winning trade books from a wide range of genres
- Embeds thoughtful professional development

i-Ready® *Diagnostic*

Built on the Common Core and integrated with the ***Ready*** program, ***i-Ready Diagnostic*** helps teachers track student growth, pointing teachers toward the correct ***Ready*** lessons to use for remediation. See page A18 for details. (***i-Ready*** sold separately.)

Supporting the Implementation of the Common Core

The Common Core State Standards (CCSS) were developed to make sure that by the time students graduate from high school, they are college- and career-ready. Therefore, the creators of the standards started with the expectations they had for students at the end of 12th grade and worked down to kindergarten. As a result of this backward design approach, the CCSS are more rigorous than most current standards. The creators of the standards want students at every grade to be creative and critical readers and writers. At the end of each grade, students are expected to independently read and comprehend increasingly complex text. Not only are most current textbooks lacking alignment to the CCSS, they also lack the levels of complex text identified in the CCSS. ***Ready*® *Common Core*** is here to help.

Using *Ready* to Support the Transition to the Common Core

As a Supplement to a Textbook

Your classroom textbook may not have been developed for the Common Core. It may not have all the resources you need to meet these challenging standards. In addition, the passages in textbooks often do not reflect the levels of text complexity required by the Common Core, and the activities and questions do not reflect the rigor of the standards. By supplementing with ***Ready***, you'll be able to address all of these gaps and deficiencies.

With a Balanced Literacy/ Reading Workshop Curriculum

Because every standard in ***Ready Common Core*** has been addressed with clear, thoughtful pedagogy, you can use ***Ready*** as the main structure of an interactive read aloud program. Any other materials aligned to the Common Core can be woven into the curriculum.

With *i-Ready*® *Diagnostic*

If you are an ***i-Ready*** subscriber, you can administer the ***i-Ready Diagnostic*** as a cross-grade-level assessment to pinpoint instructional needs and address them with ***Ready Common Core***. For more on this, see page A18.

Helpful Resources for the Transition to the Common Core

http://www.corestandards.org/
The main website for the Common Core. Here you'll find the full text of the standards, plus frequently asked questions and resources.

http://www.smarterbalanced.org/* and *http://www.parcconline.org
The testing consortia creating Common Core assessments for future implementation.

http://www.ascd.org/common-core-state-standards/common-core.aspx
A helpful list of all of ASCD's resources on the Common Core, as well as a link to ASCD's free EduCore digital tool, which was funded by a grant from the Bill & Melinda Gates Foundation. A repository of evidence-based strategies, videos, and supporting documents that help educators transition to the Common Core.

http://www.reading.org/resources/ResourcesByTopic/CommonCore-resourcetype/CommonCore-rt-resources.aspx
Links to helpful articles about the Common Core from *Reading Today Online*.

http://www.engageny.org/
Hosted by the New York State Education Department (NYSED), this site features curriculum resources and professional development materials to support the transition to the Common Core.

Answering the Demands of the Common Core with *Ready*®

THE DEMANDS OF THE COMMON CORE	HOW *READY*® DELIVERS
High-Quality Texts: It's important that students are exposed to well-crafted texts that are worth reading closely and exhibit exceptional craft and thought or provide useful information.	The nine trade books in ***Ready*** were carefully chosen to match the rigor and quality of read aloud text in Appendix B. The list includes award-winning authors Patricia Polacco, Kevin Henkes, and Patricia Lauber as well as several information books from the highly regarded Let's-Read-and-Find-Out Science series. See page A9 for more information about text complexity.
Read Aloud Texts: Students can gain comprehension skills by listening to texts being read that are of higher complexity than what they can normally read.	***Ready*** offers Read Aloud lessons in which teachers read the texts and then unpack the key details step by step, giving students access to concepts and vocabulary beyond what they could manage independently.
Wide Range of Genres; Emphasis on Nonfiction: Students must read a true balance of authentic literary and informational texts. Success in college and the real world requires that students master the skills needed to read a variety of informational texts.	The trade books and Projectables in ***Ready*** encompass a range of genres and text types, including realistic fiction, folktale, poetry, fantasy, reference, science, and biography. See page A11 for a list of the trade books and Projectables.
Intentional, Close Reading: Careful, close readings of complex texts teach students how to gather evidence and build knowledge.	Each ***Ready*** Teacher Resource Book lesson contains a Close Reading activity in which teachers prompt students with higher-level text-dependent questions, and then lead students to closely examine words and pictures to find the answers. See more on page A10.
Text-Based Evidence: Students' interpretations and comprehension of the text must be supported by the words in the text.	***Ready*** Turn and Talk activities require students to back up their answers with evidence directly from the text. Instruction throughout the Teacher Resource Book reinforces the importance of quoting from the text to substantiate interpretations.
Building Content Knowledge: Students should view reading as an opportunity to learn new information.	The informational trade books in ***Ready*** relate to grade-appropriate science and social studies content. Students deepen their knowledge of the content in Read Aloud Student Book pages by completing tasks such as drawing, writing, and completing graphic organizers.
Integrated ELA Instruction: It's important that teachers use the texts as a source of rich language arts instruction, as opposed to isolated skill instruction.	***Ready*** lessons provide students with consistent contextualized opportunities for speaking and listening as well as writing in response to a text. Foundational Reading and Language standards are addressed in activities that draw on words taken directly from the trade books.

Why Emphasize Complex Text?

Research has shown that the complexity levels of the texts in current classrooms are far below what is required for college- and career-readiness. A major emphasis of the Common Core State Standards (CCSS) is for students to encounter appropriately complex texts at each grade level in order to develop the mature language skills and conceptual knowledge they need for success in school and life. Instructional materials should meet this challenge with rich and rigorous texts at each grade level.

How do I Introduce Complex Text to K–1 Students?

At grades K–1, rich, interactive read aloud text is an important part of the curriculum. Students at these levels can listen to and comprehend much more complex material than they can read independently. The CCSS provide the following information about read aloud text:

> "Read-aloud selections should be ... at levels of complexity **well above what students can read on their own**." (Coleman & Pimentel, Revised Publishers Criteria, 2012, p. 5)

> "Children in the early grades (particularly K–2) should participate in **rich, structured conversations** with an adult in response to the written texts that are read aloud, orally **comparing and contrasting** as well as **analyzing** and **synthesizing**, in the manner called for by the Standards." (Common Core State Standards, 2010, p. 33)

> "By reading a story or nonfiction selection aloud, teachers allow children to experience written language **without the burden of decoding**, granting them access to content that they may not be able to read and understand by themselves. Children are then **free to focus their mental energy on the words and ideas presented in the text**, and they will eventually be better prepared to tackle rich written content on their own." (Common Core State Standards, 2010, Appendix A)

Read Aloud Trade Books in *Ready*®

Given the CCSS emphasis on read aloud text, ***Ready Common Core*** bases standard instruction on high-quality trade books that are read aloud. The trade book selections were influenced by the read-aloud exemplars listed in CCSS Appendix B. Not only do the trade books align with the complexity levels of these exemplars, but they also draw on the same, or comparable, authors and series, including Tomie DePaola, Kevin Henkes, Claire Llewellyn, Wendy Pfeffer, Patricia Lauber, and the Let's-Read-and-Find-Out Science series. See a complete list of the trade books on page A11.

Close-Up on Close Reading

What Is Close Reading?

According to PARCC, "[Research] links the close reading of complex text—whether the student is a struggling reader or advanced—to significant gains in reading proficiency." (PARCC, 2011) The purpose of close reading is to unpack the meaning in a text by examining and interpreting the author's choices. Although this seems like a highly sophisticated practice, even emerging readers can begin to understand that authors choose their words carefully, organize their sentences thoughtfully, and make intentional decisions about the placement of words, pictures, and other features.

Close Reading Instruction in *Ready® Common Core*

Every ***Ready Common Core*** Teacher Resource Book lesson features a Close Reading activity (see below). Through this activity, teachers model and guide students to apply close reading strategies to specific sections of the read aloud text. Key features of the Close Reading activity include the following:

Multiple readings: The instructional design of ***Ready*** requires multiple readings of the text. Students first explore a text through Read Aloud Lessons, which focus on literal comprehension of key details. Then, in Focus Lessons, students revisit the text while applying specific CCSS Reading Literature or Informational Text standards. The Close Reading feature in every lesson guides students to reread the text a third time, zooming in on specific words, phrases, and illustrations to make inferences, analyze the author's purpose, or find evidence to support a claim about the text.

Text-dependent questions: "The purposes of text-dependent questions are to prompt rereading, encourage the use of textual evidence to support answers, and deepen comprehension using the analytic processes." (Fisher, Frey, & Lapp, 2012) In ***Ready*** Close Reading activities, students answer a range of questions from literal to inferential (e.g. *Why do you think the author chose this word? What is the story's message?*) To answer such questions, students must revisit the text and choose precise details in the words and pictures and use them to defend their ideas.

Text-based discussion: Each ***Ready*** Close Reading activity allows students to develop and use academic and domain-specific language while engaging in focused talk around one aspect of the text. Open-ended questions allow students the opportunity to make claims, defend them with text evidence, and respectfully discuss conflicting ideas, all resulting in a deeper understanding of the text.

1. Teachers define the goal for students so they listen with a purpose in mind as a small portion of the text is revisited. Often this goal is a strategy that good readers utilize during close reading.

2. Teachers give targeted prompts that lead students to a key understanding about the text or the author's intentions. Students must always use text evidence to answer questions directly or support their interpretations.

3. Teachers close the activity by helping students "connect the dots" between the ideas highlighted in the prompts in order to achieve a deeper understanding of the text.

Close Reading

1 • Remind children that thinking about a character's problem can help them figure out the message. Reread the following paragraphs. Prompt children to locate details about the problem and solution:

(paragraph 4) **What words show that Abel has a problem?** *(It is already past noon; oh dear; he still had to make the cake.)*

2 **What is Abel's problem?** *(He is running out of time to get ready.)*

(paragraphs 9–16) **What details tell more about Abel's problem?** *(He is embarrassed to be behind; the house is still a mess; the cake is ruined.)*

(paragraphs 18–21) **How is Abel's problem solved?** *(Chester says they can make another cake.)*

3 • Discuss whether children think that Chester will help Abel now, and what evidence makes them think so. Then have children tell what Abel learned from the solution to his problem.

Trade Books and Projectables in *Ready*®

The Common Core emphasizes the importance of selecting rigorous, high-quality texts that reward students for their work. To encourage students to dig deeply during their readings of texts, ***Ready*** focuses instruction on a set of popular, well-respected trade books, both literature and informational text. Chosen for their range of genres as well as their text complexity, these trade books offer ample opportunities for close reading and practicing Common Core skills. In addition, Projectables, short text selections, provide extra genre and skill support. Located at the end of the Teacher Resource Book (see pages 205–216) and as PDFs in the Teacher Toolbox, Projectables are designed to be displayed with lessons that feature specific skills. The following chart shows the genre of each text, and the ***Ready*** lessons in which each title appears.

Trade Books and Projectables	Genre	*Ready*® Lessons
*The Empty Pot,** by Demi	Folktale	A, 1, 2, 3, 5, 11, 12
The Polar Bear Son: An Inuit Tale, by Lydia Dabcovich	Legend	B, 1, 4, 9, 11, 18
*My Rotten Redheaded Older Brother,** by Patricia Polacco	Realistic Fiction	C, 2, 5, 12, 17
*Mice and Beans,** by Pam Muñoz Ryan	Fantasy	D, 3, 4, 17, 18
Who Eats What? Food Chains and Food Webs, by Patricia Lauber	Science	E, 6, 7, 16
Nic Bishop: Butterflies and Moths, by Nic Bishop	Science	F, 6, 7, 8, 11, 19, 21
*Elizabeth Leads the Way: Elizabeth Cady Stanton and the Right to Vote,** by Tanya Lee Stone	Biography	G, 8, 11, 13, 19, 21
Mike Mulligan and His Steam Shovel, by Virginia Lee Burton	Fantasy	H, 10, 11, 12, 18
Earthworms, by Claire Llewellyn and Barrie Watts	Reference Book	I, 11, 13, 14, 16, 19, 21
Projectable 1: *Happy Birthday Surprise!* by Stephen Krensky	Fable	5, 18
Projectable 2: *Sometimes,* by Laura Hidalgo	Poem	9
Projectable 3: *I'm Staying Home From School Today,* by Kenn Nesbitt	Poem	10
Projectable 4: *Famous Women: Susan B. Anthony*	Biography (Website)	15, 16, 21
Projectable 5: *Upsetting the Balance,* by David Fein	Persuasive (Science)	20

*Since this book does not have page numbers, we identified page numbers to reference in the student and teacher lessons. In ***Ready***, page 1 is considered the first right-hand page opposite the inside front cover of the trade book (see sample below) regardless of whether or not this page includes text.

Using *Ready*® Common Core

The easy-to-use Teacher Resource Book contains best-practice instructional techniques to help you teach each new Common Core reading standard effectively. Much more than just an answer key to the ***Ready*** Student Book, this resource has the embedded professional development you'll need to teach students research-based strategies to conquer the challenges of reading complex text. Using the read aloud trade books as the vehicle to drive instruction, the ***Ready*** program enables you to help students develop proficiency in each Common Core reading standard by reading and revisiting these engaging, authentic literary and informational texts—utilizing a proven-effective, gradual-release approach that builds student confidence.

Teacher Resource Book

Get professional development right when you need it—while you're teaching a new standard. Proven-effective teaching strategies and tips throughout the Teacher Resource Book help you transition to the more rigorous standards, and every lesson plan gives you an easy-to-use set of tools to coordinate the trade books with the instruction presented in the ***Ready*** program.

Trade Books

Provide students with the opportunity to apply Common Core reading standards throughout nine high-quality, authentic texts spanning a range of genres, topics, and text types.

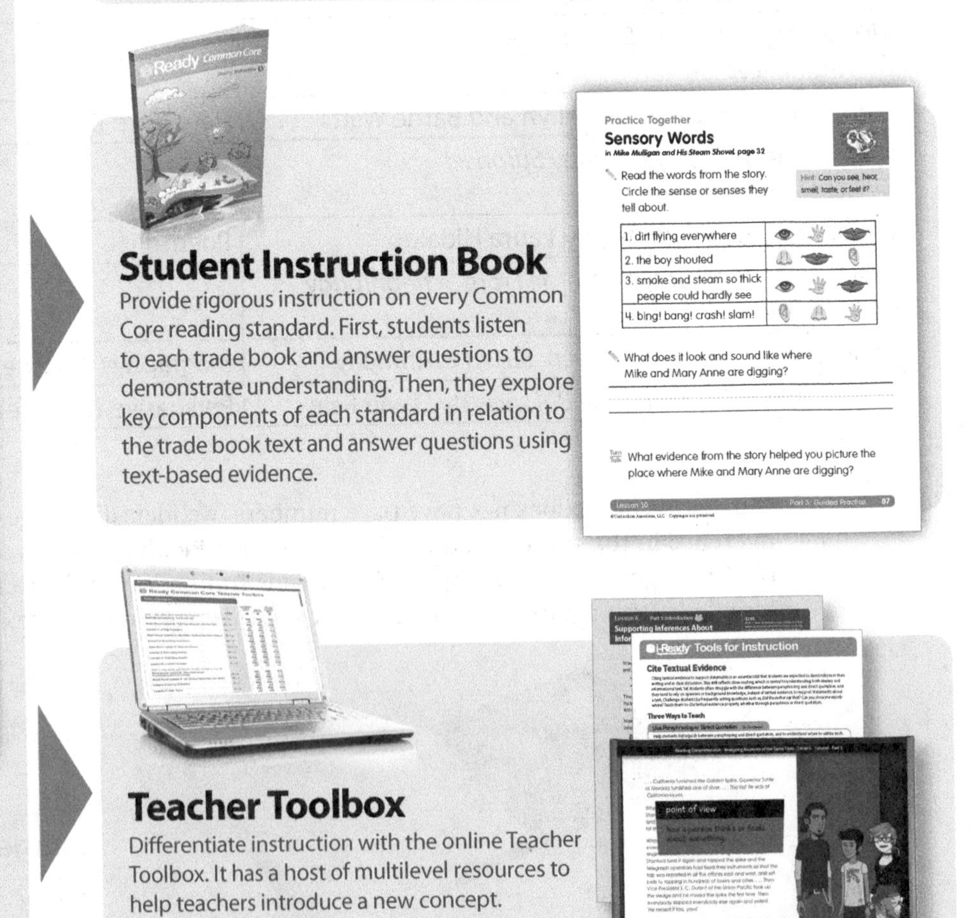

Student Instruction Book

Provide rigorous instruction on every Common Core reading standard. First, students listen to each trade book and answer questions to demonstrate understanding. Then, they explore key components of each standard in relation to the trade book text and answer questions using text-based evidence.

Teacher Toolbox

Differentiate instruction with the online Teacher Toolbox. It has a host of multilevel resources to help teachers introduce a new concept.

Year-Long Pacing Guide for Grade 1

The pacing chart below shows how ***Ready Common Core*** fits into the curriculum throughout the year. Each "week" is based on three days of Lesson instruction at 30 minutes per day, leaving time for teachers to revisit or reinforce concepts as needed.

Week	*Ready®* *Common Core* Lesson	Minutes per Week
1	Read Aloud Lesson A: *The Empty Pot*	90
2	Read Aloud Lesson B: *The Polar Bear Son*	90
3	Lesson 1: Asking Questions	90
4	Read Aloud Lesson C: *My Rotten Redheaded Older Brother*	90
5	Lesson 2: Describing Characters	90
6	Read Aloud Lesson D: *Mice and Beans*	90
7	Lesson 3: Describing Setting	90
8	Lesson 4: Describing Events	90
9	Lesson 5: Central Message	90
	Unit 1 Check	**30 (1 day)**
10	Read Aloud Lesson E: *Who Eats What?*	90
11	Read Aloud Lesson F: *Butterflies and Moths*	90
12	Lesson 6: Asking Questions	90
13	Lesson 7: Main Topic	90
14	Read Aloud Lesson G: *Elizabeth Leads the Way*	90
15	Lesson 8: Describing Connections	90
	Unit 2 Check	**30 (1 day)**
16	Lesson 9: Feeling Words	90
17	Read Aloud Lesson H: *Mike Mulligan and His Steam Shovel*	90
18	Lesson 10: Sensory Words	90
19	Lesson 11: Types of Books	90
20	Lesson 12: Who Is Telling the Story?	90
	Unit 3 Check	**30 (1 day)**
21	Read Aloud Lesson I: *Earthworms*	90
22	Lesson 13: Finding Word Meanings	90
23	Lesson 14: Text Features	90
24	Lesson 15: More Text Features	90
25	Lesson 16: Words and Pictures	90
	Unit 4 Check	**30 (1 day)**
26	Lesson 17: Story Words and Pictures	90
27	Lesson 18: Comparing Characters	90
	Unit 5 Check	**30 (1 day)**
28	Lesson 19: Words with Pictures	90
29	Lesson 20: Identifying Reasons	90
30	Lesson 21: Comparing Two Texts	90
	Unit 6 Check	**30 (1 day)**

Teaching with *Ready*® *Common Core*

To support teachers in effectively introducing the read aloud text as well as teaching the Common Core State Standards, ***Ready Common Core*** contains two types of lessons: Read Aloud Lessons and Focus Lessons. Learn more about each type of lesson here.

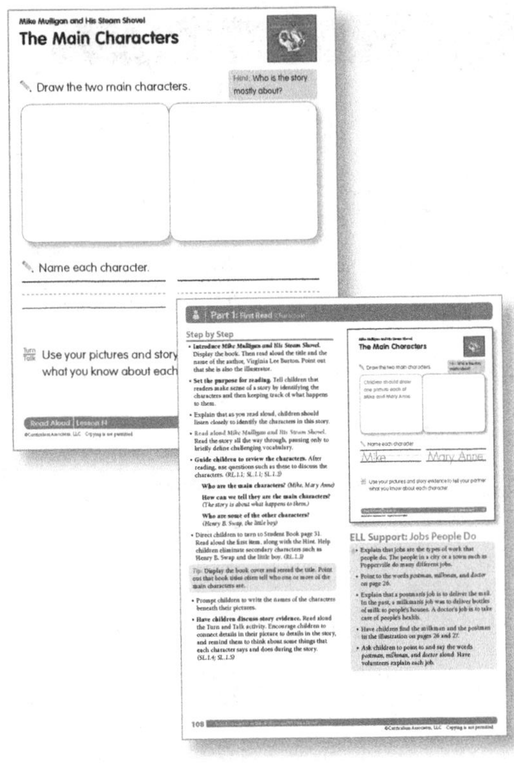

Mike Mulligan and His Steam Shovel

The Main Characters

Draw the two main characters.

Hint: Who is the story mostly about?

Name each character.

Use your pictures and story ... what you know about each ...

Read Aloud | Lesson 14

Part 1: First Read

Step by Step

- **Introduce *Mike Mulligan and His Steam Shovel*.** Display the book. Then read aloud the title and the name of the author, Virginia Lee Burton. Point out that she is also the illustrator.
- **Set the purpose for reading.** Tell children that readers make sense of a story by identifying the characters and then keeping track of what happens to them.
- Explain that as you read aloud, children should listen closely to identify the characters in this story.
- Read aloud *Mike Mulligan and His Steam Shovel*. Read the story all the way through, pausing only to briefly define challenging vocabulary.
- **Guide children to review the characters.** After reading, use questions such as these to discuss the characters. (RL.1.1; SL.1.1; SL.1.3)

  Who are the main characters? *(Mike, Mary Anne)*

  How can we tell they are the main characters? *(The story is about what happens to them.)*

  Who are some of the other characters? *(Henry B. Swap, the little boy)*
- Direct children to turn to Student Book page 31. Read aloud the first item, along with the Hint. Help children eliminate secondary characters such as Henry B. Swap and the little boy. (RL.1.3)

Tip: Display the book cover and reread the title. Point out that book titles often tell who one or more of the main characters are.

- Prompt children to write the names of the characters beneath their pictures.
- **Have children discuss story evidence.** Read aloud the Turn and Talk activity. Encourage children to connect details in their picture to details in the story, and remind them to think about some things that each character says and does during the story. (SL.1.4; SL.1.5)

The Main Characters

Draw the two main characters.

Children should draw one picture each of Mike and Mary Anne.

Name each character

Mike Mary Anne

Use your pictures and story evidence to tell your partner what you know about each character.

ELL Support: Jobs People Do

- Explain that jobs are the types of work that people do. The people in a city or a town such as Popperville do many different jobs.
- Point to the words *postman*, *milkman*, and *doctor* on page 26.
- Explain that a postman's job is to deliver the mail. In the past, a milkman's job was to deliver bottles of milk to people's houses. A doctor's job is to take care of people's health.
- Have children find the milkman and the postman in the illustration on pages 26 and 27.
- Ask children to point to and say the words *postman*, *milkman*, and *doctor* aloud. Have volunteers explain each job.

108

Read Aloud Lessons

Read Aloud Lessons provide a comprehensive introduction to each trade book in the program. After a brief review of critical vocabulary and new concepts, teachers read the entire book aloud. Over the next two days, teachers revisit the book in smaller chunks, calling students' attention to the key details needed to comprehend and ultimately retell the text. This introduction prepares students to dig deeper into the key details, craft and structure, and integration of knowledge and ideas in each text as they proceed through each Focus Lesson.

Literature Read Aloud Lessons guide students to identify the main characters, key events in the beginning, middle, and end of a story, and the problem and solution.

Informational Text Read Aloud Lessons guide students to identify the main topic and key details in a text while calling their attention to the various structures and purposes of informational text.

Suggested Daily Pacing

The models below show how to pace a Read Aloud Lesson over a period of three days. The optional features give you the flexibility to make the best choices for your allotted instructional time.

Ready Common Core Read Aloud Lesson

	Day 1 (30 minutes)		Day 2 (30 minutes)		Day 3 (30 minutes)
Teacher Resource Book	**Introduction: Critical Vocabulary and New Concepts**	**Part 1: First Read**	**Part 2: Reread for Meaning**	**Part 3: Reread for Meaning**	**Part 4: Reread for Meaning** **Retell the Text**
Student Book Literature Lesson OR Informational Lesson		**Characters**	**In the Beginning**	**In the Middle**	**At the End**
		Explore the Text	**Key Details**	**Key Details**	**Key Details**
Optional Teacher Resource Book Features		**ELL Support**	**Tier Two Vocabulary**	**Tier Two Vocabulary**	**Integrating Foundational Skills** **Additional Activities**

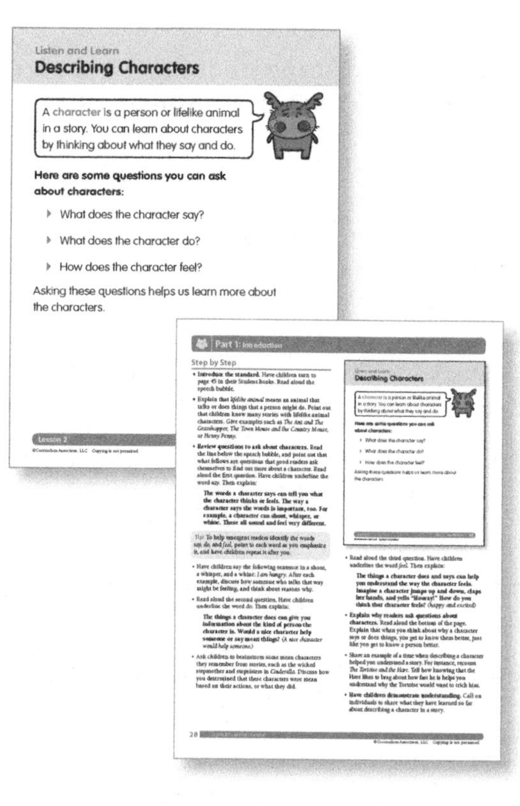

Focus Lessons

Each ***Ready*** Focus Lesson targets a specific CCSS Reading Literature or Informational Text standard. Through a gradual release of responsibility, teachers model the habits of active readers and guide students to practice these habits—first with guidance and then independently. Each lesson includes the following components:

- **Listen and Learn (Introduction):** Teachers introduce the standard and key academic language. Students learn the important questions to ask or steps to follow as they apply the standard to text.
- **Practice Together (Modeled Instruction):** Teachers think aloud as they model applying the standard to select trade book pages. Then they model how to apply the standard in the related Student Book activities.
- **Practice Together (Guided Practice):** Teachers ask a series of targeted questions that help students apply the standard to another text selection. Students discuss the Student Book activities together before recording their answers independently.
- **Practice by Myself (Independent Practice):** Teachers read aloud a third text selection as well as the Student Book activities. Students work independently to apply the standard, and then conclude by discussing their work together and reflecting on the skill.

Suggested Daily Pacing

The model below shows how to pace a Focus Lesson over a period of three days. The optional feature gives you the flexibility to make the best choices for your allotted instructional time.

Ready Common Core Focus Lesson

	Day 1 (30 minutes)		*Day 2 (30 minutes)*		*Day 3 (30 minutes)*
Teacher Resource Book	**Tap Children's Prior Knowledge**	**Part 1: Introduction**	**Part 2: Modeled Instruction**	**Part 3: Guided Practice**	**Part 4: Independent Practice**
Student Book		**Listen and Learn**	**Practice Together**	**Practice Together**	**Practice by Myself**
Optional Teacher Resource Book Features					**Differentiated Instruction**

Connecting with the *Ready*® Teacher Toolbox

Designed for use with ***Ready*® *Common Core***, the Teacher Toolbox provides a host of multilevel resources teachers can use to differentiate instruction. If you purchased the Teacher Toolbox, you should have received an insert with access codes and information. Please contact Customer Service at (800)-225-0248 if you need this information. Visit *www.teacher-toolbox.com* to get started.

The Common Core builds on skills covered in the previous year's standards. Of course, many students will not have mastered those standards, and most students could use a review. ***Ready Common Core*** allows you to access lessons from previous ***Ready*** grades through the Teacher Toolbox.

How Do I Use the Teacher Toolbox?

Lessons are conveniently organized to match your print materials, making it easy to find additional resources for teaching the skills and standards associated with each lesson. All of these resources are perfect for use with any interactive whiteboard or other computer projection screen.

Available for Grades K–8

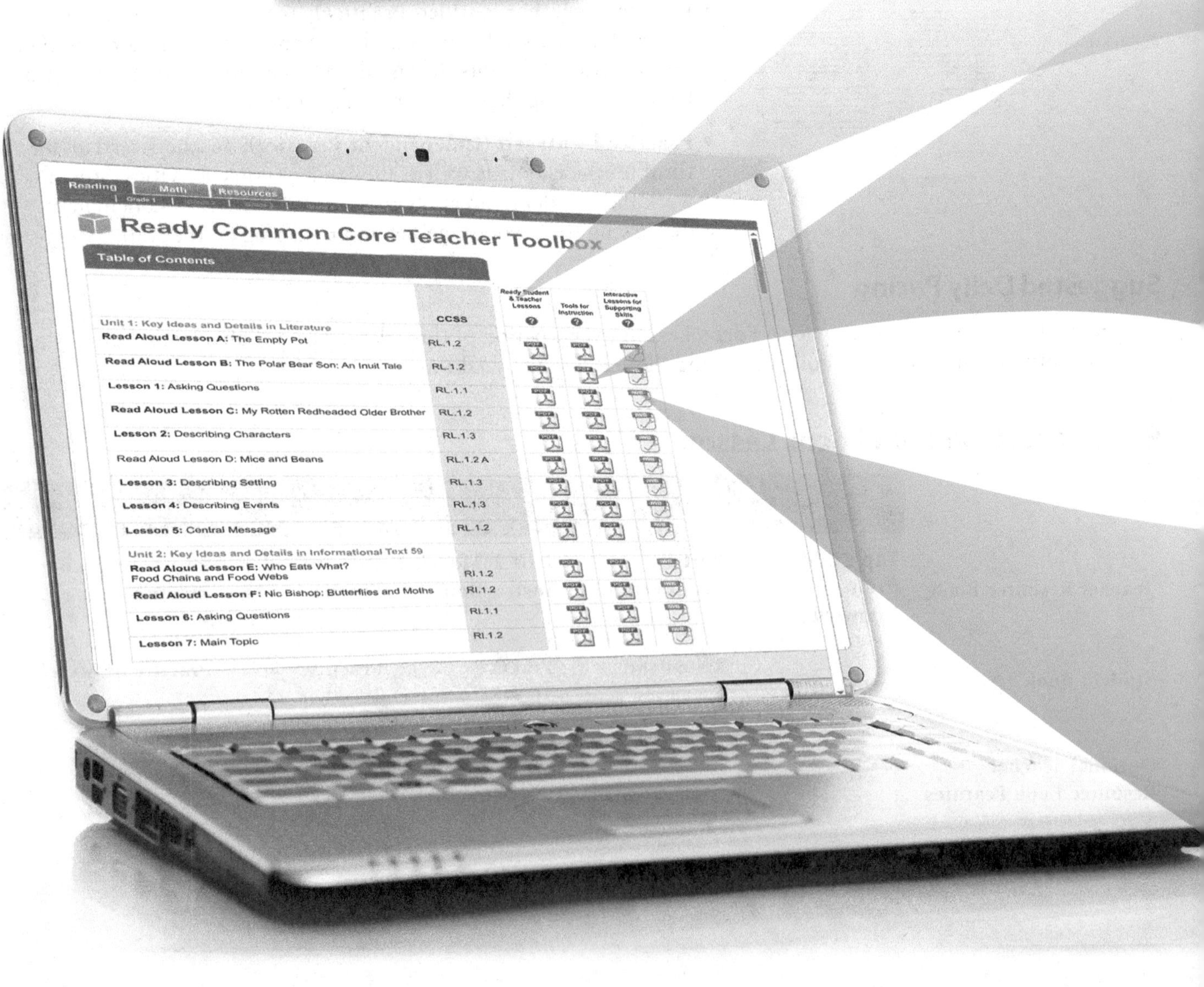

Listen and Learn

Describing Characters

A character is a person or lifelike animal in a story. You can learn about characters by thinking about what they say and do.

Here are some questions you can ask about characters:

- What does the character say?
- What does the character do?
- How does the character feel?

Asking these questions helps us learn more about the characters.

Part 1: Introduction 45

i-Ready Tools for Instruction

Diagnostic & Instruction

Describe Characters

When students listen to or read a literary text, they follow the plot based on what characters think, say, and do throughout the story. Learning to relate characters and their actions to real people engages readers with the story and contributes to comprehension. However, early readers tend to make an artificial distinction between the way people think and act in real life versus the way characters think and act in literature, particularly when the characters are not human. To help students learn to identify and describe characters, model and provide practice recognizing characters and noticing details that tell more about them. Teach students to think about how characters in stories are like people in real life.

Step by Step 20–30 minutes

1. Explain and discuss characters.
   - Hold up a familiar story, such as *Little Bear,* by Else Holmelund Minarik. Ask, *Who is this story about?* (Little Bear)
   - Say, *Little Bear is a character in this story. A character is someone who is part of a story. Because the story is about Little Bear, we call him the main character. Can you think of another character in the book* Little Bear? (Mother Bear)
   - Call attention to the bear characters in *Little Bear,* and point out that story characters can be people, animals, or even machines or objects, such as the little train engine in *The Little Engine that Could.* Explain that readers use their imaginations to think about how these characters behave like people in real life.

     I can see that Little Bear is an animal, but he talks, and he asks his mother to make him something warm to wear. Plus, we can see in this picture that Mother Bear is wearing a dress. This makes me think that the characters in this story are like people in real life, because real bears don't talk or wear clothes.

   - Invite students to suggest additional ways that Little Bear and Mother Bear are like real people. Then continue the discussion with a second familiar text that has human characters. Discuss how the characters talk, think, and behave like people in everyday life.
2. Teach and model describing characters.
   - Select a new read aloud, and take a picture walk to help students preview the characters.
   - Say, *As I read, I'm going to stop to think about the characters in this story. First I'll think about how the characters are like people in real life.*
   - As you read aloud, pause to identify characters and to think about what they say and do, as well as how they are like real people. The following example is based on *Chester's Way,* by Kevin Henkes.

     In this story, Chester is a young mouse, but in a lot of ways, he reminds me of a real child. He likes peanut butter and rides a bike with training wheels. I can see that Chester has feelings like a real child, too. He gets excited to play with his best friend, Wilson.

www.i-ready.com Reading Comprehension | Levels K–1 | Describe Characters | Page 1 of 2

Ready® Lessons

Ready® lessons make it easy for teachers to focus on particular skills, or even reteach skills that students may not have mastered at earlier grade levels. What you get:

- Every lesson in this book is available as an individual PDF file, which you can project for whole-class and small-group use.
- Prerequisite student lesson PDFs—and the accompanying Teacher Resource Book lesson—from prior grades are available to administer as remediation.

Tools for Instruction

Research-based best-practice routines and activities for the classroom and small groups provide ways to teach or review standards and prerequisite skills.

Guided Interactive Tutorials

Guided interactive tutorials give teachers another engaging way to provide whole-class or small-group instruction. Lessons follow a consistent structure of explicit instruction and guided practice. Immediate corrective feedback continuously supports students.

Using *i-Ready*® *Diagnostic* with *Ready*® *Common Core*

If you have already purchased ***i-Ready*® *Diagnostic***, you can use its robust reporting to monitor students' overall and domain-specific reading proficiency as they move through ***Ready*® *Common Core***. Specifically, use the Diagnostic Results for a Student report and the Instructional Groupings report to identify Next Step skills for student instruction.

Available for Grades K–12

Diagnostic Results for a Student

Each student's Diagnostic Results report gives teachers insight into the performance of that student, with clear next steps for instruction with detailed recommendations and resources in each domain.

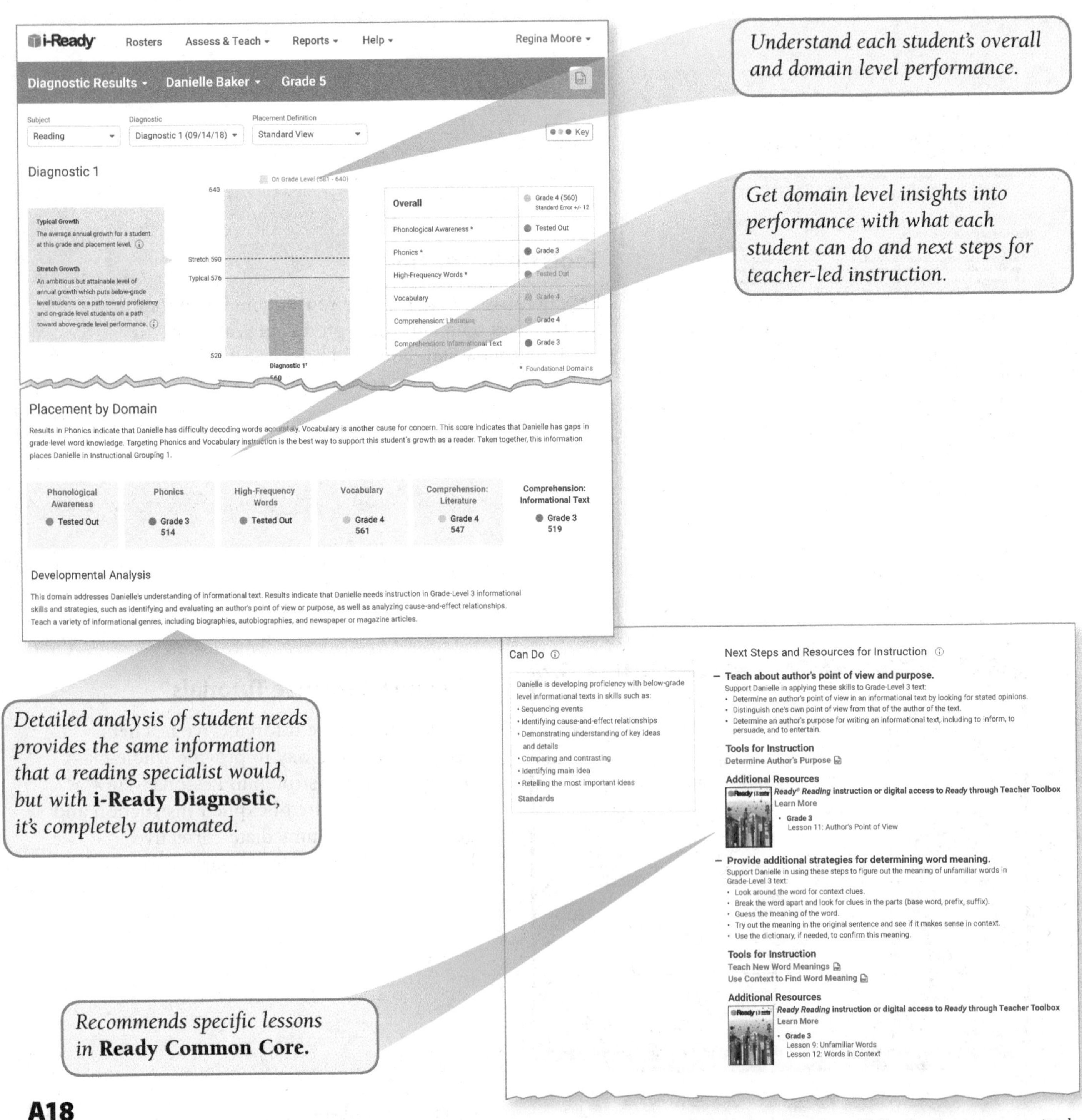

Instructional Groupings

The **Instructional Groupings** report shows teachers exactly how to group students so that students who are struggling with the same skills get the most out of small-group instruction. The report also gives effective instructional recommendations and resources for each group profile.

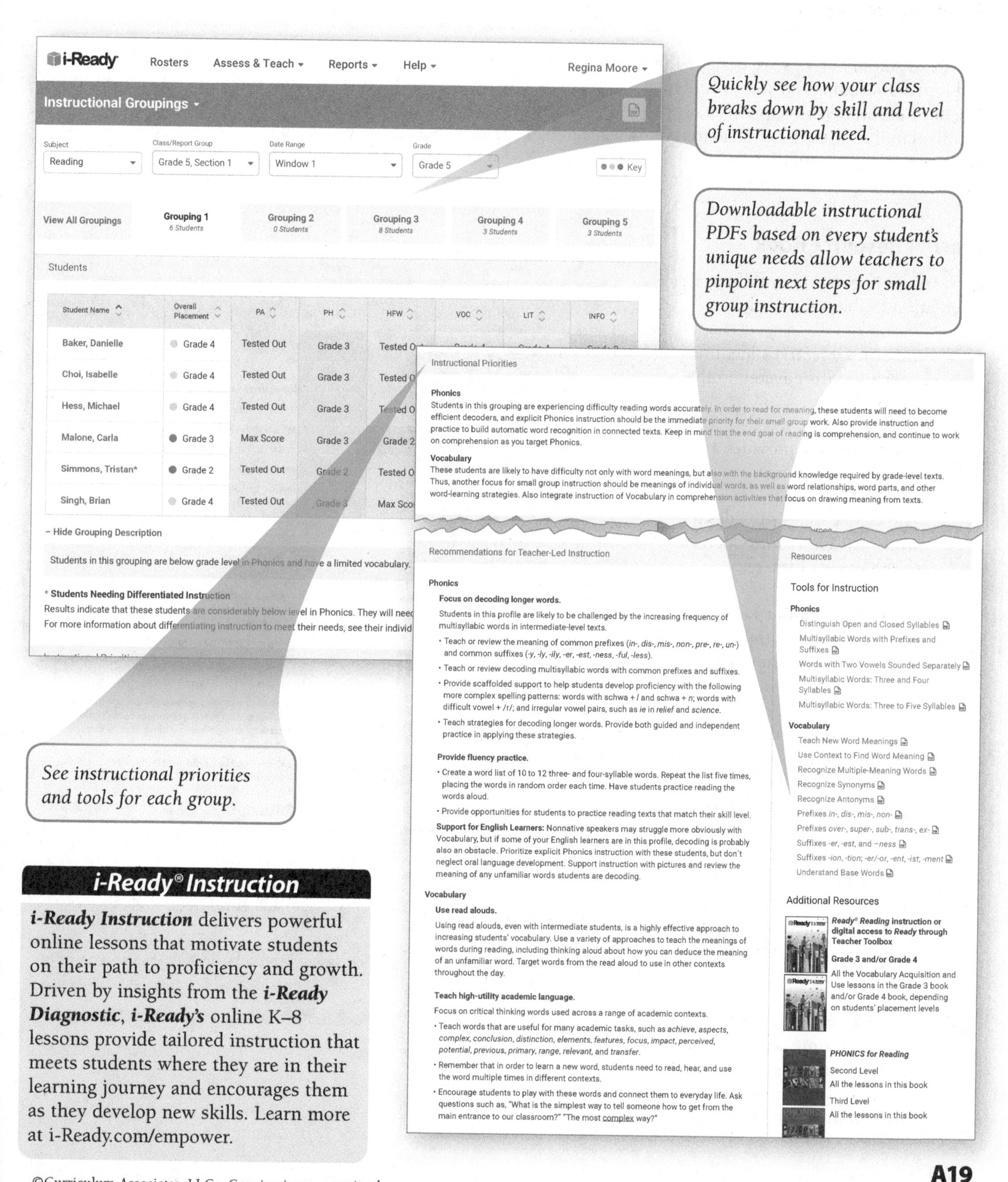

i-Ready® Instruction

i-Ready Instruction delivers powerful online lessons that motivate students on their path to proficiency and growth. Driven by insights from the ***i-Ready Diagnostic***, ***i-Ready's*** online K–8 lessons provide tailored instruction that meets students where they are in their learning journey and encourages them as they develop new skills. Learn more at i-Ready.com/empower.

Features of *Ready*® *Common Core*

This section guides teachers through the key features of the Teacher Resource Book and the Student Book. Numbered boxes call out and describe the features. Use this section to familiarize yourself with the overall structure of the ***Ready Common Core*** Read Aloud Lessons (pages A20–A27) and Focus Lessons (pages A28–A33).

Read Aloud Lessons

The Read Aloud Lessons are designed to help teachers effectively introduce the nine trade books (five literature and four informational texts) to students. There is one lesson for each trade book, and each six-page lesson in the Teacher Resource Book supports a four-page lesson in the Student Book. The Read Aloud Lessons help students become familiar with the content and knowledgeable of the key details in the trade book. These read aloud texts, once introduced to students, are then used as the vehicle for students' understanding and application of the standards in the Focus Lessons.

Teacher Resource Book

Each lesson begins with a full-page orientation to the trade book.

1. **Lesson Objectives** identify specific skills covered in the lesson.
2. The **Summary** provides an overview of the text.
3. The **Genre** focus provides a student-friendly introduction to the genre of the text.
4. **Critical Vocabulary** includes words that are central to students' understanding of the text.
5. **New Concepts** provides background information on a key concept in the book that might be unfamiliar to your students.
6. The ***Ready Teacher Toolbox*** chart provides an overview of related resources available online in the ***Ready Teacher Toolbox***.
7. **CCSS Focus** identifies the Common Core State Standard featured in the lesson, as well as additional standards covered in activities in the Teacher Resource Book.

Read Aloud Lesson H (Student Book pages 31–34)

Mike Mulligan and His Steam Shovel

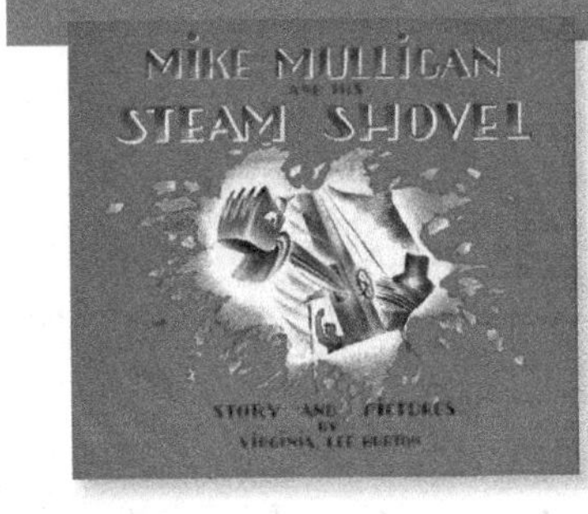

Lesson Objectives

You will read aloud *Mike Mulligan and His Steam Shovel*, which children will revisit in later lessons. Children will:

- Answer questions about key details in the story.
- Describe characters and major events, using key details.
- Retell the story, including key details.

About the Text

Summary

Mike Mulligan and his steam shovel, Mary Anne, had been digging together for years until new shovels came along and took away all their jobs. When Mike and his steam shovel get a chance to dig a cellar for a new town hall in the country, they prove that they can still be useful.

Genre: Fantasy

- *Mike Mulligan and His Steam Shovel* is a type of story called a fantasy. Remind children that in a fantasy, animals, or in this case machines, act like people.
- Use the cover illustration to point out that the steam shovel has eyes and a mouth, like a person.

Critical Vocabulary

- Prior to reading, briefly define the following words:
  - **steam shovel** (p. 3) a machine that digs big holes
  - **cellar** (p. 13) an underground room; a basement
  - **furnace** (p. 39) a machine that heats a building
  - **janitor** (p. 39) a person who cleans and takes care of a building
- As you read, pause to point to the words as you encounter them, and review their definitions.

Word Bank

- To support children in writing about the story, display a word bank containing the Critical Vocabulary and the characters' names (*Mike* and *Mary Anne*).
- Add other important story words, such as *Popperville* and *town hall*, on subsequent readings.

New Concepts: Energy Sources

- When first introducing the book, explain that some machines, such as refrigerators, get their power from electricity, while other machines, such as cars, get their power from gasoline.
- Explain that Mary Anne gets her power from steam, a form of power that isn't used much anymore.

Ready Teacher Toolbox Teacher-Toolbox.com

	Prerequisite Skills	RL.1.2
Ready Lessons		✓
Tools for Instruction	✓✓	✓
Interactive Tutorials	✓✓	

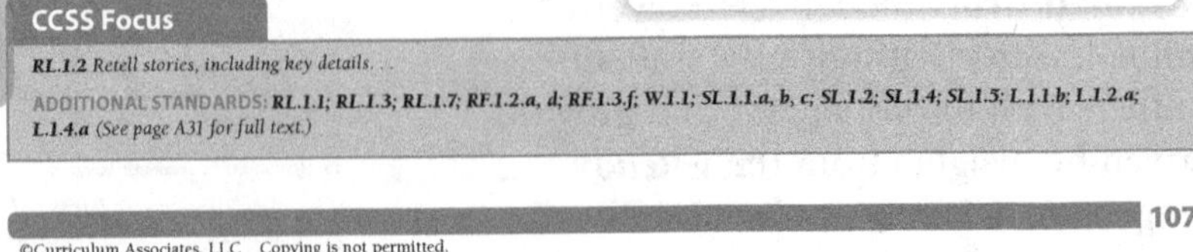

CCSS Focus

RL.1.2 *Retell stories, including key details. . .*

ADDITIONAL STANDARDS: ***RL.1.1; RL.1.3; RL.1.7; RF.1.2.a, d; RF.1.3.f; W.1.1; SL.1.1.a, b, c; SL.1.2; SL.1.4; SL.1.5; L.1.1.b; L.1.2.a; L.1.4.a*** *(See page A31 for full text.)*

107

Each of the five Read Aloud Lessons for Literature introduces students to a literature trade book used in the program. These lessons emphasize story elements. In Part 1, students listen as the teacher reads the entire trade book and then they identify the main characters in the story.

Student Book

Students draw and label the main character(s) from the story, reinforcing their understanding of story elements.

Hints provide guidance to help students stay focused and complete the task correctly.

3 **Turn and Talk** prompts students to make explicit connections to the story, telling a partner which details in their picture match details from the story.

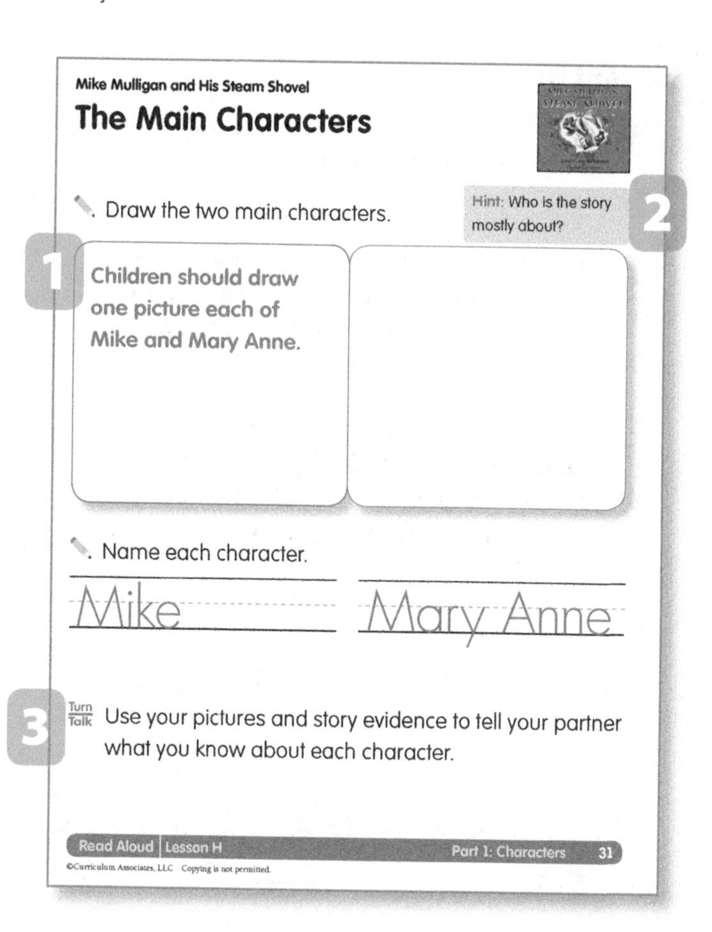

Mike Mulligan and His Steam Shovel

The Main Characters

Draw the two main characters.

Hint: Who is the story mostly about?

Children should draw one picture each of Mike and Mary Anne.

Name each character.

Mike | Mary Anne

Turn Talk Use your pictures and story evidence to tell your partner what you know about each character.

Read Aloud | Lesson H Part 1: Characters 31

©Curriculum Associates, LLC Copying is not permitted.

Part 1: First Read (Characters)

Step by Step

- **Introduce *Mike Mulligan and His Steam Shovel*.** Display the book. Then read aloud the title and the name of the author, Virginia Lee Burton. Point out that she is also the illustrator.
- **Set the purpose for reading.** Tell children that readers make sense of a story by identifying the characters and then keeping track of what happens to them.
- Explain that as you read aloud, children should listen closely to identify the characters in this story.
- Read aloud *Mike Mulligan and His Steam Shovel*. Read the story all the way through, pausing only to briefly define challenging vocabulary.
- **Guide children to review the characters.** After reading, use questions such as these to discuss the characters. *(RL.1.1; SL.1.1; SL.1.2)*

  Who are the main characters? *(Mike, Mary Anne)*

  How can we tell they are the main characters? *(The story is about what happens to them.)*

  Who are some of the other characters? *(Henry B. Swap, the little boy)*
- Direct children to turn to Student Book page 31. Read aloud the first item, along with the Hint. Help children eliminate secondary characters such as Henry B. Swap and the little boy. *(RL.1.3)*

Tip: Display the book cover and reread the title. Point out that book titles often tell who one or more of the main characters are.

- Prompt children to write the names of the characters beneath their pictures.
- **Have children discuss story evidence.** Read aloud the Turn and Talk activity. Encourage children to connect details in their picture to details in the story, and remind them to think about some things that each character says and does during the story. *(SL.1.4; SL.1.5)*

ELL Support: Jobs People Do

- Explain that jobs are the types of work that people do. The people in a city or a town such as Popperville do many different jobs.
- Point to the words *postman*, *milkman*, and *doctor* on page 26.
- Explain that a postman's job is to deliver the mail. In the past, a milkman's job was to deliver bottles of milk to people's houses. A doctor's job is to take care of people's health.
- Have children find the milkman and the postman in the illustration on pages 26 and 27.
- Ask children to point to and say the words *postman*, *milkman*, and *doctor* aloud. Have volunteers explain each job.

108 Read Aloud Lesson H: *Mike Mulligan and His Steam Shovel*

Teacher Resource Book

1 **Step by Step** guides students through each lesson part. Bulleted, bold text highlights the instructional moves in each part of the lesson.

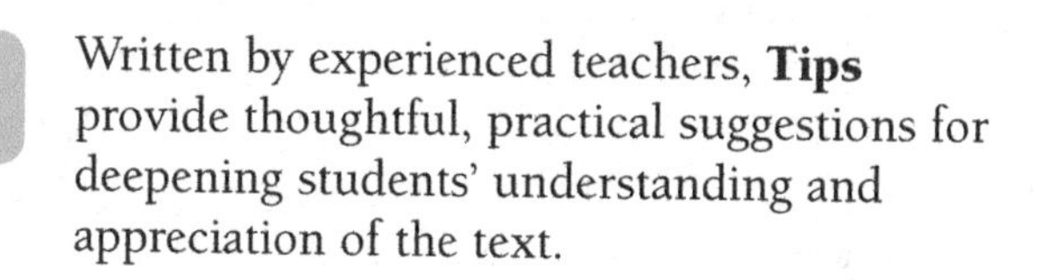

2 Written by experienced teachers, **Tips** provide thoughtful, practical suggestions for deepening students' understanding and appreciation of the text.

3 **ELL Support** provides background on concepts, content, and potentially unfamiliar words to help make text more accessible to English Language Learners.

In Part 2, students listen as the teacher rereads the beginning of the trade book aloud. The teacher then uses prompts provided in the Teacher Resource Book to guide students through answering questions about the key details in this part of the story.

Student Book

1 Students use text evidence to draw a picture about an important story event.

2 Students gain critical writing practice by using complete sentences to describe the important story event shown in their pictures.

3 **Turn and Talk** employs peer talk and interaction to answer text-related questions using evidence from the story.

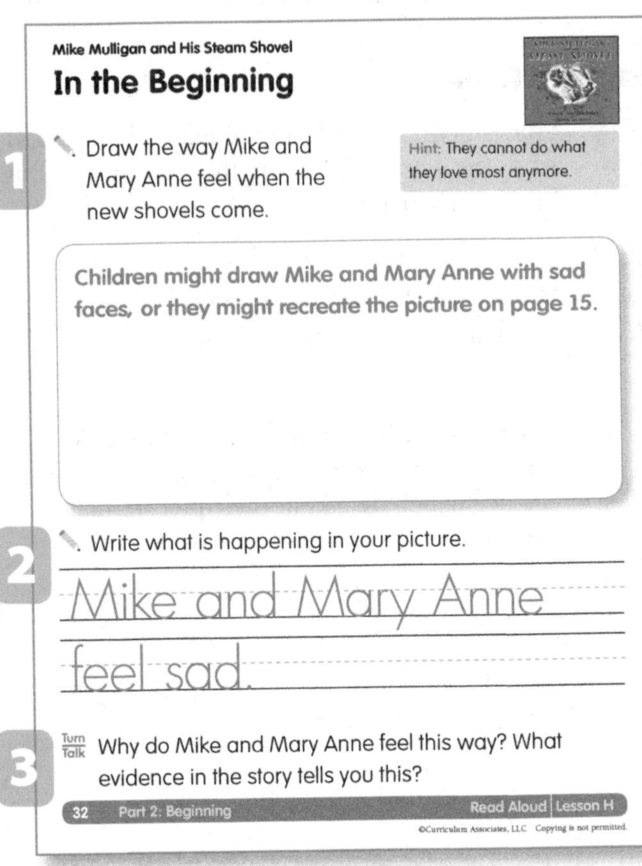

Mike Mulligan and His Steam Shovel

In the Beginning

1 Draw the way Mike and Mary Anne feel when the new shovels come.

Hint: They cannot do what they love most anymore.

Children might draw Mike and Mary Anne with sad faces, or they might recreate the picture on page 15.

2 Write what is happening in your picture.

Mike and Mary Anne feel sad.

3 Turn Talk Why do Mike and Mary Anne feel this way? What evidence in the story tells you this?

32 Part 2: Beginning Read Aloud | Lesson H

©Curriculum Associates, LLC Copying is not permitted.

Part 2: Reread for Meaning (Beginning)

Step by Step

- **Reread and discuss the beginning.** Read pages 3–17 aloud. Use questions such as these to guide discussion. *(RL.1.1; SL.1.1; SL.1.2)*

  Pages 5–13: What do Mike and Mary Anne help build? *(canals, railways, highways, landing fields)*

  Pages 14–15: Why are Mike and Mary Anne sad? *(New shovels came and took all the jobs.)*

  Page 17: What problem do Mike and Mary Anne have? *(No one wants steam shovels anymore.)*

- Use the Close Reading activity to help children look for evidence in the illustrations.
- **Focus on a key detail.** Direct children to turn to Student Book page 32. Read aloud the first item and the Hint. Recall when and why Mike and Mary Anne were happy, and help children understand why the new shovels change that. *(RL.1.3)*
- Prompt children to complete the second item.

Tip: Scaffold for emerging writers by providing a sentence starter: *Mike and Mary Anne feel____.*

- **Have children discuss story evidence.** Read aloud the Turn and Talk activity. Encourage children to connect ideas in the beginning of the story in order to explain why Mike and Mary Anne are sad. *(SL.1.4)*

Mike Mulligan and His Steam Shovel

In the Beginning

Draw the way Mike and Mary Anne feel when the new shovels come.

Hint: They cannot do what they love most anymore.

Children might draw Mike and Mary Anne with sad faces, or they might recreate the picture on page 15.

Write what is happening in your picture.

Mike and Mary Anne feel sad.

Turn Talk Why do Mike and Mary Anne feel this way? What evidence in the story tells you this?

32 Part 2: Beginning Read Aloud | Lesson H

- Discuss the most important details from this part of the story. Encourage children to use their Student Book pages to recall details.

Tier Two Vocabulary: *Proud of*

- Have children recall who Mike Mulligan is proud of. *(Mary Anne)* Guide them to point to the phrase *proud of* in the story as they give their answers.
- Work with children to determine that the phrase *proud of* means "feeling very good about yourself or someone you know."
- Provide an example of a time when you were proud of the class. You may say *I was proud of our class when we won the Class of the Month award.*
- Then have volunteers name a time when they were proud of themselves. Discuss examples and non-examples, such as breaking a rule or not telling the truth. *(L.1.5.c)*

Close Reading

- Remind children that good readers look for evidence in the words and pictures.
- Display the illustration on page 15, and read the writing on the fence. Prompt:

  What details do you notice? *(Mary Anne is crying and Mike looks sad.)*

  How does this picture help you understand Mike and Mary Anne's problem? *(The writing on the fence tells what Mike and Mary Anne are sad about. No one wants steam shovels anymore.)* *(RL.1.7)*

Read Aloud Lesson H: *Mike Mulligan and His Steam Shovel* 109

Teacher Resource Book

1 Suggested prompts guide students to identify important story events and extract key ideas from the trade book. Questions build toward a gradual understanding of the text's meaning.

2 Students work toward a retelling of the entire story by reviewing the most important details from each part, using their Student Book pictures and **Turn and Talk** conversations for support.

3 **Tier Two Vocabulary** provides students practice with key words or phrases from the trade book that are likely to be encountered in other contexts.

4 **Close Reading** engages students in strategies for extracting meaning from the text. Sometimes this activity is a deep dive into text details; other times it's a broader look at the text structure or organization.

In Part 3, students listen as the teacher rereads the middle of the trade book aloud. Students once again draw, write about, and discuss key details in this part of the story.

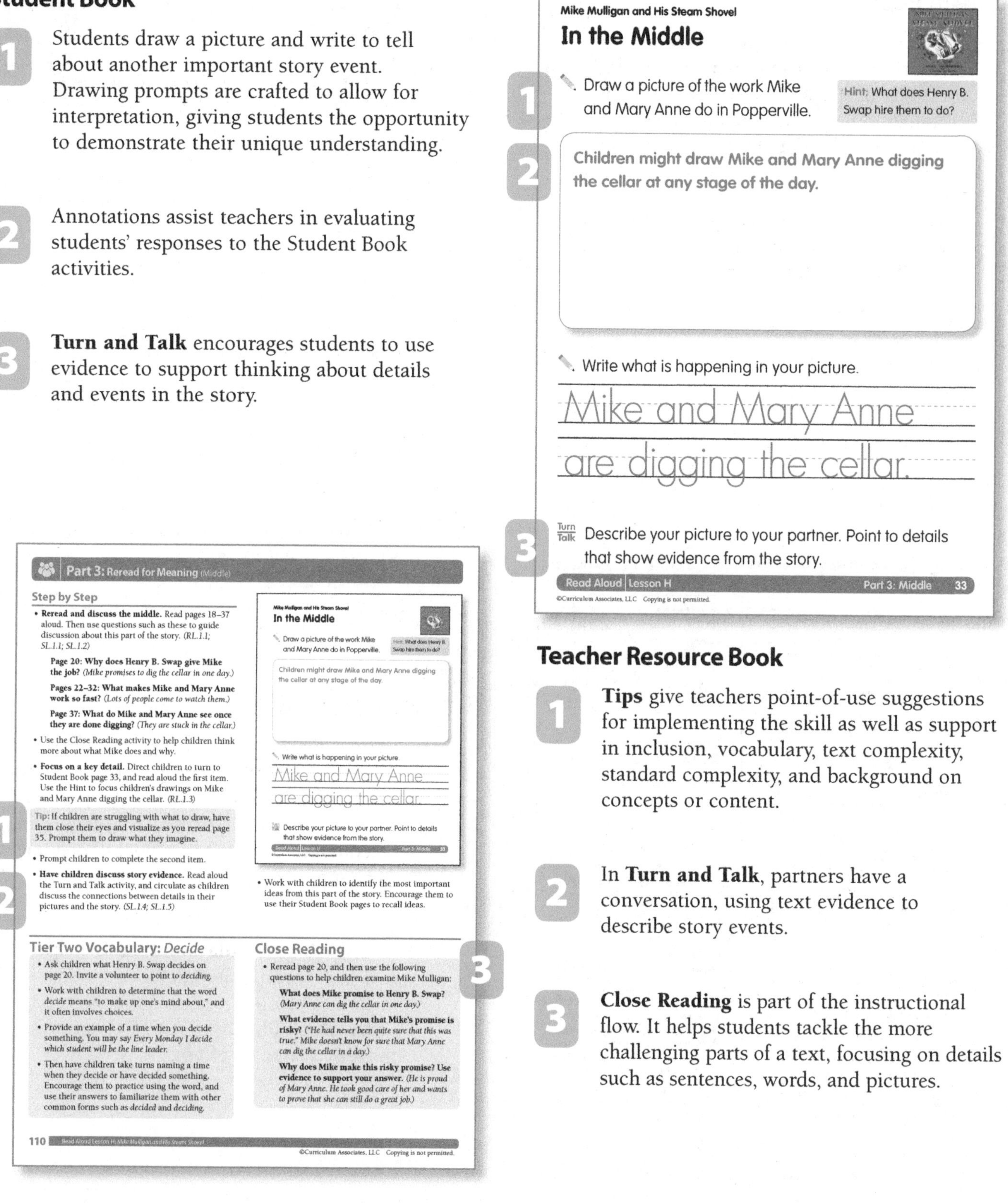

Student Book

1 Students draw a picture and write to tell about another important story event. Drawing prompts are crafted to allow for interpretation, giving students the opportunity to demonstrate their unique understanding.

2 Annotations assist teachers in evaluating students' responses to the Student Book activities.

3 **Turn and Talk** encourages students to use evidence to support thinking about details and events in the story.

Mike Mulligan and His Steam Shovel

In the Middle

1. Draw a picture of the work Mike and Mary Anne do in Popperville.

Hint: What does Henry B. Swap hire them to do?

2. Children might draw Mike and Mary Anne digging the cellar at any stage of the day.

Write what is happening in your picture.

Mike and Mary Anne are digging the cellar.

3. Turn Talk Describe your picture to your partner. Point to details that show evidence from the story.

Read Aloud | Lesson H Part 3: Middle 33

©Curriculum Associates, LLC Copying is not permitted.

Part 3: Reread for Meaning (Middle)

Step by Step

- **Reread and discuss the middle.** Read pages 18–37 aloud. Then use questions such as these to guide discussion about this part of the story. *(RL.1.1; SL.1.1; SL.1.2)*

  Page 20: Why does Henry B. Swap give Mike the job? *(Mike promises to dig the cellar in one day.)*

  Pages 22–32: What makes Mike and Mary Anne work so fast? *(Lots of people come to watch them.)*

  Page 37: What do Mike and Mary Anne see once they are done digging? *(They are stuck in the cellar.)*
- Use the Close Reading activity to help children think more about what Mike does and why.
- **Focus on a key detail.** Direct children to turn to Student Book page 33, and read aloud the first item. Use the Hint to focus children's drawings on Mike and Mary Anne digging the cellar. *(RL.1.3)*

1 Tip: If children are struggling with what to draw, have them close their eyes and visualize as you reread page 35. Prompt them to draw what they imagine.

- Prompt children to complete the second item.
- **2** **Have children discuss story evidence.** Read aloud the Turn and Talk activity, and circulate as children discuss the connections between details in their pictures and the story. *(SL.1.4; SL.1.5)*

Mike Mulligan and His Steam Shovel
In the Middle
Draw a picture of the work Mike and Mary Anne do in Popperville.
Hint: What does Henry B. Swap hire them to do?
Children might draw Mike and Mary Anne digging the cellar at any stage of the day.
Write what is happening in your picture.
Mike and Mary Anne are digging the cellar.
Describe your picture to your partner. Point to details that show evidence from the story.

- Work with children to identify the most important ideas from this part of the story. Encourage them to use their Student Book pages to recall ideas.

Tier Two Vocabulary: ***Decide***

- Ask children what Henry B. Swap decides on page 20. Invite a volunteer to point to *deciding.*
- Work with children to determine that the word *decide* means "to make up one's mind about," and it often involves choices.
- Provide an example of a time when you decide something. You may say *Every Monday I decide which student will be the line leader.*
- Then have children take turns naming a time when they decide or have decided something. Encourage them to practice using the word, and use their answers to familiarize them with other common forms such as *decided* and *deciding.*

3 **Close Reading**

- Reread page 20, and then use the following questions to help children examine Mike Mulligan:

  What does Mike promise to Henry B. Swap? *(Mary Anne can dig the cellar in one day.)*

  What evidence tells you that Mike's promise is risky? *("He had never been quite sure that this was true." Mike doesn't know for sure that Mary Anne can dig the cellar in a day.)*

  Why does Mike make this risky promise? Use evidence to support your answer. *(He is proud of Mary Anne. He took good care of her and wants to prove that she can still do a great job.)*

110 Read Aloud Lesson H: Mike Mulligan and His Steam Shovel

©Curriculum Associates, LLC Copying is not permitted.

Teacher Resource Book

1 **Tips** give teachers point-of-use suggestions for implementing the skill as well as support in inclusion, vocabulary, text complexity, standard complexity, and background on concepts or content.

2 In **Turn and Talk**, partners have a conversation, using text evidence to describe story events.

3 **Close Reading** is part of the instructional flow. It helps students tackle the more challenging parts of a text, focusing on details such as sentences, words, and pictures.

In Part 4, students listen as the teacher rereads the end of the trade book aloud. The teacher checks comprehension as students ask and answer questions about this part of the story. The teacher then guides students in a retelling of the text.

Student Book

Students draw a picture and write a description that captures a critical moment at the end of the story. Often this prompt is crafted to help students think about the solution to the character's main problem.

2 **Turn and Talk** prompts guide children to return to the story to make connections to specific details they heard.

Mike Mulligan and His Steam Shovel

At the End

1 Draw what Mike and Mary Anne are doing at the end of the story.

Hint: What are their new jobs?

Children should draw Mike and Mary Anne in the basement of the town hall. Details might show Mike taking care of the building and steam coming from Mary Anne.

Write what is happening in your picture.

Mike and Mary Anne are staying in the town hall.

2 Turn Talk Explain your drawing. What details from the story did you include in your picture?

34 Part 4: End Read Aloud Lesson H

Part 4: Reread for Meaning (End)

Step by Step

- **Reread and discuss the end.** Read pages 38–44 aloud. Discuss the way the story ends, using questions such as these. *(RL.1.1; SL.1.1; SL.1.2)*

  Page 39: What idea does the little boy have? *(He thinks Mary Anne should stay in the cellar to be the furnace and Mike should stay to be the janitor.)*

  Page 39: How does this idea solve Mike and Mary Anne's problem from earlier in the story? *(They have work to do now. People want them again.)*

  Page 44: How do Mike and Mary Anne feel now? *(They feel happy.)*

- Use the Close Reading activity to identify evidence that the problem is solved.
- **Focus on a key detail.** Direct children to turn to Student Book page 34, and read aloud the first item. Use the Hint to help children understand that Mike and Mary Anne are staying in the town hall. *(RL.1.3)*
- Prompt children to complete the second item.

Tip: Support developing writers by providing additional lined paper for children who wish to describe their pictures in more detail.

- **Have children discuss story evidence.** Read aloud the Turn and Talk activity. Encourage children to recall particular words and phrases from the text to explain their drawings. *(SL.1.4; SL.1.5)*

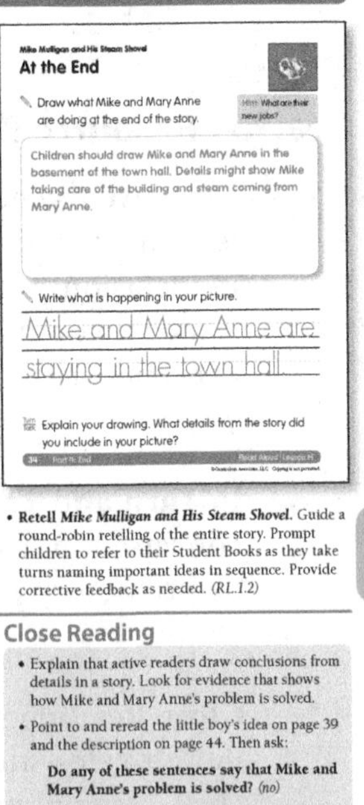
Mike Mulligan and His Steam Shovel
At the End
Draw what Mike and Mary Anne are doing at the end of the story.
Hint: What are their new jobs?
Children should draw Mike and Mary Anne in the basement of the town hall. Details might show Mike taking care of the building and steam coming from Mary Anne.
Write what is happening in your picture.
Mike and Mary Anne are staying in the town hall.
Explain your drawing. What details from the story did you include in your picture?

- **Retell *Mike Mulligan and His Steam Shovel*.** Guide a round-robin retelling of the entire story. Prompt children to refer to their Student Books as they take turns naming important ideas in sequence. Provide corrective feedback as needed. *(RL.1.2)*

Integrating Foundational Skills

Use these tasks as opportunities to integrate foundational skills into your reading of *Mike Mulligan and His Steam Shovel*.

1 Have children practice sounding out each sound in the following words: *had, get, dug, way, let, pay*. Help them to identify which words have a short vowel sound and which have a long vowel sound. *(Short vowel sound: had, get, dug, let; Long vowel sound: way, pay)* *(RF.1.2.a; RF.1.2.d)*

2 Reread and display the following words: *happened, everybody, talking, best, leave, keeping, smiled, quite*. Ask children to tell which words have an inflectional ending, such as *-ing, -ed,* or *-s*. *(happened, talking, keeping, smiled)* *(RF.1.3.f)*

Close Reading

- Explain that active readers draw conclusions from details in a story. Look for evidence that shows how Mike and Mary Anne's problem is solved.
- Point to and reread the little boy's idea on page 39 and the description on page 44. Then ask:

  Do any of these sentences say that Mike and Mary Anne's problem is solved? *(no)*

  How do these sentences help us to understand that the problem is solved? *(The sentences show how it was solved. The little boy explains the kind of work they will do, and the last page shows that Mike and Mary Anne are happy in the cellar. They are not sad anymore.)*

Read Aloud Lesson H: Mike Mulligan and His Steam Shovel 111

Teacher Resource Book

1 **Retell the text.** To reinforce the content of the story, students participate in a class-wide retelling that reviews the most important ideas and events in sequence. Students are encouraged to use their Student Book pages for support.

2 **Integrating Foundational Skills** helps teachers incorporate brief foundational skill activities using words from the target page span covered in Part 4. CCSS codes are provided at point of use.

Additional Activities

Teacher Resource Book

Additional Activities provide meaningful text-based Writing, Speaking and Listening, and Language activities. CCSS codes are identified at point of use next to each activity, allowing the teacher to easily integrate standards instruction.

Additional Activities RA Lesson H

Writing Activity

Write an Opinion *(W.1.1)*

- Direct children to look back at the pictures they drew on page 34 of their Student Books and ask them to think about the way the story ends. Discuss children's opinions about the end of the story. Ask: *Do you like the way this story ends? Why or why not?*
- Ask children to write a sentence stating whether they liked or did not like the way the story ends. Encourage them to include the title of the book. Then ask children to write a sentence explaining why they did or did not like the way the story ends.
- Invite volunteers to read aloud their writing.

Speaking and Listening Activity

Get into Character *(SL.1.4)*

- Brainstorm with children what they know about Henry B. Swap. Encourage them to describe the way he thinks, feels, and acts. Then do the same with Mike Mulligan. Write children's ideas in two columns on chart paper.
- Have children work in pairs to act out a conversation between Mike Mulligan and Henry B. Swap. One child will pretend to be Mike Mulligan, and the other will pretend to be Henry B. Swap.
- Encourage children to use what they know from the conversation that takes place in the story, but also to add in observations that aren't written. For instance, Henry B. Swap might say, "Mike is never going to finish this job, and I will get it for free!"
- Invite volunteers to share their reenactments with the class.

Language Activity

Common and Proper Nouns *(L.1.1.b; L.1.2.a)*

- Remind children that a *noun* is a word that names a person, place, or thing. Explain that there are different kinds of nouns—common nouns and proper nouns.
- Turn to page 17 of *Mike Mulligan and His Steam Shovel*, and point out the words *shovels* and *town*. Explain that these are common nouns because they name general things. They could refer to any kind of shovel, or any town.
- Then point out the words *Mary Anne* and *Popperville* and say: *These are examples of proper nouns. A proper noun names a specific person, place, or thing. A proper noun begins with a capital letter, no matter where it is in a sentence. Names are examples of proper nouns.*
- Using examples from the story, work with children to pair proper nouns with their common nouns. *(Mary Anne/shovel; Popperville/town; Mike Mulligan/man)*

112 Read Aloud Lesson H: *Mike Mulligan and His Steam Shovel*

Read Aloud Lesson—Informational Text

Each of the four Read Aloud Lessons for Informational Text introduces students to an informational text trade book used in the program. These lessons emphasize main topics and key details in the informational texts. In Part 1, students listen as the teacher reads the entire trade book. Then they identify the main topic of the book as well as some interesting features they noticed. In Part 2, students listen as the teacher rereads a section of the trade book. Students identify and discuss key details in this part of the book.

Student Book

1. In Part 1, students complete a sentence starter that allows them to express their big takeaway from the book, whether it is a description of the main topic or a particularly interesting detail.

2. Following a teacher-led discussion about the book's text features, students record the unique features of the book. Doing so helps them begin to recognize the different ways information can be presented.

3. During **Turn and Talk**, students review key concepts and details by telling a partner what they learned from the book.

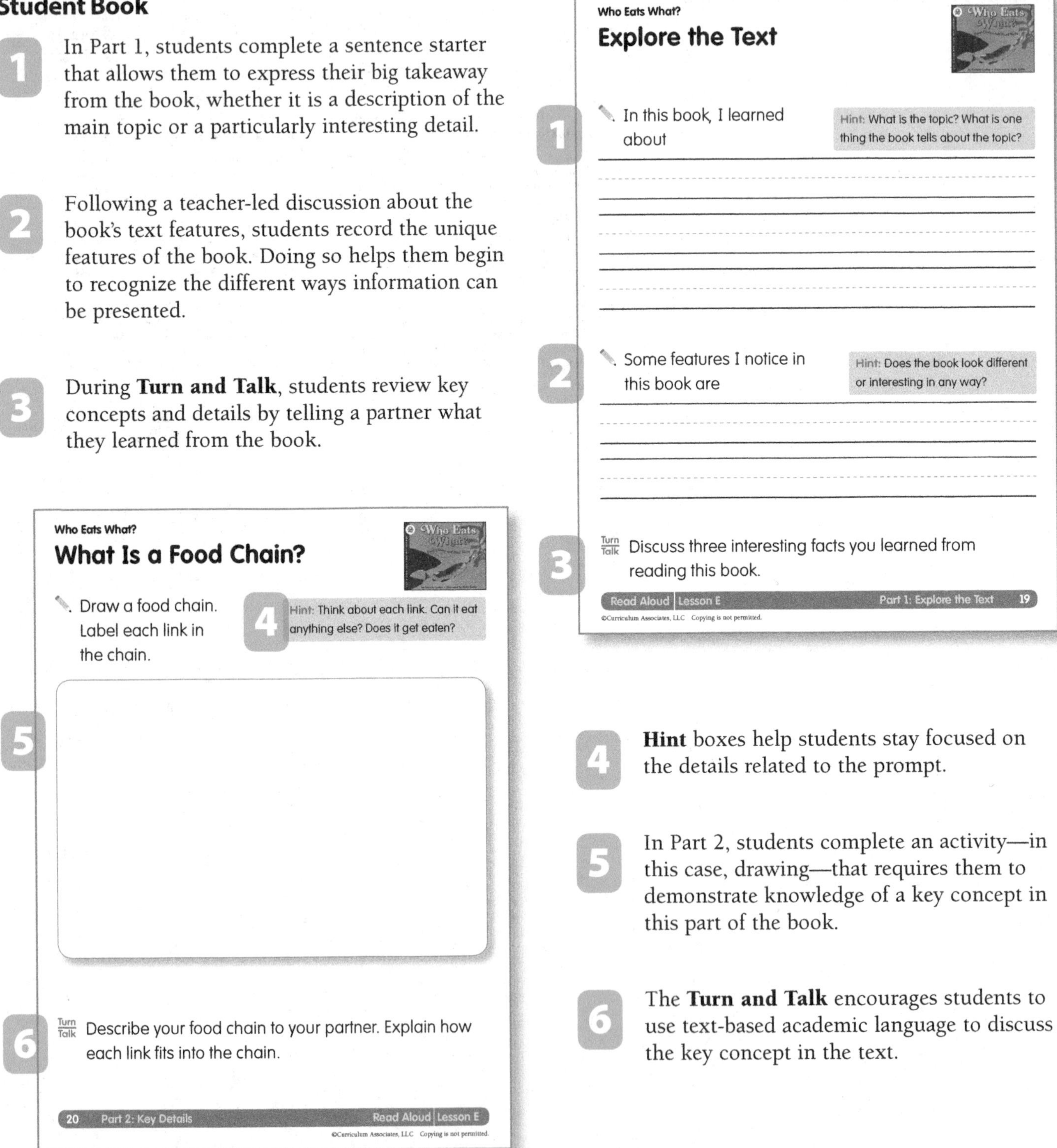

Who Eats What?

Explore the Text

1 In this book, I learned about

Hint: What is the topic? What is one thing the book tells about the topic?

2 Some features I notice in this book are

Hint: Does the book look different or interesting in any way?

3 Turn Talk Discuss three interesting facts you learned from reading this book.

Read Aloud | Lesson E Part 1: Explore the Text 19

©Curriculum Associates, LLC Copying is not permitted.

Who Eats What?

What Is a Food Chain?

5 Draw a food chain. Label each link in the chain.

4 Hint: Think about each link. Can it eat anything else? Does it get eaten?

6 Turn Talk Describe your food chain to your partner. Explain how each link fits into the chain.

20 Part 2: Key Details Read Aloud | Lesson E

©Curriculum Associates, LLC Copying is not permitted.

4. **Hint** boxes help students stay focused on the details related to the prompt.

5. In Part 2, students complete an activity—in this case, drawing—that requires them to demonstrate knowledge of a key concept in this part of the book.

6. The **Turn and Talk** encourages students to use text-based academic language to discuss the key concept in the text.

Read Aloud Lesson—Informational Text

In Parts 3 and 4, students listen as the teacher rereads two more sections of the trade book aloud. Students ask and answer questions about the key details in these parts of the text. The teacher then guides students in a review of the important details in the entire book.

Student Book

1 In Parts 3 and 4, students continue to focus on recalling details and demonstrating their understanding by writing, drawing, or completing a graphic organizer related to details in each part of the text.

2 Each **Turn and Talk** provides students with an opportunity to talk about each other's thinking as they answer a question using evidence from the book.

Who Eats What?

Food Chains Are Alike and Different

1 How is every food chain alike?

Hint: What do all food chains begin with?

Why does an animal need plants if it doesn't eat them?

Hint: How does a food chain work?

2 Turn Talk Talk to your partner about how one plant or animal might be part of more than one food chain. Together, list three examples.

Read Aloud | Lesson E Part 3: Key Details 21

Who Eats What?

Breaking the Chain

1 Complete each sentence in the flow chart to show how a food chain can be broken.

Humans hunted all of the

So nothing was left to

This caused the sea urchins to

2 Turn Talk What would happen to the animals in the ocean if the kelp went away? Use text evidence to explain your answer.

22 Part 4: Key Details Read Aloud | Lesson E

Focus Lessons

Each of the twenty-one Focus Lessons targets a specific Grade 1 Common Core State Standard for Literature or Informational Text. Nine trade books, which are introduced to students in the Read Aloud Lessons, are used as the vehicle for students' understanding and application of the standards in the Focus Lessons. The gradual-release instructional design of the Focus Lessons allows students to take increasing responsibility for applying the standard to the Read Aloud text as the lesson progresses.

The Focus Lessons begin with a brief prior knowledge activity in the Teacher Resource Book and end with differentiated instruction suggestions and an explanation of how the Grade 1 standard connects to the overarching Anchor Standard. Each six-page lesson in the Teacher Resource Book supports a four-page lesson in the Student Book. Student Book activities vary from lesson to lesson. The structure of the activity on the three practice pages within an individual lesson is the same, however, so students become familiar with the activity format as they progress through a lesson. This allows students to gradually work toward completing the pages on their own.

Teacher Resource Book

1. **CCSS** identifies the Common Core State Standard featured in the lesson.
2. **Required Read Alouds** list the trade books used in the lesson.
3. **Lesson Objectives** identify specific skills covered in the lesson.
4. **The Learning Progression** helps teachers see the standard in context.
5. **Prerequisite Skills** lists critical concepts and skills required for success with a given lesson.
6. **Tap Children's Prior Knowledge** provides a quick activity to activate students' knowledge of prerequisite and related skills, laying the foundation for the featured standard.
7. The ***Ready Teacher Toolbox*** chart provides an overview of related resources available online in the ***Ready Teacher Toolbox***.
8. **Additional CCSS** identifies additional standards covered in the lesson.

Lesson 2 (Student Book pages 45–48)

Describing Characters

CCSS

RL.1.3: Describe characters . . . in a story, using key details.

Required Read Alouds: A (*The Empty Pot*); C (*My Rotten Redheaded Older Brother*)

Lesson Objectives

- Identify words and phrases that indicate characters' feelings.
- Use words and pictures to support conclusions about characters in a story.
- Describe characters' words and actions using key details.
- Understand how describing a character can help you better understand a story.

The Learning Progression

- **Grade K:** CCSS RL.K.3 requires children to identify characters in a story with prompting and support.
- **Grade 1: CCSS RL.1.3 builds on the Grade K standard by having children work more independently at using key details and illustrations in a story to identify and describe the characters.**
- **Grade 2:** CCSS RL.2.3 expands upon the scope of the standard by having children describe how characters in a story respond to major events and challenges.

Prerequisite Skills

- Identify characters with prompting and support.
- Identify key details with prompting and support.
- Retell story details with prompting and support.

Tap Children's Prior Knowledge

- Remind children that the characters in a story are the people or animals the story is about. Ask children to name some characters from stories they have read recently. Write their suggestions on the board.
- Explain that realistic characters are like people in real life, while made-up characters do things real people or animals couldn't do. For example, Junie B. Jones is a realistic character and Martha, the talking dog, is a made-up character. Have children identify other realistic and made-up characters in the list.
- Tell children that understanding story characters is a lot like understanding people in real life. Say: *Imagine you saw a friend sitting alone in the corner and crying. What would you think? (The friend is sad.)*
- Discuss that paying attention to the things a friend says or does helps you understand how that friend is feeling. Explain that the same is true with both realistic and made-up characters in a story: paying attention to what characters say and do will help children understand them.
- Tell children that in this lesson, they will learn to describe characters based on what they say and do.

Ready *Teacher Toolbox* Teacher-Toolbox.com

	Prerequisite Skills	*RL.1.3*
Ready Lessons	✓	✓
Tools for Instruction	✓	✓
Interactive Tutorials		✓

Additional CCSS

RL.1.1; RL.1.2; RL.1.7; SL.1.1; SL.1.3; SL.1.4; L.1.1; L.1.2 (See page A38 for full text.)

27

The Listen and Learn page introduces the standard in student-friendly language, defines important academic vocabulary, and lists questions and strategies good readers use when applying the targeted standard to text. Students listen and follow along in their Student Books as the teacher reads the page aloud.

Student Book

Each Listen and Learn page introduces the standard with child-friendly explanations of academic vocabulary.

Bulleted text provides strategies that proficient readers use to access text.

3

The conclusion provides a rationale for why and how good readers use the concept developed in the lesson.

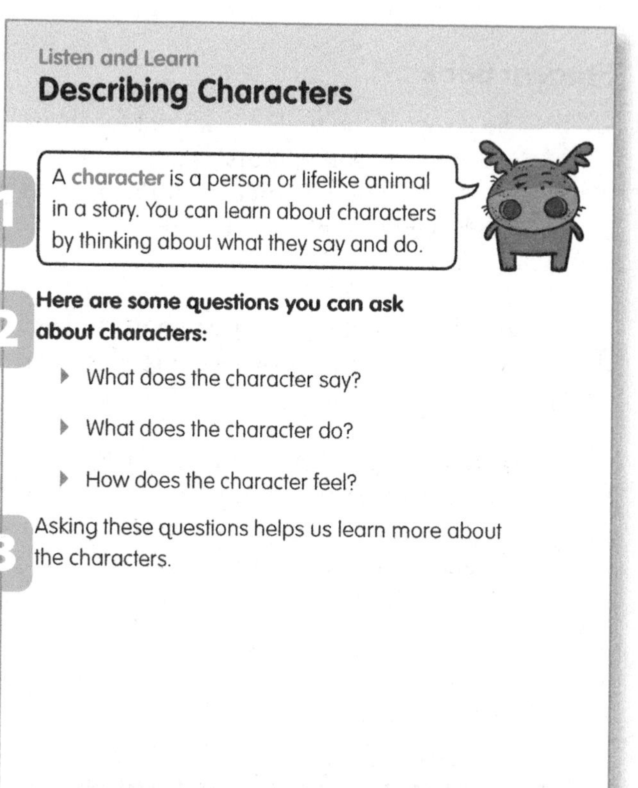

Listen and Learn

Describing Characters

1 A **character** is a person or lifelike animal in a story. You can learn about characters by thinking about what they say and do.

2 **Here are some questions you can ask about characters:**

- What does the character say?
- What does the character do?
- How does the character feel?

3 Asking these questions helps us learn more about the characters.

Lesson 2 Part 1: Introduction 45

©Curriculum Associates, LLC Copying is not permitted.

Part 1: Introduction

Step by Step

1

- **Introduce the standard.** Have children turn to page 45 in their Student Books. Read aloud the speech bubble.
- Explain that *lifelike animal* means an animal that talks or does things that a person might do. Point out that children know many stories with lifelike animal characters. Give examples such as *The Ant and The Grasshopper, The Town Mouse and the Country Mouse,* or *Henny Penny.*
- **Review questions to ask about characters.** Read the line below the speech bubble, and point out that what follows are questions that good readers ask themselves to find out more about a character. Read aloud the first question. Have children underline the word *say.* Then explain:

  The words a character says can tell you what the character thinks or feels. The way a character says the words is important, too. For example, a character can shout, whisper, or whine. These all sound and feel very different.

2

Tip: To help emergent readers identify the words *say, do,* and *feel,* point to each word as you emphasize it, and have children repeat it after you.

- Have children say the following sentence in a shout, a whisper, and a whine: *I am hungry.* After each example, discuss how someone who talks that way might be feeling, and think about reasons why.
- Read aloud the second question. Have children underline the word *do.* Then explain:

  The things a character does can give you information about the kind of person the character is. Would a nice character help someone or say mean things? *(A nice character would help someone.)*

- Ask children to brainstorm some mean characters they remember from stories, such as the wicked stepmother and stepsisters in *Cinderella.* Discuss how you determined that these characters were mean based on their actions, or what they did.

Listen and Learn

Describing Characters

A character is a person or lifelike animal in a story. You can learn about characters by thinking about what they say and do.

Here are some questions you can ask about characters:

- What does the character say?
- What does the character do?
- How does the character feel?

Asking these questions helps us learn more about the characters.

- Read aloud the third question. Have children underline the word *feel.* Then explain:

  The things a character does and says can help you understand the way the character feels. Imagine a character jumps up and down, claps her hands, and yells "Hooray!" How do you think that character feels? *(happy and excited)*

- **Explain why readers ask questions about characters.** Read aloud the bottom of the page. Explain that when you think about why a character says or does things, you get to know them better, just like you get to know a person better.
- Share an example of a time when describing a character helped you understand a story. For instance, recount *The Tortoise and the Hare.* Tell how knowing that the Hare likes to brag about how fast he is helps you understand why the Tortoise would want to trick him.

3

- **Have children demonstrate understanding.** Call on individuals to share what they have learned so far about describing a character in a story.

28 Lesson 2: Describing Characters

©Curriculum Associates, LLC Copying is not permitted.

Teacher Resource Book

1

Step by Step walks students through the Listen and Learn page. It encourages them to interact with the text, often directing them to mark it by underlining or circling key terms.

2

A point-of-use **Tip** may provide teachers with instructional strategies in developing academic vocabulary.

3

Students tell in their own words what they have learned so far about the standard.

In Part 2, students listen as the teacher reads aloud a short passage from a designated trade book. The teacher uses think-aloud support to model how to apply the standard to the text. The teacher then models completing the Student Book page. Students practice applying the standard and then complete the Student Book page, using the teacher's modeling as their guide.

Student Book

1 The cover of the trade book used for this part of the lesson appears in the corner of the page to remind students of the book to which they're applying the skill.

2 Text-dependent questions support students in a close reading or close listening of the text.

3 **Turn and Talk** poses a standard-based question for partner- and whole-class discussion. It challenges students to find text evidence to explain their answers.

Practice Together

Describing Characters

in *The Empty Pot*, pages 26–27

THE EMPTY POT

What does the Emperor do when the children come?

Hint: What do the children bring?

How does the Emperor feel?

Hint: What detail tells about the Emperor's face?

Turn Talk What evidence from the story tells you how the Emperor feels?

46 Part 2: Modeled Instruction | Lesson 2

©Curriculum Associates, LLC Copying is not permitted.

Part 2: Modeled Instruction

Step by Step

- **Review Part 1; preview Part 2.** Ask volunteers to share questions they can ask about characters in a story. Have children turn to Student Book page 46.
- **Revisit *The Empty Pot*.** Invite children to briefly retell the story, using pages 3–6 of their Student Books. *(RL.1.2)*
- **Model describing characters.** Explain that you are going to model asking questions about characters. Read aloud pages 26–27 of *The Empty Pot*. Then point to evidence in the text and pictures as you think aloud:

  I will ask myself what the Emperor says and does: First, he looks at the flowers slowly. Next, he frowns, then he does not say a word. I'll use that evidence to figure out how the Emperor feels. The words and pictures tell me that the Emperor is frowning. I think that means he feels unhappy. *(RL.1.7)*

Tip: Help children infer the Emperor's feelings. Have them frown. Ask how they feel when they make this face. Then ask how the Emperor feels.

- Read aloud each question and Hint on Student Book page 46. Discuss the answers to these questions.
- **Model writing your responses.** Model how to write the answers in complete sentences, and have children write their responses. *(RL.1.1; L.1.1; L.1.2.)*
- Use the Close Reading activity to analyze the Emperor's feelings and connect them to important events in the story.
- **Have children demonstrate understanding.** Have partners complete the Turn and Talk activity. Circulate, and prompt children to recall words, phrases, and picture evidence that helped them describe the Emperor's actions and feelings.
- Invite volunteers to share their evidence in class discussion. *(SL.1.1; SL.1.4)*

Practice Together

Describing Characters

in *The Empty Pot*, pages 26–27

What does the Emperor do when the children come?

Hint: What do the children bring?

The Emperor looks at the flowers and frowns.

How does the Emperor feel?

Hint: What detail tells about the Emperor's face?

The Emperor is unhappy.

What evidence from the story tells you how the Emperor feels?

Close Reading

- Help children recognize that by asking questions about the Emperor's actions, they can learn more about him and better understand the story. Reread pages 26–27. Then prompt:

  What do we know about the Emperor so far? *(He loves flowers. He needs to choose a successor. He gave each child a seed to grow.)*

  Why is it surprising that he frowns and doesn't say a word? *(Since he loves flowers, you would expect him to be happy to see all the flowers. Also he should be excited to see the children because he wants to pick a successor.)*

- Remind children that later, they learn that the Emperor frowned and said nothing because he was disappointed. He realized that the children had all cheated and that he couldn't trust them to take his place.

Lesson 2: Describing Characters 29

©Curriculum Associates, LLC Copying is not permitted.

Teacher Resource Book

1 The teacher uses a think-aloud to model how to apply the standard to the text.

2 Point-of-use **Tips** address student needs by anticipating confusion and providing guidance.

3 Teachers model how to complete the Student Book page.

4 **Close Reading** features engage students in a strategy that helps them extract meaning from the text for a specific purpose. Some **Close Readings** take a deep dive into text details, while others prompt students to take a broader look at some aspect of the text structure or organization.

In Part 3, students listen as the teacher reads aloud a selection from a second designated trade book. As part of the gradual-release instructional design, the teacher uses prompts provided in the Teacher Resource Book to guide students through applying the standard to the text selection.

Student Book

1. The activity format is continued throughout the lesson. The predictable page structure supports student mastery of the standard.

2. **Hints** provide clues that draw students back to the text to find evidence that supports the answer to the prompt.

Practice Together

Describing Characters

***in My Rotten Redheaded Older Brother*, pages 18–21**

What does Richie do at this point in the story?

Hint: What two things does Richie say about rhubarb?

How does Treesha feel about Richie?

Hint: What does Treesha say and do?

Turn Talk What evidence from the story tells you how Treesha feels about Richie?

Lesson 2 Part 3: Guided Practice 47

©Curriculum Associates, LLC Copying is not permitted.

Teacher Resource Book

1. The teacher revisits the second trade book and then reads aloud the targeted section of the story for this part of the lesson.

2. The teacher transitions from modeling to using questions to guide students in applying the standard to the text. The teacher then guides students to answer questions in the Student Book. Together, they review and discuss their responses.

3. The teacher guides students to answer the **Turn and Talk** question, and then they review and discuss their responses.

Part 3: Guided Practice

Step by Step

- **Review Parts 1–2; preview Part 3.** Have children recall questions they can ask about characters in a story. Direct them to Student Book page 47. Explain that you will guide them through this page.
- **Revisit *My Rotten Redheaded Older Brother*.** Have children briefly retell the story, using pages 11–14 of their Student Books. *(RL.1.2)*
- **Guide children to describe characters.** Tell children that as they listen to this part of the story, they will ask questions about what Richie and Treesha do and say, and use this evidence to identify how they feel about each other. Read aloud pages 18–21 of the story. Prompt children as you read:

  What does Richie say about rhubarb at first (page 18)? *(It's the sourest stuff on this planet.)*

  What does Treesha do, and why (page 19)? *(She challenges him to a rhubarb eating contest. She thinks she can beat him because he doesn't like rhubarb.)*

Tip: Explain that rhubarb tastes very sour, like lemon, so it would be hard to eat a lot of it at once. Share that not everyone likes eating sour foods, but Treesha does, and she thinks Richie doesn't.

  What does Richie say about rhubarb now (page 20)? *(He says he loves it.)*

  What does Treesha say about how she feels about Richie (page 21)? *(She says she can't stand him.)*

- **Guide children to write responses.** Read aloud each question on the Student Book page. Use the Hints to help children answer the questions. Discuss the answers and have children write them in complete sentences. *(RL.1.1; L.1.1; L.1.2)*
- Use the Close Reading activity to further describe the relationship between the main characters and to help prepare children for the Turn and Talk activity.
- **Have children demonstrate understanding.** Have partners do the Turn and Talk activity. Remind children to use evidence from the Close Reading discussion to support their ideas. Invite volunteers to share their answers. *(SL.1.1; SL.1.4)*

Practice Together

Describing Characters

in My Rotten Redheaded Older Brother, pages 18–21

What does Richie do at this point in the story?

Hint: What two things does Richie say about rhubarb?

He tricks Treesha. He eats more rhubarb than her.

How does Treesha feel about Richie?

Hint: What does Treesha say and do?

Treesha is mad at Richie.

What evidence from the story tells you how Treesha feels about Richie?

Close Reading

- Guide children to look closer at what Richie and Treesha say to each other in this part of the story.
- Read aloud page 21, emphasizing the tone of Richie and Treesha's words. Then prompt:

  Why does Treesha call her brother by his full name here? *(When you are very mad at someone, you sometimes use their first and last name instead of their nickname or first name.)*

  Why is it important that the author used the word *screamed*? *(When you scream at someone, you are usually very angry.)*

  What does the phrase *little twerp* tell you about the way Richie feels about Treesha? *(Calling someone by this name is making fun of them. You make fun of people you don't like and want to annoy.)*

- Discuss how this evidence tells more about the way Richie and Treesha feel about each other.

30 Lesson 2: Describing Characters

In Part 4, students listen as the teacher reads aloud a different passage from the trade book used in Part 3. As the final step of the gradual-release model, students apply the standard by completing the Student Book page independently. Students then discuss their work together, reflecting on their learning.

Student Book

As the final step of the gradual-release model, students are now prepared to work independently to answer text-dependent questions and demonstrate their understanding of the standard.

Practice by Myself

Describing Characters

in *My Rotten Redheaded Older Brother*, pages 31–32

1 What does Richie do to help Treesha?

Hint: What does Bubbie say that Richie did?

How does Richie feel about what happened to Treesha?

Hint: What words tell how Richie talks about the accident?

Turn Talk What evidence from the story tells you how Richie feels about Treesha's accident?

48 Part 4: Independent Practice Lesson 2

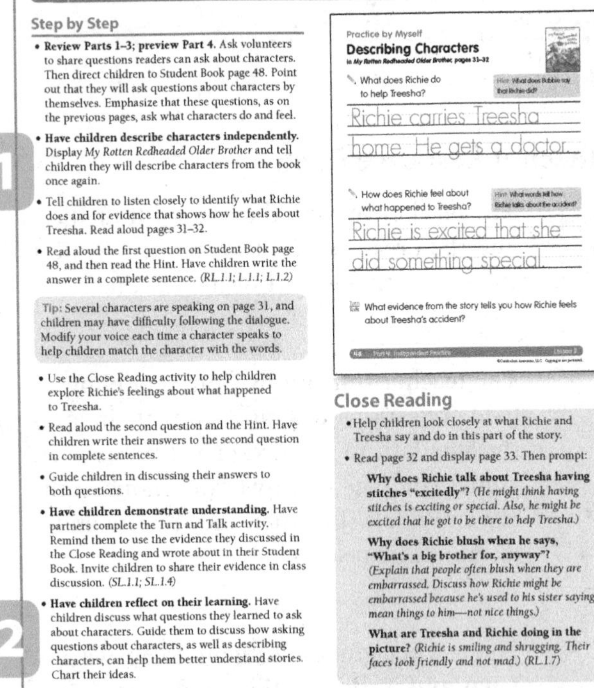

Part 4: Independent Practice

Step by Step

1

- **Review Parts 1–3; preview Part 4.** Ask volunteers to share questions readers can ask about characters. Then direct children to Student Book page 48. Point out that they will ask questions about characters by themselves. Emphasize that these questions, as on the previous pages, ask what characters do and feel.
- **Have children describe characters independently.** Display *My Rotten Redheaded Older Brother* and tell children they will describe characters from the book once again.
- Tell children to listen closely to identify what Richie does and for evidence that shows how he feels about Treesha. Read aloud pages 31–32.
- Read aloud the first question on Student Book page 48, and then read the Hint. Have children write the answer in a complete sentence. *(RL.1.1; L.1.1; L.1.2)*

Tip: Several characters are speaking on page 31, and children may have difficulty following the dialogue. Modify your voice each time a character speaks to help children match the character with the words.

- Use the Close Reading activity to help children explore Richie's feelings about what happened to Treesha.
- Read aloud the second question and the Hint. Have children write their answers to the second question in complete sentences.
- Guide children in discussing their answers to both questions.
- **Have children demonstrate understanding.** Have partners complete the Turn and Talk activity. Remind them to use the evidence they discussed in the Close Reading and wrote about in their Student Book. Invite children to share their evidence in class discussion. *(SL.1.1; SL.1.4)*

2

- **Have children reflect on their learning.** Have children discuss what questions they learned to ask about characters. Guide them to discuss how asking questions about characters, as well as describing characters, can help them better understand stories. Chart their ideas.

Practice by Myself

Describing Characters

in *My Rotten Redheaded Older Brother*, pages 31–32

What does Richie do to help Treesha?

Hint: What does Bubbie say that Richie did?

Richie carries Treesha home. He gets a doctor.

How does Richie feel about what happened to Treesha?

Hint: What words tell how Richie talks about the accident?

Richie is excited that she did something special.

What evidence from the story tells you how Richie feels about Treesha's accident?

Close Reading

- Help children look closely at what Richie and Treesha say and do in this part of the story.
- Read page 32 and display page 33. Then prompt:

Why does Richie talk about Treesha having stitches "excitedly"? *(He might think having stitches is exciting or special. Also, he might be excited that he got to be there to help Treesha.)*

Why does Richie blush when he says, "What's a big brother for, anyway"? *(Explain that people often blush when they are embarrassed. Discuss how Richie might be embarrassed because he's used to his sister saying mean things to him—not nice things.)*

What are Treesha and Richie doing in the picture? *(Richie is smiling and shrugging. Their faces look friendly and not mad.)* (RL.1.7)

Lesson 2: Describing Characters 31

©Curriculum Associates, LLC Copying is not permitted.

Teacher Resource Book

1 Students apply the standard to a different passage from the second trade book.

2 The lesson closes with students reflecting on their learning to reinforce the standard. They discuss what questions they learned to ask about the standard.

Focus Lesson

Differentiated Instruction

1 **Assessment and Remediation** provides activities that support students who have difficulty understanding the concepts of the standard. The standard is broken down into its essential elements, and activities address each potential difficulty.

2 The goal of **Connect to the Anchor Standard** is to show teachers how to anticipate the way students will use the standard with more complex texts as they move up through the grades. The activities, using the same trade books as in the lesson, are a bit more challenging, showing how the standard becomes gradually more complex.

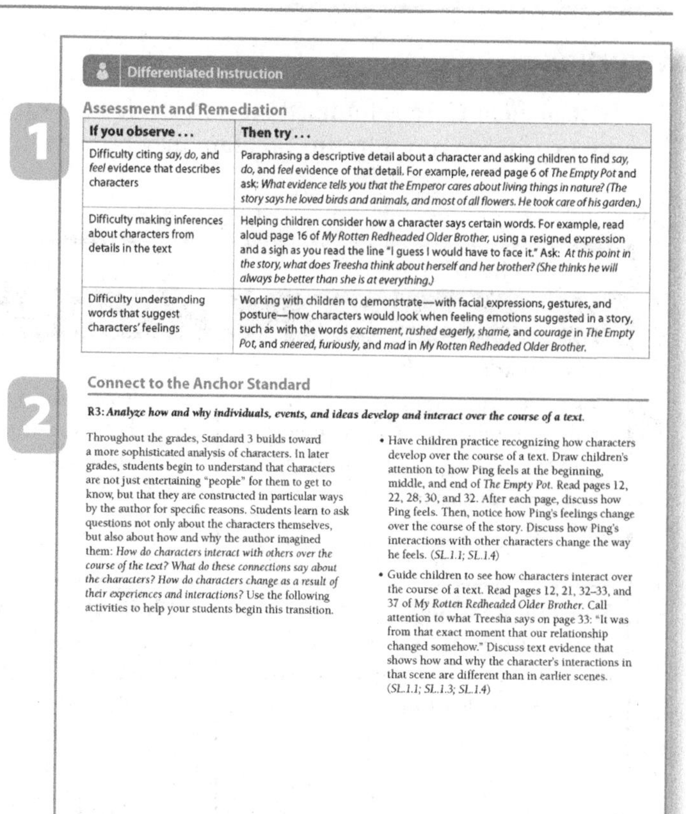

Differentiated Instruction

Assessment and Remediation

If you observe . . .	Then try . . .
Difficulty citing *say, do,* and *feel* evidence that describes characters	Paraphrasing a descriptive detail about a character and asking children to find *say, do,* and *feel* evidence of that detail. For example, reread page 6 of *The Empty Pot* and ask: *What evidence tells you that the Emperor cares about living things in nature? (The story says he loved birds and animals, and most of all flowers. He took care of his garden.)*
Difficulty making inferences about characters from details in the text	Helping children consider how a character says certain words. For example, read aloud page 16 of *My Rotten Redheaded Older Brother,* using a resigned expression and a sigh as you read the line "I guess I would have to face it." Ask: *At this point in the story, what does Treesha think about herself and her brother? (She thinks he will always be better than she is at everything.)*
Difficulty understanding words that suggest characters' feelings	Working with children to demonstrate—with facial expressions, gestures, and posture—how characters would look when feeling emotions suggested in a story, such as with the words *excitement, rushed eagerly, shame,* and *courage* in *The Empty Pot,* and *sneered, furiously,* and *mad* in *My Rotten Redheaded Older Brother.*

Connect to the Anchor Standard

R3: ***Analyze how and why individuals, events, and ideas develop and interact over the course of a text.***

Throughout the grades, Standard 3 builds toward a more sophisticated analysis of characters. In later grades, students begin to understand that characters are not just entertaining "people" for them to get to know, but that they are constructed in particular ways by the author for specific reasons. Students learn to ask questions not only about the characters themselves, but also about how and why the author imagined them: *How do characters interact with others over the course of the text? What do these connections say about the characters? How do characters change as a result of their experiences and interactions?* Use the following activities to help your students begin this transition.

- Have children practice recognizing how characters develop over the course of a text. Draw children's attention to how Ping feels at the beginning, middle, and end of *The Empty Pot.* Read pages 12, 22, 28, 30, and 32. After each page, discuss how Ping feels. Then, notice how Ping's feelings change over the course of the story. Discuss how Ping's interactions with other characters change the way he feels. *(SL.1.1; SL.1.4)*
- Guide children to see how characters interact over the course of a text. Read pages 12, 21, 32–33, and 37 of *My Rotten Redheaded Older Brother.* Call attention to what Treesha says on page 33: "It was from that exact moment that our relationship changed somehow." Discuss text evidence that shows how and why the character's interactions in that scene are different than in earlier scenes. *(SL.1.1; SL.1.3; SL.1.4)*

32 Lesson 2: Describing Characters

©Curriculum Associates, LLC Copying is not permitted.

Unit Check

Unit Checks are given at the end of each unit to assess students' understanding of the unit standards.

- Questions include both multiple-choice and short-response items that assess the unit's standards.
- Teacher Resource Book support includes an introduction to answering multiple-choice questions as well as a series of test-taking strategies that students can use during multiple-choice tests.
- Correct and incorrect answers are fully explained in the Answer Analysis.

Unit 1 Check

Listen closely as your teacher reads. Then answer the questions.

. Who is the character in the story?

A a little girl

B a boy named Ping

C a mother

. What does Ping like to do?

A draw pictures

B play with his friends

C grow flowers

. What is the setting of the story?

A a long time ago, in China

B a few years ago, on a farm

C right now, in China

61

©Curriculum Associates, LLC Copying is not permitted.

Supporting Research

Overview

Ready*® *Common Core is founded on research from a variety of federal initiatives, national literacy organizations, and literacy experts. As a result, this program may be used in support of several instructional models.

Ready® Uses . . .	Examples	Research Says . . .
Instructional Strategies		
Close Reading Close reading refers to the slow, deliberate reading of short pieces of text, focusing solely on the text itself, in order to achieve a deep understanding.	**TRB:** Close Reading activities in every lesson help students focus on and discuss the most important elements of the text.	"Close reading and gathering knowledge from specific texts should be at the heart of classroom activities and not be consigned to the margins when completing assignments." (Coleman & Pimentel, Revised Publishers' Criteria, 2012, p. 8)
Multiple Readings Through reading a text more than once, students are able to access different levels of its meaning.	**TRB:** Read Aloud Lessons allow teachers to read the trade books in their entirety and then reread to review key ideas. Focus Lessons require students to revisit each trade book multiple times in order to apply particular Common Core skills.	"Students should be asked to glean the information they need from multiple readings of a text, each with a specific purpose. In particular, aligned curriculum should explicitly direct . . . teachers to return to these portions in read-alouds." (Coleman & Pimentel, Revised Publishers' Criteria, 2012, p. 8)
Text-Dependent Questions Questions that are text-dependent can be answered only by information contained in the text itself, not personal opinion or background knowledge.	**SB:** Questions in each ***Ready*** lesson are text-dependent. Students are required to support answers with evidence from the text.	"Materials that accompany texts should ask students to think about what they have read or heard and then ask them to draw evidence from the text in support of their ideas about the reading." (Coleman & Pimentel, Revised Publishers' Criteria, 2012, p. 7)
Citing Textual Evidence Students become actively engaged as they provide evidence directly from the text to support their inferences.	**SB:** Questions in the ***Ready*** lessons specifically require students to cite evidence from the text to support their answers.	"Students cite specific evidence when offering an oral or written interpretation of a text. They use relevant evidence when supporting their own points in writing and speaking . . ." (Common Core State Standards, 2010, p. 7)
Building Content Knowledge Texts that are of high quality and substance allow students to build content knowledge as they develop and strengthen their reading skills.	**SB:** Students deepen their content knowledge by drawing, writing, and completing graphic organizers based on newly learned concepts. **TRB:** Read Aloud Informational Text Lessons relate to grade-appropriate science and social studies content and feature a close review of new concepts and vocabulary, as well as scaffolding for students to practice applying text-based academic language in discussion and Student Book activities.	"Students establish a base of knowledge across a wide range of subject matter by engaging with works of quality and substance." (Common Core State Standards, 2012, p. 7)

Ready® Uses . . .	Examples	Research Says . . .
Instructional Strategies (continued)		
Direct Instruction Scripted lesson plans include explicit step-by-step instruction of reading and learning strategies and lesson objectives.	**TRB:** Parts 1–4 of each lesson provide teachers with scaffolded, step-by-step, explicit instructions to help students meet each lesson objective.	"The research demonstrates that the types of questions, the detailed step-by-step breakdowns, and the extensive practice with a range of examples . . . will significantly benefit students' comprehension." (Gersten & Carnine, 1986, p. 72)
Scaffolded Instruction Scaffolded instruction is the gradual withdrawal of support through modeled, guided, and independent instruction.	**SB:** Activities are structured consistently from Parts 2–4 so that students can gain confidence working independently in Part 4 after practicing with the teacher in Parts 2–3. **TRB:** The gradual-release model provides appropriate support that is gradually withdrawn as students gain mastery of the standard.	"Scaffolded instruction optimizes student learning by providing a supportive environment while facilitating student independence." (Larkin, 2002)
Prior Knowledge Prior knowledge activities activate knowledge from previous experiences.	**TRB:** Tap Children's Prior Knowledge at the beginning of each Focus Lesson engages students in a discussion to review known concepts that are related to the new skill.	"Research clearly emphasizes that for learning to occur, new information must be integrated with what the learner already knows." (Rumelhart, 1980)
An Integrated Model of Literacy The processes of communication (reading, writing, listening, and speaking) are closely connected, a fact which should be reflected in literacy instruction.	**TRB:** Read Aloud Lessons give teachers opportunities to integrate Foundational Reading standards into text selections. Furthermore, Additional Activities in these lessons allow students to apply text knowledge to the areas of Writing, Speaking & Listening, and Language.	"While the Standards delineate specific expectations in reading, writing, speaking, listening, and language, each standard need not be a separate focus for instruction. Often, several standards can be addressed by a single, rich task." (Common Core State Standards, 2010, p. 5)
Instructional Features		
Complex Text A major emphasis of the Common Core State Standards is for students to encounter appropriately complex texts at each grade level in order to develop the skills and conceptual knowledge they need for success in school and life.	**TRB:** All read aloud texts in ***Ready*** were carefully selected based on the Common Core requirements for complexity and guided by the text examplars listed in Appendix B of the Standards.	"To grow, our students must read lots, and more specifically, they must read lots of 'complex' texts—texts that offer them new language, new knowledge, and new modes of thought." (Adams, 2009, p. 182)

Ready® Uses . . .	Examples	Research Says . . .
Instructional Features (continued)		
Balance of Informational and Literary Text The Common Core State Standards align with the requirements of the National Assessment of Educational Progress (NAEP) in calling for a greater emphasis on informational text.	**SB:** Six units alternate Literary and Informational text. Genres include realistic fiction, folktale, poetry, fantasy, reference, science, and biography. **TRB:** The Read Aloud Lesson opener introduces the characteristics of each genre.	"Most of the required reading in college and workforce training programs is informational in structure and challenging in content . . . . the Standards follow NAEP's lead in balancing the reading of literature with the reading of informational texts. . . ." (Common Core State Standards, 2010, pp. 4–5. See also National Assessment Governing Board, 2008)
ELL Support Some teaching strategies that have been proven to be effective for English learners include scaffolded instruction, use of graphic organizers, and modeling of language by teachers and peers.	**SB:** Features such as Hints and Turn and Talk partner discussions support English learners throughout the lesson. **TRB:** In Read Aloud Lessons, ELL Support boxes provide linguistic instruction pertinent to the unique content in each particular trade book.	Researchers state that one of the best practices for teaching ELL students is to model standard pronunciation and grammar. (Mohr & Mohr, 2007)
General Academic Vocabulary (Tier Two) General academic, or Tier Two, words are words a reader encounters in rich, complex texts of all types.	**TRB:** Tier Two Vocabulary boxes in Read Aloud Lessons support the teacher in helping students use text-based strategies to figure out the meanings of challenging words.	"Tier Two words are frequently encountered in complex written texts and are particularly powerful because of their wide applicability to many sorts of reading. Teachers thus need to be alert to the presence of Tier Two words and determine which ones need careful attention." (Common Core State Standards, Appendix A, 2010, p. 33. The three-tier model of vocabulary is based on the work of Beck, McKeown, & Kucan, 2002, 2008)
Answer Explanations for Students As a part of scaffolded instruction, students receive immediate feedback on their answer choices and the reasoning behind correct and incorrect answers.	**TRB:** In every Unit Check, answer explanations are given for each question.	Research (Pashler et al. 2007) has shown that when students receive direct instruction about the reasons why an answer choice is correct or incorrect, they demonstrate long-term retention and understanding of newly learned content.

References

Adams, M. J. (2009). The challenge of advanced texts: The interdependence of reading and learning. In Hiebert, E. H. (ed.), *Reading more, reading better: Are American students reading enough of the right stuff?* (pp. 183–189). New York, NY: Guilford.

Beck, I. L., McKeown, M. G., & Kucan, L. (2002). *Bringing words to life: Robust vocabulary instruction.* New York, NY: Guilford.

Beck, I. L., McKeown, M. G., & Kucan, L. (2008). *Creating robust vocabulary: Frequently asked questions and extended examples.* New York, NY: Guilford.

Boyles, N. (2012/2013). Closing in on close reading. *Educational Leadership,* 70(4), 36–41.

Coleman, D., & Pimentel, S. (2012). *Revised Publishers' Criteria for the Common Core State Standards in English Language Arts and Literacy, Grades K–2.* Accessed at: *http://www.corestandards.org/resources.*

Fisher, D., Frey, N., & Lapp, D. (2012). *Text complexity: Raising rigor in reading.* Washington, DC: International Reading Association.

Gersten, R., & Carnine, D. (1986). Direct instruction in reading comprehension. *Educational Leadership,* 43(7), 70–79.

Hess, K. K., Carlock, D., Jones, B., & Walkup, J. R. (2009). *What exactly do "fewer, clearer, and higher standards" really look like in the classroom? Using a cognitive rigor matrix to analyze curriculum, plan lessons, and implement assessments.* Accessed at: *http://www.nciea.org/cgi-bin/pubspage.cgi?sortby=pub_date.*

Larkin, M. (2002). *Using scaffolded instruction to optimize learning.* ERIC Digest ED474301 2002-12-00. Retrieved from *www.eric.ed.gov.*

Mohr, K., & Mohr, E. (2007). *Extending English language learners' classroom interactions using the response protocol.* Accessed at: *http://www.readingrockets.org/article/26871.*

National Assessment Governing Board. (2008). *Reading framework for the 2009 National Assessment of Educational Progress.* Washington, D.C.: U.S. Government Printing Office.

National Governors Association Center for Best Practices and Council of Chief State School Officers. (2010). *Common Core State Standards for English Language Arts and Literacy in History/Social Studies, Science, and Technical Subjects.* Accessed at: *http://www.corestandards.org/the-standards.*

———. *English Language Arts Appendix A.* Accessed at: *http://www.corestandards.org/the-standards.*

Partnership for Assessment of Readiness for College and Careers. (2011). *PARCC model content frameworks: English language arts/literacy grades 3–11.* Accessed at: *http://www.parcconline.org/parcc-model-content-frameworks.*

Pashler, H., Bain, P., Bottge, B., Graesser, A., Koedinger, K., McDaniel, M., & Metcalfe, J. (2007). *Organizing instruction and study to improve student learning* (NCER 2007–2004). Washington, D.C.: National Center for Education Research, Institute of Education Sciences, U.S. Department of Education. Retrieved from *http://ncer.ed.gov.*

Rumelhart, D. E. (1980). Schemata: the building blocks of cognition. In Spiro, R. J., Bruce, B. C., & Brewer Erlbaum, W. F. (eds.), *Theoretical issues in reading comprehension* (pp. 33–58).

Smarter Balanced Assessment Consortium. (2012). *General Item Specifications.* Accessed at: *http://www.smarterbalanced.org/wordpress/wp-content/uploads/2012/05/TaskItemSpecifications/ItemSpecifications/GeneralItemSpecifications.pdf.*

Correlation Charts

Common Core State Standards Coverage by *Ready*®

The chart below correlates each Common Core State Standard to each ***Ready*® *Common Core*** lesson that offers comprehensive instruction on that standard. Use this chart to determine which lessons your students should complete based on their mastery of each standard.

Common Core State Standards for Grade 1—Reading Standards		***Ready Common Core*** **Student Lesson(s)**	**Additional Coverage in Teacher Resource Book Lesson(s)**
Reading Standards for Literature			
Key Ideas and Details			
RL.1.1	Ask and answer questions about key details in a text.	1	A, B, C, D, H, 2, 3, 4, 17, 18
RL.1.2	Retell stories, including key details, and demonstrate understanding of their central message or lesson.	A, B, C, D, H, 5	1, 2, 4, 5, 9, 10, 11, 12, 17, 18
RL.1.3	Describe characters, settings, and major events in a story, using key details.	2, 3, 4	A, B, C, D, H, 5, 17, 18
Craft and Structure			
RL.1.4	Identify words and phrases in stories or poems that suggest feelings or appeal to the senses.	9, 10	3, 17
RL.1.5	Explain major differences between books that tell stories and books that give information, drawing on a wide reading of a range of text types.	11	—
RL.1.6	Identify who is telling the story at various points in a text.	12	19
Integration of Knowledge and Ideas			
RL.1.7	Use illustrations and details in a story to describe its characters, setting, or events.	17	B, C, D, H, 1, 2, 3, 4, 11, 12, 18
RL.1.8	(Not applicable to literature)	N/A	N/A
RL.1.9	Compare and contrast the adventures and experiences of characters in stories.	18	—
Range of Reading and Level of Text Complexity			
RL.1.10	With prompting and support, read prose and poetry of appropriate complexity for grade 1.	All Lessons	
Reading Standards for Informational Text			
Key Ideas and Details			
RI.1.1	Ask and answer questions about key details in a text.	6	E, F, G, I, 7, 8, 13, 16
RI.1.2	Identify the main topic and retell key details of a text.	E, F, G, I, 7	6, 8, 11, 13, 14, 16, 20, 21
RI.1.3	Describe the connection between two individuals, events, ideas, or pieces of information in a text.	8	E, F, G
Craft and Structure			
RI.1.4	Ask and answer questions to help determine or clarify the meaning of words and phrases in a text.	13	—
RI.1.5	Know and use various text features (e.g., headings, tables of contents, glossaries, electronic menus, icons) to locate key facts or information in a text.	14, 15	—
RI.1.6	Distinguish between information provided by pictures or other illustrations and information provided by the words in a text.	16	—

Common Core State Standards for Grade 1—Reading Standards		*Ready Common Core* Student Lesson(s)	Additional Coverage in Teacher Resource Book Lesson(s)
Reading Standards for Informational Text (continued)			
Integration of Knowledge and Ideas			
RI.1.7	Use the illustrations and details in a text to describe its key ideas.	19	E, G, 6, 8, 11, 13
RI.1.8	Identify the reasons an author gives to support points in a text.	20	—
RI.1.9	Identify basic similarities in and differences between two texts on the same topic (e.g., in illustrations, descriptions, or procedures).	21	—
Range of Reading and Level of Text Complexity			
RI.1.10	With prompting and support, read informational texts appropriately complex for grade 1.	All Lessons	

Additional Coverage of Common Core ELA Standards, Grade 1		*Ready Common Core* Teacher Resource Book Lesson(s)
Reading Standards for Foundational Skills		
Print Concepts		
RF.1.1a	Recognize the distinguishing features of a sentence (e.g., first word, capitalization, ending punctuation).	A
Phonological Awareness		
RF.1.2a	Distinguish long from short vowel sounds in spoken single-syllable words.	A, H
RF.1.2b	Orally produce single-syllable words by blending sounds (phonemes), including consonant blends.	B, F
RF.1.2c	Isolate and pronounce initial, medial vowel, and final sounds (phonemes) in spoken single-syllable words.	B
RF.1.2d	Segment spoken single-syllable words into their complete sequence of individual sounds (phonemes).	C, H
Phonics and Word Recognition		
RF.1.3a	Know the spelling-sound correspondences for common consonant digraphs.	C, F, I
RF.1.3b	Decode regularly spelled one-syllable words.	D
RF.1.3c	Know final -e and common vowel team conventions for representing long vowel sounds.	D, I
RF.1.3d	Use knowledge that every syllable must have a vowel sound to determine the number of syllables in a printed word.	E
RF.1.3e	Decode two-syllable words following basic patterns by breaking the words into syllables.	E
RF.1.3f	Read words with inflectional endings.	G, H
RF.1.3g	Recognize and read grade-appropriate irregularly spelled words.	G, I
Writing Standards		
Text Types and Purposes		
W.1.1	Write opinion pieces in which they introduce the topic or name the book they are writing about, state an opinion, supply a reason for the opinion, and provide some sense of closure.	D, H
W.1.2	Write informative/explanatory texts in which they name a topic, supply some facts about the topic, and provide some sense of closure.	F, I
W.1.3	Write narratives in which they recount two or more appropriately sequenced events, include some details regarding what happened, use temporal words to signal event order, and provide some sense of closure.	A, G
Production and Distribution of Writing		
W.1.5	With guidance and support from adults, focus on a topic, respond to questions and suggestions from peers, and add details to strengthen writing as needed.	10

Additional Coverage of Common Core ELA Standards, Grade 1		*Ready* Common Core Teacher Resource Book Lesson(s)
Writing Standards (continued)		
Research to Build and Present Knowledge		
W.1.7	Participate in shared research and writing projects (e.g., explore a number of "how-to" books on a given topic and use them to write a sequence of instructions).	B
W.1.8	With guidance and support from adults, recall information from experiences or gather information from provided sources to answer a question.	C, E
Speaking and Listening Standards		
Comprehension and Collaboration		
SL.1.1	Participate in collaborative conversations with diverse partners about grade 1 topics and texts with peers and adults in small and larger groups.	A, B, D, E, F, G, H, 1, 2, 3, 4, 5, 6, 7, 8, 9, 10, 11, 12, 13, 14, 15, 16, 17, 18, 19, 20, 21
SL.1.1a	Follow agreed-upon rules for discussions (e.g., listening to others with care, speaking one at a time about the topics and texts under discussion).	C, I
SL.1.1b	Build on others' talk in conversations by responding to the comments of others through multiple exchanges.	C, I
SL.1.2	Ask and answer questions about key details in a text read aloud or information presented orally or through other media.	A, B, C, D, E, F, G, H, I, 1, 4, 5, 6, 7, 8, 11, 12, 16, 17, 20, 21
SL.1.3	Ask and answer questions about what a speaker says in order to gather additional information or clarify something that is not understood.	E, I, 2, 14
Presentation of Knowledge and Ideas		
SL.1.4	Describe people, places, things, and events with relevant details, expressing ideas and feelings clearly.	A, B, C, D, E, F, G, H, 1, 2, 3, 4, 5, 6, 7, 9, 10, 12, 13, 16, 17, 18, 19
SL.1.5	Add drawings or other visual displays to descriptions when appropriate to clarify ideas, thoughts, and feelings.	A, B, C, D, E, F, G, H, I, 11, 12, 15
SL.1.6	Produce complete sentences when appropriate to task and situation.	C, D
Language Standards		
Conventions of Standard English		
L.1.1	Demonstrate command of the conventions of standard English grammar and usage when writing or speaking.	E, 1, 2, 3, 4, 5, 6, 7, 8, 9, 10, 12, 13, 14, 15, 16, 17, 18, 19, 20, 21
L.1.1b	Use common, proper, and possessive nouns.	H
L.1.1e	Use verbs to convey a sense of past, present, and future *(e.g., Yesterday I walked home; Today I walk home; Tomorrow I will walk home)*.	A
L.1.1f	Use frequently occurring adjectives.	C, D, F, I
L.1.1g	Use frequently occurring conjunctions (*e.g., and, but, or, so, because*).	B
L.1.1h	Use determiners (e.g., articles, demonstratives).	G
L.1.1j	Produce and expand complete simple and compound declarative, interrogative, imperative, and exclamatory sentences in response to prompts.	C, D
L.1.2	Demonstrate command of the conventions of standard English capitalization, punctuation, and spelling when writing.	F, G, I, 1, 2, 3, 4, 5, 6, 7, 8, 9, 10, 12, 13, 14, 15, 16, 17, 18, 19, 20, 21
L.1.2a	Capitalize dates and names of people.	C, E, H
L.1.2b	Use end punctuation for sentences.	C, E
Vocabulary Acquisition and Use		
L.1.4	Determine or clarify the meaning of unknown and multiple-meaning words and phrases based on *grade 1 reading and content*, choosing flexibly from an array of strategies.	13
L.1.4a	Use sentence-level context as a clue to the meaning of a word or phrase.	C, D, E, F, G, H, I, 3
L.1.4b	Use frequently occurring affixes as a clue to the meaning of a word.	C

Additional Coverage of Common Core ELA Standards, Grade 1		*Ready Common Core* Teacher Resource Book Lesson(s)
Language Standards (continued)		
Vocabulary Acquisition and Use *(continued)*		
L.1.5	With guidance and support from adults, demonstrate understanding of word relationships and nuances in word meanings.	9, 10, 13
L.1.5a	Sort words into categories (e.g., colors, clothing) to gain a sense of the concepts the categories represent.	C
L.1.5b	Define words by category and by one or more key attributes (e.g., a *duck* is a bird that swims; a *tiger* is a large cat with stripes).	F
L.1.5c	Identify real-life connections between words and their use (e.g., note places at home that are *cozy*).	A, B, C, D, E, F, G
L.1.5d	Distinguish shades of meaning among verbs differing in manner (e.g., *look, peek, glance, stare, glare, scowl*) and adjectives differing in intensity (e.g., *large, gigantic*) by defining or choosing them or by acting out the meanings.	A

Unit 1

Key Ideas and Details in Literature

The following pacing chart shows a recommended schedule for teaching the lessons in Unit 1. Each Read Aloud and Focus Lesson is taught over the course of three days. There is also time allotted in each Focus Lesson for teaching Tap Children's Prior Knowledge and Differentiated Instruction.

Day	Lesson/Activity	Time (minutes)
1	Unit 1 Opener (optional); Read Aloud Lesson A: Introduction; Part 1	30
2	Read Aloud Lesson A: Parts 2 and 3	30
3	Read Aloud Lesson A: Part 4; Additional Activities (optional)	30
4	Read Aloud Lesson B: Introduction; Part 1	30
5	Read Aloud Lesson B: Parts 2 and 3	30
6	Read Aloud Lesson B: Part 4; Additional Activities (optional)	30
7	Tap Children's Prior Knowledge; Lesson 1: Part 1	30
8	Lesson 1: Parts 2 and 3	30
9	Lesson 1: Part 4; Differentiated Instruction (optional)	30
10	Read Aloud Lesson C: Introduction; Part 1	30
11	Read Aloud Lesson C: Parts 2 and 3	30
12	Read Aloud Lesson C: Part 4; Additional Activities (optional)	30
13	Tap Children's Prior Knowledge; Lesson 2: Part 1	30
14	Lesson 2: Parts 2 and 3	30
15	Lesson 2: Part 4; Differentiated Instruction (optional)	30
16	Read Aloud Lesson D: Introduction; Part 1	30
17	Read Aloud Lesson D: Parts 2 and 3	30
18	Read Aloud Lesson D: Part 4; Additional Activities (optional)	30
19	Tap Children's Prior Knowledge; Lesson 3: Part 1	30
20	Lesson 3: Parts 2 and 3	30
21	Lesson 3: Part 4; Differentiated Instruction (optional)	30
22	Tap Children's Prior Knowledge; Lesson 4: Part 1	30
23	Lesson 4: Parts 2 and 3	30
24	Lesson 4: Part 4; Differentiated Instruction (optional)	30
25	Tap Children's Prior Knowledge; Lesson 5: Part 1	30
26	Lesson 5: Parts 2 and 3	30
27	Lesson 5: Part 4; Differentiated Instruction (optional)	30
28	Unit 1 Check	30

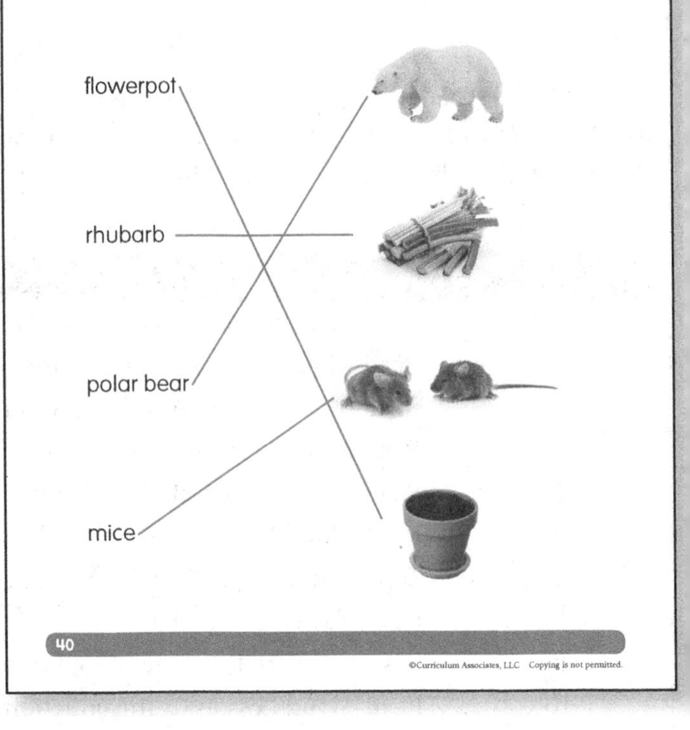

Step by Step

Explain that in this unit, children will listen to many different stories. They'll also meet many imaginary characters, young and old. Some won't even be people!

- Have children turn to page 39. Read aloud the introductory sentence and direction.
- Discuss the illustration and invite children to describe the basic story elements, including characters *(knight, horse, dragon)*; setting *(long ago outside a castle by a stream)*; and possible events in the plot.
- As necessary, encourage children to ask and answer *who, what, where, when, why,* and *how* questions for further inspiration.
- Time permitting, help children develop a simple story line to accompany the illustration.
- Then have children turn to page 40.
- Invite children to identify each picture.
- Read aloud the directions at the top of the page.
- Read aloud the word *flowerpot*. Have children say it. Then have them put a finger on the picture that matches the word. Ask them to draw a line from the word to the picture.
- Repeat the procedure for the other words.
- As time permits, discuss the initial sound in the name for each picture and the letter representing it in the matching word. Have children circle the letter.

Read Aloud Lesson A (Student Book pages 3–6)

The Empty Pot

Lesson Objectives

You will read aloud *The Empty Pot,* which children will revisit in later lessons. Children will:

- Answer questions about key details in the story.
- Describe characters and major events, using details.
- Retell the story, including key details.

About the Text

Summary

The Emperor proclaims that the child who grows the most beautiful flower from the Emperor's seeds will be his successor. Ping works hard, but his seed does not grow. When others bring flowers to the Emperor, Ping brings his empty pot. The Emperor reveals that none of the seeds could grow and rewards Ping for his honesty.

Genre: Folktale

- Explain that *The Empty Pot* is a folktale—a story from long ago that people have told again and again.
- Tell children that a folktale often teaches a lesson or explains a natural event, such as thunderstorms.

Critical Vocabulary

- Prior to reading, briefly define the following words:

  emperor (p. 6) a man who rules, or leads, a country

  successor (p. 7) a person who takes over a job for someone else

  proclamation (p. 9) an important announcement

  palace (p. 9) a large, beautiful home for a ruler

- As you read, pause to point to the words as you encounter them, and review their definitions.

Word Bank

- To support children in writing about the story, display a word bank containing the Critical Vocabulary and the characters' names *(Ping* and *the Emperor).* Point out the word *the* and the capital letter *E* in *the Emperor.*
- Add other important story words, such as *seed, empty, reward,* and *courage* on subsequent readings.

New Concepts: Leaders

- When introducing the book, explain that an emperor makes laws and protects the country he leads.
- Explain that an emperor, or any leader, must have a successor—someone to lead when the leader cannot do the job anymore. Some leaders choose a successor. Sometimes a country's people choose the next leader.

Ready *Teacher Toolbox* Teacher-Toolbox.com

	Prerequisite Skills	RL.1.2
Ready Lessons		✓
Tools for Instruction	✓ ✓	✓
Interactive Tutorials	✓ ✓	

CCSS Focus

RL.1.2 *Retell stories, including key details...*

ADDITIONAL STANDARDS: **RL.1.1; RL.1.3; RF.1.1.a; RF.1.2.a; W.1.3; SL.1.1; SL.1.2; SL.1.4; SL.1.5; L.1.1.e; L.1.5.c, d**
(See page A38 for full text.)

PART 1: First Read (Characters)

Step by Step

- **Introduce *The Empty Pot.*** Display the book. Then read aloud the title and the name of the author, Demi. Point out that she is also the illustrator.
- **Set the purpose for reading.** Tell children that they will understand a story better if they find out who the characters are and then keep track of what happens to each one.
- Explain that as you read aloud, children should listen closely to identify the characters in this story.
- **Read aloud *The Empty Pot.*** Read the story all the way through, pausing only to briefly define challenging vocabulary.
- **Guide children to review the characters.** After reading, use questions such as these to discuss the characters. *(RL.1.1; SL.1.1; SL.1.2)*

  Who are the main characters? *(Ping, the Emperor)*

  How can you tell they are the main characters? *(The most important parts of the story are about what happens to them.)*

  Who are some of the other characters? *(Ping's friend, Ping's father, other children)*

- Direct children to turn to Student Book page 3. Read aloud the first item and the Hint. Help children understand that Ping's father, friend, and the other children are less important characters. *(RL.1.3)*
- Prompt children to write the names of the characters beneath their pictures.

Tip: Children with visual difficulties may have trouble identifying characters in these detailed, elaborate illustrations. Help children isolate the characters by masking out other portions of the illustration as needed.

- **Have children discuss story evidence.** Read aloud the Turn and Talk activity. Encourage children to discuss how both the Emperor and Ping love to grow things. Direct them to the pictures of Ping and the Emperor tending to plants. *(SL.1.4; SL.1.5)*

The Empty Pot

The Main Characters

THE EMPTY POT

Draw the two main characters.

Hint: Who is the story mostly about?

Children should draw one picture each of Ping and the Emperor.

Name each character.

Ping | the Emperor

Turn Talk Use your pictures and story evidence to tell your partner what you know about each character.

ELL Support: Multiple Meanings

- Tell children that many words have more than one meaning. Explain that listening to the word in a sentence and finding clues helps us know what the word means.
- Display page 13 of *The Empty Pot*. Read aloud the first sentence.
- Point out the word *rich*. Explain that one clue to its meaning is the word *soil*. Explain that when the word *rich* describes soil, it means "full of good things" that will help a plant grow.
- Ask children if they know another meaning of the word *rich*. *(having a lot of money)* Ask them to use the word in a sentence. Then guide children to use *rich* in sentences that show the two different meanings of the word.
- Help children practice using other multiple-meaning words, such as *bat*, *fly*, *jam*, or *park*.

Step by Step

- **Reread and discuss the beginning.** Read pages 3–12 aloud. Use questions such as these to guide discussion. *(RL.1.1; SL.1.1; SL.1.2)*

  Page 7: What problem does the Emperor have? *(He is very old and needs to choose a successor.)*

  Page 8: Why does the Emperor decide to "let the flowers choose" his successor? *(because he loves flowers so much)*

  Page 10: Why do the children come to the palace? *(to get special seeds from the Emperor)*

- Use the Close Reading activity to show that readers make and update predictions based on text evidence.
- **Focus on a key detail.** Have children turn to Student Book page 4. Read aloud the first item and the Hint. Help children recall why the Emperor wants all the children to come to the palace. *(RL.1.3)*
- Prompt children to complete the second item.
- **Have children discuss story evidence.** Read aloud the Turn and Talk activity. Have children connect Ping's love of plants to how he feels about receiving his seed from the Emperor. *(SL.1.4; SL.1.5)*

Tip: Children may need to be reminded that Ping is especially good at growing flowers; reread page 3 as needed and elaborate on "burst into bloom."

The Empty Pot

In the Beginning

Draw a picture to show why Ping comes to the palace.

Hint: The Emperor gives something to each child.

Children might draw Ping receiving a seed from the Emperor, or they might recreate the image on page 12 of the story.

Write what is happening in your picture.

Ping gets a seed from the Emperor.

Turn Talk Tell how Ping feels about coming to the palace.

4 Part 2: Beginning Read Aloud | Lesson A

©Curriculum Associates, LLC Copying is not permitted.

- Discuss the proclamation and other important details from this part of the story. Guide children to use their Student Book pages to recall details.

Tier Two Vocabulary: *swarmed*

- Display and reread page 10, pointing out the word *swarmed* as you read. Discuss the illustration. Ask: *Is this a large or small group of children? Are they going together to the same place?*
- Use children's responses and context clues to help them see that the word *swarmed* means "moved together as a large group or crowd."
- Discuss together how *swarmed* tells more than *walked* or *traveled* would have. *(L.1.5.d)*
- Have children describe or demonstrate an event using the word *swarmed*. Provide an example such as, *The kids swarmed to the playground at recess.* *(L.1.5.c)*

Close Reading

- Remind children that good readers use text evidence to make predictions about a story. Reread page 9 aloud. Then prompt:

  What evidence tells you who the Emperor's successor will be? *(the child who can show the Emperor "their best in a year's time")*

  What does the Emperor seem to mean when he says "show me their best"? *(The children are given flower seeds; it seems like the Emperor means that they should grow great flowers.)*

- Reread page 31. Ask what the Emperor meant by "their best." *(being honest)* Point out that readers change their ideas when they get new evidence.

PART 3: Reread for Meaning (Middle)

Step by Step

- **Reread and discuss the middle.** Read pages 13–25 aloud. Then use questions such as these to guide discussion about this part of the story. *(RL.1.1; SL.1.1; SL.1.2)*

  Pages 13–19: What problem does Ping have? *(His seed does not grow; his pot is empty.)*

  Page 22: What does Ping's father say to help Ping? *(He says that Ping did his best and that his best is good enough for the Emperor.)*

  Page 22: What evidence shows that Ping has done his best? *(He has worked hard to take care of his seed.)*

- Use the Close Reading activity to help children make connections that identify an important idea.
- **Focus on a key detail.** Have children turn to Student Book page 5. Read aloud the first item and the Hint. Guide children to understand what Ping takes to the palace. *(RL.1.3)*
- Prompt children to complete the second item.

Tip: For children struggling with sequence, create a sequence chart of the events on pages 22–25.

- **Have children discuss story evidence.** Read aloud the Turn and Talk activity. Have children describe Ping's feelings and actions and connect them with what his father and the Emperor said. *(SL.1.4; SL.1.5)*

The Empty Pot

In the Middle

Draw a picture of what Ping takes to the palace.

Hint: What does Ping take to the Emperor?

Children might draw a picture of Ping's empty pot or of Ping walking to the palace, carrying his empty pot, similar to the illustration on page 25 of the story.

Write what is happening in your picture.

Ping takes his empty pot to the palace.

Turn Talk Tell why Ping is ashamed but goes to the palace anyway.

Read Aloud | Lesson A Part 3: Middle 5

- Work with children to identify the most important ideas in this part of the story. Display pages 13–25 as necessary and have children refer to their Student Book pages to help them.

Tier Two Vocabulary: *ashamed*

- Display and reread pages 22–23. Ask children how Ping feels about his empty pot. *(ashamed)*
- Ask children to describe what *ashamed* means, based on Ping's actions and words. Ask: *Does Ping think he has done something wrong? (yes)*
- Work with children to determine that the word *ashamed* means "sorry; embarrassed; unworthy."
- Provide a familiar example of feeling ashamed, for example, *I felt ashamed for lying to my mom.*
- Have children give examples and non-examples about when people feel ashamed. Have children practice using the word in sentences. *(L.1.5.c)*

Close Reading

- Help children make connections to identify an important idea in the story. Read aloud page 9 and then page 24. Then prompt children:

  What does the Emperor ask the children to do? *(He asks them to take the special seeds and "show me their best in a year's time.")*

  Ping's father says, "your best is good enough to present to the Emperor." How do his words connect to the Emperor's proclamation? *(The Emperor and Ping's father both say to do your best.)*

- Discuss the connection between what the Emperor seems to mean by "best" and Ping's actual efforts to do his best.

 **PART 4: Reread for Meaning** (End)

Step by Step

- **Reread and discuss the end.** Read pages 26–32 aloud. Discuss the way the story ends, using questions such as these. *(RL.1.1; SL.1.1; SL.1.2)*

  Page 31: Why does the Emperor smile after hearing Ping? *(He is happy that Ping told the truth.)*

  Pages 31–32: What happens to solve both Ping's and the Emperor's problems? *(Ping finds out that his seed couldn't grow, and the Emperor finds his successor.)*

- Use the Close Reading activity to help children use details to learn more about characters.
- **Focus on a key detail.** Have children turn to Student Book page 6. Read aloud the first item. Use the Hint to help children see that the Emperor is happy that brave Ping tells the truth. *(RL.1.3)*
- Prompt children to complete the second item.
- **Have children discuss story evidence.** Read aloud the Turn and Talk activity. Guide children to connect Ping doing his best and telling the truth to the reason why the Emperor makes Ping his successor. *(SL.1.4; SL.1.5)*

Tip: Children may find it helpful to act out this part of the story to understand how and why Ping's feelings and the Emperor's feelings change.

The Empty Pot

At the End

Draw a picture of what makes the Emperor smile.

Hint: Ping tells about trying to grow a flower.

Children should draw Ping holding his empty pot; they might also recreate the illustration on page 31 of the story.

Write what is happening in your picture.

Ping tells the truth about his pot. He has courage.

Turn Talk Tell why the Emperor chooses Ping to be his successor.

6 Part 4: End Read Aloud | Lesson A

- **Retell *The Empty Pot.*** Guide a retelling of the story, asking children to tell events in sequence. Remind them to use their Student Book pages to help them remember important events and details. Provide feedback as needed.

Integrating Foundational Skills

Use these tasks as opportunities to integrate foundational skills into your reading of *The Empty Pot*.

1. Display page 26 of the story. Help children point out the first word, the capital letter, and the period at the end of the sentence. Repeat for pages 27 and 28, having children identify capital letters that begin sentences and punctuation that ends them. *(RF.1.1.a)*
2. Have children identify short and long vowel sounds as you say these word pairs: *said/seed; had/say; big/smile; not/grow; best/be.* Repeat each vowel sound separately as needed. *(RF.1.2.a)*

Close Reading

- Explain that active readers use details to find out more about characters. Display and reread pages 30–31. Then prompt:

  Why did every child but Ping grow a flower? *(The other children cheated and used different seeds than those the Emperor gave them.)*

  Why does this make Ping special in the Emperor's eyes? *(Ping is honest, even when it is hard to be.)*

- Discuss how thinking about the things characters say and do, and why they do them, helps readers understand more about the characters.

Writing Activity

Continue the Story (*W.1.3*)

- Have children continue the story. Ask: *What do you think will happen next to Ping and the Emperor? What will Ping do to get ready to be an emperor? How will the Emperor help Ping?*
- Have children begin writing or drawing their ideas. Ask them to include two or more new events in their continuation of the story. Remind them to include details that show how Ping and the Emperor act and feel. Explain that their new story will need a good ending, too.
- Display a list of transition or sequence words for children to use as they write, such as *first, next, then, last, after,* and *finally*.
- When children have finished, have them share their new stories with each other.

Speaking and Listening Activity

Talk About Fairness (*SL.1.4*)

- Have children use story details to discuss the Emperor's proclamation and contest.
- Work with children to describe the different elements of the Emperor's plan. As needed, make sure children understand that growing the best flower wasn't what the Emperor asked the children to do; he simply asked them to do "their best."
- Then ask: *How fair was the Emperor's contest? Why do the other children cheat and use new seeds? Does this make them bad people? Why or why not?*
- Invite children to share their responses. Remind them to take turns speaking and to respond politely to each other's points.
- Have children offer their experiences of times when being honest paid off. Help them think of other story characters who benefited from being honest.

Language Activity

Verbs: Past, Present, and Future (*L.1.1.e*)

- Display and read aloud these sentences:

  I walked yesterday.
  I walk every day.
  I will walk tomorrow.

- Read the sentences with children. Then underline the words *walked, walk,* and *will walk*, reading them aloud with children as you do so.
- Explain that the underlined words are verbs, or words that tell about actions and when the actions happen.
- Tell children that the first sentence tells about the past; the second sentence tells about the present, or now; and the third sentence tells about the future.
- Have children practice using past, present, and future tense by replacing *walked, walk,* and *will walk* in each sentence with forms of these words: *plant, wait, rush, frown, cook.* Provide guidance and corrective feedback as needed.

Read Aloud Lesson B (Student Book pages 7–10)

The Polar Bear Son

THE POLAR BEAR SON
AN INUIT TALE
RETOLD AND ILLUSTRATED BY LYDIA DABCOVICH

Lesson Objectives

You will read aloud *The Polar Bear Son,* which children will revisit in later lessons. Children will:

- Answer questions about key details in the story.
- Describe characters and major events, using key details.
- Retell the story, including key details.

About the Text

Summary

A solitary old woman in an Inuit village finds and raises a polar bear cub. The bear grows up to help her hunt and fish, but when the village hunters grow jealous, she sends him away. Later, when she calls out for him, he returns, and they hunt and fish together once again.

Genre: Legend

- A legend is a story that has been told for generations. Legends usually contain some element of truth to which heroic, mythical qualities have been added.
- Think together as you read about what seems true and what seems mythical in *The Polar Bear Son.*

Critical Vocabulary

- Prior to reading, briefly define the following words:

  depend (p. 7) to trust or need someone or something

  jealous (p. 20) feeling upset because someone does or has something better

  provider (p. 20) one who takes care of someone else

  faithful (p. 36) loyal, reliable, trustworthy

- As you read, pause to point to the words as you encounter them, and review their definitions.

Word Bank

- To support children in writing about the story, display a word bank containing the Critical Vocabulary and the characters' names *(the old woman; Kunikdjuaq).*
- Add other important story words, such as *polar bear, hunter,* and *village,* on subsequent readings.

New Concepts: Gathering Food

- Explain that long ago, there were no grocery stores. Instead, people like the Inuit in *The Polar Bear Son* needed to work hard to find their own food in nature.
- Discuss some ways that people would find and gather food, including catching fish, hunting animals, and picking berries. Have children listen for ways that the old woman and Kunikdjuaq find food in the story.

Ready *Teacher Toolbox* Teacher-Toolbox.com

	Prerequisite Skills	RL.1.2
Ready Lessons		✓
Tools for Instruction	✓ ✓	✓
Interactive Tutorials	✓ ✓	

CCSS Focus

RL.1.2 *Retell stories, including key details...*

ADDITIONAL STANDARDS: **RL.1.1; RL.1.3; RL.1.7; RF.1.2.b, c; W.1.7; SL.1.1; SL.1.2; SL.1.4; SL.1.5; L.1.1.g; L.1.5.c**
(See page A38 for full text.)

Step by Step

- **Introduce *The Polar Bear Son.*** Display the book. Then read aloud the title and the name of the author, Lydia Dabcovich. Point out that she is also the illustrator.

Tip: As you introduce the book, use the information in the Author's Note on page 37 to answer any questions children may have about Inuit culture.

- **Set the purpose for reading.** Tell children that active readers pay attention to what characters in a story do, say, think, and feel.
- Explain that as you read aloud, children should listen closely to identify the characters in this story and then think about what happens to them.
- **Read aloud *The Polar Bear Son.*** Read the story all the way through, pausing only to briefly define challenging vocabulary. Help children practice saying the polar bear's name *(koo-nick-joo-uck).*
- **Guide children to review the characters.** After reading, use questions such as these to discuss the characters. *(RL.1.1; SL.1.1; SL.1.2)*

  Who are the main characters? *(the old woman; the polar bear, Kunikdjuaq)*

  How can we tell they are the main characters? *(The story tells what happens to them both.)*

  Name some of the other characters. *(the village children; the hunters)*

- Direct children to turn to Student Book page 7. Read aloud the first item. Discuss the Hint as needed and guide children to identify the main characters. *(RL.1.3)*
- Prompt children to write the names of the characters on each line below the pictures. Clarify that they may use *polar bear* or *Kunikdjuaq*. Display the Word Bank to help them spell the names.
- **Have children discuss story evidence.** Read aloud the Turn and Talk activity. Encourage children to connect their pictures to details in the story, including where the main characters live and what they do there. *(SL.1.4; SL.1.5)*

The Polar Bear Son

The Main Characters

Draw the two main characters.

Hint: Who is the story mostly about?

Children should draw one picture each of the old woman and the polar bear.

Name each character.

the old woman

the polar bear

Turn Talk Use your pictures and story evidence to tell your partner what you know about each character.

Read Aloud | Lesson B   Part 1: Characters   7

ELL Support: Words About Time

- Explain that many words and phrases in *The Polar Bear Son* help readers know when events happen.
- Read aloud the first sentence on page 18. Write the word *soon* on the board, and explain that it means "in a short time."
- Continue rereading and defining the following words and phrases about time: *in time* (p. 20), *tomorrow* (p. 23), *at once* (p. 24), *now* (p. 28), and *up to this day* (p. 36). Display each word.
- Reread the list. Help children put the words in time order, using prompts such as the following:

  Which of these words or phrases tells that something already happened? *(up to this day)*

  Which tells that something is happening? *(now)*

  Which tells that something will happen right this minute? *(at once)*

PART 2: Reread for Meaning (Beginning)

Step by Step

- **Reread and discuss the beginning.** Read pages 6–15 aloud. Use questions such as these to guide discussion. *(RL.1.1; SL.1.1; SL.1.2)*

  Pages 6–7: What problem does the old woman have? *(She has no family or sons to hunt for her. She has to depend on neighbors for food.)*

  Pages 8–9: Where does the old woman find the cub? *(out on the ice)*

  Pages 9–11: Why does she take the cub home with her? *(He is alone. She thinks his mother must have been killed.)*

- **Focus on a key detail.** Direct children to turn to Student Book page 8. Read aloud the first item and the Hint. Recall with children what the old woman does for the cub in her hut. *(RL.1.3)*
- Prompt children to complete the second item.

Tip: There are several possible answers to this prompt. Encourage children to describe their pictures as best they can in writing. Allow them to read you what they wrote and elaborate verbally if they'd like.

- Then use the Close Reading activity to help children find story evidence that tells how the cub feels.
- **Have children discuss story evidence.** Read aloud the Turn and Talk activity. Guide children to talk about how the cub feels and why. *(SL.1.4)*

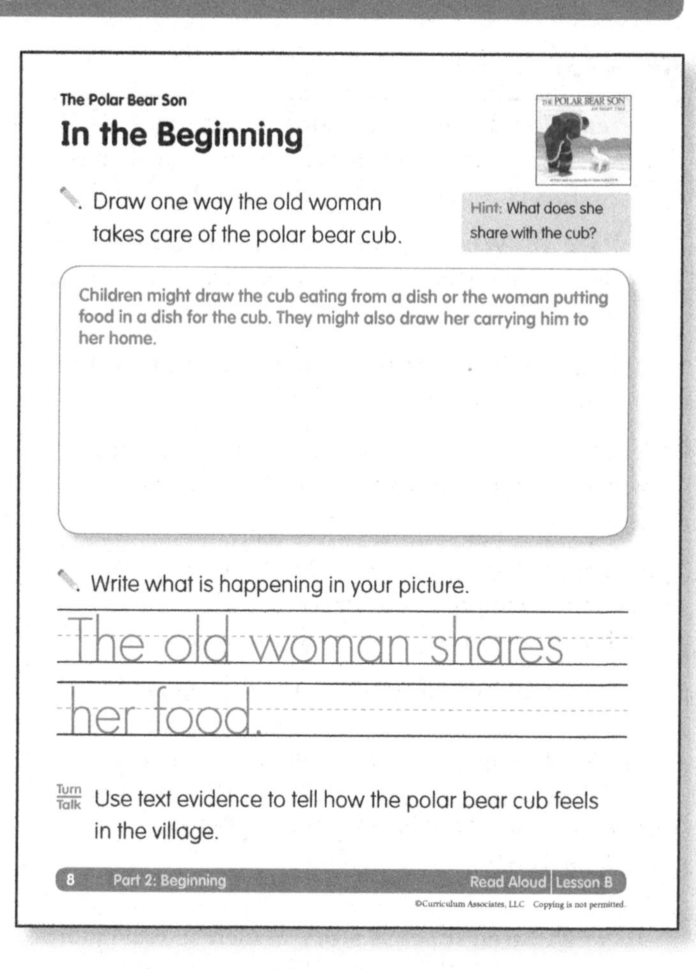

The Polar Bear Son

In the Beginning

Draw one way the old woman takes care of the polar bear cub.

Hint: What does she share with the cub?

Children might draw the cub eating from a dish or the woman putting food in a dish for the cub. They might also draw her carrying him to her home.

Write what is happening in your picture.

The old woman shares her food.

Turn Talk Use text evidence to tell how the polar bear cub feels in the village.

8 Part 2: Beginning Read Aloud | Lesson B

©Curriculum Associates, LLC Copying is not permitted.

- Discuss important details about the old woman, the cub, and the village. Encourage children to use their Student Book pages to recall details about the beginning of the story.

Tier Two Vocabulary: *tumbling*

- Read aloud the last sentence on page 14. Ask what the text and picture evidence show about the meaning of *tumbling*. *(You can do it in the snow; the bear and children are rolling and falling.)*
- Demonstrate tumbling, rolling your hands one over the other to show the motion. Help children describe *tumbling* as "rolling over and over, back and forth, or end over end."
- Use the word in a sentence, such as *I like to watch puppies tumbling when they play.*
- Have children use objects to show what *tumbling* means. Ask them to use *tumbling* in a sentence to describe what they are doing. *(L.1.5.c)*

Close Reading

- Remind children that good readers look for evidence in the words and pictures.
- Display and read aloud pages 14–15. Prompt:

  What do the words say about how the cub feels? *(He is happy with the old woman.)*

  What does the picture show about how the cub feels? *(Everyone is laughing. He seems to like playing with the children from the village.) (RL.1.7)*

  Why do you think the polar bear cub is happy in this village? *(He is not alone anymore. He has food and friends to play with.)*

PART 3: Reread for Meaning (Middle)

Step by Step

- **Reread and discuss the middle.** Read pages 16–27 aloud. Use questions such as these to guide discussion about this part of the story. *(RL.1.1; SL.1.1; SL.1.2)*

  Page 18: What do the old woman and the bear do for the village? *(They share their meat and fish with the villagers.)*

  Page 23: What problem does Kunikdjuaq face? *(The hunters want to kill him.)*

- Use the Close Reading activity to find evidence about why the hunters are upset with Kunikdjuaq.
- **Focus on a key detail.** Direct children to turn to Student Book page 9. Read aloud the first item and the Hint, helping children connect the hunters' feelings to what happens to Kunikdjuaq. *(RL.1.3)*
- Prompt children to complete the second item.

Tip: Scaffold by providing sentence frames for children to complete as they draw, write, and talk to their partners: *Kunikdjuaq is leaving because* ____. *The hunters are jealous because* ____.

- **Have children discuss story evidence.** Read aloud the Turn and Talk activity. Have children discuss why the hunters are upset. Recall that the old woman is sharing her food and encourage them to talk about why this does not please the hunters. *(SL.1.4; SL.1.5)*

The Polar Bear Son

In the Middle

Draw Kunikdjuaq's reason for leaving the village.

Hint: How do the hunters feel about Kunikdjuaq?

Children should draw one or more hunters with angry expressions.

Write what is happening in your picture.

The hunters are jealous and angry.

Turn Talk Use text evidence to discuss why the hunters feel this way.

Read Aloud | Lesson B Part 3: Middle 9

- Work with children to recall the most important details in this part of the story. Remind them to use their Student Book pages to help them recall ideas.

Tier Two Vocabulary: *warn*

- Reread page 20 aloud. Point out the word *warn* and read it aloud with children. Then prompt:

  Are the children going to tell the old woman about something good or bad? *(bad)*

- Use children's responses to discuss that *warn* means "to tell someone about something bad or dangerous that might happen."
- Give an example such as *We warn each other if something is about to fall off a shelf.*
- Have children take turns telling when they would warn someone. Guide them to say sentences with *warn* as well as *warned* and *warns.* *(L.1.5.c)*

Close Reading

- Reread page 20, and then use the following questions to discuss the hunters' feelings:

  Why are the hunters angry? *(because Kunikdjuaq is better at hunting than they are)*

  What makes the hunters jealous of the old woman? *(They are jealous that she has found such a good provider to find food and help her.)*

  What do the hunters decide to do? *(They decide to kill Kunikdjuaq.)*

- Help children understand that characters' feelings often give clues about why they say or do things.

PART 4: Reread for Meaning (End)

Step by Step

- **Reread and discuss the end.** Read pages 28–36 aloud. Discuss the way the story ends, using questions such as these. *(RL.1.1; SL.1.1; SL.1.2)*

  Pages 28–31: Where do the old woman and Kunikdjuaq meet again? *(far out on the ice, away from the village)*

  Pages 32–36: How is the old woman's problem solved? *(She sends Kunikdjuaq away, but visits him. They still share food and take care of each other.)*

- **Focus on a key detail.** Have children turn to Student Book page 10. Read aloud the first item and provide support using the Hint. Remind children that Kunikdjuaq cannot come back to the village. *(RL.1.3)*
- Prompt children to complete the second item.
- Use the Close Reading activity to find evidence that shows how Kunikdjuaq is faithful.
- **Have children discuss story evidence.** Read aloud the Turn and Talk activity. Have children use what they drew to help them respond to the prompt. *(SL.1.4, SL.1.5)*
- **Retell *The Polar Bear Son.*** Guide a retelling in which small groups act out the story. Choose one child to be the narrator. Form groups of six to eight children and assign the roles of old woman, Kunikdjuaq, children, and hunters. Have each group choose locations for the village and far out on the ice.

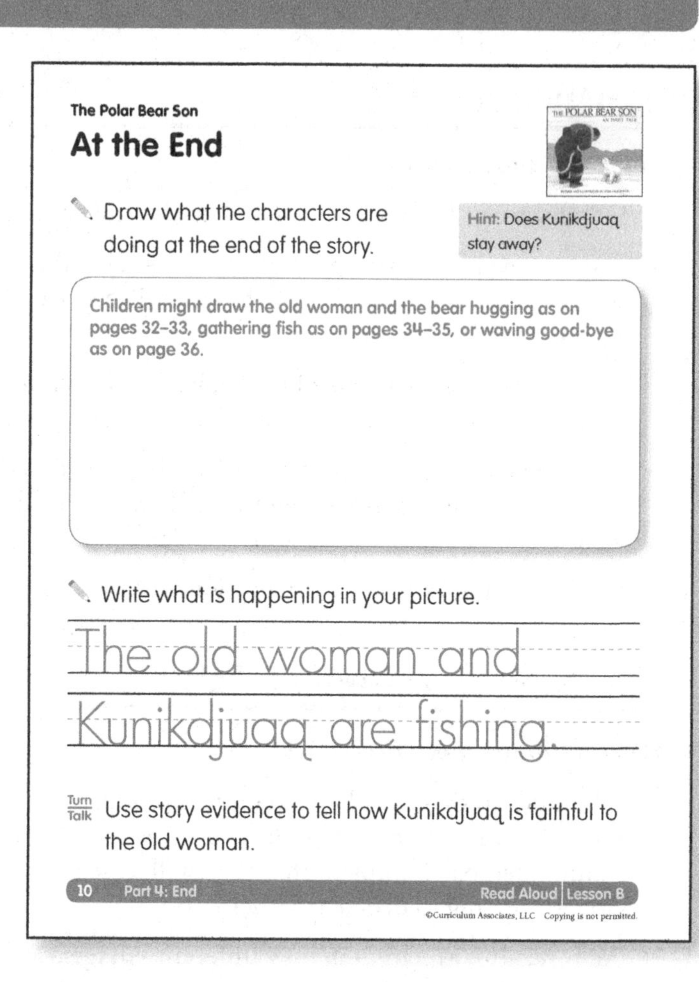

The Polar Bear Son

At the End

Draw what the characters are doing at the end of the story.

Hint: Does Kunikdjuaq stay away?

Children might draw the old woman and the bear hugging as on pages 32–33, gathering fish as on pages 34–35, or waving good-bye as on page 36.

Write what is happening in your picture.

The old woman and Kunikdjuaq are fishing.

Turn Talk Use story evidence to tell how Kunikdjuaq is faithful to the old woman.

10 Part 4: End Read Aloud | Lesson B

©Curriculum Associates, LLC Copying is not permitted.

- Display the book and page through it. Have the narrator describe each event, and then pause for groups to act out the event. Encourage children to add details that the narrator might have omitted.

Integrating Foundational Skills

Use these tasks as opportunities to integrate foundational skills into your reading of *The Polar Bear Son.*

1. Say the following sets of phonemes and have children blend them to say the word that appears in the text: /s/ /ē/ /d/; /h/ /ō/ /m/; /k/ /ŭ/ /b/; /p/ /l/ /ā/; /s/ /l/ /ī/ /d/; /r/ /ĕ/ /s/ /t/; /t/ /ī/ /m/; /s/ /n/ /ō/; /l/ /ĕ/ /f/ /t/. *(seed; home; cub; play; slide; rest; time; snow; left) (RF.1.2.b)*
2. Say each of the following words from the text, one at a time: *hut, day, back, son, him, grew, keep, house, fed, meat, big, hunt, ice.* Have children isolate and pronounce each phoneme in the word. *(RF.1.2.c)*

Close Reading

- Read aloud page 36. Use these questions to have children find evidence that Kunikdjuaq is faithful.

  What happens when the old woman calls Kunikdjuaq? *(He comes running to meet her.)*

  What does he bring her and why? *(He brings salmon and seal for her to eat and to take home.)*

  How do these events show that Kunikdjuaq is faithful? *(They show that the old woman can still depend on Kunikdjuaq to provide food for her.)*

- Have children summarize the evidence by completing the following sentence: *Kunikdjuaq is faithful because ______.*

Writing Activity

Research and Write *(W.1.7)*

- Tell children that you will research and write about a topic together.
- Display several on-level nonfiction books related to *The Polar Bear Son,* such as books about the Arctic, polar bears, other Arctic animals, or the Inuit. Page through each book and help children identify its main topic or topics. Record each topic.
- Have children choose one of the topics for the shared writing. Read aloud the books or sections of books on the topic. Have children tell you what facts or ideas they hear, and record them on chart paper.
- Once the facts and ideas are recorded, begin a shared writing on a new piece of chart paper. Ask children to suggest a title for their writing that tells what the topic is. Guide them to dictate sentences on the topic. Help them put the sentences in a logical order.
- Invite children to provide illustrations for the shared writing. Then read it aloud together.

Speaking and Listening Activity

Have a Village Meeting *(SL.1.1)*

- Tell children that the old woman in *The Polar Bear Son* wants to convince the village to bring Kunikdjuaq back. Explain that they will have a village meeting to decide whether to do this.
- First, recall with children how different villagers felt about Kunikdjuaq.
- Next, form two groups of children: one group that wants to bring Kunikdjuaq back, and one group that is against it.
- Help each group decide on three points they want to make in the discussion, such as *Kunikdjuaq is not dangerous. He brings food for everyone. He plays with us.* Record ideas on chart paper.
- Review discussion rules such as listening carefully, taking turns, and staying on topic.
- Remind children not to simply recite their own points but to respond to the comments of others as well. Also remind them to ask questions if they do not understand something that is said.
- After the discussion, have children vote on whether to bring Kunikdjuaq back to the village.

Language Activity

Conjunctions *(L.1.1.g)*

- Display this sentence from page 34 of *The Polar Bear Son*: "They ate some of it together, and the old woman took the rest home with her."
- Point out the word *and.* Explain that this word can be used to combine, or put together, two sentences into one sentence.
- Using self-stick notes—one with a period and one with a capital T—show children how the above sentence can be split into two sentences, each with its own end punctuation: *They ate some of it together. The old woman took the rest home with her.*
- Read each sentence aloud. Then remove the self-stick notes and read the combined sentence aloud once more.
- Repeat with the last sentence on page 23 and the fourth sentence on page 24, working with children to have them find *and,* split the sentence, and then recombine the sentence.
- Finally, provide oral practice, having children combine these pairs of sentences: *The old woman called Kunikdjuaq. He came to meet her; The children loved to play. The cub played with them.*

Lesson 1 (Student Book pages 41–44)
Asking Questions

CCSS

RL.1.1: Ask and answer questions about key details in a text.

Required Read Alouds: *A (The Empty Pot); B (The Polar Bear Son)*

Lesson Objectives

- Recognize that key details are important pieces of information in a story.
- Use both text and pictures to identify key details in stories, including characters, settings, and events.
- Ask and answer questions about key details.

The Learning Progression

- **Grade K:** CCSS RL.K.1 expects children to ask and answer questions about key details in a story with prompting and support.
- **Grade 1: CCSS RL.1.1 advances the Grade K standard by having children work more independently to ask and answer questions about key details in a story.**
- **Grade 2:** CCSS RL.2.1 furthers the standard by having children ask and answer a widening range of questions about key details to demonstrate their understanding of the text.

Prerequisite Skills

- Understand that a detail is a piece of information.
- Understand how to ask questions with prompting and support.
- Answer questions about key details with prompting and support.
- Identify characters, settings, and major events in a story with prompting and support.

Tap Children's Prior Knowledge

- Remind children that a detail is a piece of information. Explain that sometimes noticing details can help us understand something better. For example, identifying a detail about a person, such as how tall they are, or if they have grey hair, might help us understand how old the person is.
- Explain that one way to uncover details is to ask questions. Share that many questions start with the words *who, what, when, where,* and *why.*
- Display a page from a picture book that shows a character. Challenge children to brainstorm questions they can ask about details in the picture that would help them know more about the character. Write the questions and underline the question words.
- Prompt children to group their questions by question words. If not all question words are represented, help children brainstorm questions for the missing words. Review the questions, and explain that by asking and answering them, you learn important details about the character.
- Explain that you ask questions about lots of things you read in stories. Tell children that in this lesson, they will learn how to ask and answer questions to find details in stories.

Ready *Teacher Toolbox* — Teacher-Toolbox.com

	Prerequisite Skills	*RL.1.1*
Ready Lessons	✓	✓
Tools for Instruction		✓
Interactive Tutorials		✓

Additional CCSS

RL.1.2; RL.1.7; SL.1.1; SL.1.2; SL.1.4; L.1.1; L.1.2 *(See page A38 for full text.)*

Part 1: Introduction

Step by Step

- **Introduce the standard.** Have children turn to page 41 in their Student Books. Read aloud the speech bubble.
- **Review questions and identify question words.** Read the line below the speech bubble, and point out that what follows are questions good readers ask to figure out key details.
- Read aloud the first question, and have children underline the word *Who*. Then explain:

> **One key detail is who the story is about. So I ask *who* to find the people or animals the story tells about. These people or animals are called the characters.**

Tip: To help emergent readers recognize the questions readers ask, point to and emphasize the word *Who* as you read the first question aloud. Repeat for the words *Where, What, When,* and *Why.*

- Read aloud the second question, and have children underline the word *Where*. Then explain:

> **Another key detail is where a story happens. I ask *where* to find out where the characters are. Characters can go to different places in a story, so I need to pay attention and keep asking *where?***

- Read aloud the third question and example, and have children underline the words *What, When,* and *Why.* Then explain:

> **Another key detail is what happens in a story. I ask *what* to find out what the characters are doing. I can also ask *when* and *why* questions to help me understand the things the characters do.**

- **Explain why readers ask and answer questions.** Read aloud the bottom of the page. Explain how asking and answering questions helps readers develop a deeper understanding of a story:

> **Asking *who, where, what, when,* and *why* helps you understand more about the characters and what they do. Once you know these key details, you can see how they fit together and then you can make sense of the story.**

Listen and Learn

Asking Questions

A **key detail** is an important piece of information. Asking and answering questions helps you notice key details.

Here are some questions you can ask about the key details in a story:

- Who are the characters?
- Where are the characters?
- What are the characters doing?
  Think about:
  When are they doing this?
  Why are they doing this?

Asking and answering questions about key details helps you understand how the parts of the story fit together.

Lesson 1 Part 1: Introduction 41

- Share a time when asking and answering questions helped you understand key details. For example, when reading *Little Red Riding Hood*, you might have asked questions about a character's appearance to figure out if Little Red Riding Hood was visiting her grandmother or the wolf in disguise.
- Explain that some questions are easy to answer because the answers are right there in the book. Other questions are harder because you have to search for the answer. Share that in this lesson, children will be learning to ask both easy and hard questions.
- **Have children demonstrate understanding.** Call on individuals to share what they have learned so far about asking questions about key details in a story. Encourage them to give brief examples of questions they can ask about familiar classroom read-alouds.

Part 2: Modeled Instruction

Step by Step

- **Review Part 1; preview Part 2.** Ask volunteers to share questions they can ask to find key details in a story. Have children turn to Student Book page 42.
- **Revisit *The Polar Bear Son*.** Invite children to briefly retell the story, using pages 7–10 of their Student Books. *(RL.1.2)*
- **Model asking questions to find key details.** Explain that you are going to model asking questions. Read aloud pages 8–11 of *The Polar Bear Son*. Think aloud:

  First I'll ask, *Who is in the story so far?* I'll look at the text and the pictures to see who is in the story. I notice that the words say *old woman* and *a little white polar bear cub*. I see that the pictures show these characters, too. I think the story is about the woman and the cub.

  Now I know that the old woman is a character, I'll ask, *What does she do?* Oh! The answer is right here. She took him (the cub) home. *(RL.1.7)*

- Read aloud the first Student Book page question and Hint. Remind children that characters can be humans or animals. Discuss the answer to this question.
- Then read aloud the second question and Hint. Discuss the answer to this question.
- **Model writing your responses.** Model how to write the answers to the first and second questions. *(L.1.1; L.1.2)*

Tip: Have early emergent writers dictate answers or write one- or two-word answers. Have more proficient writers write complete sentences.

- Use the Close Reading activity to model asking additional questions about these pages in the story.
- **Have children demonstrate understanding.** Have partners complete the Turn and Talk activity. If children need support, remind them to ask questions beginning with the words *who, where, what, when,* or *why*. Circulate and check that children's questions address key story details. *(SL.1.1; SL.1.4)*
- Have volunteers share questions they asked. Discuss where children found answers to the questions.

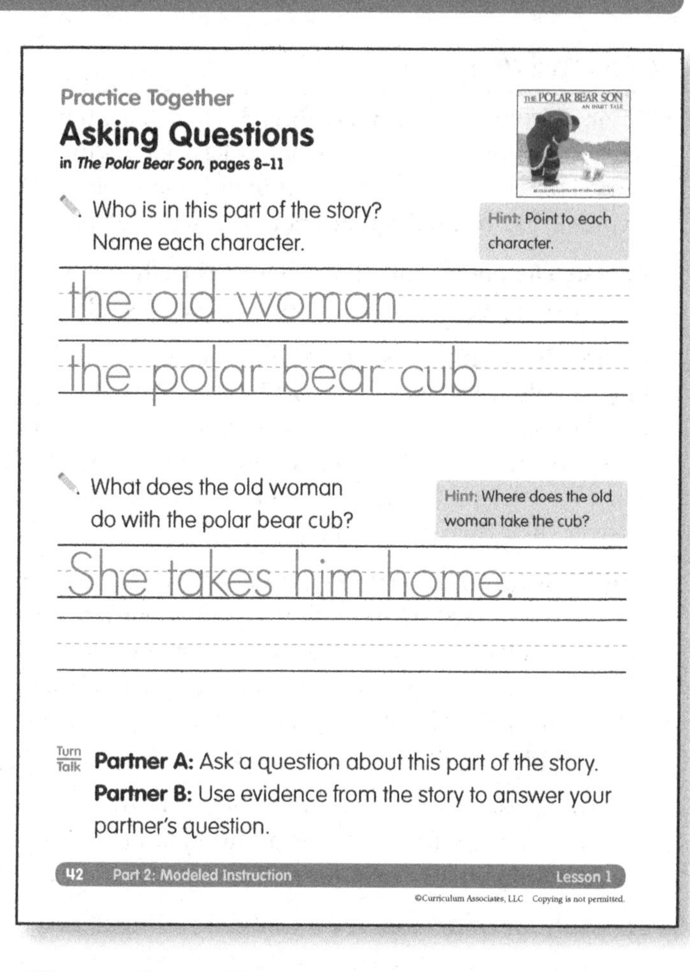

Practice Together

Asking Questions

in *The Polar Bear Son*, pages 8–11

Who is in this part of the story? Name each character.

Hint: Point to each character.

the old woman

the polar bear cub

What does the old woman do with the polar bear cub?

Hint: Where does the old woman take the cub?

She takes him home.

Turn Talk **Partner A:** Ask a question about this part of the story.
Partner B: Use evidence from the story to answer your partner's question.

42 Part 2: Modeled Instruction Lesson 1

©Curriculum Associates, LLC Copying is not permitted.

Close Reading

- Remind children that asking questions can help them learn about characters. Reread pages 9–11 of *The Polar Bear Son*. Tell children to look closely at the pictures as they listen. Then prompt:

  Where are the characters? *(They are out on the ice.)*

  Why does the woman take the cub? *(She thinks his mother was killed.)*

  What does the woman do when the cub is in her arms? *(She smiles.)*

- Have children discuss why the woman is smiling, based on what they have learned so far. Help them understand that she was lonely and now she has found a friend.
- Guide children to see how asking and answering questions about evidence in the words and pictures helped them learn more about the woman and the cub.

Part 3: Guided Practice

Step by Step

- **Review Parts 1–2; preview Part 3.** Have children recall questions they can ask about key details in a story. Direct them to turn to Student Book page 43. Explain that you will guide them through this page.
- **Revisit *The Empty Pot.*** Have children briefly retell the story, using pages 3–6 of their Student Books. *(RL.1.2)*
- **Guide children to ask questions in order to find key details.** Read aloud pages 12–14 of *The Empty Pot.* As you read, guide children to ask *Who is in this part of the story* and *What does Ping do with his seed?* Then have them use text and picture evidence to answer their questions. *(SL.1.2)*
- **Guide children to write responses.** Read aloud each question on the Student Book page, along with the Hints. Discuss the answers. Have children write the characters' names to answer the first question. Then have them write the answer to the second question in a complete sentence. *(L.1.1; L.1.2)*
- Use the Close Reading activity to help children practice asking and answering additional questions and to help prepare them for the Turn and Talk.
- **Have children demonstrate understanding.** Have partners complete the Turn and Talk activity.
- Tell children that it is okay if they repeat some of the same questions they just discussed or that were on the Student Book page. Emphasize that the important thing is that each child is practicing asking and answering questions. *(SL.1.1; SL.1.4)*

Tip Have children switch roles so those who were Partner A for Part 2 are now Partner B and will answer questions. Children who were Partner B now become Partner A and will ask the questions.

- Circulate and check that children's questions address key story details.
- Have volunteers share questions they asked, and discuss where children found answers to the questions. If children couldn't find the answers in the given pages, discuss strategies they used to find them.

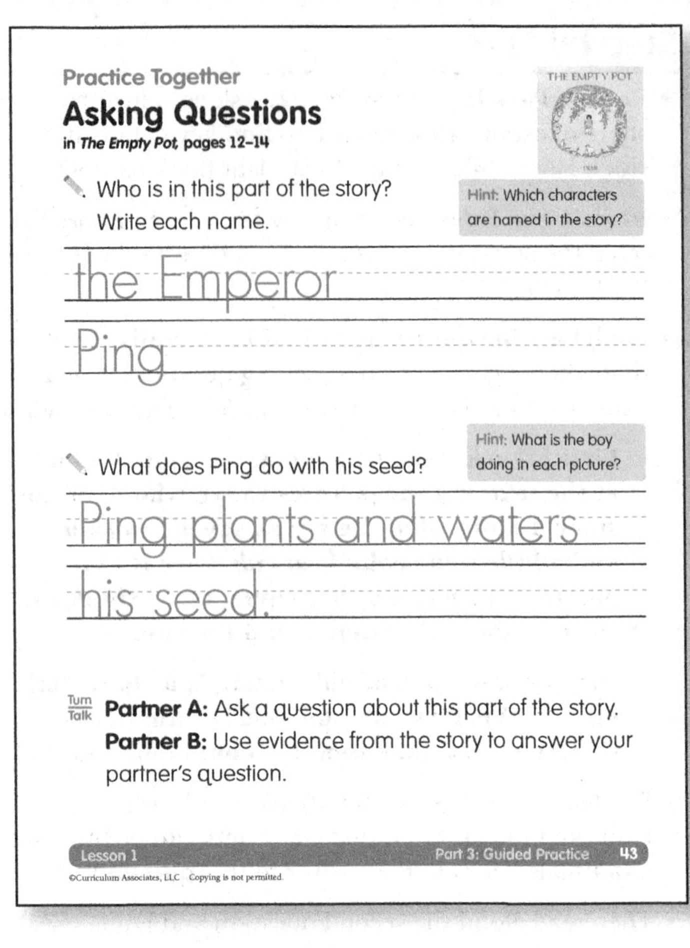
Practice Together

Asking Questions

in *The Empty Pot*, pages 12–14

Who is in this part of the story? Write each name.

Hint: Which characters are named in the story?

the Emperor

Ping

What does Ping do with his seed?

Hint: What is the boy doing in each picture?

Ping plants and waters his seed.

Turn Talk **Partner A:** Ask a question about this part of the story.
Partner B: Use evidence from the story to answer your partner's question.

Lesson 1 Part 3: Guided Practice 43

Close Reading

- Remind children that asking and answering questions can help them learn more about characters. Encourage them to ask and answer other questions about pages 12–14 of *The Empty Pot*, such as the following:

  Why was Ping "the happiest child of all"? *(He was sure that he could grow the most beautiful flower.)*

  Where is Ping in the picture on page 12? *(He is at the Emperor's palace.)*

  Why does Ping fill his flowerpot with rich soil? *(He knows it will help the seed grow.)*

  Why did Ping water his seed every day? *(He thought that water would help it grow.)*

- Guide children to see how asking and answering questions about evidence in the words and pictures helped them learn more about Ping and the reasons for his actions.

Part 4: Independent Practice

Step by Step

- **Review Parts 1–3; preview Part 4.** Invite a volunteer to tell why it is important to ask and answer questions. Then direct children to Student Book page 44.
- Explain that children will ask and answer questions by themselves, but they are the same questions they answered on previous pages. The first question asks *who,* and the answers are characters. The second question is about what a character is doing.
- **Have children ask and answer questions independently.** Display *The Empty Pot* and tell children they will ask and answer questions about another part of the book.
- Ask children to listen for who is in this part of the story and what each character does. Read aloud pages 28–30. Have children touch their noses when they hear a character's name.
- Read aloud the first question on the Student Book page along with the Hint. Have children write the names of the characters.
- Read aloud the second question and the Hint. Remind children that "using your own words" means telling about something the way you would say it, not simply repeating every word the text says. Have children write their answers in complete sentences. *(L.1.1; L.1.2)*

Tip: Discuss how asking questions can help define unfamiliar words. For example, model figuring out the meaning of *shame* by asking questions about "hung his head" and "expecting to be punished."

- Use the Close Reading activity to help children use text and picture evidence to practice asking and answering questions.
- Discuss answers to the first and second questions.
- **Have children demonstrate understanding.** Have partners complete the Turn and Talk activity. Challenge them to ask and answer *why* questions such as *Why does Ping become the successor? (SL.1.1; SL.1.4)*
- **Have children reflect on their learning.** Guide children in a discussion about why asking and answering questions about key details helps them better understand stories. Chart their ideas.

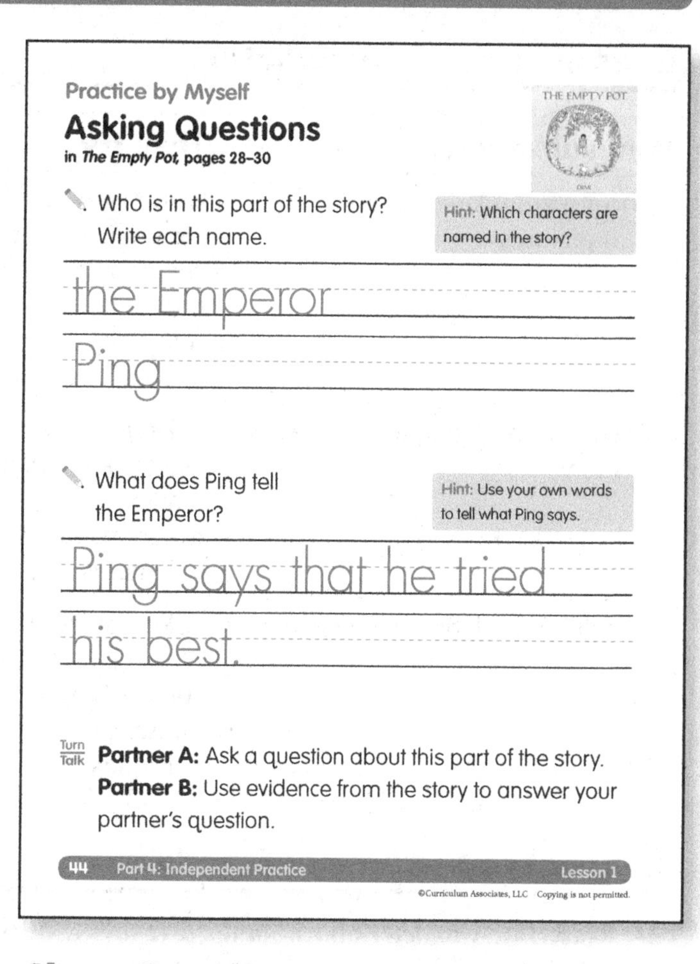

Practice by Myself

Asking Questions

in *The Empty Pot,* pages 28–30

Who is in this part of the story? Write each name.

Hint: Which characters are named in the story?

the Emperor

Ping

What does Ping tell the Emperor?

Hint: Use your own words to tell what Ping says.

Ping says that he tried his best.

Turn Talk **Partner A:** Ask a question about this part of the story.
Partner B: Use evidence from the story to answer your partner's question.

44 Part 4: Independent Practice Lesson 1

©Curriculum Associates, LLC Copying is not permitted.

Close Reading

- Remind children that asking and answering questions can help them learn more about characters. Encourage them to ask and answer other questions about pages 28–30 of *The Empty Pot,* such as the following:

  Why does Ping expect to be punished? *(He brings an empty pot instead of a flower.)*

  Why are the children laughing? *(They all grew flowers and Ping did not. The children are making fun of him.)*

  Why does Ping say he put the seed in a better pot with better soil? *(He wants the Emperor to know that he tried everything he could to make the seed grow.)*

- Explain that when readers ask questions about why things happen, they may find some answers directly in the text or pictures. To answer other questions, they may have to combine text and picture evidence with what they know.

Assessment and Remediation

If you observe . . .	Then try . . .
Difficulty formulating questions about pictures	Identifying details in a picture and asking questions about them. Display a picture from a story book. Remind children that pictures have details. Help children describe the details by asking, *What do you see?* and *What do you notice about ______?* Then guide children to ask questions. Start with questions that have answers right in the pictures, and work up to more inferential questions, such as *Why does the character look sad?*
Difficulty formulating *who* and *what* questions	Asking questions about pantomimes. Choose two volunteers. In a whisper, assign each volunteer an activity to pantomime, such as sweeping the floor or reading a book. Have children pantomime for the class. Guide children to ask questions such as *Who is sweeping?* and *What is Elisa doing?* Choose new volunteers and have children ask *who* and *what* questions on their own.
Difficulty formulating *why* questions	Asking story characters why they do things. Assign four children to act out *The Three Little Pigs* as you retell it. Model how to ask the first pig questions such as *Why did you leave home?* and *Why did you use straw to build your house?* Guide children to ask the other two pigs and the wolf additional *why* questions.

Connect to the Anchor Standard

R1: *Read closely to determine what the text says explicitly and to make logical inferences from it; cite specific textual evidence when writing or speaking to support conclusions drawn from the text.*

Throughout the grades, Standard 1 builds toward a more advanced understanding of what it means to ask and answer questions. In later grades, readers transition from "right there" questions to asking more in-depth questions that pair close reading with metacognitive thinking: *What evidence can I find directly in the text? What is the author telling me that's not directly stated? How can I add up clues in the text to understand what it doesn't say directly? Why did the author choose to describe certain details and leave out others?* Use the following activities to help your students begin this transition.

- Work with children to make inferences from explicit information in the text. Draw a character web for the Emperor from *The Empty Pot*. Reread pages 6–7 and 31–32. Guide children to identify explicit details, such as *loved flowers, tended a garden, very old*. Add these to the web. Then talk about how to read "between the lines" to make inferences. For instance, determine that the Emperor is kind, smart, and patient, and add these to the web. Discuss how the text supports this second level of detail. *(SL.1.1; SL.1.2; SL.1.4)*
- Have children draw conclusions. Reread page 20 in *The Polar Bear Son*. Ask: *What do the children do when they hear the hunters' plan? (They run and warn the old woman.)* Build from the literal to the inferential by asking how the children feel about Kunikdjuaq. *(They care about him.)* Discuss how adding up clues in the text helps fill in details that are not stated directly. *(SL.1.1; SL.1.2; SL.1.4)*

Read Aloud Lesson C (Student Book pages 11–14)

My Rotten Redheaded Older Brother

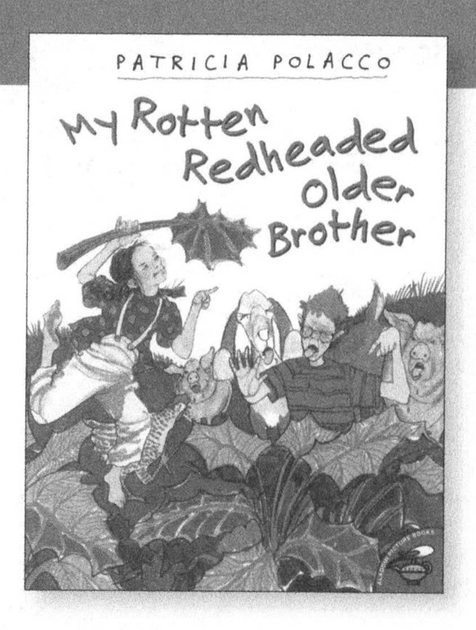

Lesson Objectives

You will read aloud *My Rotten Redheaded Older Brother,* which children will revisit in later lessons. Children will:

- Answer questions about key details in the story.
- Describe characters and major events, using key details.
- Retell the story, including key details.

About the Text

Summary

Treesha's older brother Richard beats her at everything. When the carnival comes, Treesha is determined to be the best at riding the merry-go-round, but she gets dizzy and passes out. When Richard shows what a big brother he can be, they both realize they have a special relationship.

Genre: Realistic Fiction

- *My Rotten Redheaded Older Brother* is realistic fiction. Explain that realistic fiction stories have characters and events that could happen in real life.
- Use the story title to help children recognize the sibling rivalry, which is common in real-life families.

Critical Vocabulary

- Prior to reading, briefly define the following words:

  ordinary (p. 8) normal or usual; not special

  record (p. 14) the best performance; the top

  challenged (p. 14) tested or questioned; asked someone to be part of a contest or game

  incredible (p. 26) hard to believe; amazing

- As you read, pause to point to the words as you encounter them, and review their definitions.

Word Bank

- To support children in writing about the story, display a word bank containing the Critical Vocabulary and the characters' names *(Treesha; Richard; Bubbie).*
- Add other important story words, such as *carnival, merry-go-round* and *carousel,* on subsequent readings.

New Concepts: Traveling Carnivals

- Explain that an important part of the story happens at a traveling carnival—an amusement park that moves from place to place. A carnival has rides, such as merry-go-rounds (or carousels) and Ferris wheels. Often there are food and game booths, too.
- Display pages 26–27 and identify some carnival features.

Ready *Teacher Toolbox* Teacher-Toolbox.com

	Prerequisite Skills	RL.1.2
Ready Lessons		✓
Tools for Instruction	✓ ✓	✓
Interactive Tutorials	✓ ✓	

CCSS Focus

RL.1.2 *Retell stories, including key details...*

ADDITIONAL STANDARDS: **RL.1.1; RL.1.3; RL.1.7; RF.1.2.d; RF.1.3.a; W.1.8; SL.1.1.a, b; SL.1.2; SL.1.4; SL.1.5; SL.1.6; L.1.1.f, j; L.1.2.a, b; L.1.4.a, b; L.1.5.a, c** *(See page A38 for full text.)*

Step by Step

- **Introduce *My Rotten Redheaded Older Brother*.** Display the book. Then read aloud the title and the name of the author, Patricia Polacco. Point out that she is also the illustrator.
- **Set the purpose for reading.** Tell children that readers make sense of a story by identifying the characters and then keeping track of what happens to them.
- Explain that as you read aloud, children should listen closely to identify the characters in this story.
- **Read aloud *My Rotten Redheaded Older Brother*.** Read the story all the way through, pausing only to briefly define challenging vocabulary.
- **Guide children to review the characters.** After reading, use questions such as these to discuss the characters. *(RL.1.1; SL.1.1; SL.1.2)*

  Who are the main characters? *(Treesha, Richard)*

  How can we tell they are the main characters? *(The story tells what happens to them both.)*

  Name some of the other characters. *(Bubbie; Mom; Grandpa)*

Tip: If children are confused about whether Bubbie is a main character, remind them that the story events are not about Bubbie and what happens to her.

- Direct children to turn to Student Book page 11. Read aloud the first item. Discuss the Hint and have children identify and draw the two main characters. *(RL.1.3)*
- Prompt children to write the names of the characters beneath their pictures.
- **Have children discuss story evidence.** Read aloud the Turn and Talk activity. Encourage children to connect their pictures to details in the story, including how the characters' feelings about each other change from the beginning of the story to the end. *(SL.1.4; SL.1.5)*

My Rotten Redheaded Older Brother

The Main Characters

Draw the two main characters.

Hint: Who is the story mostly about?

Children should draw one picture each of Treesha and Richard.

Name each character.

Treesha   Richard

Turn Talk Use your pictures and evidence from the story to tell your partner what you know about each character.

Read Aloud | Lesson C   Part 1: Characters   11

ELL Support: Comparing Words

- Reread pages 16–17, emphasizing the words ending in *-est*. Point to and read aloud the word *longest*. Then write *long, longer,* and *longest*.
- Point to and underline the endings *-er* and *-est*. Explain that adding these endings to words lets us compare one thing to another.
- Display three objects of different lengths. Describe each object as follows: *The [object 1] is long. The [object 2] is longer. The [object 3] is longest.* Have children repeat after you.
- Continue with other story words, such as *fast, high, far, dirty,* and *loud*. Point out the spelling changes in *farther, farthest, dirtier,* and *dirtiest*.
- Have children use the comparative forms in oral sentences about Treesha and Richard. You might also wish to discuss these irregular comparatives: *good/better/best; bad/worse/worst; more/most. (L.1.1.f; L.1.4.b)*

PART 2: Reread for Meaning (Beginning)

Step by Step

- **Reread and discuss the beginning.** Read pages 8–17 aloud. Use questions such as these to guide discussion. *(RL.1.1; SL.1.1; SL.1.2)*

  Pages 12–13: What does Treesha say is the worst thing about Richard? *(He is always telling her that he can do everything better than she can.)*

  Pages 12–17: Does Richard keep quiet about what he can do better? Explain. *(No. He brags about what he does better and teases Treesha.)*

  Pages 16–17: What is Treesha's problem? *(She can't do anything better than her brother.)*

- **Focus on a key detail.** Ask children to turn to Student Book page 12. Read aloud the first item and the Hint. Help children recall what Treesha says about her brother on page 15. *(RL.1.3)*
- Use the Close Reading activity to find story evidence that shows how Treesha feels about Richard.

Tip: Pause to remind children that Treesha is telling the story, so readers see Richard the way Treesha—someone who is mad at him—describes him.

- Prompt children to complete the second item.
- **Have children discuss story evidence.** Read aloud the Turn and Talk activity. Guide children to talk about story evidence that shows how Treesha feels about competing with her brother. *(SL.1.4; SL.1.5)*

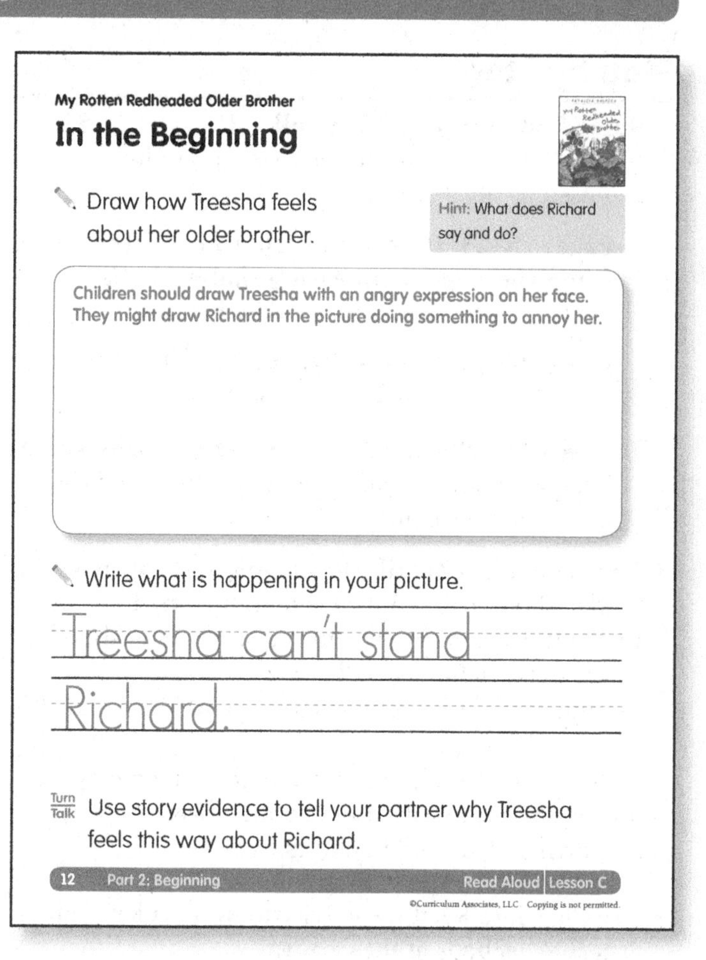

My Rotten Redheaded Older Brother

In the Beginning

Draw how Treesha feels about her older brother.

Hint: What does Richard say and do?

Children should draw Treesha with an angry expression on her face. They might draw Richard in the picture doing something to annoy her.

Write what is happening in your picture.

Treesha can't stand Richard.

Turn Talk Use story evidence to tell your partner why Treesha feels this way about Richard.

12 Part 2: Beginning Read Aloud | Lesson C

©Curriculum Associates, LLC Copying is not permitted.

- Discuss details about Treesha, Richard, and their relationship. Have children use their Student Book pages to recall the beginning of the story.

Tier Two Vocabulary: *equal*

- Read aloud pages 16–17. Point to the word *equal*.
- Ask children to tell in what subject they usually hear the word *equal*. *(math)* Invite a volunteer to use blocks to demonstrate something that is equal, based on what he or she knows about math.
- Guide children to express that *equal* means "the same." Then explain that *to have an equal* means "to be the same as another in some way." Give examples, such as *My grandmother's meatballs are so good, they have no equal.*
- Have children use *equal* to describe how Treesha and Richie feel about each other. Then invite them to use the word in their own examples.

Close Reading

- Help children look for important details in the story illustrations. *(RL.1.7)*
- Display pages 10–13, and read them aloud. Then prompt:

  What is Richard doing on page 10? *(He is keeping Treesha's doll away from her.)*

  How does Treesha look in the illustration on page 13? *(angry; annoyed; upset)*

  How do these pictures support what Treesha says about Richard? *(She says that she can't stand him, and that he is always saying he does things better than her. The pictures show that.)*

Step by Step

- **Reread and discuss the middle.** Read pages 18–29 aloud. Use questions such as these to guide discussion. *(RL.1.1; SL.1.1; SL.1.2)*

  Pages 18–23: How does Richard trick Treesha when she asks about eating rhubarb? *(He doesn't tell her that he loves eating rhubarb.)*

  Pages 24–25: What is Treesha's wish? *(to do something better than her brother)*

  Pages 26–29: How does Treesha decide to solve her problem? *(by riding the merry-go-round for longer than Richard)*

- **Focus on a key detail.** Direct children to turn to Student Book page 13. Read aloud the first item and the Hint. Help children connect Treesha's wish to be better than Richard with her carousel ride. Then prompt children to complete the second item. *(RL.1.3)*

Tip: Make sure children understand that a merry-go-round is a ride with different animals that go up and down and around in circles.

- Use the Close Reading activity to find evidence about Treesha's feelings at the carnival.
- **Have children discuss story evidence.** Read aloud the Turn and Talk activity. Ask how Treesha's feelings are different from the beginning of the story. *(She is sure she will beat her brother. Before, she felt like she couldn't.) (SL.1.4; SL.1.5)*

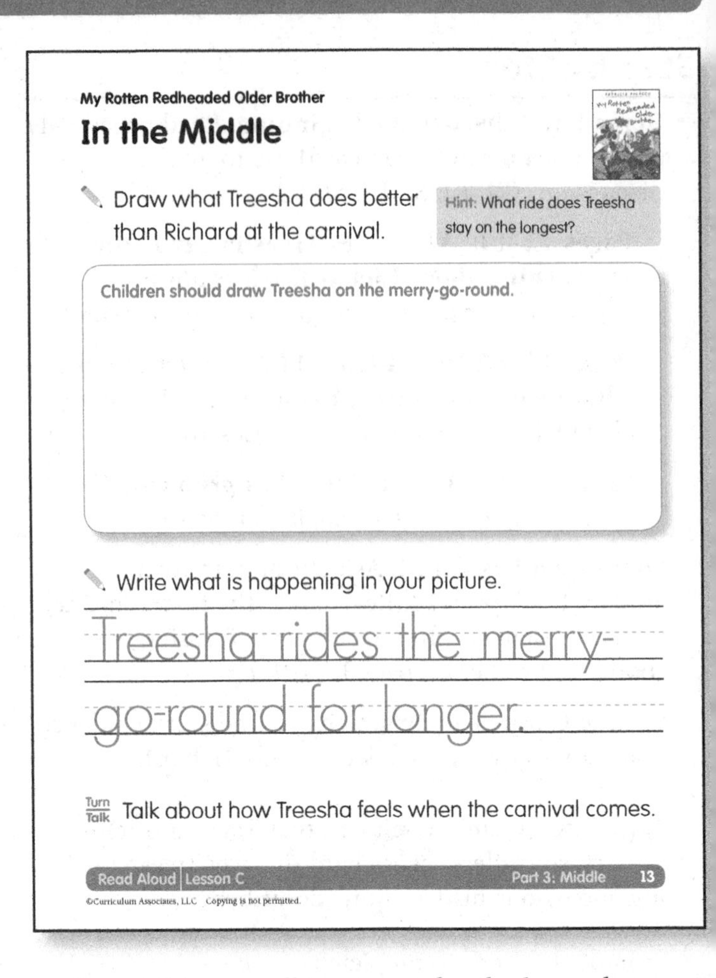
My Rotten Redheaded Older Brother

In the Middle

Draw what Treesha does better than Richard at the carnival.

Hint: What ride does Treesha stay on the longest?

Children should draw Treesha on the merry-go-round.

Write what is happening in your picture.

Treesha rides the merry-go-round for longer.

Turn Talk Talk about how Treesha feels when the carnival comes.

Read Aloud | Lesson C Part 3: Middle 13

©Curriculum Associates, LLC Copying is not permitted.

- Have children recall important details about what Treesha and Richard say and do in this part of the story. Encourage them to use their Student Book pages.

Tier Two Vocabulary: *announced*

- Read page 20, and point to the word *announced*. Have children repeat it a few times.
- Work with children to name words that might replace *announced*, such as *said, called,* or *told me*.
- Guide children to understand that *announced* means "to tell something aloud; to let everyone know something." Give an example such as this: *The principal announced that our class had won the school spirit award.*
- Have children take turns giving examples of something that might be announced. Guide them to use other forms of the word, such as *announce* and *announces*. *(SL.1.6; L.1.1.j; L.1.4.a; L.1.5.c)*

Close Reading

- Display and reread pages 28–29, and then use the following questions to discuss Treesha's actions and feelings:

  What does Treesha say to Richard? *(She knew she could ride the carousel longer than he could.)*

  How is Treesha feeling? *(proud)*

  What is different about Treesha in this part of the story? *(She feels proud of herself for being better than Richard at something. She isn't angry or annoyed.)*

- Discuss whether Treesha's wish came true.

PART 4: Reread for Meaning (End)

Step by Step

- **Reread and discuss the end.** Read pages 30–36 aloud. Discuss the way the story ends, using questions such as these. *(RL.1.1; SL.1.1; SL.1.2)*

  Pages 30–31: What happens to Treesha when she steps off the merry-go-round? *(She falls, and Richard carries her home and gets the doctor.)*

  Pages 32–33: What is the special thing that Richard says Treesha does? *(She passed out.)*

Tip: Clarify that *passed out* means "fainted," or fell asleep for a few seconds after becoming very dizzy. It is special because it does not happen often.

  Pages 34–36: How does Treesha's wish come true differently than she thought? *(She did do something better than Richard, but she also sees that he is a good brother who loves her.)*

- **Focus on a key detail.** Have children turn to Student Book page 14. Read aloud the first item and provide support using the Hint.
- Prompt children to complete the second item. Then use the Close Reading activity to have children find evidence about the characters' feelings. *(RL.1.3)*
- **Have children discuss story evidence.** Read aloud the Turn and Talk activity. Have children recall how Treesha and Richard felt at the beginning and why their feelings change at the end. *(SL.1.4; SL.1.5)*

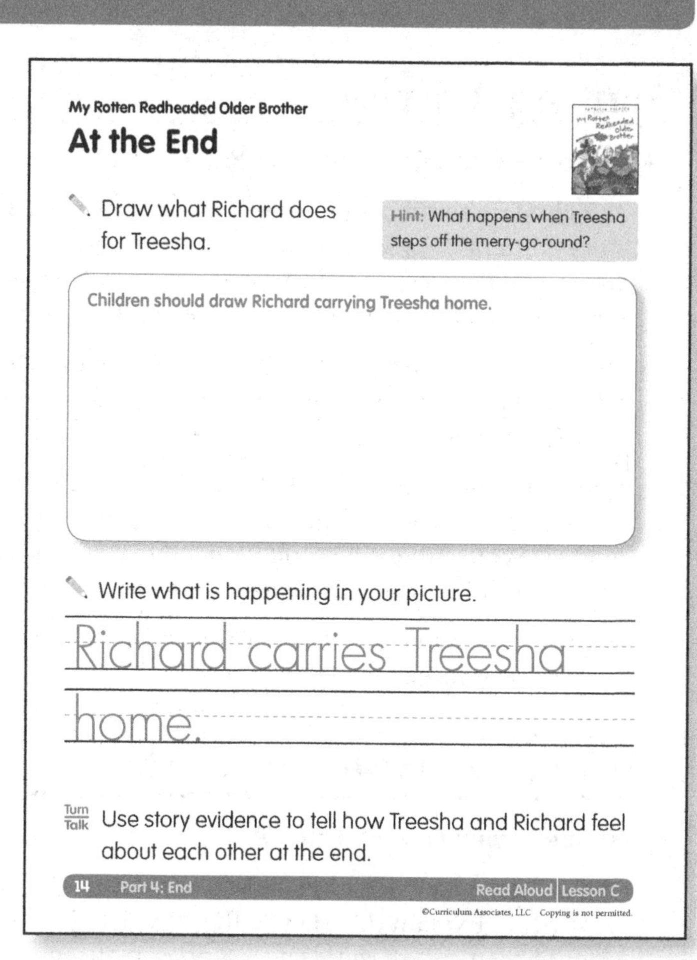

My Rotten Redheaded Older Brother

At the End

Draw what Richard does for Treesha.

Hint: What happens when Treesha steps off the merry-go-round?

Children should draw Richard carrying Treesha home.

Write what is happening in your picture.

Richard carries Treesha home.

Turn Talk Use story evidence to tell how Treesha and Richard feel about each other at the end.

14 Part 4: End Read Aloud | Lesson C

©Curriculum Associates, LLC Copying is not permitted.

- **Retell *My Rotten Redheaded Older Brother.*** Guide a round-robin retelling of the entire story. Prompt children to refer to their Student Books as they take turns naming important ideas in sequence. Provide corrective feedback as needed.

Integrating Foundational Skills

Use these tasks as opportunities to integrate foundational skills into your reading of *My Rotten Redheaded Older Brother.*

1. Have children segment words into their individual sounds. Say *sit*. Have children segment as follows: /s/ /ĭ/ /t/. Continue with these words: *laugh, like, not, can, make, sick, climb, bite, slap, wish, fell, run, pick, sleep.* *(RF.1.2.d)*
2. Display these digraphs: *sh, th, ch.* Tell children they will listen to a word and write the sound they hear at the beginning. Use these words: *she, thank, show, chew, they, child, shoot, then, chirp.* Check children's work after each word. *(RF.1.3.a)*

Close Reading

- Read aloud pages 31–32. Use these questions to have children find evidence that Treesha and Richard's feelings have changed.

  What two things does Treesha thank Richie for doing? *(for carrying her home and for saying she did something special)*

  What does Richie say about what he did? *(He says what he did is what a big brother is for. He is supposed to help his little sister.)*

  How are Treesha's and Richie's feelings different now? *(Treesha isn't angry or annoyed. Richie is being nice to Treesha.)*

Writing Activity

Write to Answer a Question (*W.1.8; L.1.2.a, b*)

- Ask children to think about someone in their lives with whom they have shared experiences like those in the story. Prompt: *Do you have a brother, sister, cousin, or friend that the story events remind you of? For example, you might know someone older than you who can do things better. Or you might argue with a brother or sister even though you really love him or her.* Have children discuss their ideas with a partner.
- Display the following writing prompt: *Tell how a relationship in your life is like Treesha and Richard's relationship.* If any children need support, offer an alternative such as an example from a familiar book or an appropriate television show or movie.
- Help children dictate or write two to three sentences to tell how their relationship is like the one in the book. As needed, provide sentence starters and refer children to the Word Bank. Guide children to observe language conventions by capitalizing the names of people and any dates they use in their responses. Help them use end punctuation correctly as well.
- Invite children to share their writing with the class, and discuss how Treesha and Richard's relationship is similar to children's own experiences.

Speaking and Listening Activity

Describe Family Fun (*SL.1.1.a, b*)

- Tell children they will have a discussion about family fun. Explain that they will use evidence from *My Rotten Redheaded Older Brother* to discuss the following prompt: *What is fun about being part of Treesha and Richard's family?*
- You might want to display and discuss the Polacco family photos on pages 2–3 prior to the discussion.
- Form children into small groups. Have each group discuss a few ideas they want to share with the class. Help them write down these ideas so they can refer to them during the discussion.
- Before the discussion begins, review the rules such as listening carefully, taking turns to speak, and staying on topic. Remind children not to simply tell about their own ideas but to respond to the ideas and comments of others.
- As children speak, clarify that they should ask questions if they do not understand something that is said.
- After the discussion, have children give a brief summary of the ideas they talked about.

Language Activity

I Challenge You! (*L.1.5.a, c*)

- Review the Critical Vocabulary with children, and recall that Treesha and Richard were always having contests of many different kinds.
- Then explain that children are going to play a game called "I Challenge You!"
- Form children into small groups. Ask each small group to think of a challenge they want to give another group, such as "Name six red things in the classroom" or "Name as many furry things as you can in thirty seconds."
- Check in with each group to make sure their proposed challenge is clear and able to be accomplished in the classroom within the given time span.
- Have each group take turns challenging the other groups. Help children present their challenges in complete sentences and help all groups keep track of whether each challenge was successfully met.

Lesson 2 (Student Book pages 45–48)

Describing Characters

CCSS

RL.1.3: Describe characters . . . in a story, using key details.

Required Read Alouds: *A (The Empty Pot); C (My Rotten Redheaded Older Brother)*

Lesson Objectives

- Identify words and phrases that indicate characters' feelings.
- Use words and pictures to support conclusions about characters in a story.
- Describe characters' words and actions using key details.
- Understand how describing a character can help you better understand a story.

The Learning Progression

- **Grade K:** CCSS RL.K.3 requires children to identify characters in a story with prompting and support.
- **Grade 1: CCSS RL.1.3 builds on the Grade K standard by having children work more independently at using key details and illustrations in a story to identify and describe the characters.**
- **Grade 2:** CCSS RL.2.3 expands upon the scope of the standard by having children describe how characters in a story respond to major events and challenges.

Prerequisite Skills

- Identify characters with prompting and support.
- Identify key details with prompting and support.
- Retell story details with prompting and support.

Tap Children's Prior Knowledge

- Remind children that the characters in a story are the people or animals the story is about. Ask children to name some characters from stories they have read recently. Write their suggestions on the board.
- Explain that realistic characters are like people in real life, while made-up characters do things real people or animals couldn't do. For example, Junie B. Jones is a realistic character and Martha, the talking dog, is a made-up character. Have children identify other realistic and made-up characters in the list.
- Tell children that understanding story characters is a lot like understanding people in real life. Say: *Imagine you saw a friend sitting alone in the corner and crying. What would you think? (The friend is sad.)*
- Discuss that paying attention to the things a friend says or does helps you understand how that friend is feeling. Explain that the same is true with both realistic and made-up characters in a story: paying attention to what characters say and do will help children understand them.
- Tell children that in this lesson, they will learn to describe characters based on what they say and do.

Ready *Teacher Toolbox* Teacher-Toolbox.com

	Prerequisite Skills	*RL.1.3*
Ready Lessons	✓	✓
Tools for Instruction	✓	✓
Interactive Tutorials		✓

Additional CCSS

RL.1.1; RL.1.2; RL.1.7; SL.1.1; SL.1.3; SL.1.4; L.1.1; L.1.2 (See page A38 for full text.)

Part 1: Introduction

Step by Step

- **Introduce the standard.** Have children turn to page 45 in their Student Books. Read aloud the speech bubble.
- Explain that *lifelike animal* means an animal that talks or does things that a person might do. Point out that children know many stories with lifelike animal characters. Give examples such as *The Ant and The Grasshopper, The Town Mouse and the Country Mouse,* or *Henny Penny.*
- **Review questions to ask about characters.** Read the line below the speech bubble, and point out that what follows are questions that good readers ask themselves to find out more about a character. Read aloud the first question. Have children underline the word *say.* Then explain:

  The words a character says can tell you what the character thinks or feels. The way a character says the words is important, too. For example, a character can shout, whisper, or whine. These all sound and feel very different.

Tip: To help emergent readers identify the words *say, do,* and *feel,* point to each word as you emphasize it, and have children repeat it after you.

- Have children say the following sentence in a shout, a whisper, and a whine: *I am hungry.* After each example, discuss how someone who talks that way might be feeling, and think about reasons why.
- Read aloud the second question. Have children underline the word *do.* Then explain:

  The things a character does can give you information about the kind of person the character is. Would a nice character help someone or say mean things? *(A nice character would help someone.)*

- Ask children to brainstorm some mean characters they remember from stories, such as the wicked stepmother and stepsisters in *Cinderella.* Discuss how you determined that these characters were mean based on their actions, or what they did.

Listen and Learn

Describing Characters

A **character** is a person or lifelike animal in a story. You can learn about characters by thinking about what they say and do.

Here are some questions you can ask about characters:

- What does the character say?
- What does the character do?
- How does the character feel?

Asking these questions helps us learn more about the characters.

Lesson 2 Part 1: Introduction 45

- Read aloud the third question. Have children underline the word *feel.* Then explain:

  The things a character does and says can help you understand the way the character feels. Imagine a character jumps up and down, claps her hands, and yells "Hooray!" How do you think that character feels? *(happy and excited)*

- **Explain why readers ask questions about characters.** Read aloud the bottom of the page. Explain that when you think about why a character says or does things, you get to know them better, just like you get to know a person better.
- Share an example of a time when describing a character helped you understand a story. For instance, recount *The Tortoise and the Hare.* Tell how knowing that the Hare likes to brag about how fast he is helps you understand why the Tortoise would want to trick him.
- **Have children demonstrate understanding.** Call on individuals to share what they have learned so far about describing a character in a story.

Part 2: Modeled Instruction

Step by Step

- **Review Part 1; preview Part 2.** Ask volunteers to share questions they can ask about characters in a story. Have children turn to Student Book page 46.
- **Revisit *The Empty Pot*.** Invite children to briefly retell the story, using pages 3–6 of their Student Books. *(RL.1.2)*
- **Model describing characters.** Explain that you are going to model asking questions about characters. Read aloud pages 26–27 of *The Empty Pot.* Then point to evidence in the text and pictures as you think aloud:

  I will ask myself what the Emperor says and does: First, he looks at the flowers slowly. Next, he frowns, then he does not say a word. I'll use that evidence to figure out how the Emperor feels. The words and pictures tell me that the Emperor is frowning. I think that means he feels unhappy. *(RL.1.7)*

Tip: Help children infer the Emperor's feelings. Have them frown. Ask how they feel when they make this face. Then ask how the Emperor feels.

- Read aloud each question and Hint on Student Book page 46. Discuss the answers to these questions.
- **Model writing your responses.** Model how to write the answers in complete sentences, and have children write their responses. *(RL.1.1; L.1.1; L.1.2.)*
- Use the Close Reading activity to analyze the Emperor's feelings and connect them to important events in the story.
- **Have children demonstrate understanding.** Have partners complete the Turn and Talk activity. Circulate, and prompt children to recall words, phrases, and picture evidence that helped them describe the Emperor's actions and feelings.
- Invite volunteers to share their evidence in class discussion. *(SL.1.1; SL.1.4)*

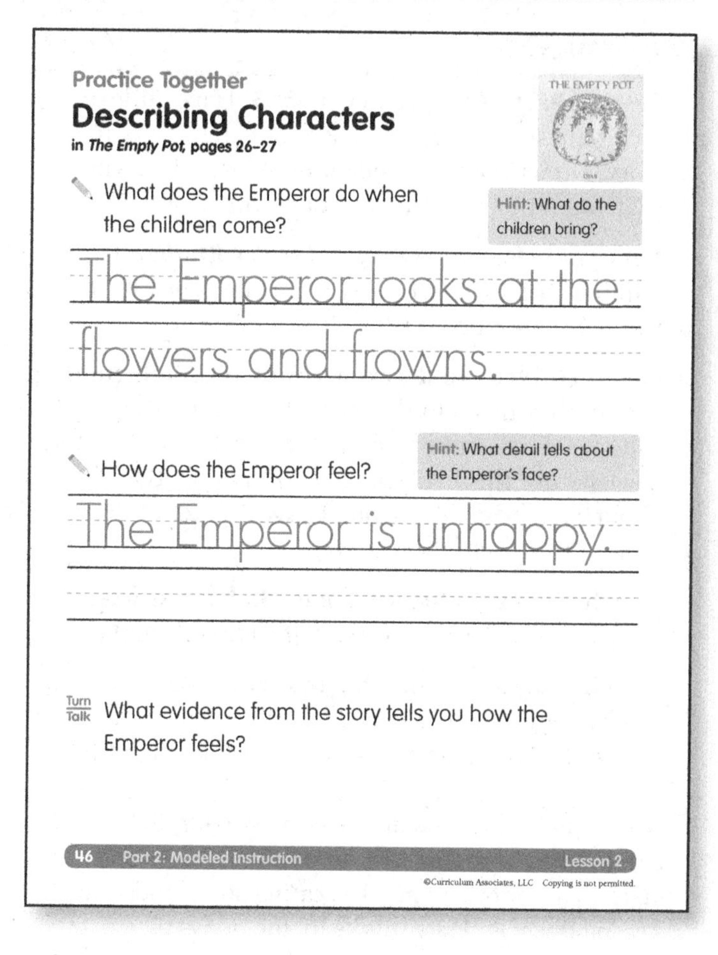

Practice Together

Describing Characters

in *The Empty Pot,* pages 26–27

What does the Emperor do when the children come?

Hint: What do the children bring?

The Emperor looks at the flowers and frowns.

How does the Emperor feel?

Hint: What detail tells about the Emperor's face?

The Emperor is unhappy.

Turn Talk What evidence from the story tells you how the Emperor feels?

46 Part 2: Modeled Instruction Lesson 2

©Curriculum Associates, LLC Copying is not permitted.

Close Reading

- Help children recognize that by asking questions about the Emperor's actions, they can learn more about him and better understand the story. Reread pages 26–27. Then prompt:

  What do we know about the Emperor so far? *(He loves flowers. He needs to choose a successor. He gave each child a seed to grow.)*

  Why is it surprising that he frowns and doesn't say a word? *(Since he loves flowers, you would expect him to be happy to see all the flowers. Also he should be excited to see the children because he wants to pick a successor.)*

- Remind children that later, they learn that the Emperor frowned and said nothing because he was disappointed. He realized that the children had all cheated and that he couldn't trust them to take his place.

Part 3: Guided Practice

Step by Step

- **Review Parts 1–2; preview Part 3.** Have children recall questions they can ask about characters in a story. Direct them to Student Book page 47. Explain that you will guide them through this page.
- **Revisit *My Rotten Redheaded Older Brother.*** Have children briefly retell the story, using pages 11–14 of their Student Books. *(RL.1.2)*
- **Guide children to describe characters.** Tell children that as they listen to this part of the story, they will ask questions about what Richie and Treesha do and say, and use this evidence to identify how they feel about each other. Read aloud pages 18–21 of the story. Prompt children as you read:

  What does Richie say about rhubarb at first (page 18)**?** *(It's the sourest stuff on this planet.)*

  What does Treesha do, and why (page 19)**?** *(She challenges him to a rhubarb eating contest. She thinks she can beat him because he doesn't like rhubarb.)*

Tip: Explain that rhubarb tastes very sour, like lemon, so it would be hard to eat a lot of it at once. Share that not everyone likes eating sour foods, but Treesha does, and she thinks Richie doesn't.

  What does Richie say about rhubarb now (page 20)**?** *(He says he loves it.)*

  What does Treesha say about how she feels about Richie (page 21)**?** *(She says she can't stand him.)*

- **Guide children to write responses.** Read aloud each question on the Student Book page. Use the Hints to help children answer the questions. Discuss the answers and have children write them in complete sentences. *(RL.1.1; L.1.1; L.1.2)*
- Use the Close Reading activity to further describe the relationship between the main characters and to help prepare children for the Turn and Talk activity.
- **Have children demonstrate understanding.** Have partners do the Turn and Talk activity. Remind children to use evidence from the Close Reading discussion to support their ideas. Invite volunteers to share their answers. *(SL.1.1; SL.1.4)*

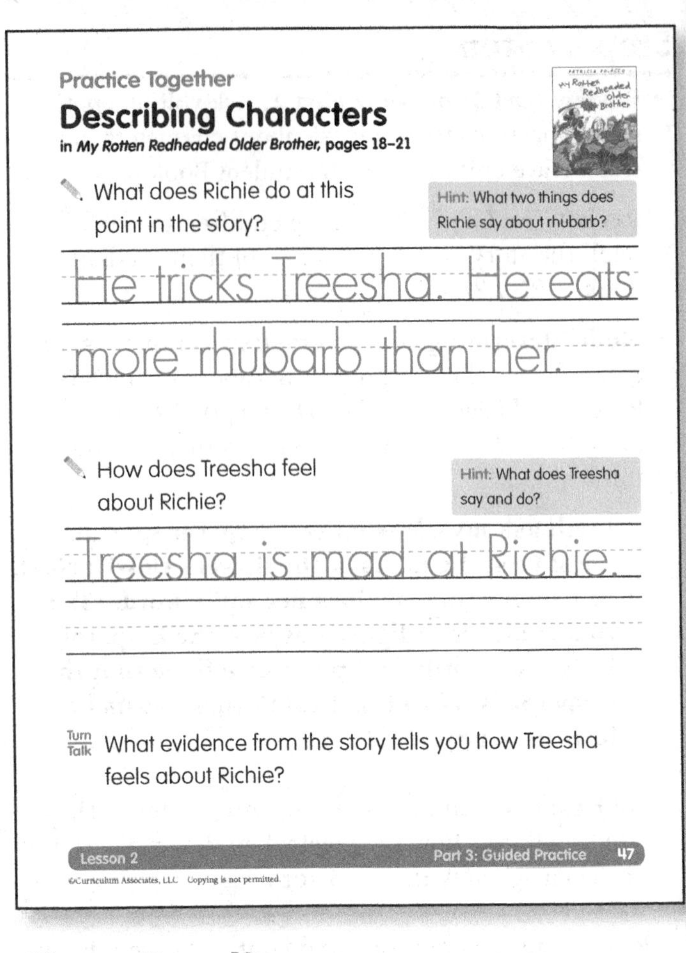
Practice Together

Describing Characters

in *My Rotten Redheaded Older Brother,* pages 18–21

What does Richie do at this point in the story?

Hint: What two things does Richie say about rhubarb?

He tricks Treesha. He eats more rhubarb than her.

How does Treesha feel about Richie?

Hint: What does Treesha say and do?

Treesha is mad at Richie.

Turn Talk: What evidence from the story tells you how Treesha feels about Richie?

Lesson 2 — Part 3: Guided Practice 47

©Curriculum Associates, LLC Copying is not permitted.

Close Reading

- Guide children to look closer at what Richie and Treesha say to each other in this part of the story.
- Read aloud page 21, emphasizing the tone of Richie and Treesha's words. Then prompt:

  Why does Treesha call her brother by his full name here? *(When you are very mad at someone, you sometimes use their first and last name instead of their nickname or first name.)*

  Why is it important that the author used the word *screamed*? *(When you scream at someone, you are usually very angry.)*

  What does the phrase *little twerp* tell you about the way Richie feels about Treesha? *(Calling someone by this name is making fun of them. You make fun of people you don't like and want to annoy.)*

- Discuss how this evidence tells more about the way Richie and Treesha feel about each other.

Part 4: Independent Practice

Step by Step

- **Review Parts 1–3; preview Part 4.** Ask volunteers to share questions readers can ask about characters. Then direct children to Student Book page 48. Point out that they will ask questions about characters by themselves. Emphasize that these questions, as on the previous pages, ask what characters do and feel.
- **Have children describe characters independently.** Display *My Rotten Redheaded Older Brother* and tell children they will describe characters from the book once again.
- Tell children to listen closely to identify what Richie does and for evidence that shows how he feels about Treesha. Read aloud pages 31–32.
- Read aloud the first question on Student Book page 48, and then read the Hint. Have children write the answer in a complete sentence. *(RL.1.1; L.1.1; L.1.2)*

Tip: Several characters are speaking on page 31, and children may have difficulty following the dialogue. Modify your voice each time a character speaks to help children match the character with the words.

- Use the Close Reading activity to help children explore Richie's feelings about what happened to Treesha.
- Read aloud the second question and the Hint. Have children write their answers to the second question in complete sentences.
- Guide children in discussing their answers to both questions.
- **Have children demonstrate understanding.** Have partners complete the Turn and Talk activity. Remind them to use the evidence they discussed in the Close Reading and wrote about in their Student Book. Invite children to share their evidence in class discussion. *(SL.1.1; SL.1.4)*
- **Have children reflect on their learning.** Have children discuss what questions they learned to ask about characters. Guide them to discuss how asking questions about characters, as well as describing characters, can help them better understand stories. Chart their ideas.

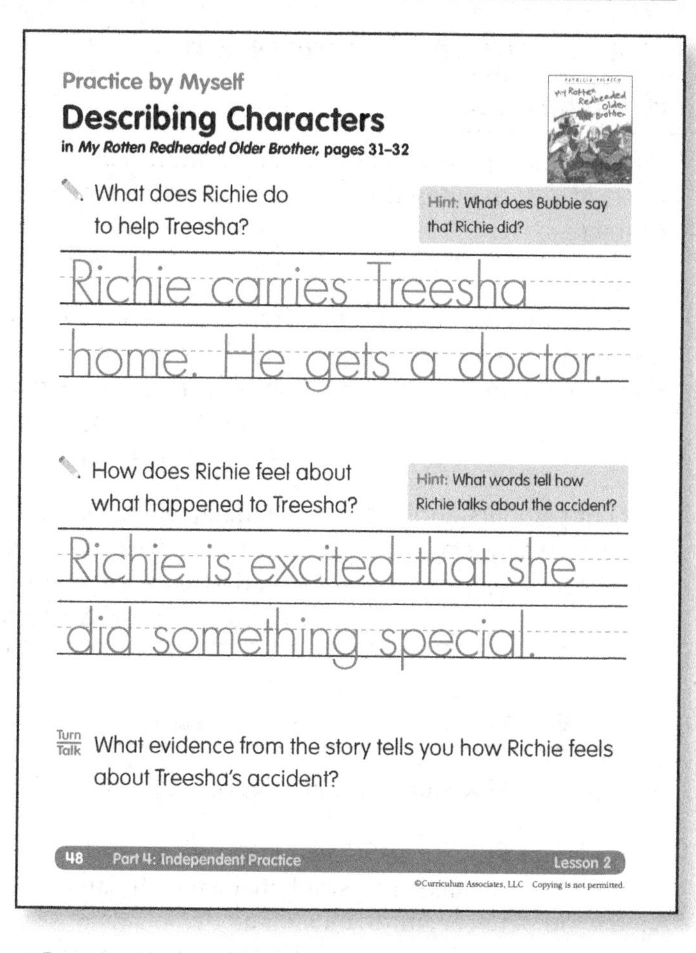

Practice by Myself

Describing Characters

in *My Rotten Redheaded Older Brother*, pages 31–32

What does Richie do to help Treesha?

Hint: What does Bubbie say that Richie did?

Richie carries Treesha home. He gets a doctor.

How does Richie feel about what happened to Treesha?

Hint: What words tell how Richie talks about the accident?

Richie is excited that she did something special.

Turn Talk What evidence from the story tells you how Richie feels about Treesha's accident?

48 Part 4: Independent Practice Lesson 2

©Curriculum Associates, LLC Copying is not permitted.

Close Reading

- Help children look closely at what Richie and Treesha say and do in this part of the story.
- Read page 32 and display page 33. Then prompt:

  Why does Richie talk about Treesha having stitches "excitedly"? *(He might think having stitches is exciting or special. Also, he might be excited that he got to be there to help Treesha.)*

  Why does Richie blush when he says, "What's a big brother for, anyway"? *(Explain that people often blush when they are embarrassed. Discuss how Richie might be embarrassed because he's used to his sister saying mean things to him—not nice things.)*

  What are Treesha and Richie doing in the picture? *(Richie is smiling and shrugging. Their faces look friendly and not mad.) (RL.1.7)*

Differentiated Instruction

Assessment and Remediation

If you observe . . .	Then try . . .
Difficulty citing *say, do,* and *feel* evidence that describes characters	Paraphrasing a descriptive detail about a character and asking children to find *say, do,* and *feel* evidence of that detail. For example, reread page 6 of *The Empty Pot* and ask: *What evidence tells you that the Emperor cares about living things in nature? (The story says he loved birds and animals, and most of all flowers. He took care of his garden.)*
Difficulty making inferences about characters from details in the text	Helping children consider how a character says certain words. For example, read aloud page 16 of *My Rotten Redheaded Older Brother,* using a resigned expression and a sigh as you read the line "I guess I would have to face it." Ask: *At this point in the story, what does Treesha think about herself and her brother? (She thinks he will always be better than she is at everything.)*
Difficulty understanding words that suggest characters' feelings	Working with children to demonstrate—with facial expressions, gestures, and posture—how characters would look when feeling emotions suggested in a story, such as with the words *excitement, rushed eagerly, shame,* and *courage* in *The Empty Pot,* and *sneered, furiously,* and *mad* in *My Rotten Redheaded Older Brother.*

Connect to the Anchor Standard

R3: *Analyze how and why individuals, events, and ideas develop and interact over the course of a text.*

Throughout the grades, Standard 3 builds toward a more sophisticated analysis of characters. In later grades, students begin to understand that characters are not just entertaining "people" for them to get to know, but that they are constructed in particular ways by the author for specific reasons. Students learn to ask questions not only about the characters themselves, but also about how and why the author imagined them: *How do characters interact with others over the course of the text? What do these connections say about the characters? How do characters change as a result of their experiences and interactions?* Use the following activities to help your students begin this transition.

- Have children practice recognizing how characters develop over the course of a text. Draw children's attention to how Ping feels at the beginning, middle, and end of *The Empty Pot.* Read pages 12, 22, 28, 30, and 32. After each page, discuss how Ping feels. Then, notice how Ping's feelings change over the course of the story. Discuss how Ping's interactions with other characters change the way he feels. *(SL.1.1; SL.1.4)*
- Guide children to see how characters interact over the course of a text. Read pages 12, 21, 32–33, and 37 of *My Rotten Redheaded Older Brother.* Call attention to what Treesha says on page 33: "It was from that exact moment that our relationship changed somehow." Discuss text evidence that shows how and why the character's interactions in that scene are different than in earlier scenes. *(SL.1.1; SL.1.3; SL.1.4)*

Read Aloud Lesson D (Student Book pages 15–18)

Mice and Beans

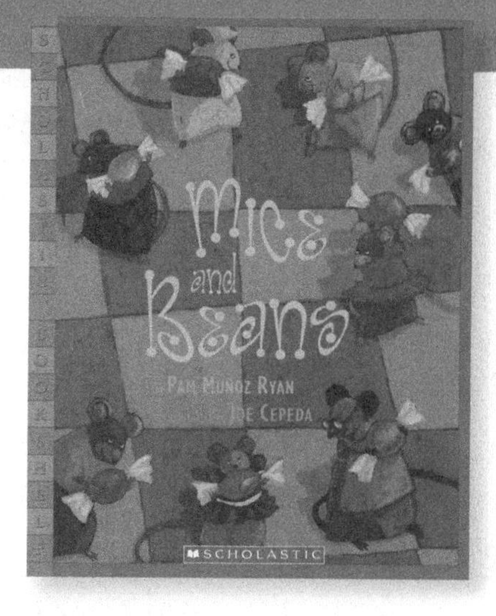

Lesson Objectives

You will read aloud *Mice and Beans,* which children will revisit in later lessons. Children will:

- Answer questions about key details in the story.
- Describe characters and major events, using key details.
- Retell the story, including key details.

About the Text

Summary

Rosa María plans a party and sets mousetraps. Each day, though, both a party item and her mousetraps are missing. Rosa María thinks she is forgetful, but sneaky mice are the problem. On party day, when a piñata is mysteriously filled with candy, she discovers the mice are helpers after all.

Genre: Fantasy

- *Mice and Beans* is a fantasy. Explain that characters in a fantasy do or say things that cannot happen in real life.
- Point out the mice on the cover wearing clothes and glasses. Discuss that mice would not do this in real life.

Critical Vocabulary

- Prior to reading, briefly define the following words:

  set (p. 5) to get something ready to use

  checked (p. 6) looked closely at

  missing (p. 6) gone; disappeared

- As you read, pause to point to the words as you encounter them, and review their definitions.

Word Bank

- To support children in writing about the story, display a word bank containing the Critical Vocabulary and the characters' names *(Rosa María* and *the mice).*
- Add other important story words, such as *mousetrap, cupboard,* and *piñata,* on subsequent readings.

New Concepts: The Game of Piñata

- Explain that a piñata is a breakable container, usually in the shape of an animal, filled with surprises such as candy, toys, and confetti.
- The piñata is hung from a tree branch or other object that allows it to swing.
- Children take turns being blindfolded and trying to break the piñata with a stick.

Ready *Teacher Toolbox* Teacher-Toolbox.com

	Prerequisite Skills	RL.1.2
Ready Lessons		✓
Tools for Instruction	✓ ✓	✓
Interactive Tutorials	✓ ✓	

CCSS Focus

RL.1.2 *Retell stories, including key details…*

ADDITIONAL STANDARDS: **RL.1.1; RL.1.3; RL.1.7; RF.1.3.b, c; W.1.1; SL.1.1; SL.1.2; SL.1.4; SL.1.5; SL.1.6; L.1.1.f, j; L.1.4.a; L.1.5.c**
(See page A38 for full text.)

PART 1: First Read (Characters)

Step by Step

- **Introduce *Mice and Beans*.** Display the book. Then read aloud the title and the name of the author, Pam Muñoz Ryan. Read aloud the name of the illustrator, Joe Cepeda.
- **Set the purpose for reading.** Tell children that readers understand a story by identifying characters and paying attention to what they do and say.
- Explain that as you read aloud, children should listen and look closely to identify the characters.
- **Read aloud *Mice and Beans*.** Read the story all the way through, pausing only to briefly define challenging vocabulary.

Tip: Be sure to draw children's attention to the mice in the pictures in order to explain what happens. The pictures carry many details that are not in the text.

- **Guide children to review the characters.** After reading, use questions such as these to discuss the characters. *(RL.1.1; SL.1.1; SL.1.2)*

  Who are the main characters? *(Rosa María, the mice)*

  How can we tell they are the main characters? *(The story is about what happens to them.)*

  How do we find out what the mice do? *(by looking at the pictures)*

  Who are some of the other characters? *(Little Catalina, Rosa María's other family members)*

- Direct children to turn to Student Book page 15. Read aloud the first item and the Hint. Help children realize that the mice are main characters, even though they never say anything. *(RL.1.3)*
- Prompt children to write the names of the characters beneath their pictures.
- **Have children discuss story evidence.** Read aloud the Turn and Talk activity. Remind children to connect details in their picture to details in the story. Encourage them to look closely at the expressions on the faces of the mice and to notice where Rosa María is looking in each illustration. *(SL.1.4; SL.1.5)*

Mice and Beans

The Main Characters

Draw the main characters.

Hint: Who is the story mostly about?

Children should draw one picture each of Rosa María and the mice.

Name the characters.

Rosa María | the mice

Turn Talk Use your pictures and evidence from the story to tell your partner what you know about the main characters.

Read Aloud | Lesson D Part 1: Characters 15

ELL Support: Bilingual Dictionary

- Tell children that they will make a bilingual dictionary together. Provide printer paper for the activity.
- Page through the story, pointing out Spanish words. Ask children to use context and what they know to figure out what each word means. Use the Glossary and Pronunciation Guide on page 32 to guide discussion.
- Create an entry for each word, using a separate piece of paper. Have volunteers come up and write the word or definition in the entry. Leave room for drawing as needed.
- Once all the words are on paper, have children help you arrange the pages in alphabetical order.
- Have children draw pictures for entries that lend themselves to illustration. If possible, bind the pages into a classroom Bilingual Dictionary.

PART 2: Reread for Meaning (Beginning)

Step by Step

- **Reread and discuss the beginning.** Read pages 2–13 aloud. Use questions such as these to guide discussion. *(RL.1.1; SL.1.1; SL.1.2)*

  Pages 2–5: What is Rosa María planning? *(a seventh birthday party for her granddaughter)*

  Pages 6–7: What two things are missing on Monday? *(a matching napkin and a mousetrap)*

  Pages 12–13: What is Rosa María's problem? *(Her things keep disappearing as she plans the party.)*

Tip: Children may need to review each spread with you to identify what the mice have done each day.

- **Focus on a key detail.** Have children turn to Student Book page 16. Read aloud the first item and provide support using the Hint. Remind children what Rosa María's mother told her about mice on page 2. *(RL.1.3)*
- Prompt children to complete the second item.
- Use the Close Reading activity to help children use picture evidence to find details that may not be in the text.
- **Have children discuss story evidence.** Read aloud the Turn and Talk activity. As needed, remind children that the mice are measuring the mousetrap on page 4. It looks like they are going to build something with it. *(SL.1.4; SL.1.5)*

Mice and Beans

In the Beginning

Draw what Rosa María does each night before going to bed.

Hint: What does Rosa María not want in her house?

Children should draw Rosa María setting a mousetrap.

Write what is happening in your picture.

Rosa María sets a mousetrap.

Turn Talk: Tell what happens to the mousetrap each night.

16 Part 2: Beginning — Read Aloud | Lesson D

©Curriculum Associates, LLC Copying is not permitted.

- Help children identify and discuss the connection between Rosa María's problem and the mice's actions. Encourage children to use their Student Book pages to recall details.

Tier Two Vocabulary: *vanished*

- Display pages 8–9 and read the second and third paragraphs aloud. Point out the word *vanished.*
- Ask children what happened to the mousetrap on other days. *(It was gone; it was missing; it disappeared.)* Based on these details, ask children what they think the word *vanished* means. *("gone; missing; disappeared")*
- Provide an example, such as *The bubble broke and vanished into the air.*
- Then have children use *vanished* to describe other familiar situations, such as what happens to the picture when the TV is turned off or how a cookie seems to disappear. *(L.1.1.j; L.1.4.a; L.1.5.c)*

Close Reading

- Remind children that good readers use picture evidence to find details that may not be in the text. Display pages 2–5.

  What is the mouse on page 3 wearing and doing? *(an apron and glasses like Rosa María's; waving good-bye) (RL.1.7)*

  What are the mice on page 4 wearing and doing? *(hard hats for construction; measuring the mousetrap)*

  What are the mice on page 5 doing? *(They are looking at Rosa María's list and making their own.)*

- Discuss how these details give important clues about the mice as characters.

Step by Step

- **Reread and discuss the middle.** Read pages 14–25 aloud. Then use questions such as these to guide discussion about this part of the story. *(RL.1.1; RL.1.7; SL.1.1; SL.1.2)*

  Pages 14–17: What keeps happening to Rosa María? *(Things disappear; she has to set new mousetraps.)*

  Pages 18–19: What do the mice see? *(The bag of candy is still full; they realize that Rosa María has not filled the piñata.)*

  Pages 20–21: Describe what is happening in the picture. *(The mice are filling the piñata with candy.)*

Tip: On page 19, point out that the Spanish word *dulces* on the full bag means "candy." Discuss how this helps you understand that Rosa María was not ready.

- Use the Close Reading activity to help children find evidence of what Rosa María forgot to do.
- **Focus on a key detail.** Have children turn to Student Book page 17. Read aloud the first item, and provide support using the Hint. *(RL.1.3)*
- Prompt children to complete the second item.
- **Have children discuss story evidence.** Read aloud the Turn and Talk activity. Have children recall story evidence that explains what Rosa María forgets to do before the party. *(SL.1.4; SL.1.5)*

Mice and Beans

In the Middle

Draw what surprises Rosa María at the party.

Hint: What happens when Little Catalina breaks the piñata?

Children should draw the piñata breaking open and candy spilling out. They might show Little Catalina breaking the piñata.

Write what is happening in your picture.

The piñata breaks. It is full of candy.

Turn Talk Tell your partner the one thing Rosa María forgot to do.

Read Aloud | Lesson D Part 3: Middle 17

- Discuss important details about Rosa María, the mice, and the party. Encourage children to use their Student Book pages to recall details as a group.

Tier Two Vocabulary: *collect*

- Display pages 24–25 and read aloud the third paragraph. Point to the word *collect*.
- Ask children to describe or demonstrate what the children in the illustration are doing with the candy, such as picking it up or gathering it.
- Work together to determine that the word *collect* in this context means "to pick up or gather."
- Provide an example of a time when you wanted to collect something. You may say, *I decided to collect all the pencils and put them away.*
- Then guide children to use *collect* in sentences of their own. *(L.1.1.j; L.1.4.a; L.1.5.c)*

Close Reading

- Display and reread pages 18–19, and then use these questions to have children find evidence about what Rosa María forgot to do.

  What are the mice sitting next to on the table? *(Rosa María's to-do list)*

  Which item on the list hasn't been done yet? *(FILL PIÑATA)*

  What other clues do the mice see? *(a full bag of candy; an empty piñata)*

  What do the mice know? *(that Rosa María forgot to fill the piñata)*

PART 4: Reread for Meaning (End)

Step by Step

- **Reread and discuss the end.** Read pages 26–31 aloud. Discuss the way the story ends, using the questions below. *(RL.1.1; RL.1.7; SL.1.1; SL.1.2)*

  Pages 26–27: What does Rosa María see on the floor? *(pieces of candy)*

  Pages 28–29: What makes Rosa María change her mind about mice? *(She realizes they helped her, so she changes her mother's saying to "there's room in the house … even for a mouse.")*

  Pages 30–31: What have the mice done with Rosa María's missing items and mousetraps? *(They have used them to have a birthday party.)*

Tip: Explain to children that the ellipses on page 29 tell readers that the sentence continues on the next page. On page 30, the ellipses are repeated so that readers know that this is the rest of the sentence.

- **Focus on a key detail.** Have children turn to Student Book page 18. Read aloud the first item, and provide support using the Hint. *(RL.1.3)* Prompt children to complete the second item.
- Use the Close Reading activity to have children use evidence to make connections.
- **Have children discuss story evidence.** Read aloud the Turn and Talk activity. Have children explain Rosa María's decision based on what the mice have done for her. *(SL.1.4; SL.1.5)*

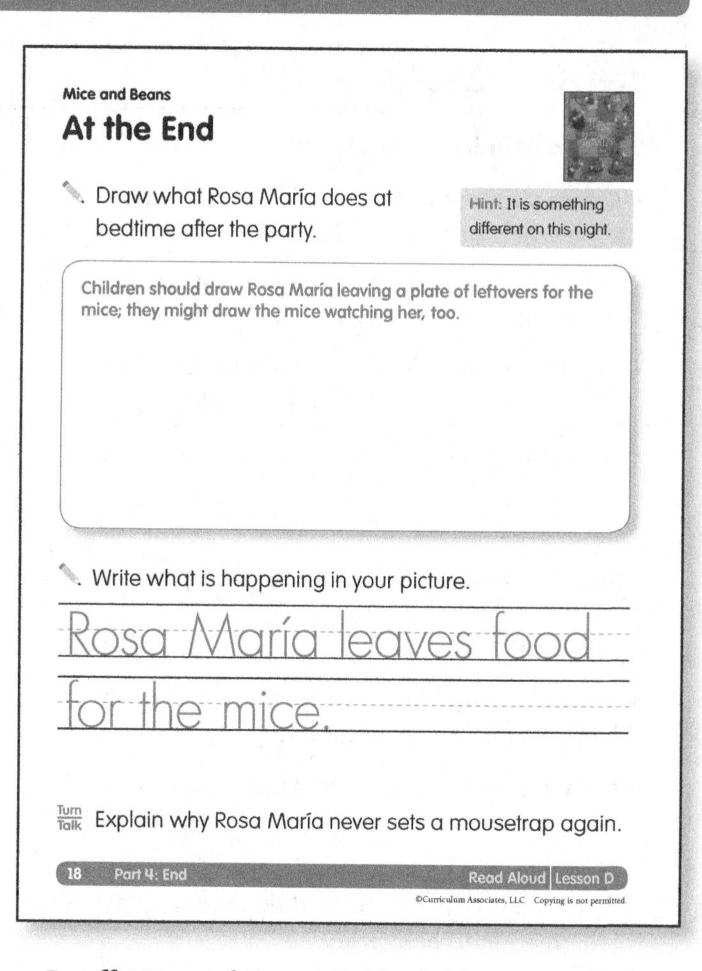

Mice and Beans

At the End

Draw what Rosa María does at bedtime after the party.

Hint: It is something different on this night.

Children should draw Rosa María leaving a plate of leftovers for the mice; they might draw the mice watching her, too.

Write what is happening in your picture.

Rosa María leaves food for the mice.

Turn Talk Explain why Rosa María never sets a mousetrap again.

18 Part 4: End Read Aloud | Lesson D

©Curriculum Associates, LLC Copying is not permitted.

- **Retell *Mice and Beans*.** Guide children to retell the story. Remind them that it takes place over one week; encourage them to tell what happens on each day to help them tell events in sequence. Prompt children to refer to their Student Books as needed.

Integrating Foundational Skills

Use these tasks as opportunities to integrate foundational skills into your reading of *Mice and Beans*.

1. Display one-syllable words and ask children to take turns decoding them. Use words such as the following: *had, still, swept, set, did, help, much, did, off, went, bed.* *(RF.1.3.b)*
2. Display these words: *cake, time, home.* Have children underline the vowels. Point out the vowel_*e* spelling pattern. Ask children if this pattern gives the word a short or long vowel sound. *(long)* Then display these words and have children read them: *mice, late, wipe, case, rice, white, home, stove, made, like, rope.* *(RF.1.3.c)*

Close Reading

- Explain that active readers make connections. Have children find evidence that shows what happened to Rosa María's missing items. Read aloud the last sentence of the story, and display the illustration on pages 30–31.

  What missing items can you see? *(candy, mini piñata made of piñata feathers, candle, wooden spoon, piece of cake, mousetraps)*

  How have the mice used the mousetraps? *(They made a swing set, which is the same gift Rosa María gave to Little Catalina at her party.)*

  Who is the mouse birthday party for? *(the mouse in the blue dress)*

Writing Activity

Write an Opinion (*W.1.1*)

- Direct children to look back at their Student Book pages and think about the story. Discuss their opinions about the story events. Then ask: *What is your favorite part of the story? Why do you like it the best?*
- Ask children to write a sentence stating their favorite part of the story. Encourage them to include the title of the book. Then ask children to write a sentence explaining why they like that part the best.
- Provide sentence starters for children as needed, such as *My favorite part of* Mice and Beans *is* ____________________ and *I like it best because* ____________________.
- Invite volunteers to read aloud their writing.

Speaking and Listening Activity

Lend a Hand (*SL.1.2*)

- Recall *Mice and Beans* with children. Ask them how the mice helped Rosa María.
- Have children think about times when they or someone they know helped another person.
- Have children turn and talk with a partner to share their experiences and discuss why it can be worthwhile to help others.
- After partners have finished sharing, invite individual children to share their ideas with the group. Encourage partners to lend a hand if their partner needs help remembering the details of the ideas they wanted to share.
- You might also have children tell their partner's story about helping rather than their own.

Language Activity

Adjectives (*L.1.1.f; SL.1.6*)

- Explain to children that an adjective is a word that describes something else. Tell them that there are many kinds of adjectives.
- Tell children that color words, such as *red* or *blue*, are one kind of adjective. Other adjectives tell about size. Some adjectives tell how things look, smell, taste, sound, or feel.
- Read aloud some examples from the story and have children identify the adjectives:
  "Rosa María lived in a tiny house." *(tiny)*
  "She loved to cook big meals." *(big)*
  "She dipped the tortillas in red sauce." *(red)*
- Next, have children use the following adjectives in sentences out loud: *tiny, big, little, large, fat, thin, plump, soft, hard, sweet, sour, loud, strong.*
- Then have children say a sentence with an adjective and tell which word is the adjective.

Lesson 3 (Student Book pages 49–52)

Describing Setting

CCSS

RL.1.3: Describe . . . settings . . . in a story, using key details.

Required Read Alouds: A *(The Empty Pot)*; D *(Mice and Beans)*

Lesson Objectives

- Recognize that a setting is when and where events in a story take place.
- Describe a setting based on key details in the text and the pictures.
- Understand how describing a setting can help you better understand a story.

The Learning Progression

- **Grade K:** CCSS RL.K.3 requires children to identify settings in a story with prompting and support.
- **Grade 1: CCSS RL.1.3 builds on the Grade K standard by having children work more independently, using illustrations and key details in a story to identify and describe settings.**
- **Grade 2:** CCSS RL.2.3 expands upon the scope of the standard by having children use their understanding of the connections between setting and other story elements as they describe how characters respond to challenges and events.

Prerequisite Skills

- Understand concepts of *when* and *where*.
- Identify a setting with prompting and support.
- Retell story details with prompting and support.

Tap Children's Prior Knowledge

- Display the heading *Words That Tell When*. Then ask children questions about when they do things. For example, ask: *When do you go to school? When is your birthday?* or *When is school vacation?*
- Record answers beneath the heading. Continue to give prompts that will generate words for days of the week, months of the year, seasons, times of day, and other *when* words such as *before, after, daytime, nighttime,* and *long ago.*
- Guide children to sort the list of words into categories by asking, *Which words have something in common? What should we call this group?* Work with children to organize the words into groups and give each group a heading, such as *Seasons. (L.1.5)*
- Repeat the exercise with *Words That Tell Where*. Ask questions such as *Where do you go each day of the week?* or *Where are we now?* Record children's answers and together sort the words into categories.
- Explain that just like in real life, stories can happen in different places and at different times. Tell children that in this lesson, they will think about where characters are and when they do things. Be sure to keep the word lists on display so you can refer to them throughout the lesson.

Ready *Teacher Toolbox* — Teacher-Toolbox.com

	Prerequisite Skills	RL.1.3
Ready Lessons	✓	✓
Tools for Instruction		✓
Interactive Tutorials		✓

Additional CCSS

RL.1.1; RL.1.2; RL.1.7; SL.1.1; SL.1.4; L.1.1; L.1.2 *(See page A38 for full text.)*

Part 1: Introduction

Step by Step

- **Introduce the standard.** Have children turn to page 49 in their Student Books. Read aloud the speech bubble.
- **Review questions about setting.** Read the line below the speech bubble. Point out that what follows are questions readers can ask about the setting of a story.
- Read aloud the first question. Have children underline the word *where*. Explain that a story happens in at least one place, but usually more than one. Review the *Words That Tell Where* list from page 39. Use some of the words to give an example such as the following:

  The characters in a story might start at home and then go to the park, so we would say one part of the story takes place at home, and another part takes place at the park. Home and the park are both settings in the story.

- Read aloud the second question, and have children underline the word *when*. Explain that a story might happen in a short time, such as one day at school, or over a long time, such as a year. Review the *Words that Tell When* list from page 39.
- Read aloud the third question. Have children underline the phrase *look like*. Explain that authors and illustrators include details that show what a setting looks, sounds, and feels like. These details help readers picture where the story is happening.

Tip: Explain that words that describe what something looks like are called *sensory words*. Guide students to understand that we call them *sensory* because many of the details relate to our five senses.

- **Explain why readers ask questions about the setting.** Read aloud the bottom of the page. Explain that thinking about and describing a setting can help readers follow the story events and develop a deeper understanding of the story. Then give examples such as these:

  If a story takes place on a dark and stormy night, you might expect something scary to happen, or that there is a mystery to solve.

Listen and Learn

Describing Setting

The **setting** is where and when a story takes place, or happens. Details in the story tell you about the setting.

Here are some questions you can ask about the setting of a story:

- Where does the story take place?
- When does the story take place?

  Think about:

  season of the year — time of day
  now or long ago — day of the week

- What does the setting look like?

Understanding where and when a story happens helps you to make connections between important story details.

Lesson 3 — Part 1: Introduction 49

If a story starts in summer, then moves through fall, winter, and spring, you know that a lot of time is passing. You might expect characters to do different things as the seasons change. You might also expect characters to change or grow.

- Share an example of a time when describing a setting helped you understand a story. For instance, explain that knowing that the forest in Hansel and Gretel is dark, thick, and very big helped you understand why the children get lost, and why they are scared.
- **Have children demonstrate understanding.** Call on individuals to share what they have learned so far about describing a setting in a story. Encourage them to give brief examples of settings from familiar classroom read-alouds.

Step by Step

- **Review Part 1; preview Part 2.** Ask volunteers to share questions they can ask about settings in a story. Have children turn to Student Book page 50.
- **Revisit *Mice and Beans.*** Invite children to briefly retell the story, using pages 15–18 of their Student Books. *(RL.1.2)*
- **Model describing setting.** Explain that you are going to model asking questions about setting. Read aloud pages 8–9 of *Mice and Beans.* Then think aloud:

  I'm going to look for where and when this part of the story happens. The first word is *Tuesday*, so I know *when* it happens. Now I'll look for *where* it happens. Rosa María walks to the market. That's one place. Next she stops at the *pastelería*. That is another place.

- Continue thinking about each sentence, and identify Rosa María's kitchen as the third setting. Read aloud the first Student Book page question and Hint, and have children recall the three settings. *(RL.1.1)*

Tip: Point out that when the words don't name the setting, the details help you identify it. For example, you used the details *washed the dishes* and *hurried to the cupboard* to identify the setting as the kitchen.

- Read aloud the second question and the Hint. Discuss the answer to this question.
- **Model writing your responses.** Model how to write the answers to the first and second questions in complete sentences. Have children write their own responses. *(L.1.1; L.1.2)*
- Use the Close Reading activity to help children recognize multiple settings.
- **Have children demonstrate understanding.** Have partners complete the Turn and Talk activity. If children need support, prompt them:

  Name all the things that Rosa María does on this day. *(She goes to the market, pastelería, and home.)*

  It sounds like she does a lot. How do we describe someone's day if they do a lot of things? *(busy)*

- Invite children to share their evidence from the Turn and Talk in class discussion. *(RL.1.7; SL.1.1; SL.1.4)*

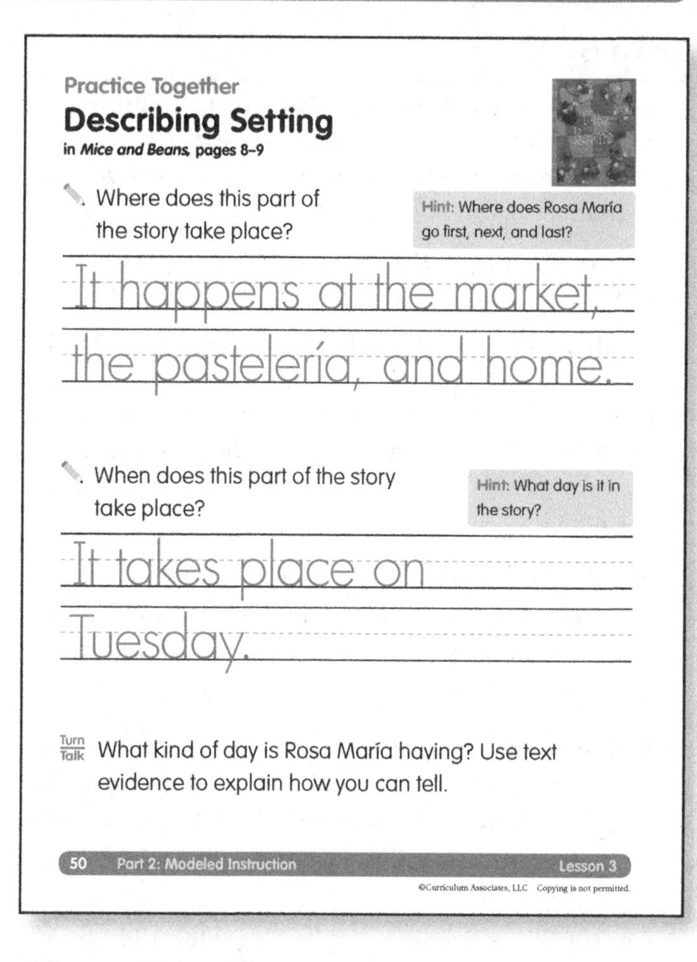
Practice Together

Describing Setting

in *Mice and Beans*, pages 8–9

Where does this part of the story take place?

Hint: Where does Rosa María go first, next, and last?

It happens at the market, the pastelería, and home.

When does this part of the story take place?

Hint: What day is it in the story?

It takes place on Tuesday.

Turn Talk What kind of day is Rosa María having? Use text evidence to explain how you can tell.

50 Part 2: Modeled Instruction Lesson 3

©Curriculum Associates, LLC Copying is not permitted.

Close Reading

- Explain that most stories have more than one setting, not just throughout the whole book, but sometimes even on the same page. Reread page 7. Prompt children:

  Name all the places Rosa María has gone today. *(She went to the market, the pastelería, and home.)*

  What happens at each place? *(She bought groceries at the market, bought the cake at the pastelería, and at home in the kitchen, she did dishes and then checked the mousetrap and realized it was missing.)*

- Explain to children that since the setting can change so many times, it's important to ask questions about the setting frequently.

Part 3: Guided Practice

Step by Step

- **Review Parts 1–2; preview Part 3.** Have children recall questions they can ask about settings in a story. Direct them to turn to Student Book page 51. Explain that you will guide them through this page.
- **Revisit *The Empty Pot*.** Have children briefly retell the story, using pages 3–6 of their Student Books. *(RL.1.2)*
- **Guide children to describe the setting.** Read aloud page 3 of *The Empty Pot*. Remind children that to learn about setting, they ask *where* and *when* questions. Ask children to describe the setting on the page using these questions. *(The story takes place a long time ago in China.)*

Tip: Explain that folktales, or stories told for many years, often start with *a long time ago* or *once upon a time*. Discuss why folktales might begin with these phrases. Ask: *Why is time used in both examples?*

- **Guide children to write responses.** Read aloud each question on the Student Book page. Use the Hints to help children answer the questions. Discuss answers and have children write them in complete sentences. *(RL.1.1; L.1.1; L.1.2)*
- Use the Close Reading activity to guide children to provide a more detailed description of the setting in this part of the story.
- **Have children demonstrate understanding.** Explain to children that the Turn and Talk questions require them to combine details from the text with what they already know. Invite volunteers to share their answers. *(SL.1.1; SL.1.4)*
- If children need support, prompt them:

  What details did you use to describe the setting? *(There are flowers and plants everywhere; the air smells like flowers; the people are all gardening.)*

  What does this tell us about what is important to the people who live in this setting? *(The people like flowers and trees; they like to grow and care for plants; they care about nature.)*

- Through class discussion, guide children to understand that the setting tells readers how much the people love and value flowers. Remind them that since they know the whole story of *The Empty Pot*, they know that this detail is important.

Practice Together

Describing Setting

in *The Empty Pot*, pages 3–5

THE EMPTY POT

Where does the story take place?

Hint: Which word names a place?

It takes place in China.

When does the story take place?

Hint: Which words tell about a time?

It takes place a long time ago.

Turn Talk What does the setting tell you about the people in the story? Why does it help to know this?

Lesson 3 Part 3: Guided Practice 51

©Curriculum Associates, LLC Copying is not permitted.

Close Reading

- Tell children that they should look closely for text details that can help them describe the setting.
- Have them close their eyes and try to picture what the words describe as you reread pages 3–5 of *The Empty Pot*. Then prompt:

  Which words describe what the setting looks and smells like? *(Everyone planted flowers everywhere; the air smelled like perfume.)*

- Move around the room slowly and show the pictures from these pages. Then prompt:

  What do you notice about the setting in the pictures? *(There are lots of trees and flowers.)*

- Have children use these details to practice describing the setting in their own words.

Step by Step

- **Review Parts 1–3; preview Part 4.** Invite a volunteer to tell why describing a setting is important. Then direct children to turn to Student Book page 52. Point out how the questions on this page are similar to the others on setting. The first question asks *where* and the second asks *when*.
- **Have children describe a setting independently.** Display *The Empty Pot* and tell children they will describe another setting in the book.
- Tell children to listen for evidence that tells where and when this part of the story takes place. Read aloud pages 20–21.
- Read aloud the first question on the Student Book page, and then read the Hint. Have children write the answer in a complete sentence. *(RL.1.1; L.1.1; L.1.2)*
- Read aloud the second question and the Hint. Have children write the answer in a complete sentence.
- Discuss the answers to both questions.
- Use the Close Reading activity to prepare children to answer the Turn and Talk questions.

Tip: Explain to children that noticing what is missing from a description or illustration of the setting can be important. For example, on pages 20–21, discuss why it is significant that Ping is not in the pictures.

- **Have children demonstrate understanding.** Have partners complete the Turn and Talk activity. Ask children to recall evidence that describes how much time has passed since the children first went to get seeds.
- Invite volunteers to share why it is important that so much time has passed. *(The Emperor had said that children had a "year's time" to grow their seeds. Since it is now spring, a year has passed and it is time for children to show their pots to the Emperor.)*
- **Have children reflect on their learning.** Have children discuss what they learned about setting. Guide them to identify questions they can ask about setting and tell how describing the setting can help them better understand stories. Chart their ideas.

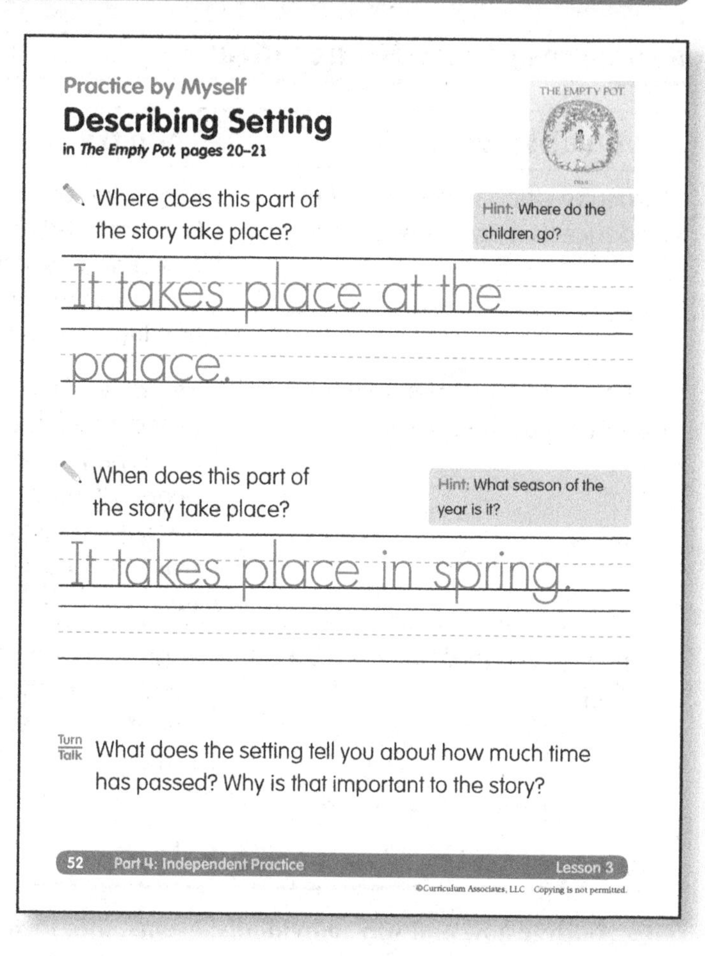
Practice by Myself

Describing Setting

in *The Empty Pot*, pages 20–21

Where does this part of the story take place?

Hint: Where do the children go?

It takes place at the palace.

When does this part of the story take place?

Hint: What season of the year is it?

It takes place in spring.

Turn Talk What does the setting tell you about how much time has passed? Why is that important to the story?

52 Part 4: Independent Practice Lesson 3

©Curriculum Associates, LLC Copying is not permitted.

Close Reading

- Discuss with children that in *The Empty Pot*, the change in setting from one season to another is very important.
- Read aloud page 20 and prompt:

  When does this part of the story take place? *(spring)*
- Display pages 18 and 19, and prompt:

  Look closely at the illustrations. What is the season on page 18? *(fall)*

  What is the season on page 19? *(winter)*
- Read aloud page 9 and prompt:

  How much time did the children have to grow their seeds? *(a year's time)*
- Discuss with children that when the setting of the story changes to the spring, it is important because it means that the year is over and their time to grow the flowers is up.

Differentiated Instruction

Assessment and Remediation

If you observe . . .	Then try . . .
Difficulty citing *where* and *when* evidence that describes a setting	Reviewing examples of *where* and *when* words from the charts children brainstormed on page 39. Then reread pages 3, 10, and 13 of *The Empty Pot,* one sentence at a time. After each sentence, ask children which word or words tell *where* or *when.* Then have children examine the pictures closely, looking for clues that tell *where* or *when.*
Difficulty making inferences from details about the setting	Revisiting descriptions of the setting and asking what children can guess based on what they already know about the descriptions. For example, read aloud page 5 of *The Empty Pot.* Ask: *What do the words say about where the people planted flowers? (They planted them everywhere.)* Then ask: *What does this tell you about the people? (They loved flowers.) What does it tell you about what kind of place they live in? (It is pretty and smells fresh.) What do you think the weather is like? (There is a lot of sun and rain for plants to grow. It is warm.)*
Difficulty recognizing changes in setting	Paging through *The Empty Pot* and asking where the characters are on each page. Guide children to answer using text and picture clues. Help them understand that sometimes the text tells readers that the setting changes, but other times readers have to figure it out based on clues in the pictures.

Connect to the Anchor Standard

R3: *Analyze how and why individuals, events, and ideas develop and interact over the course of a text.*

Throughout the grades, Standard 3 teaches students not only to identify and describe a setting, but to analyze its importance in character and plot development. In later grades, students transition from recognizing the surface-level details of where and when a story takes place to asking higher-level questions about a setting's function and influence: *Is the setting just a backdrop, or does it play a role in the plot? How does the setting affect the characters' state of mind? Why did the author choose this particular time and place to set the story? How would the story be different if the setting changed? How does the setting in this text compare to the setting in another text?* Use the following activities to help your students begin this transition.

- Guide children to connect setting details in pictures with story events. Reread pages 18–21 in *Mice and Beans.* Have children look at the picture and tell where it shows. *(the kitchen)* Then, point out the *piñata* with an open hole and the words *FILL PIÑATA.* Discuss how these clues help you know that Rosa María has forgotten to fill the *piñata,* and why it is important for readers to see the mice in the kitchen. *(SL.1.1; SL.1.4)*
- Explain that even when the setting is very simple, it still tells about the characters. Reread pages 28–29 in *The Empty Pot.* Discuss how the text, along with the lack of detail in the pictures, tell about Ping's conversation with the Emperor. Guide children to see that the circles are almost as empty as Ping's empty pot, and Ping even looks like a small seed. Discuss how the blank setting helps you understand how difficult this moment is for Ping, whose offering is as empty as the circle he stands in. *(SL.1.1; SL.1.4)*

Lesson 4 (Student Book pages 53–56)
Describing Events

CCSS

RL.1.3: Describe . . . major events in a story, using key details.

Required Read Alouds: B (*The Polar Bear Son*); D (*Mice and Beans*)

Lesson Objectives

- Understand that a story has events.
- Identify major story events in sequence.
- Use details to describe major story events.
- Understand how describing events can help you understand a story.

The Learning Progression

- **Grade K:** CCSS RL.K.3 requires children to identify major events in a story with prompting and support.
- **Grade 1: CCSS RL.1.3 builds on the Grade K standard by having children work more independently to identify and then describe major story events using key details.**
- **Grade 2:** CCSS RL.2.3 expands on the standard by requiring children to not only identify and describe major story events, but also to describe how characters respond and react to them.

Prerequisite Skills

- Identify characters in a story with prompting and support.
- Identify events in a story with prompting and support.
- Retell familiar stories, including the beginning, middle, and end.
- Use the words *first, next,* and *last* to tell the order of events.

Tap Children's Prior Knowledge

- Remind children that an *event* is something that happens. Point out that they know how to identify events and describe the order in which they happen.
- Explain that events happen every day, and that they happen in an order that makes sense. Name a daily class routine, such as going to lunch. Discuss the events involved, and record them on the board. *(First we line up; next we walk to the lunchroom; then we eat lunch; last we return to the classroom.)*
- Point out that the words *first, next,* and *last* tell the order of events. Prompt:

  Listen again and decide if the events make sense: *First we eat lunch. Next we line up. Then we walk to the lunchroom. Last we return to the classroom.*

- Talk about what happens if you put events out of order, helping children understand that they don't make sense. If children have difficulty, have them act out each event as you narrate the sequence again.
- Explain that events in stories happen in a certain order so that they make sense. Explain that in this lesson, children will tell what important events happen and use details from the story to describe, or tell more about, the events.

Ready *Teacher Toolbox* — Teacher-Toolbox.com

	Prerequisite Skills	RL.1.3
Ready Lessons	✓	✓
Tools for Instruction		✓
Interactive Tutorials		✓

Additional CCSS

RL.1.1; RL.1.2; RL.1.7; SL.1.1; SL.1.2; SL.1.4; L.1.1; L.1.2 (See page A38 for full text.)

Part 1: Introduction

Step by Step

- **Introduce the standard.** Have children turn to page 53 in their Student Books. Read aloud the speech bubble, and remind children that key details are important pieces of information.
- **Guide children to describe events in order.** Have children listen as you read aloud the example. Point out that what follows are questions that good readers ask to describe important events in a story. Read aloud the first question. Help children underline the words *first, next,* and *last*. Then explain:

  To tell about what happens first, I start at the beginning. I look for an event. It can be something a character does or says, something that happens to a character, or something that changes.

- Reread the example, and have children raise their hands when they hear the first thing that happens. *(Piglet goes for a long bike ride with his mom.)*
- Read aloud the second question and help children underline the word *important*. Explain that good readers decide which events are most important:

  I ask, *Would the story make sense without this event?* If this event were not in the story, I wouldn't know that Piglet and his mom are on a bike ride. Then the next sentence wouldn't make sense! So, I know that this event is important.

- Read aloud the third question. Help children underline the word *details*. Explain that details tell more about events and make them more interesting. Guide children to identify the details that tell about Piglet's bike ride. *(long; with his mom; he wears his helmet and rides on the right.)*
- Return to the first question and ask what happens next. *(After a while Piglet gets terribly hungry.)* Together decide if the event is important. *(Yes it is, because it explains why they go home.)* Identify the details. (Terribly *tells that Piglet is very, very hungry.)*

Tip: Help children separate events and details by acting out the example. After each sentence, ask: *Are you doing a new thing? Did something change?*

- Continue, guiding children to identify the last important event and the details. (Event: *He and his mom go home and eat lunch;* Details: *Piglet has his favorite, a peanut-butter-and-pickle pie.)*

Listen and Learn

Describing Events

An **event** is something that happens in a story. You can use **key details** to describe an event, or tell more about it.

Look at the example. Then ask the questions:

Piglet goes for a long bike ride with his mom. He wears his helmet and rides on the right. After a while Piglet gets terribly hungry. He and his mom go home and eat lunch. Piglet has his favorite—a peanut-butter-and-pickle pie.

- What happens first, next, or last?
- How important is this event?
- What details tell about the event?

Describing important events helps you make sense of a story. It can help you understand, remember, and retell the story.

Lesson 4 Part 1: Introduction 53

- **Explain why readers describe events.** Read aloud the bottom of the page. Prompt children:

  What happens if you tell the events of the story out of order? (Read the example out of order.) *(The story doesn't make sense.)*

  What happens if you read only the details? (Read only the details.) *(It doesn't make sense.)*

- Share an example of how describing events and details helped you understand a story. Recount *Stone Soup*. Explain that one event is "The villagers say they don't have food to share." Then there is a series of events where the soldier asks for a little at a time. Knowing the details of each event helps you see how the soldier gets the villagers to share.
- **Have children demonstrate understanding.** Ask volunteers to share what they have learned about describing story events.

Part 2: Modeled Instruction

Step by Step

- **Review Part 1; preview Part 2.** Call on volunteers to share questions they can ask to describe story events. Have children turn to Student Book page 54.
- **Revisit *Mice and Beans*.** Invite children to briefly retell the story, using pages 15–18 of their Student Books. *(RL.1.2)*
- **Model describing events.** Explain that you are going to model asking questions to help you identify and describe events. Read aloud page 11 of *Mice and Beans*. Then think aloud:

  I read that first, Rosa María prepares *enchiladas*. Then I read what she does with *tortillas*, sauce, and cheese. I ask myself, *Is Rosa María making two different dishes?* No, I think both sentences tell about one event: making the *enchiladas*.

  Is this event important? Well, every day Rosa María does something to get ready for the party. Making *enchiladas* is one of those things, so it is important. The details tell how she makes them.

- Read the next three sentences. Continue modeling:

  Next, Rosa María notices missing feathers. I've noticed that things keep disappearing from Rosa María's house, so I think this is an important event. The next two sentences tell more details.

- Read aloud the questions and the Hints on Student Book page 54. Point out the words *first* and *next* mean children should look for events in order from the beginning of the page. Discuss answers.
- **Model writing your responses.** Model how to write the answers in complete sentences. Have children write their own responses. *(L.1.1; L.1.2)*
- Use the Close Reading activity to help children use details to describe additional events.

Tip: Help children distinguish important events. Discuss the three biggest events from the page. After each event, ask: *Would the next part of the story make sense without this event?*

- **Have children demonstrate understanding.** Assign the Turn and Talk activity. Have partners tell what details show the event "The mousetrap disappeared." Ask children to share their ideas. *(SL.1.1; SL.1.4)*

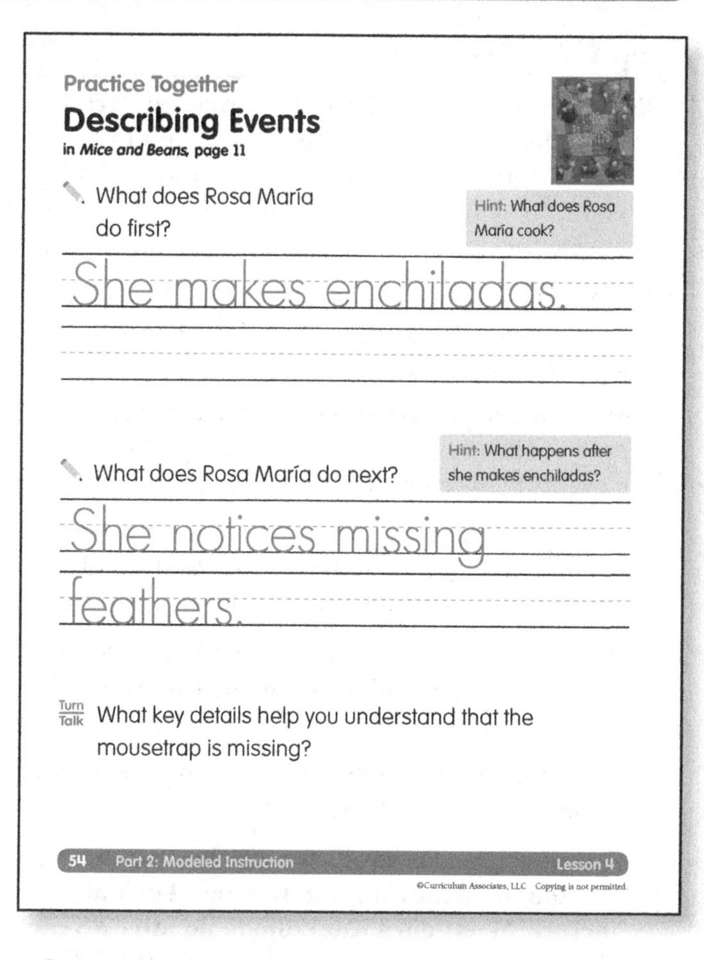

Practice Together

Describing Events

in *Mice and Beans*, page 11

What does Rosa María do first?

Hint: What does Rosa María cook?

She makes enchiladas.

What does Rosa María do next?

Hint: What happens after she makes enchiladas?

She notices missing feathers.

Turn Talk What key details help you understand that the mousetrap is missing?

54 Part 2: Modeled Instruction Lesson 4

©Curriculum Associates, LLC Copying is not permitted.

Close Reading

- Tell children that sometimes a story tells clearly what events happen. Other times, readers have to think about the details to figure out the events.
- Read aloud paragraphs 3–5 and prompt children:

  What does Rosa María do in this part of the story? (Rosa María mops up sauce and checks the mousetrap.)

  What change do the words "But it was gone again!" tell about? *(The mousetrap disappeared.)*

  What is the most important event in this part? Why? *(The mousetrap is gone. It is important because the words that tell about it are big, this same event has happened before, and the next sentences wouldn't make sense without this event.)*

- Continue identifying and evaluating events on page 11. Explain that noticing details and using them to figure out important events helps readers understand what is happening in a story.

Part 3: Guided Practice

Step by Step

- **Review learning from Parts 1–2; preview Part 3.** Have children recall questions they can ask to describe story events. Direct them to Student Book page 55, and explain that you will help them complete this page.
- **Revisit *The Polar Bear Son.*** Have children briefly retell the story, using pages 7–10 of their Student Books. *(RL.1.2)*
- **Guide children to describe important events.** Remind children that sometimes they need to figure out events by piecing story details together.
- Have children listen for details that describe how characters change and what they do. Read aloud pages 16–18 of *The Polar Bear Son.* Prompt children:

  What do the words "Spring, summer, and long dark winter passed" and "spring came again" mean? *(A whole year passes.) (RL.1.1)*

  How does Kunikdjuaq change in that year? *(He grows quickly; He gets big and strong.)*

  Think about the words "he was big and strong enough to go hunting and fishing." Look at the picture. What does Kunikdjuaq do after a year? *(He hunts and fishes for the old woman.) (RL.1.7)*

Tip: To help children distinguish between events and details, write each sentence from page 16 on a strip of paper. Together, sort the strips into events and details, cutting the strips into pieces as needed.

- **Guide children to write responses.** Read aloud each question and Hint on the Student Book page. Use the Hints to help children answer the questions. Discuss answers and have children write them in complete sentences. *(L.1.1; L.1.2)*
- Use the Close Reading activity to show how noticing changes helps readers identify important events.
- **Have children demonstrate understanding.** Assign the Turn and Talk activity. Have partners decide whether a year passing is an important event in the story and give reasons for their answers. Remind children to support their decisions with evidence from the story. *(SL.1.1; SL.1.4)*

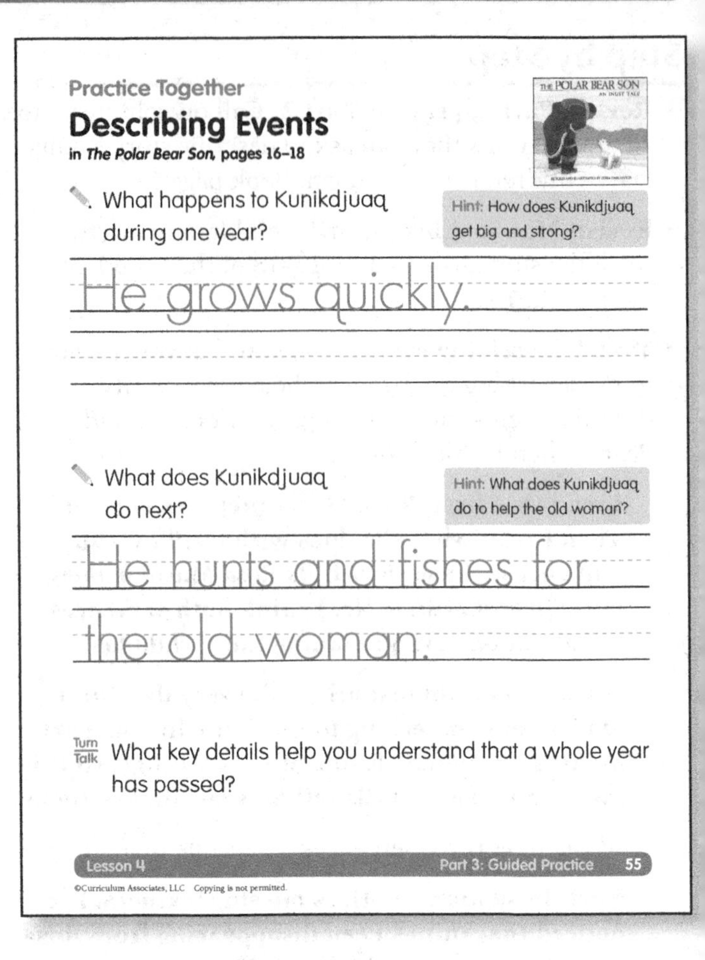

Practice Together

Describing Events

in *The Polar Bear Son,* pages 16–18

What happens to Kunikdjuaq during one year?

Hint: How does Kunikdjuaq get big and strong?

He grows quickly.

What does Kunikdjuaq do next?

Hint: What does Kunikdjuaq do to help the old woman?

He hunts and fishes for the old woman.

Turn Talk What key details help you understand that a whole year has passed?

Lesson 4 Part 3: Guided Practice 55

©Curriculum Associates, LLC Copying is not permitted.

Close Reading

- Explain that noticing when things change in a story can help readers identify important events:

  Often when a character does something new or different, it is an important event.

- Remind children of how *The Polar Bear Son* started by reading aloud page 7. Then read page 18. Ask:

  What is different for the old woman? *(Before she didn't have anyone to hunt for her and had to get food from her neighbors. Now she has plenty and can share with the village.)*

  Is this change, or new event, important to the story? How do you know? *(Yes it is. The old woman helped the bear at first and now he is helping her; the hunters getting jealous only makes sense because the bear hunts so well.)*

- Point out that the last sentence on page 18 tells the words the old woman said when she shared with the village, but it does not tell a new event.

Part 4: Independent Practice

Step by Step

- **Review Parts 1–3; preview Part 4.** Discuss why good readers describe important story events.
- Direct children to turn to Student Book page 56. Explain that they will write about events by themselves. Point out that the questions on this page are like the ones on previous pages—they ask about events by identifying what characters do.
- **Have children describe events independently.** Display *The Polar Bear Son* and tell children that they will describe events in another part of the book.
- Ask children to listen for events by noticing what the characters do and say. Read aloud pages 24–27 of *The Polar Bear Son.* Have partners discuss what events they heard.
- Next have children use picture details to help them determine the important events. Circulate and display the pages. Ask children to decide which event details on each page are the most important.
- Read aloud the questions on the Student Book page, along with the Hints. Have children write their answers in complete sentences. *(L.1.1; L.1.2)*

Tip: If children have trouble identifying the important events, use stick-on notes to cover up the second paragraph on each page. Then reread the pages and ask: *Does the story still make sense?*

- Use the Close Reading activity to combine word and picture evidence to identify important events.
- **Have children demonstrate understanding.** Have partners do the Turn and Talk activity. Give everyone a chance to look closely and identify text and picture details that show how the characters feel about the events. *(the words "crying bitterly" and "sadly"; the expressions on the characters' faces)*
- Ask volunteers to share their ideas with the class. *(SL.1.1; SL.1.4)*
- **Have children reflect on their learning.** Discuss what readers can do to separate events from details, and why it is important to do so. Help them see that naming important events helps them understand, remember, and retell a story, while noticing key details helps them better understand each event.

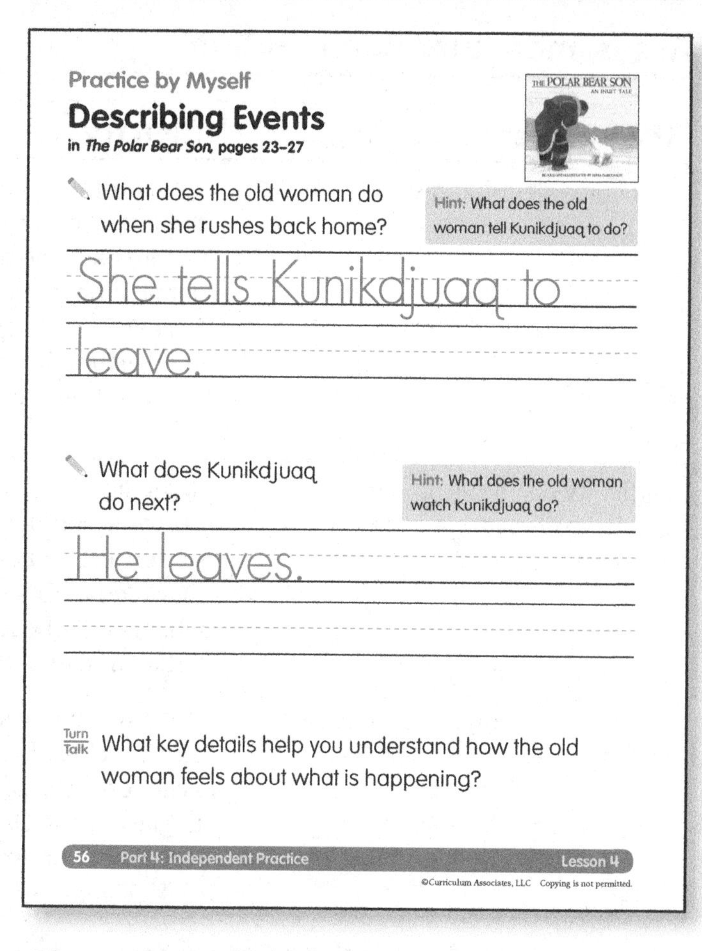

Practice by Myself

Describing Events

in *The Polar Bear Son,* pages 23–27

What does the old woman do when she rushes back home?

Hint: What does the old woman tell Kunikdjuaq to do?

She tells Kunikdjuaq to leave.

What does Kunikdjuaq do next?

Hint: What does the old woman watch Kunikdjuaq do?

He leaves.

Turn Talk What key details help you understand how the old woman feels about what is happening?

56 Part 4: Independent Practice Lesson 4

Close Reading

- Tell children that readers can use word and picture evidence to find important story events. Reread page 24 and prompt children:

  What events do the words tell about? *(The old woman rushes home; she tells Kunikdjuaq to leave; she cries and asks him not to forget her.)*

  What event details does the picture show? *(The old woman is saying something important to Kunikdjuaq. She and the children look sad.)*

  What is the most important part of the picture? (Frame different parts to help children decide.) *(the old woman talking to the bear) (RL.1.7)*

  What is the most important event? How do you know? *(The old woman tells Kunikdjuaq to leave. Almost all of the details tell more about this event.)*

- Have children use evidence to describe the most important event on page 27. Guide them to use everything they know about the story to decide.

Assessment and Remediation

If you observe . . .	Then try . . .
Difficulty identifying story events	Providing additional practice. Choose a volunteer to relate something he or she did recently. Prompt the child to tell what happened first, next, and last. Record each event in a numbered list. If an event doesn't include much detail, prompt the child to add details with questions such as the following: *Did this event happen quickly or slowly? How did you feel when this event happened? What did it look like when this event happened?* Work with the other children to name events and details from the volunteer's story.
Difficulty distinguishing major events from minor events	Rereading page 2 of *Mice and Beans.* Point out that several things are described on this page, but there is only one important event. Read each sentence, one at a time, and ask: *If I take this sentence out, would the story still make sense?* Cover unneeded sentences with stick-on notes. At the end, read what is still uncovered and help children understand that having a party for Little Catalina is the most important event.
Difficulty putting story events in order	Using a sequencing activity to help children order events. Retell a familiar story, such as *The Fox and the Crow.* Ask: *What happened first?* and record the event on a slip of paper. Continue with questions for the next events and the last event. Distribute the slips of paper, and ask children to put them in the correct order. Encourage them to add drawings to each event.

Connect to the Anchor Standard

R3: *Analyze how and why individuals, events, and ideas develop and interact over the course of a text.*

Throughout the grades, Standard 3 builds to a more complex understanding of story events. In later grades, students transition from identifying and describing story events to understanding how the plot unfolds in a deliberate manner. In looking at exposition, rising action, climax, falling action, and resolution, they will analyze how events develop and interact over the course of a text. They will ask in-depth questions such as: *How did one event lead to the next? How do characters' actions affect events? If the events were told in a different order, would they still make sense? Is the plot believable?* Use the following activities to help your students begin this transition.

- Help children connect events from different parts of the story. Reread page 16, pages 28–31, and pages 34–36 of *The Polar Bear Son.* Ask children to tell what happens in each passage. Discuss how Kunikdjuaq learns to hunt for the old woman early on, so he knows how to provide for her year after year. Have children use text evidence to explain how these events are able to continue despite challenges from the hunters. *(SL.1.1; SL.1.2; SL.1.4)*
- Reread page 2 of *Mice and Beans.* Call attention to the saying "When there's room in the heart, there's room in the house, except for a mouse." Then reread page 29 and discuss how Rosa María has changed her mother's saying. Ask children to tell how the events in the story caused Rosa María to change her mind.

Lesson 5 (Student Book pages 57–60)

Central Message

CCSS

RL.1.2: . . . demonstrate understanding of [the] central message or lesson.

Required Read Alouds: *Projectable 1: (Happy Birthday Surprise!); A (The Empty Pot); C (My Rotten Redheaded Older Brother)*

Lesson Objectives

- Identify the relationship between important story events and the central message.
- Identify the relationship between a character's goal or problem and the central message.
- Use text evidence to determine the central message of a story.
- Understand that readers can learn important lessons by thinking about a story's message.

The Learning Progression

- **Grade K:** CCSS RL.K.2 expects children to retell familiar stories, including key details, with prompting and support.
- **Grade 1: CCSS RL.1.2 advances the Grade K standard by having children work more independently to retell stories, including key details, and use that information to determine the central message or lesson.**
- **Grade 2:** CCSS RL.2.2 broadens the standard by having children recount a variety of stories, including fables and folktales from a range of cultures, and then determine their main message, lesson, or moral.

Prerequisite Skills

- Identify characters in a story.
- Distinguish main events from minor events.
- Retell stories, including key details.

Tap Children's Prior Knowledge

- Ask children if they have ever made mistakes. Explain that people usually learn from their mistakes.
- Give an example of a mistake you made and what you learned. For example, tell about a time you didn't put on a painting smock and then you got paint on your favorite shirt. Ask: *What do you think I learned? (to wear a smock every time you paint)*
- Invite a few children to share examples of mistakes and what they learned from them. Point out that the things we learn from mistakes can be called *lessons,* and that lessons are important things to know in life.
- Explain that making a mistake isn't the only way to learn a lesson. People learn lessons by listening to advice, watching other people, and even from common sayings. Share a few examples, such as "Look before you leap," and discuss the lesson. *(Think about what might happen before you take action.)*
- Finally, explain that one great thing about reading stories is that we can learn important lessons without making mistakes ourselves! Tell children that they will learn to figure out the lessons in different stories.

Ready *Teacher Toolbox* Teacher-Toolbox.com

	Prerequisite Skills	RL.1.2
Ready Lessons	✓	✓
Tools for Instruction	✓✓	✓
Interactive Tutorials	✓	

Additional CCSS

RL.1.2; RL.1.3; SL.1.1; SL.1.2; SL.1.4; L.1.1; L.1.2 *(See page A38 for full text.)*

Step by Step

- **Introduce the standard.** Have children turn to page 57 in their Student Books. Read aloud the speech bubble.
- Explain that in a story, sometimes the author wants the reader to learn an important lesson. That lesson is the *message* of the story.
- **Review questions about central message.** Read the line below the speech bubble. Point out that what follows are questions that good readers ask themselves to figure out the message of a story.
- Read aloud the first question. Have children circle the phrase *important events*. Remind children that they already know that stories have a beginning, a middle, and an end, and how to identify important events. Explain:

  The central message is an important lesson that the author wants to teach. The most important events in a story are clues to the author's message.

- Read aloud the second question. Have children circle the words *problem* and *goal*. Ask volunteers to share problems they have solved or goals they have reached.
- Explain that, just like people in real life, characters in stories can have problems or goals:

  Notice what characters do to solve a problem or reach a goal. Paying attention to how characters act can help you figure out the story's message.

- Read aloud the third and fourth questions. Point out the word *lesson* in each question and have children circle it. Remind children that people learn lessons by trying things, making mistakes, and trying again.
- **Explain why readers identify a story's message.** Read aloud the bottom of the page. Then prompt:

  Think of when you started school and had to learn the rules. You probably made a few mistakes before you figured out how to act. When you think about what a character is trying to do and the mistakes he or she makes, you can learn a lesson.

Listen and Learn

Central Message

Stories can teach us lessons about life. The **message** is a story's lesson. Thinking about events helps you find the message.

To figure out the message, ask these questions about characters and events:

- What are the most important events in the story?
- Does a character solve a problem, do something hard, or reach an important goal?
- What lesson does the character learn?
- What lesson do you learn?

You can learn about a story and about life by thinking about the story's message.

Lesson 5 Part 1: Introduction 57

- Then share a time when you learned a lesson about life from a story. You might tell about a familiar fable, such as *The Lion and the Mouse (Little friends can make a big difference.)* Or you might choose to tell about a book you have read. For example:

  I read about people who sailed to the Antarctic, where it is very cold. Their ship got trapped in the ice and they couldn't sail back! Everyone had to try hard and work together to get over the frozen ocean back to land. I learned that it is important to try hard and work together in difficult situations.

Tip: Point out that in fables like *The Lion and the Mouse,* the author tells the message at the end of the story, where it is called a *moral*. In other stories, readers have to figure out the message by thinking about events.

- **Have children demonstrate understanding.** Ask children to explain what they have learned so far about figuring out a story's message.

Part 2: Modeled Instruction

Step by Step

- **Review Part 1; preview Part 2.** Call on volunteers to share steps they can take to identify a story's message. Have children turn to Student Book page 58.
- **Read *Happy Birthday Surprise!*** Invite children to listen as you read aloud the story on pages 205–206. Then have children briefly retell the story by telling the important events at the beginning, middle, and end of the story. *(RL.1.2)*
- **Model identifying important events.** Read aloud the first activity and the Hint on Student Book page 58. Think aloud:

  The first event is an important one: it tells what Abel is trying to do. I need this event to tell the story. The second event tells about something Abel does. But I don't need this detail in order to tell the story. I will cross it out.

Tip: Discuss why the omitted event is not important. Prompt children to tell whether the story would have ended differently if Abel hadn't sneezed.

- Have children cross out the second event. Continue discussing events together, crossing out the fourth event. Reread the remaining events together and have children decide if they tell the whole story. *(RL.1.3)*
- **Model determining the story's message.** Remind children that the important events in a story are clues to the story's message. Tell them they can think about the events to figure out what lesson the author wants to teach. Think aloud:

  When I retell the important events, I see that Abel learns that he should have asked for help. I think Abel's lesson is the same as the message—it is the lesson the author wants to teach.

- **Model writing your response.** Read aloud the second activity, along with the Hint. Have children restate the lesson Abel learns. Model how to write the answer. *(L.1.1; L.1.2)*
- Use the Close Reading activity to relate the details of Abel's problem to the central message.
- **Have children demonstrate understanding.** Have partners complete the Turn and Talk activity by telling about events in the story that show the lesson. Have the class share ideas. *(SL.1.1; SL.1.2)*

Practice Together

Central Message

in *Happy Birthday Surprise!*

PROJECTABLE

Happy Birthday Surprise!

Choose the three most important events from the story. Cross out the other events.

Hint: Which three events tell the whole story?

- Abel tries to plan the party by himself.
- ~~Abel sneezes from the dust.~~
- Abel can't get everything done on his own.
- ~~Abel mixes eggs, flour, and sugar.~~
- Chester comes early and helps.

Write the message of the story.

Hint: How can Able solve his problem?

Ask for help when you need it.

Turn Talk What evidence from the story helped you figure out the message?

58 Part 2: Modeled Instruction Lesson 5

Close Reading

- Remind children that thinking about a character's problem can help them figure out the message. Reread the following paragraphs. Prompt children to locate details about the problem and solution:

  (paragraph 4) **What words show that Abel has a problem?** *(It is already past noon; oh dear; he still had to make the cake.)*

  What is Abel's problem? *(He is running out of time to get ready.)*

  (paragraphs 9–16) **What details tell more about Abel's problem?** *(He is embarrassed to be behind; the house is still a mess; the cake is ruined.)*

  (paragraphs 18–21) **How is Abel's problem solved?** *(Chester says they can make another cake.)*

- Discuss whether children think that Chester will help Abel now, and what evidence makes them think so. Then have children tell what Abel learned from the solution to his problem.

Step by Step

- **Review Parts 1–2; preview Part 3.** Have children recall what readers can do to find a story's message. Direct them to Student Book page 59. Explain that you will guide them through this page.
- **Revisit *The Empty Pot*.** Have children retell the story, using pages 3–6 of their Student Books. *(RL.1.2)*
- **Guide children to identify important events.** Read aloud the directions and Hint for the first activity.
- Read aloud each event and have children repeat it. Have children decide if they need the event to tell the story. If the answer is "no," have children cross out the event. *(RL.1.3)*

Tip: Help children distinguish important events by comparing them. For example, ask: *Is the story mostly about how the Emperor loves birds and animals, or mostly about Ping trying to grow a seed?*

- **Guide children to identify the story's message.** Have children listen as you read aloud pages 29–32. Then read aloud the directions and Hint for the second activity. Prompt children:

  What does the empty pot show about Ping's goal? *(He was not able to grow a flower.)*

  What hard thing does Ping do when he goes to the Emperor? *(Ping tells the Emperor he tried his best, but could not grow a flower.)*

  What does the Emperor say about the difficult thing Ping did? *(He admires his courage and rewards him with his kingdom.)*

- Discuss the message or lesson Ping learns when he is rewarded for telling the truth.
- **Guide children to write a response.** Have children state the message in their own words and then write it in a complete sentence. *(L.1.1; L.1.2)*
- Use the Close Reading activity to identify evidence to support a story's unstated message.
- **Have children demonstrate understanding.** Have partners do the Turn and Talk activity. Encourage them to notice what Ping says and how he looks in the pictures. Invite them to share their evidence. *(SL.1.1; SL.1.2)*

Practice Together

Central Message

in *The Empty Pot* pages 29–32

THE EMPTY POT

Choose the three most important events from the story. Cross out the other events.

Hint: Which events do you need to tell the story?

- ~~The Emperor loves birds and animals.~~
- Ping does his best, but his seed doesn't grow.
- ~~The children put on their best clothes.~~
- Ping tells the truth about his empty pot.
- The Emperor gives Ping his kingdom.

Write the message of the story.

Hint: What does Ping learn?

Tell the truth, even when it is hard.

Turn Talk What evidence from the story helped you figure out the message?

Lesson 5 Part 3: Guided Practice 59

Close Reading

- Tell children that when an author doesn't tell a story's message, they can look for the message in the words and pictures near the end of the story. Reread pages 31–32 and prompt children:

  What does the Emperor do that shows what he thinks of Ping? *(He smiles and says Ping is the one person worthy of being Emperor.)*

  What does it mean that the Emperor says, "where you got your seeds I do not know"? *(The children with flowers used different seeds than the ones they were given. They were dishonest.)*

  What do you think the words "empty truth" mean? *(They mean the truth about the empty pot, and that the truth is hard to tell.)*

  What does the Emperor do to reward Ping? *(He makes him Emperor of all the land.)*

- Discuss what this evidence shows about the lesson the author wants to teach.

Part 4: Independent Practice

Step by Step

- **Review Parts 1–3; preview Part 4.** Discuss why it is important to figure out the message of a story. Direct children to Student Book page 60. Explain that on this page, as on previous pages, children will choose important events and write the central message.
- **Revisit *My Rotten Redheaded Older Brother*.** Have children briefly retell the story, using pages 11–14 of their Student Books. *(RL.1.2)*
- **Have children determine the message independently.** Read page 35 from the story. Then read the directions and Hint for the first activity on Student Book page 60.
- Read aloud the first event and have children repeat it. Remind children to ask themselves, *Can I tell the story without this event?* Have them cross out the events that are not important. *(RL.1.3)*
- Read aloud the directions and the Hint for the second activity. Remind children that Treesha is telling the story. Reread page 35 and prompt:

  What does Treesha say about wishes? *(Sometimes wishes come true differently than you think they will.)*

  What was different than Treesha expected? *(She wanted to do something better than Richie, but she ended up getting hurt.)*

  What does Bubbie say about Treesha's thoughts on wishes? *(You must be careful what you wish for because it might come true.)*

Tip: Point out that Bubbie tells Treesha the lesson that is the story's central message.

- **Guide children to write a response.** Tell children to decide what Treesha learns and write the message in a complete sentence. *(L.1.1; L.1.2)*
- Use the Close Reading activity to guide children in generating the story's message.
- **Have children demonstrate understanding.** Have partners do the Turn and Talk activity, using events and clues from the story. Invite children to share ideas with the class. *(SL.1.1; SL.1.2)*
- **Have children reflect on their learning.** Have children discuss what they learned about finding the central message and how it helps them understand stories. Chart their ideas.

Practice by Myself

Central Message

in *My Rotten Redheaded Older Brother*, page 35

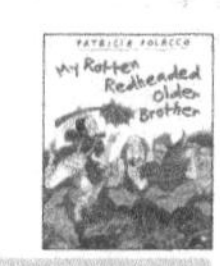

Choose the three most important events from the story. Cross out the other events.

Hint: Which events could you take away and still tell the story?

- ~~Richie laughs a rotten laugh.~~
- Treesha wishes to do something better than her brother.
- Treesha beats Richie at the merry-go-round.
- Treesha gets dizzy and hurt, but Richie helps her.
- ~~The family sleeps outside.~~

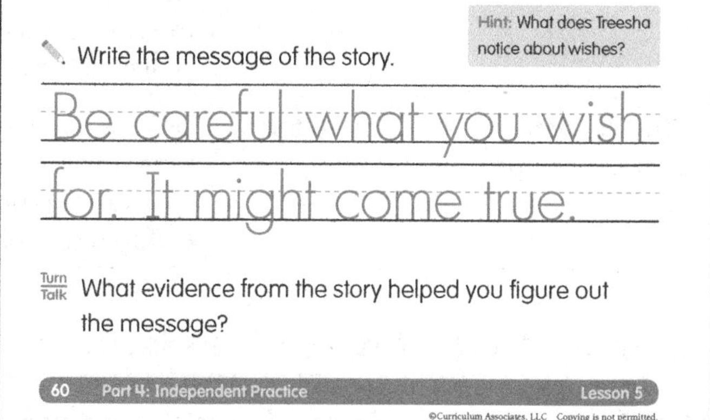

Write the message of the story.

Hint: What does Treesha notice about wishes?

Be careful what you wish for. It might come true.

Turn Talk What evidence from the story helped you figure out the message?

60 Part 4: Independent Practice Lesson 5

©Curriculum Associates, LLC Copying is not permitted.

Close Reading

- Remind children that revisiting a character's goals can help them figure out a story's message.
- Read aloud the end of page 24 and prompt:

  What do the words "I'd show him!" tell you about Treesha's goal? *(She wants to do something better than Richie to prove to him that she can.)*
- Read aloud page 26 and prompt:

  How does Treesha expect her wish to come true? *(She thinks she is going to do something so incredible that Richie will have to notice.)*
- Display pages 29 and 30 and prompt:

  What is the difference between what Treesha expects to do and what actually happens? *(She thinks she'll beat Richie at the merry-go-round, but instead she falls off, gets hurt, and Richie helps her.)*
- Discuss what lesson Treesha learns when she gets her wish in an unexpected way.

Differentiated Instruction

Assessment and Remediation

If you observe . . .	Then try . . .
Difficulty relating lessons in stories to lessons in life	Relating morals from familiar stories to children's lives. Display a list of morals from familiar fables, for example: *Look before you leap; Honesty is the best policy; Don't judge a book by its cover;* and *Don't count your chickens before they hatch.* Discuss the meaning of each moral. Give examples of how you could apply the lessons to your own life, and then have children take turns applying each moral to their own lives.
Difficulty identifying a character's goal or problem	Brainstorming a chart of goals or problems. Display the headings *Goals* and *Problems* on chart paper. Discuss the meaning of each word. Then name books children have read recently and prompt children to name goals or problems the characters have in each story. Briefly discuss whether each character achieved the goal or solved the problem, and what they learned from it.
Difficulty determining an unstated central message	Using a real-life example. Call on a volunteer to dictate a short story about a time he or she made a mistake and learned from it or tried something he or she was nervous about. Discuss what lesson the child learned, asking children to name evidence such as events, goals, problems, and solutions.

Connect to the Anchor Standard

R2: *Determine central ideas or themes of a text and analyze their development; summarize the key supporting details and ideas.*

Throughout the grades, Standard 2 advances students' understanding of central idea by introducing more sophisticated themes. Students progress from learning explicit messages in genres such as fables to inferring complex themes about moral and ethical dilemmas in genres such as myths, dramas, and poetry. They explore higher-level questions that address how these issues resonate within the text and also within a broader context: *What life lessons did the characters learn? How well did the author develop the theme? How does the theme reflect the human condition? How is the message universal?* Use the following activities to help your students begin this transition.

- Examine the secondary message in *The Empty Pot.* Reread page 23 and ask: *What has Ping's clever friend done with his seed? What does he say to Ping? (The friend has grown a great big flower and asks Ping why he hasn't grown one also.)* Then reread the last paragraph on page 31, when the Emperor speaks to the clever friend and the other children who brought flowers. Discuss the lesson the clever friend has learned. *(It does not pay to cheat or lie.) (SL.1.1; SL.1.2; SL.1.4)*
- Evaluate the message in *Happy Birthday Surprise!* Reread the story and have children act out each of Abel's tasks. Discuss whether one person can do all of these things in one day. Then ask: *Do you think Abel knew how much work it would be to throw a party?* Discuss text evidence. Have children use evidence to suggest ways Chester could have been even more helpful to Abel.

Introduction

To prepare students for the Unit Checks, you may wish to explain how to answer multiple-choice questions. To begin, write the following question on the board:

What color is the sky?

A blue

B red

C yellow

Guide students through the process of answering a multiple-choice question:

Today you will listen as I read aloud a book, and then you will answer some questions about details in the book. Some of the questions have three different answer choices. You will need to choose the best one. This kind of question is called a *multiple-choice question*. Each choice has a letter, such as A, B, or C.

When you have decided which choice is the best answer to the question, circle the letter next to that answer. *(Ask students which answer is correct. Then circle A on the board.)*

If you are not sure about an answer, you can look back at the story to help you decide. Look for words from the question that are also in the story. For example, if you were looking in a story for an answer to this question, you would look for the words *color* and *sky*.

Be sure to read the whole question and think about all of the choices before you answer. If you go too fast, you might not see that another choice is an even better answer.

If you choose two answers, it will not be counted as correct. So if you change your mind, you need to erase your old answer completely. If you have time after answering the questions, check your answers. If you need to change an answer, do so neatly and carefully.

Step by Step

- Revisit *The Empty Pot*. Have children review the main topic and key details.
- Have children follow along as you read aloud the directions on page 61 of their Student Books.

Unit 1 Check

Listen closely as your teacher reads. Then answer the questions.

Who is the character in the story?

A a little girl

(B) a boy named Ping

C a mother

What does Ping like to do?

A draw pictures

B play with his friends

(C) grow flowers

What is the setting of the story?

(A) a long time ago, in China

B a few years ago, on a farm

C right now, in China

61

- Then read aloud one or more pages from the text, as specified below, before having children complete each item. Display the appropriate pages for children to view while they read and answer each question.
- For items 1, 2, and 3, reread pages 1–3; display the illustrations.
- For item 4, reread pages 28–30; display the illustration on page 29.

Note: Read aloud each question, answer choice, and Hint before directing children to answer it.

- When children have finished, reread each question and discuss the correct answer. Point to evidence in the text and pictures. Then use the Answer Analysis to discuss the correct answer.

Answer Analysis

1 This item requires children to answer a question by identifying the main character, Ping. ***(RL.1.1, RL.1.3)***

The best answer is choice B, a boy named Ping. The story tells all about what Ping does with his flower seed. Choice A is not a good answer. Both boys and girls are given seeds by the emperor, but the story does not mention any one girl. Choice C is not a good answer. The story does mention parents and Ping's father, but it does not tell a key detail about anyone's mother.

2 This item asks children to identify a key detail that describes Ping. ***(RL.1.3)***

The best answer is choice C, "grow flowers." The words on the page say that Ping "loved flowers" and that "anything he planted burst into bloom." He must have spent lots of time growing flowers. Choices A and B, "drawing pictures" and "playing with his friends," are things a boy might like to do. The book, however, does not say these are activities that Ping likes.

3 This item asks children to identify the setting, a basic story element. ***(RI.1.3)***

The best answer is choice A, "a long time ago, in China." The story actually begins with those words, so choices B and C, "a few years ago, on a farm" and "right now, in China" are incorrect.

4 This item focuses on an important story event in the plot. ***(RL.1.2, RL.1.3)***

The best answer is choice C, "Ping becomes the Emperor." Choice A is not true. The Emperor never gets angry with Ping. And even though Ping gets very sad and starts to cry when he first talks to the Emperor, choice B is not the best answer. More things happen to Ping after that. The question asks you to name what happens last in the story. In the last sentence, the Emperor says, "I admire Ping's great courage…and make him Emperor of all the land!"

Unit 1 Check

What happens last in the story?

A The Emperor gets angry with Ping.

B Ping gets very sad.

(C) Ping becomes the Emperor.

What is the story's message?

Tell the truth, even when it is hard.

62

5 This item requires children to describe the story's central message in their own words. ***(RL.1.2)***

Sample response: Tell the truth, even when it is hard.

Remember that a story's message is the lesson the character learns. Even though he is embarrassed, Ping is the only child who tells the truth, and the Emperor sees that the other children cheated. As a result, the Emperor rewards Ping. The story message is something like "Tell the truth, even when it is hard."

Unit 2

Key Ideas and Details in Informational Text

The following pacing chart shows a recommended schedule for teaching the lessons in Unit 2. Each Read Aloud and Focus Lesson is taught over the course of three days. There is also time allotted in each Focus Lesson for teaching Tap Children's Prior Knowledge and Differentiated Instruction.

Day	Lesson/Activity	Time (minutes)
1	Unit 2 Opener (optional); Read Aloud Lesson E: Introduction; Part 1	30
2	Read Aloud Lesson E: Parts 2 and 3	30
3	Read Aloud Lesson E: Part 4; Additional Activities (optional)	30
4	Read Aloud Lesson F: Introduction; Part 1	30
5	Read Aloud Lesson F: Parts 2 and 3	30
6	Read Aloud Lesson F: Part 4; Additional Activities (optional)	30
7	Tap Children's Prior Knowledge; Lesson 6: Part 1	30
8	Lesson 6: Parts 2 and 3	30
9	Lesson 6: Part 4; Differentiated Instruction (optional)	30
10	Tap Children's Prior Knowledge; Lesson 7: Part 1	30
11	Lesson 7: Parts 2 and 3	30
12	Lesson 7: Part 4; Differentiated Instruction (optional)	30
13	Read Aloud Lesson G: Introduction; Part 1	30
14	Read Aloud Lesson G: Parts 2 and 3	30
15	Read Aloud Lesson G: Part 4; Additional Activities (optional)	30
16	Tap Children's Prior Knowledge; Lesson 8: Part 1	30
17	Lesson 8: Parts 2 and 3	30
18	Lesson 8: Part 4; Differentiated Instruction (optional)	30
19	Unit 2 Check	30

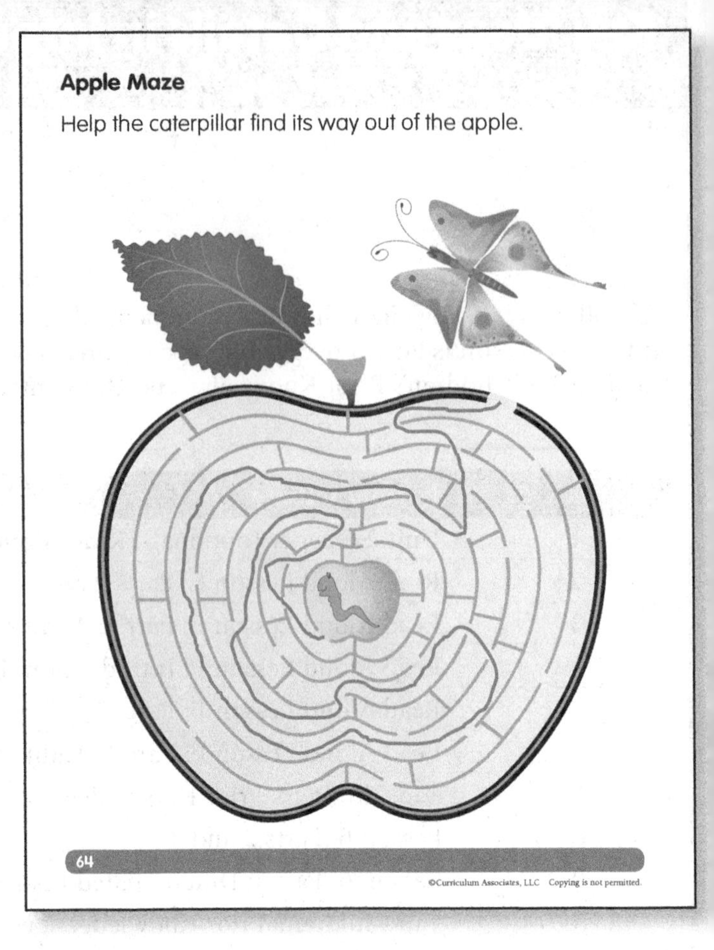

Step by Step

Explain that in this unit, children will learn about the exciting world of insects and other creatures. They will discover how they, and all living things, are connected. They will also read about a special person who made a difference.

- Have children turn to page 63. Read aloud the introductory sentences and question.
- Discuss the photo and invite children to describe what they see. *(ants building a bridge)*
- As necessary, encourage children to ask and answer *who*, *what*, *where*, *when*, *why*, and *how* questions for further inspiration.
- Time permitting, have children think of another caption that tells about the photo.
- Then have children turn to page 64.
- Read aloud the directions at the top of the page. Ask children what they know about caterpillars. You may wish to give themw a sneak peek at some of the photographs in *Butterflies and Moths.*
- Explain that the picture is a maze. Tell children to use a pencil to draw the way out of the apple. They should place the point of their pencils in the center of the apple, where the caterpillar is. Then, tell them to slowly draw a line through the maze, only through the open lines. If they get stuck, tell them they can use an eraser to get "unstuck" and try another "path."
- When children have finished the maze, invite volunteers to display their mazes.

Read Aloud Lesson E (Student Book pages 19–22)

Who Eats What?

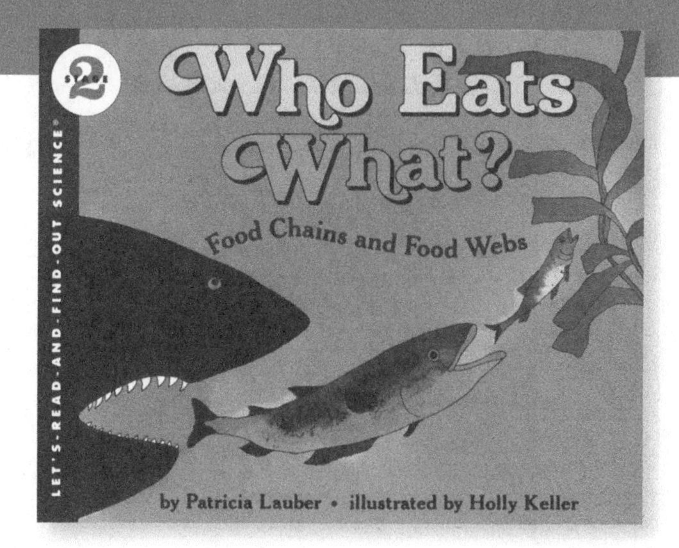

Lesson Objectives

You will read aloud *Who Eats What?* which children will revisit in later lessons. Children will:

- Identify the main topic of a text and sections within it.
- Ask and answer questions about key details.
- Identify how the information in the text is organized.

About the Text

Summary

This book explains what food chains and food webs are and what they look like on land, in the air, and in the sea. The book shows children how all living things depend on each other as part of the life cycle.

Informational Text: Science

- Explain that a science book tells facts about a science topic such as stars, the earth, or animals. Point out that *Who Eats What?* is about animals and what they eat.
- Display some informational texts from the classroom library on various topics. Guide children to identify the science texts and tell how they knew.

Critical Vocabulary

- Prior to reading, briefly define the following words:

  link (p. 6) one piece of something that connects to other pieces of the same thing

  chain (p. 6) something made by two or more pieces that are connected to each other

  fuel (p. 11) something that gives energy to something else

  branching (p. 19) spreading out in different directions

- As you read, pause to point to the words as you encounter them, and review their definitions.

Word Bank

- To support children in writing about the text, display a word bank containing the Critical Vocabulary.
- Add other important words from the text, such as *break, animals,* and *plants,* on subsequent readings.

New Concepts: Eating to Survive

- Explain that the word *survive* means "to stay alive." Tell children that all living things, both animals and plants, need to eat food to stay alive.
- Explain that for most living things, eating to survive means eating *other* living things—most animals eat and get eaten by other animals.

Ready *Teacher Toolbox* Teacher-Toolbox.com

	Prerequisite Skills	RI.1.2
Ready Lessons		✓
Tools for Instruction	✓✓	✓
Interactive Tutorials	✓	

CCSS Focus

RI.1.2 . . . *retell key details of a text.*

ADDITIONAL STANDARDS: **RI.1.1; RI.1.3; RI.1.7; RF.1.3.d, e; W.1.8; SL.1.1; SL.1.2; SL.1.3; SL.1.4; SL.1.5; L.1.1; L.1.2.a, b; L.1.4.a; L.1.5.c** *(See page A38 for full text.)*

PART 1: First Read

Step by Step

- **Introduce and explore *Who Eats What?*** Read aloud the title and the name of the author, Patricia Lauber. Read aloud the name of the illustrator, Holly Keller.
- Display the book, and ask children what they think the fish on the cover are doing. *(They are all trying to eat the thing in front of it.)*
- Turn the pages and think aloud:

  The title says this book is about food chains. I wonder what a food chain is. As I turn the pages, I see lots of pictures with arrows, called *diagrams* (pages 6–10).

  An arrow shows how one thing is connected to another, so I think that those pictures will have a lot of helpful information. And look, these pictures have labels (pages 10 and 18). **I'll make sure to read the labels when I read those pages.**

- **Read aloud *Who Eats What?*** As you read, pause to define challenging vocabulary and give children opportunities to look at the illustrations.
- **Guide a review of the text.** Direct children to turn to Student Book page 19. Read aloud the first item, and invite volunteers to offer ways to complete the sentence, based on what they heard during reading. Have children record their answers. *(RI.1.2)*
- Read aloud the second item. Display the book once more for review, and help children recall its features. Have children record their answers.

Tip: Clarify that a *feature* is a special part of the text that readers can use to find information or notice something important. Discuss how the features in *Who Eats What?* help readers in these ways.

- Read aloud the Turn and Talk activity. Tell children the facts they choose can come from any part of the book. Have each partner write or draw one of their three facts to share with the class. Invite volunteers to share their ideas. *(SL.1.1; SL.1.2; SL.1.5)*
- Ask children if they have more questions about food chains after reading the text, such as *How do green plants make their food?* or *Why did people hunt sea otters?* Discuss where you might look to find answers to these questions.

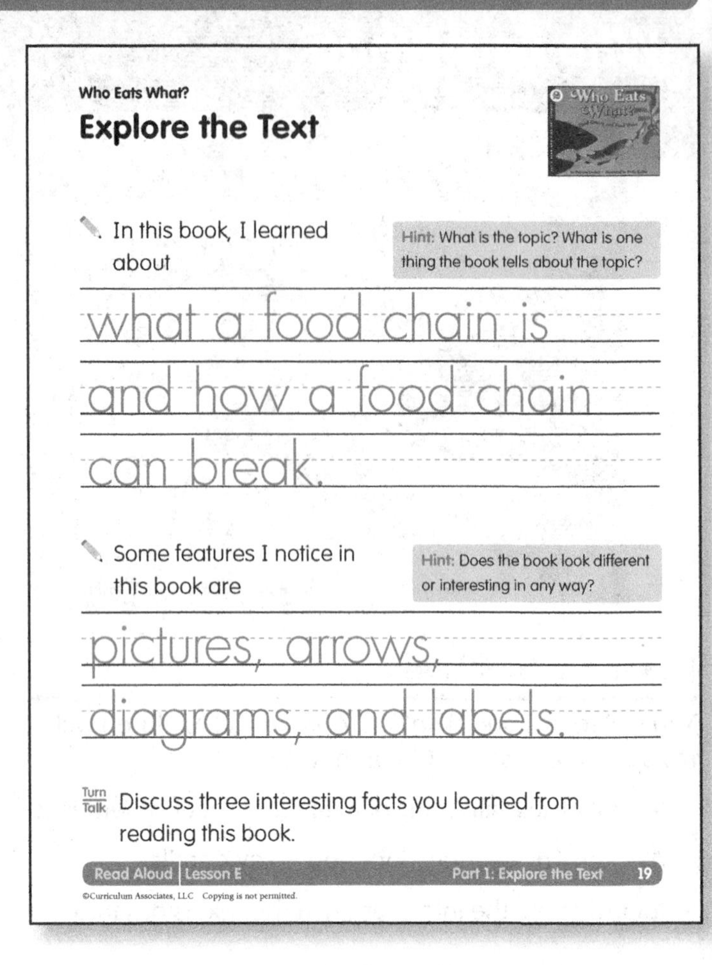

ELL Support: Animal Groups

- Explain that land and water animals are part of food chains. Display page 14 of *Who Eats What?* Ask where these animals live: on land or in water. *(on land)* Repeat for pages 20–21. *(in water)*
- Display and read aloud these sentence frames: *A ____ lives on land. A ____ lives in the water.* Create a chart with the headings *Land* and *Water.*
- One at a time, display pictures of land and water animals from *Who Eats What?* For example, use pictures of a cow, grasshopper, deer, squirrel, caterpillar, mouse, chipmunk, fish, shark, squid, whale, seal, sea otter, and sea urchin.
- Name each animal and have children repeat the name. Then have children complete a sentence frame to tell where the animal lives. Write the animal's name in the chart.
- When the chart is complete, have each child choose an animal and tell where it lives.

PART 2: Reread for Meaning

Step by Step

- **Reread to find out what a food chain is.** Explain that children will listen and look for details in order to determine what a food chain is. Instruct them to listen closely as you reread pages 4–11.
- **Have children identify key details.** Use questions such as these to guide discussion. *(RI.1.1; SL.1.1; SL.1.2)*

  Page 6: What does a food chain show? *(It shows one animal eating a plant or another animal and then getting eaten by something bigger.)*

  Page 7: What does it mean to be at the top of a food chain? *(This animal is the last eater. Nothing else eats it.)*

  Page 11: What does food do for us? *(It keeps us alive and gives us energy to do things.)*
- Use the Close Reading activity to help children understand how the illustrations support the words in the text.
- **Guide children to demonstrate understanding.** Direct children to turn to Student Book page 20. Read aloud the first activity, and then read the Hint. Prompt children to include at least three links in their food chains.

Tip: Help provide information as needed about where less obvious items, such as cheese, come from. Be sure to simplify complex items to one source as with the bread on page 10.

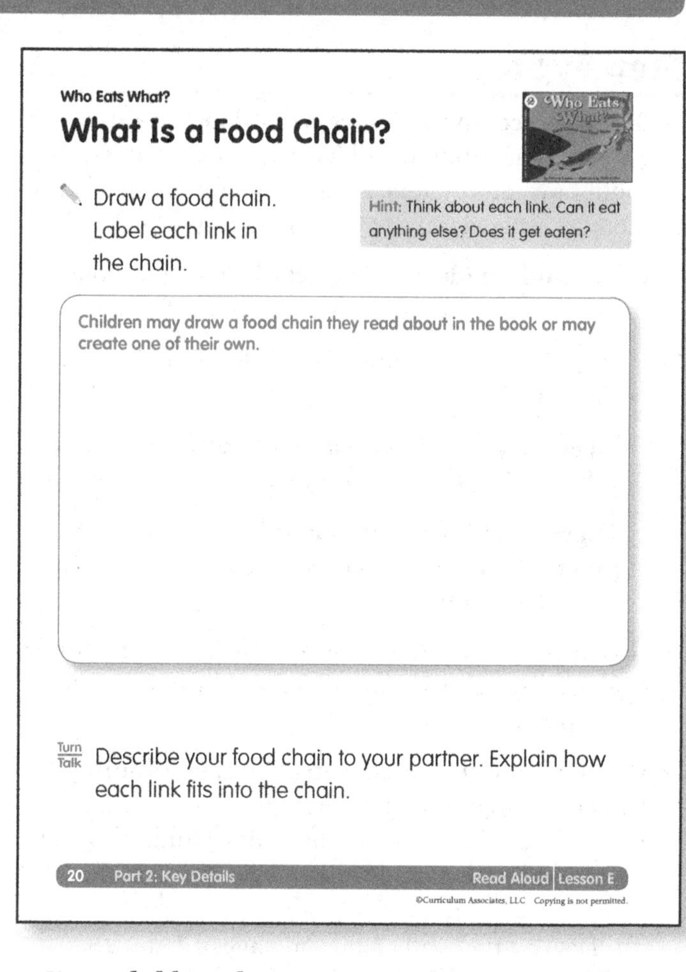
Who Eats What?

What Is a Food Chain?

Draw a food chain. Label each link in the chain.

Hint: Think about each link. Can it eat anything else? Does it get eaten?

Children may draw a food chain they read about in the book or may create one of their own.

Turn Talk Describe your food chain to your partner. Explain how each link fits into the chain.

20 Part 2: Key Details Read Aloud Lesson E

©Curriculum Associates, LLC Copying is not permitted.

- **Have children discuss text evidence.** Read aloud the Turn and Talk activity. Have partners describe evidence in the text that helped them create their food chains. Invite children to describe their drawings to the class. *(SL.1.4; SL.1.5)*

Tier Two Vocabulary: *several*

- Display the diagram on page 10. Write the first sentence on the board. Underline the word *several.*
- Ask children how many food chains are in the diagram. *(five)* Help them determine that *several* means "more than two." Then explain that *several* describes a limited amount, such as five, and *many* describes a larger amount, such as ten or more.
- Display pages 18–19. Ask children which page shows *several* food chains *(page 18)* and which shows *many. (page 19)*
- Have children use *several* to describe things in the room. For example, *I have several markers in my desk. (L.1.4.a; L.1.5.c)*

Close Reading

- Help children notice how the text and the diagram work together to present information. Display and read aloud page 10. Prompt:

  What details from the text are shown in the diagram? *(a child at the top of the food chain; labeled pictures of the food in the text)*

  What details does the diagram add? *(arrows; pictures to show the links in the food chain that the food items come from)*

  What do the text and diagram work together to explain? *(that when we eat, we become the top of several food chains) (RI.1.3; RI.1.7)*

PART 3: Reread for Meaning

Step by Step

- **Reread to compare and contrast food chains.** Explain that children will listen and look for details about how food chains are alike and different. Instruct them to listen closely as you reread pages 12–19.
- **Have children identify key details.** Use questions such as these to guide discussion. *(RI.1.1; SL.1.1; SL.1.2)*

  Page 12: What is one way all food chains are the same? *(All food chains begin with green plants.)*

  Page 12: How are green plants different from other living things? *(They make their own food.)*

  Pages 16–19: How are all animals linked to green plants? *(All animals eat green plants or eat other animals that eat plants.)*
- Use the Close Reading activity to help children find evidence that shows how all animals are linked to green plants.
- **Guide children to demonstrate understanding.** Direct children to turn to Student Book page 21. Read aloud each item and the Hints. Guide children to respond with complete sentences. *(L.1.1; L.1.2)*

Tip: Display the food chains on pages 17 and 18. Guide children to see how these food chains have been combined to make the food web on page 19. Use the chipmunk to demonstrate how an animal can be part of more than one food chain.

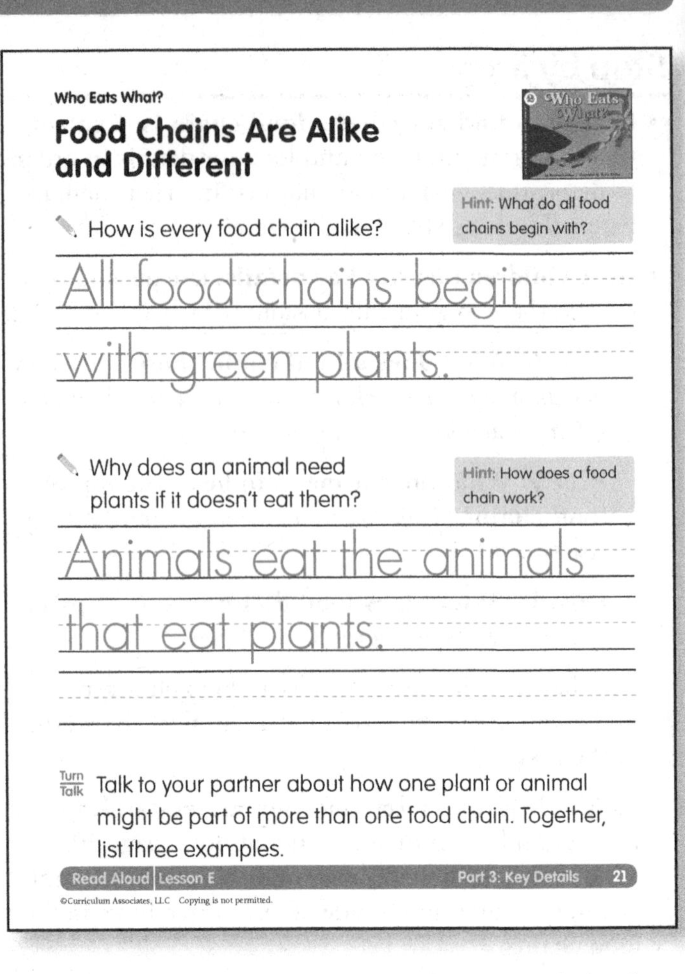
Who Eats What?

Food Chains Are Alike and Different

How is every food chain alike?

Hint: What do all food chains begin with?

All food chains begin with green plants.

Why does an animal need plants if it doesn't eat them?

Hint: How does a food chain work?

Animals eat the animals that eat plants.

Turn Talk: Talk to your partner about how one plant or animal might be part of more than one food chain. Together, list three examples.

Read Aloud | Lesson E | Part 3: Key Details 21

©Curriculum Associates, LLC Copying is not permitted.

- **Have children discuss text evidence.** Read aloud the Turn and Talk activity. Remind children to use evidence from the food chains and web in the text to help them respond. Invite children to discuss their examples with the class. *(SL.1.4)*

Tier Two Vocabulary: *depend on*

- Display and read aloud the last sentence on page 12. Underline the phrase *depend on.*
- Prompt children to discover the meaning:

  Can animals live without green plants? *(no)*

  So if they depend on green plants, what do you think *depend on* means? *(need)*
- Provide an example, such as *I depend on my car to get to school every day.* Substitute *need* into the sentence and discuss whether it still makes sense.
- Then have children describe other familiar situations using the phrase *depend on,* such as *We depend on the air to breathe.* *(L.1.4.a)*

Close Reading

- Help children use visual details to find links between animals and green plants.
- Read aloud pages 17–19, and display the diagram on page 19. Think aloud, using your finger to trace arrows on the diagram:

  The chipmunk eats nuts, berries, and buds, which are all parts of plants. The hawk doesn't eat any of these things, but it eats the chipmunk, which means it eats whatever is inside the chipmunk. This is how the hawk is connected to the plants.
- Guide children to make connections between plants and the fox, bobcat, and coyote. *(RI.1.3; RI.1.7)*

PART 4: Reread for Meaning

Step by Step

- **Reread to learn how food chains break.** Explain that children will listen and look for details about how a food chain can be broken. Instruct children to listen closely as you reread pages 28–32.
- **Have children identify key details.** Use questions such as these to guide discussion. *(RI.1.1; SL.1.1; SL.1.2)*

  Page 30: Why is kelp important to have in the ocean? *(It is the start of many food chains.)*

  Page 31: How did the killing of sea otters cause the kelp beds to die? *(There were too many sea urchins because the otters were not eating them. The sea urchins cut off too much kelp from the sea floor, and the kelp died.)*

- **Guide children to demonstrate understanding.** Direct children to turn to Student Book page 22. Read the directions aloud and explain that this flow chart shows a chain of cause-and-effect events. Guide children to complete each sentence in the chart.

Tip: Remind children that *cause* and *effect* means one event happened because of another event. Explain how each event in the flow chart happens because of the event on top of it.

- **Have children discuss text evidence.** Read aloud the Turn and Talk activity, and reread the last paragraph on page 30 to support children's discussions. Invite children to share their ideas with the class. *(SL.1.4)*

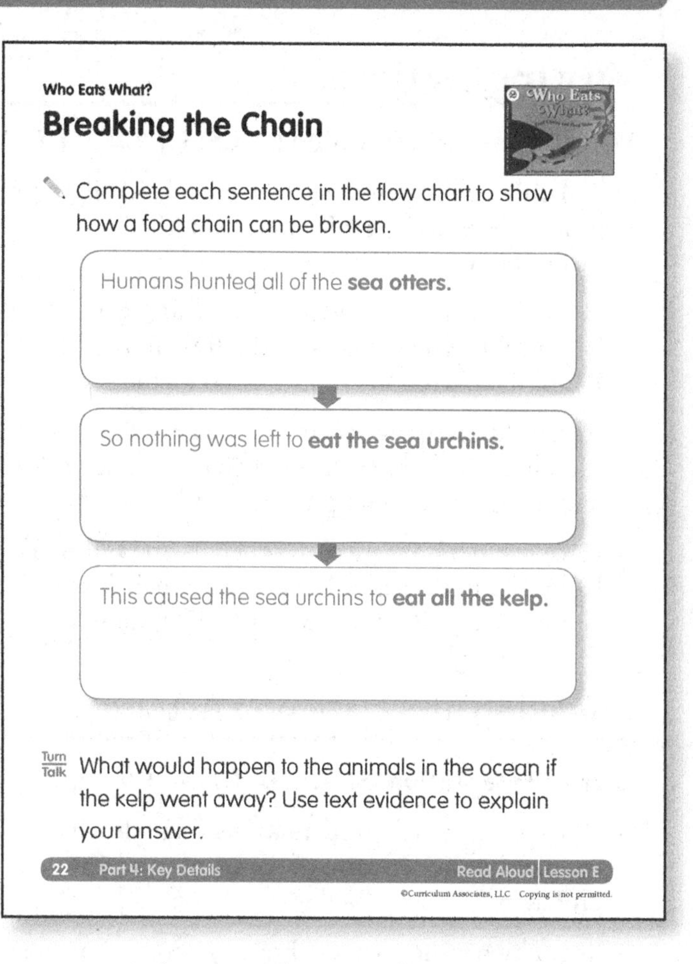

Who Eats What?

Breaking the Chain

Complete each sentence in the flow chart to show how a food chain can be broken.

Humans hunted all of the **sea otters.**

So nothing was left to **eat the sea urchins.**

This caused the sea urchins to **eat all the kelp.**

Turn Talk What would happen to the animals in the ocean if the kelp went away? Use text evidence to explain your answer.

22 Part 4: Key Details Read Aloud Lesson E

©Curriculum Associates, LLC Copying is not permitted.

- **Review *Who Eats What?*** Use the prompts in the Book Review to revisit and record important concepts from the text. Use the diagrams throughout the book to help children recall important details about food chains and food webs. *(RI.1.2)*

Integrating Foundational Skills

Use these activities to integrate foundational skills into your reading of *Who Eats What?*

1. Display and read aloud these words: *caterpillar, animal, depend, scientists, underwater, human, shrimp, branch.* Have children sort the words by number of syllables. Remind them that each syllable must have a vowel sound. *(1: shrimp, branch; 2: depend, human; 3: animal, scientists; 4: caterpillar, underwater) (RF.1.3.d)*
2. Display these words: *summer, harbor, begin, happen, insects, tuna, dinner, bobcats, otter, later.* Have children break each word into syllables and then read it aloud. *(RF.1.3.e)*

Book Review

- As children review key details from *Who Eats What?*, record their answers on chart paper. Keep the chart on hand for revisiting later.

  What does a food chain show? *(It shows how plants and animals are linked by what they eat.)*

  What does a food web show? *(It shows many different food chains and how they overlap.)*

  Why are green plants important? *(Every food chain begins with green plants. All animals need green plants to live.)*

  What can break a food chain? *(Causing changes in one or more links can break the chain.)*

Writing Activity

Write to Answer a Question *(W.1.8; L.1.2.a; L.1.2.b)*

- Tell children they will each create a food chain for an animal from *Who Eats What?* Give children in small groups a chance to look carefully at the book. Have each child choose one animal and its food chain to write about.
- Have children work independently to create a food chain for their animal. Review that every food chain begins with green plants, and tell them that their food chain should answer the question *Who eats what?* Remind children that they should include arrows and labels to help organize the links in their chain.
- Ask children to give their food chain a title, such as *A Shark's Food Chain.* Then have them write two to three sentences describing the food chain. Guide children to observe language conventions by capitalizing names and using correct end punctuation.
- Have partners review each other's work and make any suggestions or corrections that might be needed. Then have volunteers share and compare their food chains with the rest of the class. You may wish to post the food chains on a bulletin board titled *Who Ate What?*

Speaking and Listening Activity

Give a Presentation *(SL.1.3; SL.1.4; SL.1.5)*

- Have partners give presentations that tell why people should take care of the plants and animals on Earth.
- Begin by having partners brainstorm reasons why it is important to take care of plants and animals. Encourage them to use what they learned from reading *Who Eats What?* Then have them choose the best reason and draw a poster to illustrate their ideas. Remind them to title their poster.
- Have partners plan and practice presenting the posters. Help them plan with prompts such as the following: *Will you take turns speaking? Will one of you speak? What will the other partner do?* Remind speakers to begin by telling what their presentation is about.
- Have partners present to the class. Before beginning the presentations, remind children that the audience should listen carefully to each presenter. Explain that they can ask questions once the speaker has finished if they do not understand something.

Language Activity

Use Context *(L.1.4.a)*

- Have children practice using context to help them understand the meaning of words in a text.
- Explain to children that if they don't know a word, they can try looking at the words near the word, rereading or reading ahead, or using the pictures to help them figure out its meaning.
- Display and read aloud page 5 of *Who Eats What?* Point to the word *spotted.* Ask children what they think *spotted* means in this sentence, and how they know. *(It means "seen"; the wren saw the caterpillar. The picture shows that the wren has the caterpillar in its mouth.)*
- Continue with the following words and clues:

  blade (p. 15) *(It means "leaf"; the words say the grasshopper is eating a blade of grass; the picture shows the grasshopper eating a leaf of grass.)*

  bore (p. 16) *(It means "dig into"; the words say beetles bore into a tree's trunk; they are doing it to get food.)*

  disappeared (p. 30) *(It means "stopped being there"; the sea urchins destroyed the kelp.)*

Read Aloud Lesson F (Student Book pages 23–26)

Butterflies and Moths

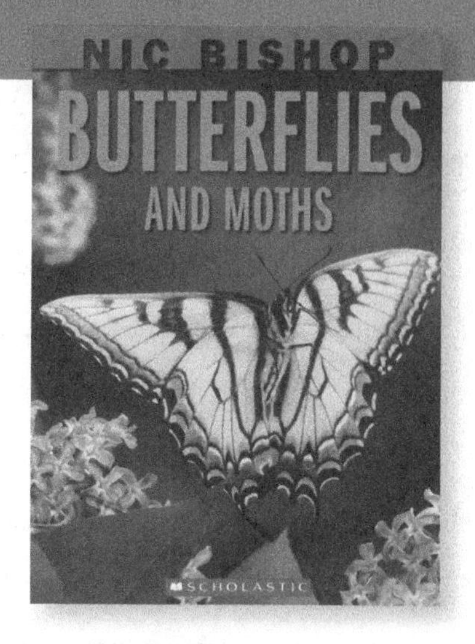

Lesson Objectives

You will read aloud *Butterflies and Moths,* which children will revisit in later lessons. Children will:

- Identify the main topic of a text and sections within it.
- Ask and answer questions about key details.
- Identify how the information in the text is organized.

About the Text

Summary

This book's text and close-up photographs present basic information and fun facts about butterflies and moths, including what they look like, how they hide from enemies, and their amazing transformation from egg to adult.

Informational Text: Science

- Explain that a science book tells facts about a science topic. Point out that a science book often has features such as photographs, captions, and large bold type to help readers understand information.
- Help children notice ways that this science book is different from another science book, *Who Eats What?*

Critical Vocabulary

- Prior to reading, briefly define the following words:

  creature (p. 5) an animal

  hatches (p. 11) breaks free from its eggshell

  enclosed (p. 21) inside of something; covered completely

  scales (p. 25) hard, flat, thin, plate-like pieces that cover the wings of a moth or butterfly

- As you read, pause to point to the words as you encounter them, and review their definitions.

Word Bank

- To support children in writing about the text, display a word bank containing the Critical Vocabulary.
- Add other important words from the text, such as *caterpillar* and *pupa,* on subsequent readings.

New Concepts: Animals that Transform

- Tell children that some animals begin life looking one way, but then change into something completely different as adults. Compare this process to the way a little acorn can grow up into an enormous oak tree.
- Have children listen closely for details about how butterflies and moths change as they grow from a tiny egg to a caterpillar to a pupa to a winged adult.

Ready *Teacher Toolbox* Teacher-Toolbox.com

	Prerequisite Skills	RI.1.2
Ready Lessons		✓
Tools for Instruction	✓✓	✓
Interactive Tutorials	✓	

CCSS Focus

RI.1.2 . . . *retell key details of a text.*

ADDITIONAL STANDARDS: **RI.1.1; RI.1.3; RF.1.2.b; RF.1.3.a; W.1.2; SL.1.1; SL.1.2; SL.1.4; SL.1.5; L.1.1.f; L.1.2; L.1.4.a; L.1.5.b, c**
(See page A38 for full text.)

PART 1: First Read

Step by Step

- **Introduce and explore *Butterflies and Moths*.** Read aloud the title and the name of the author, Nic Bishop. Explain that Bishop also took the photographs.
- Display the front and back covers and think aloud:

  The title tells me the topic of the book. I wonder if this bug on the front cover is a butterfly or a moth. The bug on the back looks different; it has bigger antennae and looks fatter. I wonder which one that is? Maybe this book will explain how to tell the difference.

- Turn the pages. Ask children what they see repeated on each page, including photographs, captions, and sentences in larger, colored type. Show and briefly explain the index and glossary. Discuss how these features help the reader. *(SL.1.1)*

Tip: Point out that the close-up photographs show details of the insects that we wouldn't usually see. Discuss how seeing these details can make the text more interesting and exciting to read.

- **Read *Butterflies and Moths* aloud.** As you read, pause to define challenging vocabulary, and give children opportunities to look at the photographs.
- **Guide a review of the text.** Have children turn to Student Book page 23. Read aloud the first item, and invite volunteers to complete the sentence, based on what they heard and saw during the reading. Have children record their answers. *(RI.1.2)*
- Read aloud the second item, and help children recall features you noticed together in your preview. Display the book once more for review. Have children record their answers.
- Read aloud the Turn and Talk activity. As children discuss their facts, ask them what things about the book, such as photographs or colored text, helped them remember the facts they chose. Invite children to share their ideas and discuss as a class.
- Ask children if they have any additional questions about butterflies and moths after reading the text, such as *What kinds of butterflies and moths live here where we live?* or *Are butterflies and bees friends or enemies?* Discuss where you might look to find the answers to these questions.

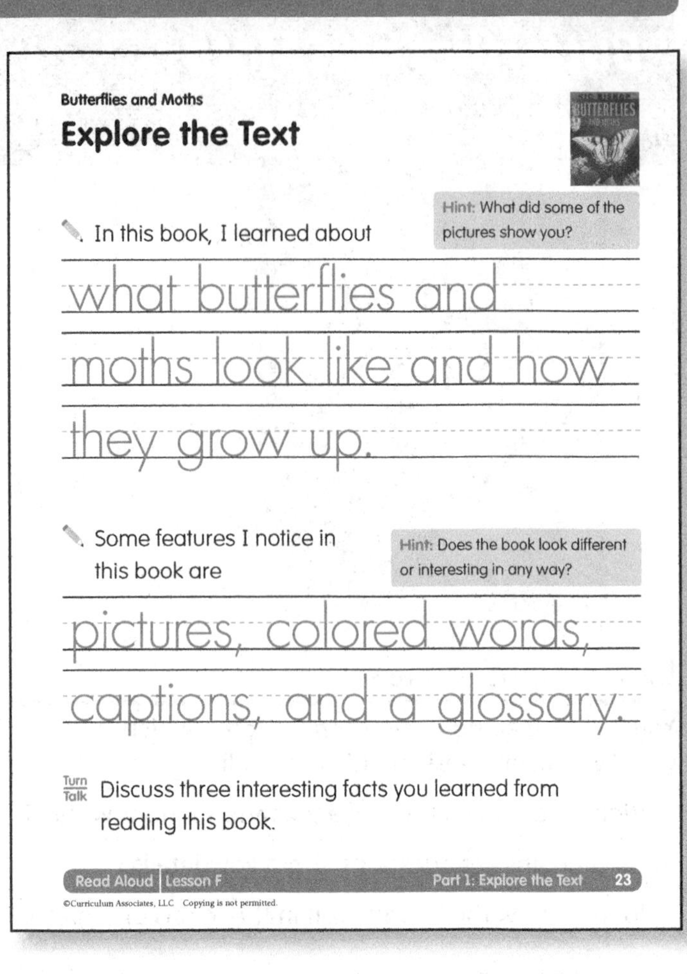
Butterflies and Moths

Explore the Text

In this book, I learned about

Hint: What did some of the pictures show you?

what butterflies and moths look like and how they grow up.

Some features I notice in this book are

Hint: Does the book look different or interesting in any way?

pictures, colored words, captions, and a glossary.

Turn Talk Discuss three interesting facts you learned from reading this book.

Read Aloud | Lesson F Part 1: Explore the Text 23

©Curriculum Associates, LLC Copying is not permitted.

ELL Support: Feature Words

- Explain that learning the names for the parts of a butterfly's and moth's body will help children understand the text.
- Display the photograph on page 27. Then copy the following words onto chart paper, and read them aloud: *head, eyes, antennae, thorax, legs.* Point out and name each body part on the photograph.
- Write the names of the body parts on stick-on notes and distribute them to children. Help children read the labels on the notes and stick the notes to the correct body parts in the photograph. Redistribute the notes until all children have had a chance to label a body part.
- Repeat the process with the photograph on page 33 and the words *proboscis, antennae, head, eyes, legs,* and *wings,* as well as with the photograph on page 24 and the words *scales* and *veins.*

PART 2: Reread for Meaning

Step by Step

- **Reread to learn about life stages.** Explain that children will listen and look for details about a butterfly's or moth's four stages of life. Instruct them to listen closely as you reread pages 10–23.

Tip: You may wish to skip pages 16–19, as these pages focus on how caterpillars avoid being eaten, not on a new stage of the life cycle.

- **Have children identify key details.** Use questions such as these to guide discussion. *(RI.1.1; SL.1.1; SL.1.2)*

  Pages 10–13: What happens in the first two stages of a butterfly's or moth's life? *(it begins as an egg; the egg hatches and a caterpillar comes out)*

  Pages 14–15: What does a caterpillar do? *(It eats, grows, and molts when it's too big for its skin.)*

  Pages 20–21: How does a caterpillar become a moth or butterfly? *(It turns into a pupa; the pupa grows into wings, legs, and a body.)*

- **Guide children to demonstrate understanding.** Direct children to turn to Student Book page 24. Read aloud the drawing prompt and Hint. Guide children to put their answers in the correct order and use the Word Bank to spell challenging words.

- **Have children discuss text evidence.** Read aloud the Turn and Talk activity. Invite partners to present their drawings to the class, explaining how the drawings are alike and different. *(SL.1.4; SL.1.5)*

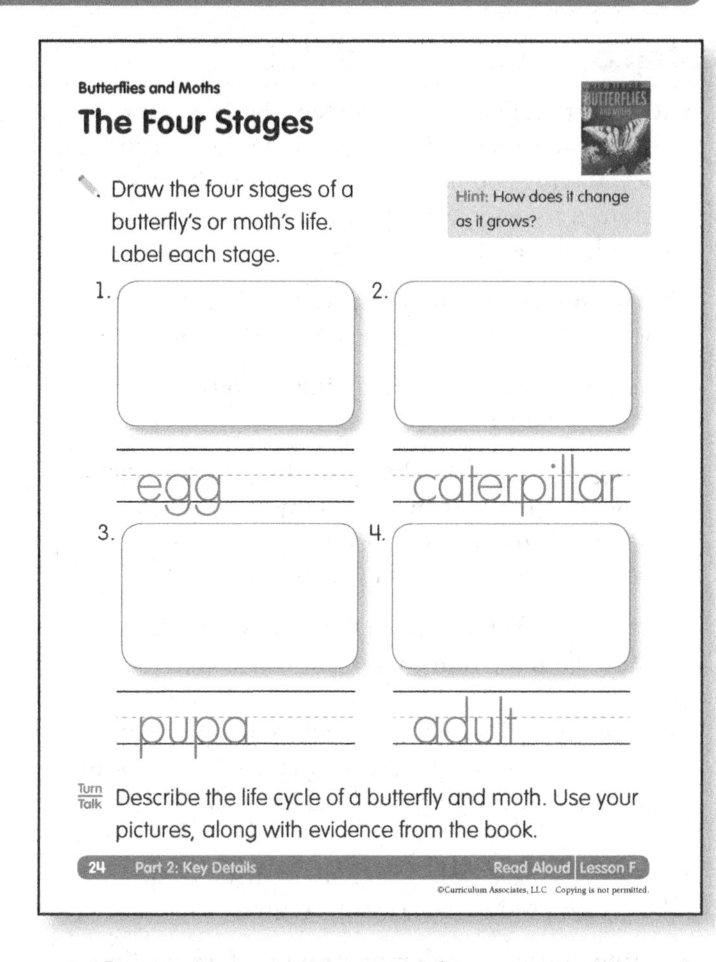

- **Reflect on text structure and features.** Use the Close Reading activity to explore how the larger, colored text helps readers pay special attention to important information.

Tier Two Vocabulary: *recognize*

- Read aloud the first two sentences on page 13. Display the word *recognize* and read it aloud. Ask children what *recognize* might mean based on the the second sentence. *(find)*
- Say another sentence, such as *I answered the phone and recognized my father's voice.* Ask children what they think *recognize* might mean now that they have heard it in two sentences. *(to know or identify)*
- Use *recognize* in more sentences, such as *At first I didn't recognize the girl, but then I realized it was my cousin.* Then have children use *recognize* in their own sentences, such as *I got off the bus when I recognized my street.* *(L.1.4.a; L.1.5.c)*

Close Reading

- Discuss how authors use text features to organize information. Display pages 20–21. Read aloud the first two paragraphs, tracking the print. Prompt:

  What is the next stage of the caterpillar's life? *(turning into a pupa)*

  Which sentence tells this? *(the colored one)*

  Why do you think the author chose to put these words in big, colored text? *(They stand out and help readers pay attention to an important fact.) (RI.1.3)*

- Use additonal examples on pages 10, 13, and 14 to reinforce the purpose of the larger, colored words.

PART 3: Reread for Meaning

Step by Step

- **Reread to learn about a special body part.** Explain that children will listen and look for details about the special wings of butterflies and moths. Instruct children to listen closely as you reread pages 24–25, including the caption on page 25.
- **Have children identify key details.** Use questions such as these to guide discussion. *(RI.1.1; SL.1.1; SL.1.2)*

  Page 25: What are the wings covered with? *(tiny, colored scales)*

  Page 25: How do the scales help butterflies and moths escape from an enemy? *(If they get caught in a web, the scales come off easily when they pull their wings away, so they can escape.)*

  Page 25: What makes the wings strong? *(long, straight tubes called veins)*

Tip: Remind children that the photograph on page 24 is enlarged to help them see details. Flip back to page 23 to show the whole wing from afar.

- Use the Close Reading activity to discuss the special language used to describe the wings.
- **Guide children to demonstrate understanding.** Direct children to turn to Student Book page 25. Read aloud the writing prompt and the Hint. Remind children to write in complete sentences. Sample answers are shown. *(L.1.1; L.1.2)*

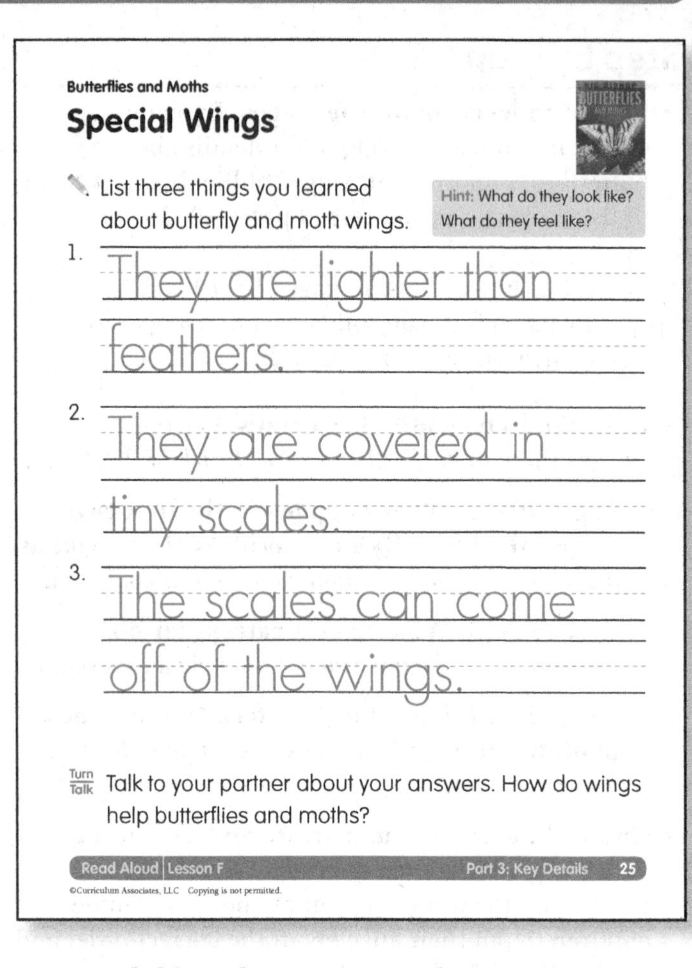
Butterflies and Moths

Special Wings

List three things you learned about butterfly and moth wings.

Hint: What do they look like? What do they feel like?

1. They are lighter than feathers.
2. They are covered in tiny scales.
3. The scales can come off of the wings.

Turn Talk Talk to your partner about your answers. How do wings help butterflies and moths?

Read Aloud | Lesson F Part 3: Key Details 25

©Curriculum Associates, LLC Copying is not permitted.

- **Have children discuss text evidence.** Read aloud the Turn and Talk activity. Encourage partners to discuss how the descriptive language helped them better understand the wings. Invite children to share their lists with the class. *(SL.1.5)*

Tier Two Vocabulary: *pattern*

- Display and read aloud the second paragraph on page 25. Point to the word *patterns* and the photo.
- Have children describe what they see in the photo. *(big orange circles, small white shapes, a black background)* Repeat with the photo on the front cover. *(black, white, grey, and orange stripes)*
- Tell children that they have described two patterns. Ask what they think the word *pattern* means. Guide them to see that *pattern* means "an arrangement of colors and shapes."
- Model making a pattern with classroom objects, such as blocks or crayons. Then have children create and describe their own patterns. *(L.1.5.c)*

Close Reading

- Explain that authors use descriptive language to help readers imagine what something is like.
- Display and reread page 25. Then prompt:

  Which words tell about the weight of the wings? *("lighter than feathers") (RI.1.3)*

  What do the words "like a piece of glass" tell about the scales? *(They are thin and breakable.)*

  How would the wings look and feel in your hand? *(brightly colored; very light; breakable)*

- Discuss whether children have a better understanding of butterfly and moth wings after thinking about what feathers and glass feel like.

PART 4: Reread for Meaning

Step by Step

- **Reread to learn about escaping from predators.** Explain that children will listen for details about ways that butterflies and moths try to stay away from predators, or animals who hunt for and eat them. Instruct children to listen closely for these details as you reread pages 38–41.
- **Have children identify key details.** Use questions such as these to guide discussion. *(RI.1.1; SL.1.1; SL.1.2)*

  Page 40: How do butterflies stay safe from birds? *(not flying in straight lines; having eyespots that confuse birds; dropping to the ground)*

  Page 40: If a bird grabs a butterfly's wing, what can help the butterfly escape? *(The scales on the wing tear off and allow it to escape.)*

Tip: Have children compare the photos on pages 34 and 41. Point out how page 34 shows the top of the blue morpho's wings and page 41 shows the bottom.

- **Guide children to demonstrate understanding.** Direct children to turn to Student Book page 26. Read aloud the directions and the completed circles of the web. Help children complete the two remaining circles.
- **Have children discuss text evidence.** Read aloud the Turn and Talk activity. Suggest that partners try demonstrating each butterfly escape. Invite volunteers to share their ideas. *(SL.1.4; SL.1.5)*

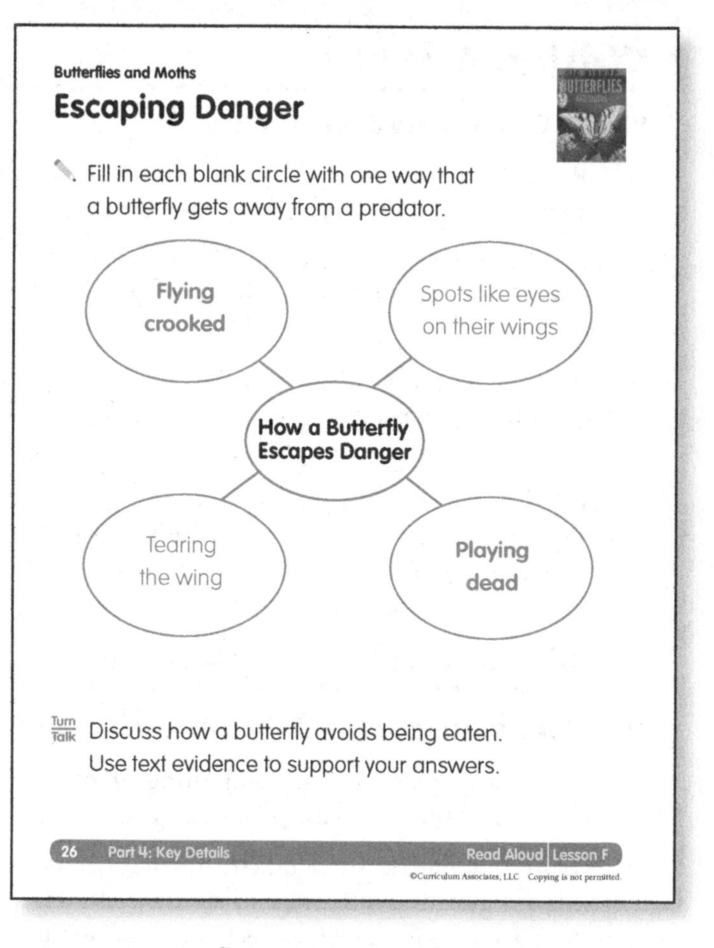

Butterflies and Moths

Escaping Danger

Fill in each blank circle with one way that a butterfly gets away from a predator.

Turn Talk Discuss how a butterfly avoids being eaten. Use text evidence to support your answers.

26 Part 4: Key Details Read Aloud | Lesson F

©Curriculum Associates, LLC Copying is not permitted.

- **Review *Butterflies and Moths.*** Use the prompts in the Book Review to revisit and record important concepts from the book. As appropriate, point out that the large, colored sentences often state topics or key details. *(RI.1.2)*

Integrating Foundational Skills

Use these activities to integrate foundational skills into your reading of *Butterflies and Moths.*

1. Say these sets of phonemes, and have children say the word: /d/ /r/ /ī/; /s/ /ī/ /z/; /d/ /ă/ /n/ /s/; /p/ /l/ /ā/ /s/; /g/ /l/ /ī/ /d/; /b/ /r/ /ī/ /t/; /f/ /l/ /ă/ /p/; /g/ /r/ /ă/ /b/; /t/ /r/ /ā/ /l/. *(dry; size; dance; place; glide; bright; flap; grab; trail) (RF.1.2.b)*
2. Display and review digraphs *sh, th, ch.* Then tell children to listen to the following words and write the sound they hear at the beginning: *chew, shiver, thorax, shelter, thing, changing, chunks.* Repeat with ending digraphs: *moth, inch, push, touch, mouth, search, munch, crush, health. (RF.1.3.a)*

Book Review

- As children review key details from *Butterflies and Moths,* record their answers on chart paper. Keep the chart on hand for later revisiting.

  How are moths different from butterflies? *(moths fly at night, have less colorful wings and fat, furry bodies)*

  What are the four life stages of a butterfly or moth? *(egg, caterpillar, pupa, butterfly/moth)*

  What are some ways caterpillars stay safe? *(colors; stinging hairs; poisons)*

  How do butterflies and moths stay safe? *(fly crooked; eyespots, play dead; tear their wings)*

Writing Activity

Write a Class Library Book *(W.1.2)*

- Tell children that they will create a class library book about butterflies and moths. Explain that each child will create one to two pages for a book that tells some information they learned about butterflies and moths.
- Have children refer to their Student Book pages and to the text to recall interesting facts about butterflies and moths. Ask each child to choose a specific topic, such as the body parts of a butterfly, to write about on their book page(s).
- Have children work independently to create their page(s). Remind them to organize their writing in the following way: write the topic, give three facts about the topic, and then write a closing thought about the topic. Give children examples of what each of these parts should look like.
- Have children share their pages with the class. Help them organize the pages into one or more books, depending on the content of each child's work. Then have children work together to choose titles and create covers as needed.

Speaking and Listening Activity

Describe a Butterfly or Moth *(SL.1.4; SL.1.5; L.1.1.f)*

- Help children practice describing things to others using important details and clear language.
- Explain that partners will take turns describing a moth or butterfly at any stage of its life cycle. The other partner will draw what is being described.
- Review the life cycle stages (egg, caterpillar, pupa, butterfly/moth). Ask individuals to decide and write down which stage they will describe.
- Have children take a few minutes to list some important details they will use in their descriptions. Remind them to use adjectives—words that tell about size, color, feel, and shape—as well as body parts and other details they will need to get a complete picture.
- Remind partners that they must listen carefully and draw only the details they hear, rather than details they recall from photographs. Ask children not to look at their partner's drawing until both partners have drawn.
- Have partners share their drawings with the class. Encourage them to discuss any improvements they would make in their descriptions after seeing their partner's drawing.

Language Activity

Sort Words *(L.1.5.b)*

- Tell children that putting things together that are alike in some way is called *sorting* them. Explain that they are going to practice sorting words into groups.
- Create a three-column chart with these heads: *Color Words, Verbs* (or *Action Words),* and *Places.*
- Organize children into three small groups. Tell each group to listen for one of the categories of words as you read aloud.
- Display and read aloud pages 4–5 of *Butterflies and Moths,* including the caption. Ask each small group to name words they heard that belong in their category.
- Record children's responses. As needed, reread the page sentence by sentence, pausing for children to identify words. *(Color Words: colorful, blues, reds, yellows; Verbs: skip, blown, dance, shimmer, glide, flying; Places: woods, fields, parks, backyards, gardens, forests, meadows)*
- Ask each group to add two or three words of their own to their category, and record responses. Display the chart for reference during other writing and language activities.

Lesson 6 (Student Book pages 65–68)

Asking Questions

CCSS

RI.1.1: Ask and answer questions about key details in a text.

Required Read Alouds: E (*Who Eats What?*); F (*Butterflies and Moths*)

Lesson Objectives

- Identify key details in informational text and text features.
- Ask *who, what, when, where, why,* and *how* questions about key details in the text.
- Answer *who, what, when, where, why,* and *how* questions with text-based evidence.
- Understand how asking and answering questions helps readers comprehend informational text.

The Learning Progression

- **Grade K:** CCSS RI.K.1 requires children to ask and answer questions about key text details with prompting and support.
- **Grade 1: CCSS RI.1.1 advances the Grade K standard by expecting children to ask and answer questions about key text details more independently.**
- **Grade 2:** CCSS RI.2.1 continues to develop the standard by expecting children to ask and answer a wide range of questions *(who, what, where, when, why, how)* to confirm understanding of key text details.

Prerequisite Skills

- Understand that informational text gives facts and information.
- Recognize and describe the relationship between illustrations and text with prompting and support.

Tap Children's Prior Knowledge

- Remind children that they have already practiced asking questions about stories. Have them name question words as they recall things they can ask about characters and events. *(who, what, when, where, why, how)*
- Review that a *fact* is something that is true or real. Then explain that children can also ask questions about facts and information. Show a photograph or website of an animal in nature, and have children look carefully at the image.
- Model how to ask questions about the animal's features, such as *How many legs does it have?* or *What color is it?* Point out that these questions are easy to answer by looking at the image. Have children ask questions about other details in the picture.
- Then explain that not all questions can be answered by using the picture details. Give examples, such as *Where does the animal live?* or *What does it eat?* Discuss where readers might find the answers to these questions. *(in the text or caption that goes with the image; in other books or magazines; on a website)*
- Review that the word *details* describes the facts and information in a book. Tell children they will learn how to ask and answer questions to find key details in an informational text.

Ready *Teacher Toolbox* Teacher-Toolbox.com

	Prerequisite Skills	*RI.1.1*
Ready Lessons	✓	✓
Tools for Instruction		✓
Interactive Tutorials		

Additional CCSS

RI.1.2; RI.1.7; SL.1.1; SL.1.2; SL.1.4; L.1.1; L.1.2 (*See page A38 for full text.*)

Part 1: Introduction

Step by Step

- **Introduce the standard.** Have children turn to Student Book page 65. Read aloud the speech bubble. Explain that *key* means "important" and that *information* means "facts and other details" that an author wants readers to understand.
- **Review asking questions about details.** Read the line below the speech bubble, and explain that the steps below tell how readers ask and answer questions in order to find key details.
- Read aloud the first bullet, along with the example words in the box. Explain that children can use these words to ask questions about key details.
- Point to and read the word *Who*. Have children repeat the word and circle it. Then have them think of a *who* question they could ask about their school, such as *Who is the principal of our school?* Ask children to share their *who* questions with a partner.
- Repeat with the remaining words. As needed, give examples such as these: *What do we do after lunch? When does school end every day? Where is the main office? Why do children go to school? How do you get to school?* Continue to have children share their questions with a partner.

Tip: If children struggle to think of questions, prompt them with more specifics topics. For example, say: *Ask a* when *question about dismissal.* or *Ask a* where *question about the main office.*

- Point out that answering these questions helps children identify key details about the school. Then explain that readers also look for key details by asking questions about the subject of the text.
- **Review answering questions about details.** Read aloud the second bullet. Explain that text features are parts of a book that give information in a place separate from the main words. Give an example, such as the words below a photograph (caption) or the big bold words at the top of a section (heading).
- Point out that sometimes the answer to a question can be found easily in the text or text features. Other times, readers have to think about the details, look in different parts of the book, or even look in other books to find the answer.

Listen and Learn

Asking Questions

A **key detail** is an important piece of information. Asking and answering questions can help you find key details.

Here is how you find key details:

- Ask a question. Begin the question with one of these words:

Who	What	When
Where	Why	How

- Look for the answer to your question. You can find it in the words or in the text features.

When you ask questions about what you read, answering your questions helps you understand the text.

Lesson 6 Part 1: Introduction 65

- **Explain why readers ask and answer questions.** Read aloud the bottom of the page. Explain that informational books have lots of details, but some—called *key details*—are more important than others. Good readers ask and answer questions as they read to be sure they understand the key details.
- Share an example of how asking and answering a question during reading helped you understand a key detail:

  As I read *Butterflies and Moths,* I asked myself, *How are they alike?* I paid close attention to words and pictures that would answer this question. Then I learned that they grow up the same way. This is a key detail.

- **Have children demonstrate understanding.** Call on volunteers to share what they have learned so far about asking and answering questions to find key details. Ask them to explain in their own words why asking and answering questions helps readers understand information.

Part 2: Modeled Instruction

Step by Step

- **Review Part 1; preview Part 2.** Call on volunteers to tell what they have learned about asking and answering questions to find key details. Have children turn to Student Book page 66.
- **Revisit *Butterflies and Moths*.** Have children briefly recall the topic and key details, using the chart created for the Book Review on Teacher Resource Book page 71. *(RI.1.2)*
- **Model asking and answering questions.** Explain that you will model asking and answering questions about a key detail. Read aloud page 13 of *Butterflies and Moths*, including the caption. Think aloud:

  This page has a lot of facts! I will ask a question to help me focus: *What are the body parts of a caterpillar?* This will help me pay attention to these details and remember all the parts.

- Reread the page, having children signal when they hear the name of a body part. If children signal when you read the words *sensors* or *taste buds*, explain that these are part of the caterpillar's mouth.
- Then model asking and answering another question:

  I'm confused about the second paragraph. I'll ask questions to figure it out: *What is the caterpillar sticking to, and why?* I'll reread and use the details to make a picture in my mind. Now I get it: the caterpillar uses its webbing and prolegs to stick to the leaf that it is eating.

- **Model writing your responses.** Read aloud the first activity on Student Book page 66. Help children recall four body parts, rereading as needed. Model writing the answers, and have children write their own. Together, name the remaining body parts that were not listed. *(glands, legs, prolegs) (L.1.1; L.1.2)*
- Read aloud the second question and the Hint. Model how to write the answer in a complete sentence.
- Use the Close Reading activity to practice asking and answering questions about text features.
- **Have children demonstrate understanding.** Assign partners the Turn and Talk activity, with partners switching roles after a few questions. Remind children that they can use Student Book page 65 for help with question words. Invite children to share their questions and answers. *(SL.1.1; SL.1.2; SL.1.4)*

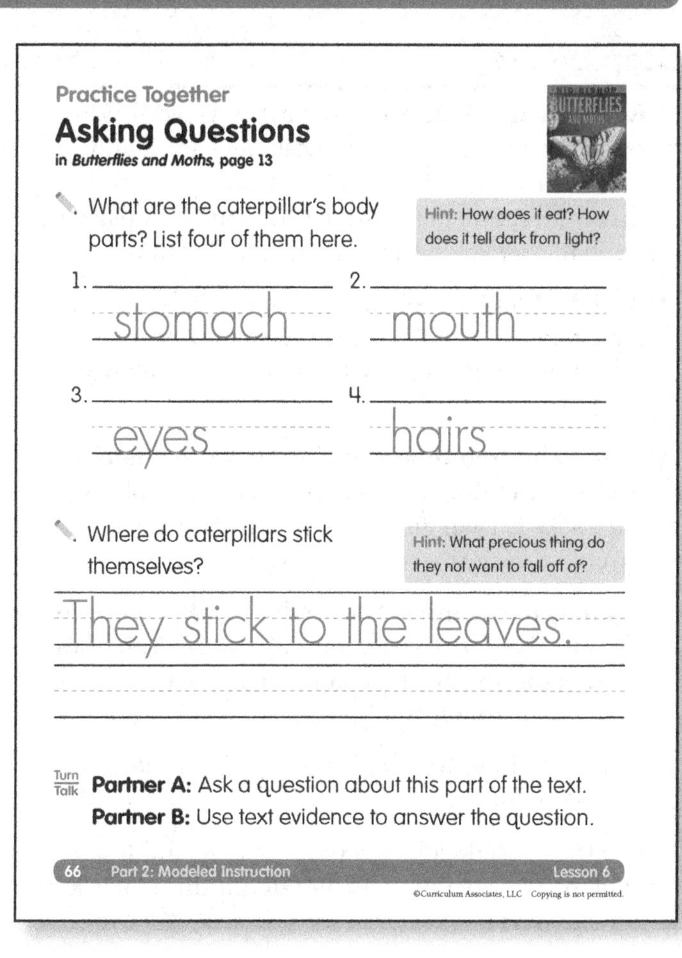

Practice Together

Asking Questions

in Butterflies and Moths, page 13

What are the caterpillar's body parts? List four of them here.

Hint: How does it eat? How does it tell dark from light?

1. stomach
2. mouth
3. eyes
4. hairs

Where do caterpillars stick themselves?

Hint: What precious thing do they not want to fall off of?

They stick to the leaves.

Turn Talk **Partner A:** Ask a question about this part of the text.
Partner B: Use text evidence to answer the question.

66 Part 2: Modeled Instruction Lesson 6

©Curriculum Associates, LLC Copying is not permitted.

Close Reading

- Remind children that photographs and text features can include key details. Display the photograph on pages 12–13 of *Butterflies and Moths*.
- Together, ask questions about the picture details. Then read the caption to look for answers:

  What are the three hairy feet? *(prolegs)*

  What are the green spiky things on the caterpillar's back? *(stingers)*

  What are the orange dots? *(spiracles for breathing)*

- Encourage children to ask *why* and *how* questions, such as *How do the prolegs help a caterpillar stick?* and *Why does a caterpillar have stingers?*
- Discuss the answers. Point out that sometimes answers can be found on the page. Other times, readers need to recall or look for details from different parts of the book to find the answers.

Part 3: Guided Practice

Step by Step

- **Review Parts 1–2; preview Part 3.** Have children recall words they can use to ask questions, and where they might look for key details to answer them. Direct them to turn to Student Book page 67. Explain that you will guide them through this page.
- **Revisit *Who Eats What?*** Have children recall the topic and key details, using the chart you created for the Book Review on Teacher Resource Book page 65. *(RI.1.2)*
- **Guide children to ask and answer questions to find key details.** Read aloud pages 10–11 of *Who Eats What?*. Then guide children to find key details. Circulate with the book as you prompt:

  Point to the milk. Where does milk come from? *(cows)* **Now trace the food chain up. Tell about each picture in the chain.** *(A cow eats grass; the cow makes milk; we drink the milk.) (RI.1.7)*

  Why is food like fuel? *(Food keeps us alive and gives us energy.)*

- Use the Close Reading activity to help children explore a key detail in greater depth through asking and answering questions.
- **Guide children to write responses.** Read aloud the first question and the Hint on Student Book page 67. Display the illustration on page 10 and help children think about the answer. Remind them to write their response in a complete sentence. *(L.1.1; L.1.2)*

Tip: Emphasize that the question asks only about the peanut-butter-and-jelly sandwich and help children focus on the appropriate picture details, excluding the milk and the apple.

- Read aloud the second question and the Hint. Discuss possible answers, and have children write their response in a complete sentence.
- **Have children demonstrate understanding.** Read aloud the Turn and Talk activity. Explain that Partner A can use questions from the Student Book page or class discussion, or use the question words on Student Book page 65 to ask new questions.
- Have partners switch roles. After a few minutes, invite children to share questions and answers with the class. *(SL.1.1; SL.1.2; SL.1.4)*

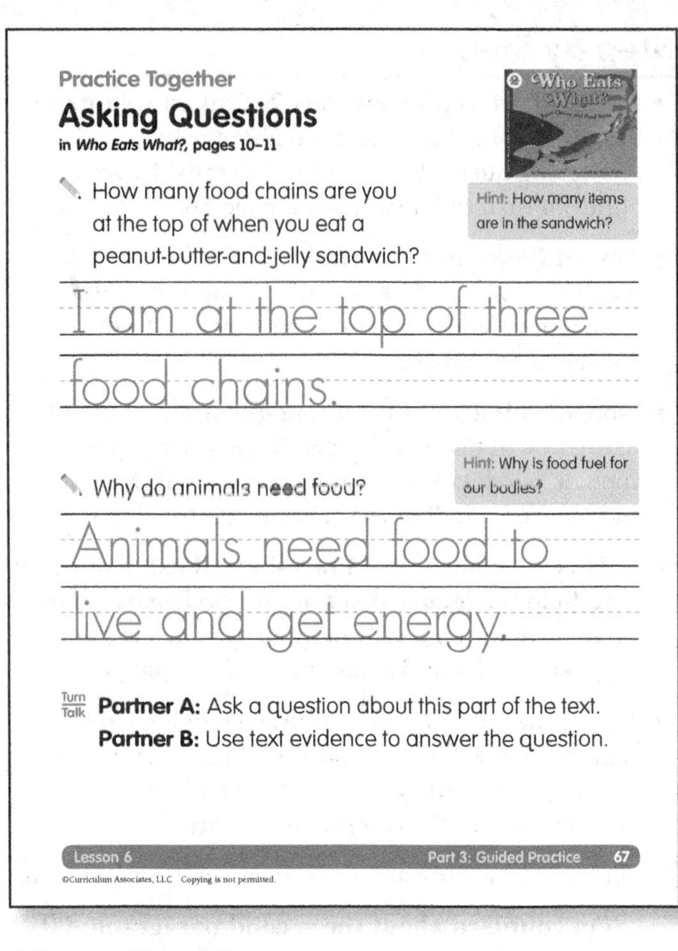

Practice Together

Asking Questions

in *Who Eats What?*, pages 10–11

How many food chains are you at the top of when you eat a peanut-butter-and-jelly sandwich?

Hint: How many items are in the sandwich?

I am at the top of three food chains.

Why do animals need food?

Hint: Why is food fuel for our bodies?

Animals need food to live and get energy.

Turn Talk **Partner A:** Ask a question about this part of the text.
Partner B: Use text evidence to answer the question.

Lesson 6 Part 3: Guided Practice 67

©Curriculum Associates, LLC Copying is not permitted.

Close Reading

- Tell children that asking questions helps readers make sense of new or confusing information.
- Read aloud the first three sentences on page 11. Then prompt children to answer with details:

  What is energy? *(It is like power. We use it to grow, move, and do things.)*

  Think about fuels like gasoline and oil. What does the author mean by saying "food is fuel"? *(Fuels like gasoline and oil give cars and houses power. Food gives us energy, or power. The author is saying that our fuel is food.)*

  To *flow* means "to move in a direction." What do the words *flow of energy* mean? (Flow of energy *means that each link in a food chain gets energy by eating another link. The energy flows from one creature to another.)*

- Discuss how asking and answering questions helps children better understand key details.

Part 4: Independent Practice

Step by Step

- **Review Parts 1–3; preview Part 4.** Discuss the term *key detail,* and have children tell how asking and answering questions helps readers understand the text. Direct children to turn to Student Book page 68.
- Tell children they will now ask and answer questions by themselves. Point out that the questions on this page, as on previous pages, ask about text details.
- **Have children ask and answer questions independently.** Display *Who Eats What?*. Tell children they will answer more questions about it.
- Ask children to listen for details that answer the question *Why are green plants important?* Then read aloud page 12. Circulate and display the illustration. Repeat, having children listen and look for details about the hawk's food chain as you read page 13.

Tip: Explain that the illustration on page 13 shows a food chain without using arrows. Discuss which type of illustration better helps readers to understand a food chain and the flow of energy.

- Use the Close Reading activity to help children look for and think about key details.
- Read aloud the first question on Student Book page 68, along with the Hint. Explain that thinking about where green plants get their energy can help children answer this question. Have children write their answers in complete sentences. *(L.1.1; L.1.2)*
- Read aloud the second question and the Hint. Explain that because there are four numbered lines, there will be four links in the hawk's food chain, starting with the hawk. Circulate and have children look at the picture before they write their answers.
- **Have children demonstrate understanding.** Have partners do the Turn and Talk activity by asking questions and finding answers about key details. Invite them to share their discussions with the class. *(SL.1.1; SL.1.2; SL.1.4)*
- **Have children reflect on their learning.** Guide children in a discussion about how asking and answering questions helps readers identify key details. Discuss how asking and answering questions about informational texts is the same as or different from asking about stories. Chart children's ideas.

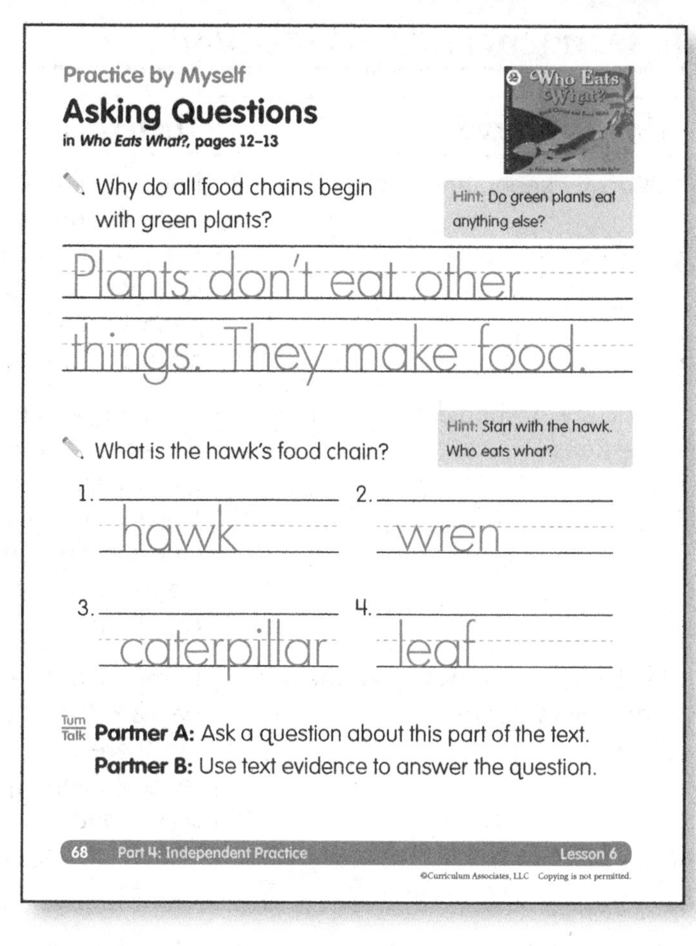
Practice by Myself

Asking Questions

in *Who Eats What?*, pages 12–13

Why do all food chains begin with green plants?

Hint: Do green plants eat anything else?

Plants don't eat other things. They make food.

What is the hawk's food chain?

Hint: Start with the hawk. Who eats what?

1. hawk
2. wren
3. caterpillar
4. leaf

Turn Talk **Partner A:** Ask a question about this part of the text.
Partner B: Use text evidence to answer the question.

68 Part 4: Independent Practice Lesson 6

©Curriculum Associates, LLC Copying is not permitted.

Close Reading

- Tell children that sometimes they need to keep reading or look back for details to answer a question. Read page 12, and think aloud:

  Wait, I don't understand. How do all animals depend on green plants if they don't eat them? I'll keep reading to look for the answer.

- Read aloud page 13, then prompt:

  What would happen to the caterpillar if it didn't have green plants to eat? *(It might die.)*

  How would that affect the wren and the hawk? *(The wren wouldn't have food and might die. Then the hawk wouldn't have food either.)*

  Think about what we read on page 12. Why do all animals depend on green plants? *(All food chains start with green plants; the food chain doesn't work without them.)*

- Discuss how reading ahead and looking back can help children find answers to questions.

Differentiated Instruction

Assessment and Remediation

If you observe . . .	Then try . . .
Difficulty generating questions	Having children make a question cue sheet. Have them trace their hands and write one question word in each finger: *What?, Where?, When?, Why?, How?* Display a detailed image from an informational text. Model asking questions about the details, beginning each question with a word from the hand. Let children take turns asking their own questions. Repeat with additional images and advance to practicing with simple text passages.
Difficulty locating details to answer questions	Providing additional practice. Display and read aloud pages 36–37 of *Butterflies and Moths.* Write questions on the board; for example: *How long does a luna moth live? Why doesn't a luna moth have a mouth? Where does the luna moth's name come from?* Explain that good readers notice important words in a question and look for those words in the text to find the answer. Help children underline the important words in each question and then locate those words in the text to find the details that answer the question.
Difficulty distinguishing key details from minor details	Comparing details in order to decide which are most important. Display pages 8–9 of *Butterflies and Moths.* Read aloud the last paragraph, and point out these sentences: "And there are weird moths, too. One feeds on the tears of sleeping animals." Ask: *Which sentence tells an exact detail? (the second one)* Repeat with other pages and details, each time discussing the reason why one detail is more important than the other.

Connect to the Anchor Standard

R1: *Read closely to determine what the text says explicitly and to make logical inferences from it; cite specific textual evidence when writing or speaking to support conclusions drawn from the text.*

Throughout the grades, Standard 1 builds toward a more advanced understaning of what it means to ask and answer questions. In later grades, readers transition from asking and answering literal questions about facts on the page to asking and answering questions that reflect inferential thinking. Furthermore, readers grow to ask themselves higher-order questions that pair close reading with metacognitive thinking: *What questions do I have about the text? What is the author telling me? What does the author want me to understand?* All the while, readers are expected to ground their answers in concrete text evidence. Use the following activities to help your students begin this transition.

- Explain that sometimes readers have to piece together details from different parts of a book in order to answer a question. Reread pages 16–19 and the bold words on page 21 of *Butterflies and Moths.* Prompt: *Why does the caterpillar need to find a safe place to turn into a pupa? (so it won't be eaten by a predator)* Point out that children had to use information from two different parts of the book to figure out the answer.
- Have children ask and answer questions to make inferences about an author's message. Display and reread pages 30–31 of *Who Eats What?* Prompt: *Why do you think the author tells this story about the kelp disappearing?* Examine together the details that show the danger of disrupting a food chain. Then ask: *What might the author be warning readers about?* Help children use the previous discussion to frame the response.

Lesson 7 (Student Book pages 69–72)

Main Topic

CCSS

RI.1.2: Identify the main topic and . . . key details of a text.

Required Read Alouds: *E (Who Eats What?); F (Butterflies and Moths)*

Lesson Objectives

- Understand that a main topic is what a text is mostly about.
- Recognize that key details are pieces of information that tell about the main topic.
- Identify the main topic and key details.
- Understand that finding the main topic and key details can help you better understand what you read.

The Learning Progression

- **Grade K:** CCSS RI.K.2 expects children to identify the main topic and retell key details of a text with prompting and support.
- **Grade 1: CCSS RI.1.2 builds on the Grade K standard by having children work more independently to identify the main topic and key details of a text.**
- **Grade 2:** CCSS RI.2.2 broadens the application of the standard by having children identify the main topic of an entire text as well as the focus of individual paragraphs within the text.

Prerequisite Skills

- Identify the main topic of a text with prompting and support.
- Identify key details of a text with prompting and support.

Tap Children's Prior Knowledge

- Remind children that information is organized in a way that makes sense to readers. Most often, details work together to describe the main topic—what the information is mostly about.
- Display the following list and read it aloud: *cats, dogs, bears, squirrels.* Ask: *What is one name we could give to tell about all the things on this list?* Invite children to give suggestions and explain their reasoning. Provide corrective feedback as needed. Then choose a name for the list, such as *Animals with Fur.*
- Guide children to see that the heading, or main topic, describes the list in a general way.
- Then explain that a key detail is an important piece of information that tells more about the main topic. Reread the animal names on the list, and ask: *How do these things tell more about the main topic? (They are examples of animals with fur.)*
- Repeat the activity with other simple lists such as classroom supplies, clothing, and seasons.
- Tell children that in this lesson, they will learn how to find the main topic and name key details in informational books.

Ready *Teacher Toolbox* Teacher-Toolbox.com

	Prerequisite Skills	RI.1.2
Ready Lessons	✓	✓
Tools for Instruction	✓	✓
Interactive Tutorials		✓

Additional CCSS

RI.1.1; SL.1.1; SL.1.2; SL.1.4; L.1.1; L.1.2 (See page A38 for full text.)

Step by Step

- **Introduce the standard.** Have children turn to page 69 in their Student Books. Read aloud the speech bubble.
- **Guide children to identify the main topic.** Have children listen as you read aloud the lines below the speech bubble and the example. Then read aloud the instructions after the first red arrow. Have children underline the words *main topic*. Explain:

  The main topic is what the text is mostly about. I'll read again and look for a sentence that tells what this whole paragraph is about.

- Reread the example, and model finding the main topic:

  I ask myself, *Is this whole paragraph about patting a dog or a cat?* Let me check the other sentences. No, I don't see patting mentioned again. So as I reread each sentence, I will ask, *Is this what the text is mostly about?*

- Continue checking each sentence. Point out how the second and third sentences are too specific—they do not tell what most of the other sentences are about.

Tip: Review the sorting and naming activity from page 79. Explain that you are looking for the sentence that would be the heading, and the other sentences would fit in the list beneath the heading.

- Identify the last sentence as the main topic, and have children underline it.
- **Guide children to identify details.** Read aloud the instructions after the second red arrow. Have children underline the word *details*. Ask:

  What does each detail in the paragraph tell about the main topic, *All pets are domestic animals?*

- Discuss responses. Point out that the first sentence asks a question about dogs and cats, which are pets. Continue discussing each detail and what it tells about pets or domestic animals.
- **Explain why readers look for the main topic and key details.** Read aloud the bottom of the page. Explain that noticing what the key details tell about helps readers recognize the main topic. Then point out that identifying both the main topic and key details helps readers understand the important ideas in a text.

Listen and Learn

Main Topic

The **main topic** is what a text is mostly about. The **key details** in the text tell more about the main topic.

Look carefully at this example. Then follow the instructions below:

Have you ever patted a dog or a cat? Dogs and cats are domestic animals. Domestic animals depend on people for food, water, and shelter. All pets are domestic animals.

- To find the main topic, look for a sentence that tells what the text is mostly about.
- Look for the details. What information tells more about the main topic?

Think about what most of the details describe. This will help you find the main topic of a text.

- Share an example of how naming the main topic and key details helped you better understand a text, such as an informational text about sharks. Think aloud:

  I read a lot of details about sharks' teeth, their coloring, and their skeletons. It was hard to keep track of the details.

  Then I read, "These features make sharks deadly predators." I realized that was the main topic!

  Now I see that teeth, coloring, and skeleton are all features that make sharks deadly predators. Knowing the main topic helped me make sense of all the different details.

- **Have children demonstrate understanding.** Call on individuals to share what they have learned so far about finding the main topic and key details in a text. Encourage them to describe how key details should tell more about the main topic.

Step by Step

- **Review Part 1; preview Part 2.** Ask volunteers to share strategies they learned to identify the main topic and key details in a text. Have children turn to Student Book page 70.
- **Revisit *Who Eats What?*** Have children briefly summarize the book, using the chart created for the Book Review on Teacher Resource Book page 65.
- **Model identifying the main topic and key details.** Explain that you will model finding the main topic and key details. Read aloud pages 4–6 of *Who Eats What?* Then think aloud:

  I ask myself, *What is the text mostly about? What do the details describe?* Each sentence on pages 4 and 5 tells what a different animal eats, but those details are very similar. Then page 6 says that the leaf, caterpillar, wren, and hawk are all linked because "together they form a food chain." I think that connection is the main topic of these pages.

Tip: Point out that the main topic is not always a single sentence, or even in the same paragraph. Write the sentences from pages 4–6 on slips of paper. Together, sort them into main topic and key details. Discuss that more than one sentence states the topic.

- Use the Close Reading activity to help children practice adding up details in order to identify the main topic.
- Read aloud the first Student Book page activity and the Hint. Determine the main topic and model how to underline it. Then read aloud the second activity and Hint. Emphasize that it asks for a detail from the book in addition to the ones listed above it in the Student Book.
- **Model writing your response.** Model writing your response in a complete sentence. Have children write their own response. *(RI.1.1; L.1.1; L.1.2)*
- **Have children demonstrate understanding.** Have partners complete the Turn and Talk activity. Prompt children to recall text and picture evidence about what happens in the food chain. Have volunteers share the topic they named. Discuss the details children found that tell about the topic. *(SL.1.1; SL.1.2; SL.1.4)*

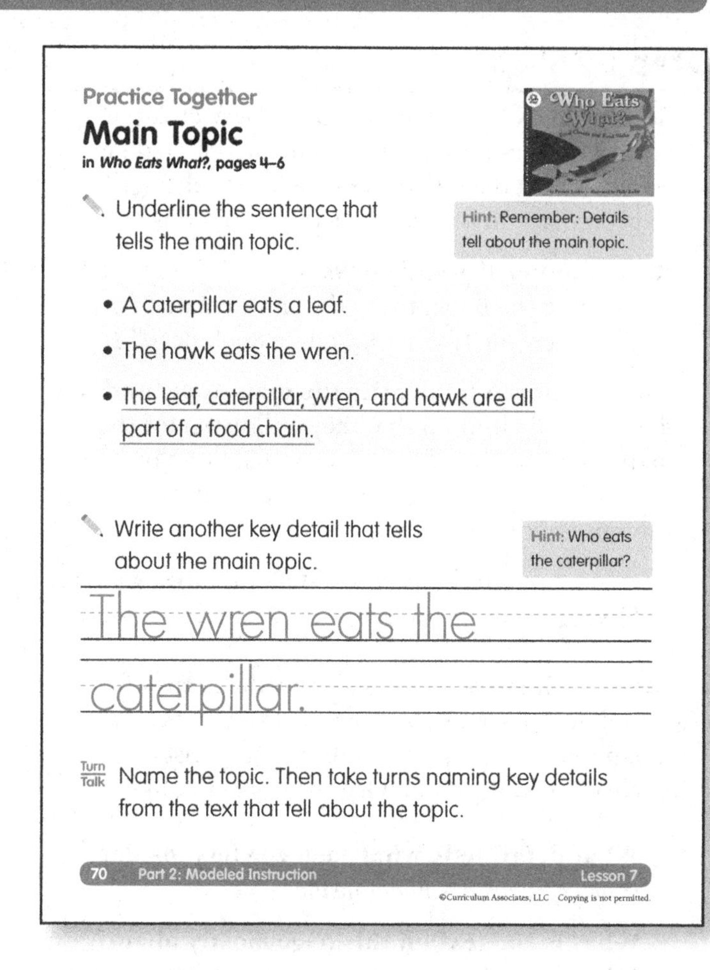
Practice Together

Main Topic

in *Who Eats What?*, pages 4–6

Underline the sentence that tells the main topic.

Hint: Remember: Details tell about the main topic.

- A caterpillar eats a leaf.
- The hawk eats the wren.
- The leaf, caterpillar, wren, and hawk are all part of a food chain.

Write another key detail that tells about the main topic.

Hint: Who eats the caterpillar?

The wren eats the caterpillar.

Turn Talk Name the topic. Then take turns naming key details from the text that tell about the topic.

70 Part 2: Modeled Instruction Lesson 7

©Curriculum Associates, LLC Copying is not permitted.

Close Reading

- Explain that thinking about how the details fit together can help readers figure out the main topic. Point to the pictures and discuss each detail as you reread pages 4–6 of *Who Eats What?* Prompt:

  (page 4) **What do the text and picture details show about the caterpillar and the leaf?** *(The caterpillar eats the leaf.)*

  (page 5) **What do the details tell about the caterpillar and the wren?** *(Later the wren eats the caterpillar.)*

  What do the details tell about the wren and the hawk? *(Still later the hawk eats the wren.)*

  (page 6) **Let's put the details together: the caterpillar eats the leaf; the wren eats the caterpillar; the hawk eats the wren. What main topic do all these details tell about?** *(The leaf, caterpillar, wren, and hawk are all linked in a food chain.)*

Part 3: Guided Practice

Step by Step

- **Review Parts 1–2; preview Part 3.** Have children recall strategies for identifying a main topic and key details. Direct them to turn to Student Book page 71. Explain that you will guide them through this page.
- **Revisit *Butterflies and Moths*.** Have children briefly summarize the book, using the chart created for the Book Review on Teacher Resource Book page 71.
- **Guide children to identify the main topic and key details.** Tell children that they will listen for the main topic and key details as you read this part of the book. Read aloud page 10 of *Butterflies and Moths.* Prompt children:

  What detail tells about what shapes the eggs are? *(An egg can be shaped like a ball, a barrel, or a saucer.)*

Tip: If children are unfamiliar with the shape of a barrel or a saucer, draw a simple sketch of each. Explain that the author uses these comparisons to help readers understand what the eggs look like.

  What detail tells what each egg has inside? *(Each egg has a tiny dot inside.)*

  What is the text on this page mostly about? *(The life of a butterfly or a moth begins with an egg.)*

- **Guide children to write responses.** Read aloud the first activity and the Hint. Have children identify the main topic by finding the sentence that the details, or other sentences, tell more about. Have children underline the main topic.
- Read aloud the second activity and the Hint. Explain that the question asks for a detail from the book that is different from the ones listed above it in the Student Book. Discuss the answer, and have children write it in a complete sentence. *(RI.1.1; L.1.1; L.1.2)*
- Use the Close Reading activity to help children distinguish the main topic from details, and to help prepare them for the Turn and Talk activity.
- **Have children demonstrate understanding.** Have partners complete the Turn and Talk activity. Remind children to use evidence from the Close Reading activity to explain what each detail describes. Invite volunteers to share their evidence. *(SL.1.1; SL.1.2; SL.1.4)*

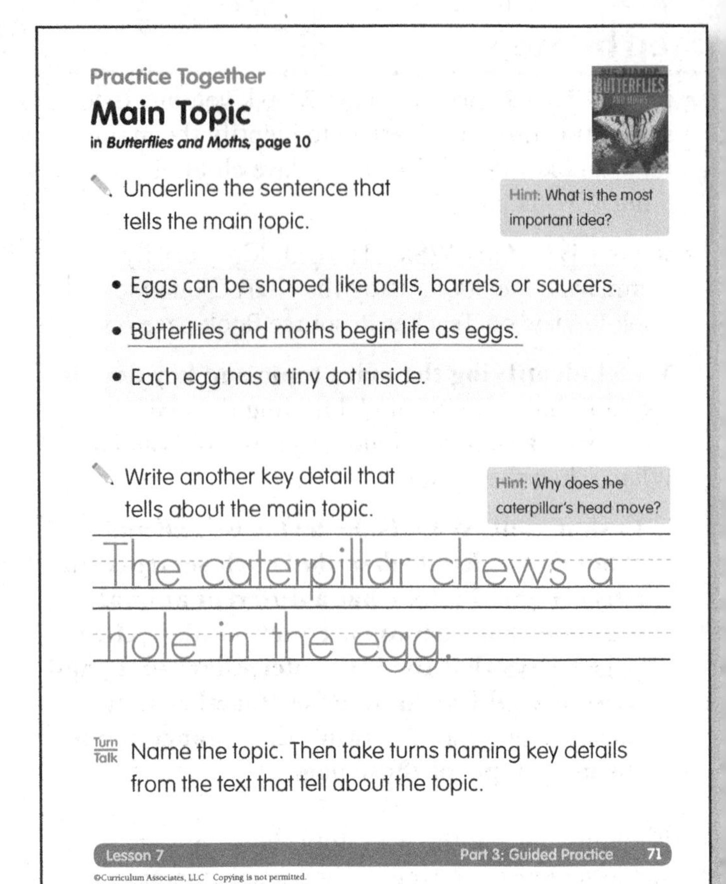
Practice Together

Main Topic

in *Butterflies and Moths*, page 10

Underline the sentence that tells the main topic.

Hint: What is the most important idea?

- Eggs can be shaped like balls, barrels, or saucers.
- Butterflies and moths begin life as eggs.
- Each egg has a tiny dot inside.

Write another key detail that tells about the main topic.

Hint: Why does the caterpillar's head move?

The caterpillar chews a hole in the egg.

Turn Talk Name the topic. Then take turns naming key details from the text that tell about the topic.

Lesson 7 Part 3: Guided Practice 71

©Curriculum Associates, LLC Copying is not permitted.

Close Reading

- Explain that sometimes main topics and details are combined in the same sentence.
- On page 10 of *Butterflies and Moths,* reread the first sentence up to the word *egg.* Then prompt:

  What does this part of the sentence tell you? *(The life of a butterfly or moth begins as an egg.)*

- Read the rest of the first sentence, beginning with the word *no.* Then prompt:

  What does this part of the sentence tell you? *(An egg is smaller than a grain of sand.)*

  Does one of these ideas tell the main topic of the whole paragraph? *(yes)*

  Which one? *(A butterfly or moth begins life as an egg.)*

- Review that you need to read the entire paragraph to figure out which part of the first sentence tells the main topic and which part is a detail.

Part 4: Independent Practice

Step by Step

- **Review Parts 1–3; preview Part 4.** Invite a volunteer to tell why it is important to identify the main topic and key details in a text. Then direct children to Student Book page 72.
- Explain that children will now find the main topic and a key detail by themselves. Point out that, as on previous pages, they will underline a main topic and then write a key detail about it.
- **Have children identify a main topic and key details independently.** Display *Butterflies and Moths* and tell children they will find the main topic and key details in another part of the book.
- Use the Close Reading activity to help children identify the main topic and details in the text.
- Read aloud the first activity and the Hint on the Student Book page. Have children find and underline the main topic.
- Read aloud the second activity and the Hint. Remind children that the question asks for a detail that is different from the ones listed above it in the Student Book. Have them write their answer in a complete sentence. *(RI.1.1; L.1.1; L.1.2)*

Tip: Point out that sometimes one sentence can contain two details. Reread the second sentence on page 18. Ask children what two details are in the sentence. *(look like bird poop; vomit green juice)*

- Discuss responses to the first and second activities.
- **Have children demonstrate understanding.** Have partners complete the Turn and Talk activity. If partners need support with naming key details, prompt them:

  Name three things caterpillars do that make them too yucky for birds to eat. *(They vomit green juice, sting with hairs, and use poisons in their bodies.)*

- Invite children to share their evidence in class discussion. *(SL.1.1; SL.1.2; SL.1.4)*
- **Have children reflect on their learning.** Guide children in a discussion about why finding the main topic and key details helps them better understand what they read. Chart their ideas.

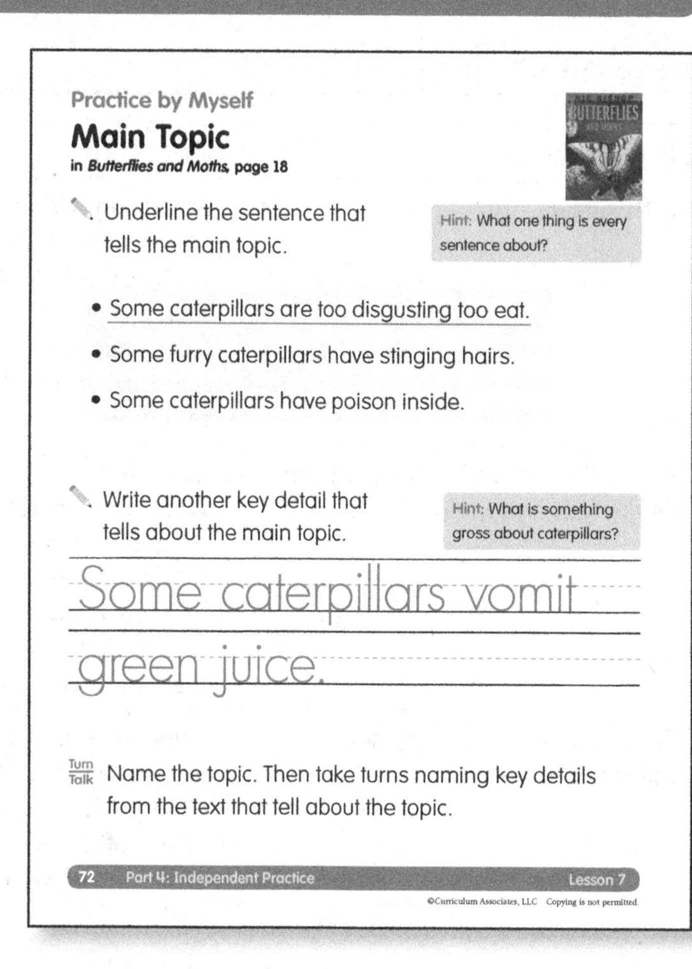
Practice by Myself

Main Topic

in *Butterflies and Moths*, page 18

Underline the sentence that tells the main topic.

Hint: What one thing is every sentence about?

- Some caterpillars are too disgusting too eat.
- Some furry caterpillars have stinging hairs.
- Some caterpillars have poison inside.

Write another key detail that tells about the main topic.

Hint: What is something gross about caterpillars?

Some caterpillars vomit green juice.

Turn Talk Name the topic. Then take turns naming key details from the text that tell about the topic.

72 Part 4: Independent Practice Lesson 7

Close Reading

- Remind children that the main topic is what a text is mostly about, and that readers can think about how details fit together to identify the topic.
- Read aloud the first paragraph on page 18 of *Butterflies and Moths.* Discuss each sentence, prompting:

  What does this detail tell you?

- Guide children to connect the details. Prompt:

  What do all of the details tell about? *(They all tell about caterpillars that are bad to eat.)*

- Reread the paragraph. Have children raise their hands when they hear a sentence that tells what the details are mostly about. *("A few caterpillars seem too disgusting to eat.")*
- Discuss how thinking about how the details fit together helped children figure out the main topic.

Differentiated Instruction

Assessment and Remediation

If you observe . . .	Then try . . .
Difficulty identifying the main topic	Practicing with created text. Write a simple summary of *Butterflies and Moths*, page 25. Include the topic sentence *Wings are amazing*, and details such as the following: *They are light but strong. They are covered in colorful scales. They have all different patterns and colors.* Read the summary aloud. Have children ask and answer the question *Which sentence tells what the text is mostly about?* Then revisit each remaining sentence to confirm whether it tells more about the topic.
Difficulty discriminating between key details and the main topic	Modeling with sentence strips. Write the sentences from page 8 of *Who Eats What?* on separate strips. Explain that you want to arrange the strips with the topic on top and the details below. Place the strips in random order, and model asking questions to decide if the placement is correct: *Does this sentence tell what all the sentences are mostly about?* Guide children to try new arrangements and ask questions about them until they determine the main topic and key details. Repeat with the sentences from page 9.
Difficulty adding up key details to identify the main topic	Using an animal riddle. Draw a word web on the board. One at a time, say and write the following clues in the outer circles: *gray, huge, tusks, trunk.* Tell children to raise a hand when they know the animal. Write *elephant* in the center of the web. Explain that the clues are details that tell about the main topic—an elephant.

Connect to the Anchor Standard

R2: Determine central ideas or themes of a text and analyze their development; summarize the key supporting details and ideas.

Throughout the grades, Standard 2 leads student from simply identifying the main topic and key details to understanding how multiple topics are interwoven in a text and how details support the important ideas. As readers transition to a more in-depth analysis, they will ask questions such as: *How do the main ideas and details of each section fit into the main idea of the entire text? How can I summarize the text so the main ideas and details are clear?* Use the following activities to help your students begin this transition.

- Explain that sometimes an author doesn't tell the reader a main topic. The reader has to add up the details to figure it out on their own. Read aloud page 40 of *Butterflies and Moths.* Ask children to tell details from the page. List them on chart paper. Reread the list and ask children what all the details tell about. Guide them to see that all the details tell about ways butterflies stay safe from predators. Have children restate this main topic in their own words. *(SL.1.1; SL.1.2; SL.1.4)*
- Guide children to trace a main topic across passages in a text in order to summarize text. Read aloud pages 11, 14, and 21–22 of *Butterflies and Moths.* Point out the main topic of these passages. *(A caterpillar hatches and grows up.)* Ask children what details tell how a caterpillar grows up. Then ask children to tell in their own words how a caterpillar becomes a butterfly.

Read Aloud Lesson G (Student Book pages 27–30)

Elizabeth Leads the Way

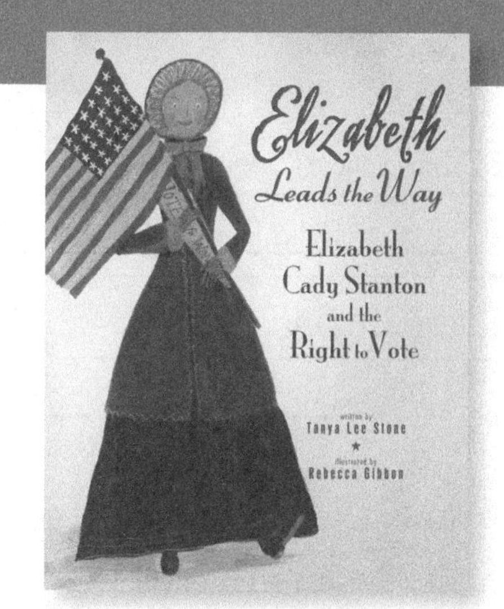

Lesson Objectives

You will read aloud *Elizabeth Leads the Way,* which children will revisit in later lessons. Children will:

- Identify the main topic of a text and sections within it.
- Ask and answer questions about key details.
- Identify how the information in the text is organized.

About the Text

Summary

This book describes the life of Elizabeth Cady Stanton, who changed American history by insisting that women should have the same rights as men. When Elizabeth bravely spoke out, she led the way for all women.

Informational Text: Biography

- Explain that a biography is a text that tells about the life of a real person, including where and when they lived and important things they did.
- Tell children that biographies are usually organized like a story. Most follow a familiar narrative structure and center around a main problem and solution.

Critical Vocabulary

- Prior to reading, briefly define the following words:

  vote (p. 5) a choice for a leader or a law

  rights (p. 5) things people are allowed to do

  waver (p. 25) to change ideas or opinions a lot; to go back and forth between one or more choices

  declaration (p. 27) an important statement or announcement

- As you read, pause to point to the words as you encounter them, and review their definitions.

Word Bank

- To support children in writing about the text, display a word bank containing the Critical Vocabulary.
- Add other important words from the text, such as *laws* and *allowed,* on subsequent readings.

New Concepts: Women's Rights

- Explain to children that women have not always had the same rights as men. Give examples, such as how women could not own land or homes and were not allowed to vote in order to make or change laws.
- As you read the book, have children listen for ways Elizabeth Cady Stanton fought for women's rights.

Ready *Teacher Toolbox* Teacher-Toolbox.com

	Prerequisite Skills	*RI.1.2*
Ready Lessons		✓
Tools for Instruction	✓ ✓	✓
Interactive Tutorials	✓	

CCSS Focus

RI.1.2 . . . *retell key details of a text.*

ADDITIONAL STANDARDS: ***RI.1.1; RI.1.3; RI.1.7; RF.1.3.f, g; W.1.3; SL.1.1; SL.1.2; SL.1.4; SL.1.5; L.1.1.h; L.1.2; L.1.4.a; L.1.5.c***
(See page A38 for full text.)

PART 1: First Read

Step by Step

- **Introduce and explore *Elizabeth Leads the Way*.** Read aloud the title and the names of the author, Tanya Lee Stone, and the illustrator, Rebecca Gibbon.
- Display the book. Ask children to think about the title and then identify the woman on the cover. *(Elizabeth Cady Stanton)* Think aloud:

  I notice that she is dressed differently than we dress nowadays, so I think Elizabeth must have lived a long time ago. I also see that she is holding an American flag and smiling. I wonder why? The title says she "leads the way." Maybe she does something important for the country.

- Turn the pages slowly and have children point out things they notice in the illustrations. Also point out the large, colored words on pages 9 and 22. Finally, pause on pages 30–31 and think aloud:

  This looks like a map of the United States. This reminds me of Elizabeth holding the American flag on the cover. I wonder if Elizabeth does something that makes a big difference.

- **Read aloud *Elizabeth Leads the Way*.** Remind children that even though this is an informational text, it is told like a story, so they should listen for Elizabeth's problem and solution. As you read, pause to define challenging vocabulary.
- **Guide a review of the text.** Direct children to turn to Student Book page 27. Read aloud the first item, and invite volunteers to offer ways to complete the sentence, based on what they heard during reading. Have children record their answers. *(RI.1.2)*
- Read aloud the second item, and help children recall the features you found together. Display the book for review. Have children record their answers.
- Read aloud the Turn and Talk activity, and ask children to tell which facts will help them remember what Elizabeth did and why. Invite children to share their ideas. *(SL.1.1)*
- Ask children if they have any additional questions about Elizabeth after reading the text, such as *What other women's rights did Elizabeth fight for?* or *What did she achieve in her lifetime?* Discuss where you might look to find the answers to these questions. Use the Author Note on page 32 as needed.

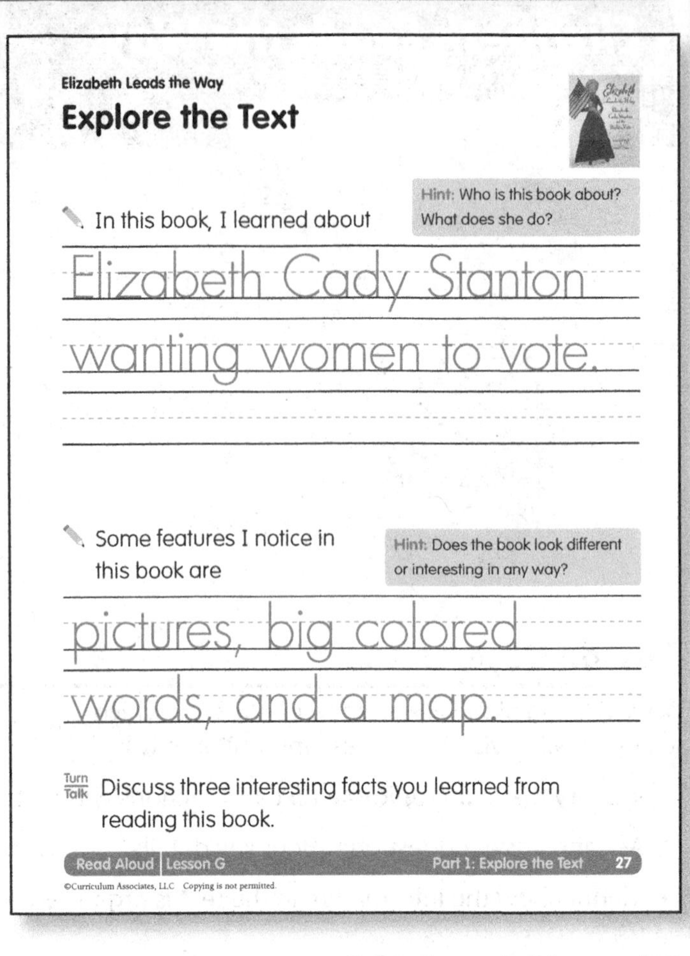
Elizabeth Leads the Way

Explore the Text

In this book, I learned about — Hint: Who is this book about? What does she do?

Elizabeth Cady Stanton wanting women to vote.

Some features I notice in this book are — Hint: Does the book look different or interesting in any way?

pictures, big colored words, and a map.

Turn Talk: Discuss three interesting facts you learned from reading this book.

Read Aloud | Lesson G — Part 1: Explore the Text — 27

ELL Support: could/should/would

- Display the following words: *could, should, would.* Read them aloud slowly, pointing to each word. Have children repeat the words after you.
- Display the following sentence frame: *I ______ catch the ball.* Write *could* in the blank and read the sentence aloud. Explain that the sentence tells what someone can do.
- Repeat with *should.* Explain that we use *should* when we think something needs to be done; for example, *I should hit the ball to help my team win.*
- Repeat with *would.* Explain that we use *would* when we talk about someone's wishes or choices; for example, *I would hit the ball if I wanted to.*
- Turn to page 9 of *Elizabeth Leads the Way.* Use *could, should,* and *would* to replace the words in the second, third, and last sentence. Discuss how the meaning of each sentence changes. Have children practice with their own sentences.

PART 2: Reread for Meaning

Step by Step

- **Reread to learn how Elizabeth grew up.** Ask children to listen and look for details about Elizabeth's life as a child and young adult. Instruct them to listen closely as you reread pages 5–13.

Tip: Help children find Elizabeth in each illustration before reading each set of pages aloud. Ask: *How old is Elizabeth here? What is she doing? What does her expression show that she feels?*

- **Have children identify key details.** Use questions such as these to guide discussion. *(RI.1.1; SL.1.1; SL.1.2)*

  Page 7: What does Elizabeth hear when she is four years old? *(A woman says life is better for boys.)*

  Page 9: Why does Elizabeth decide to show that she can do anything a boy can do? *(She is angry that women are not treated the same as men.)*

  Page 12: Why can't Elizabeth go to college to study? *(Colleges would not let girls in.)*

- **Guide children to demonstrate understanding.** Direct children to turn to Student Book page 28. Read each prompt aloud, along with the Hint. Revisit pages 7–9 as needed to help children recall the details to answer each question. Have children write their answers in complete sentences. *(L.1.1; L.1.2)*
- Use the Close Reading activity to help children use text features to find key details about Elizabeth.

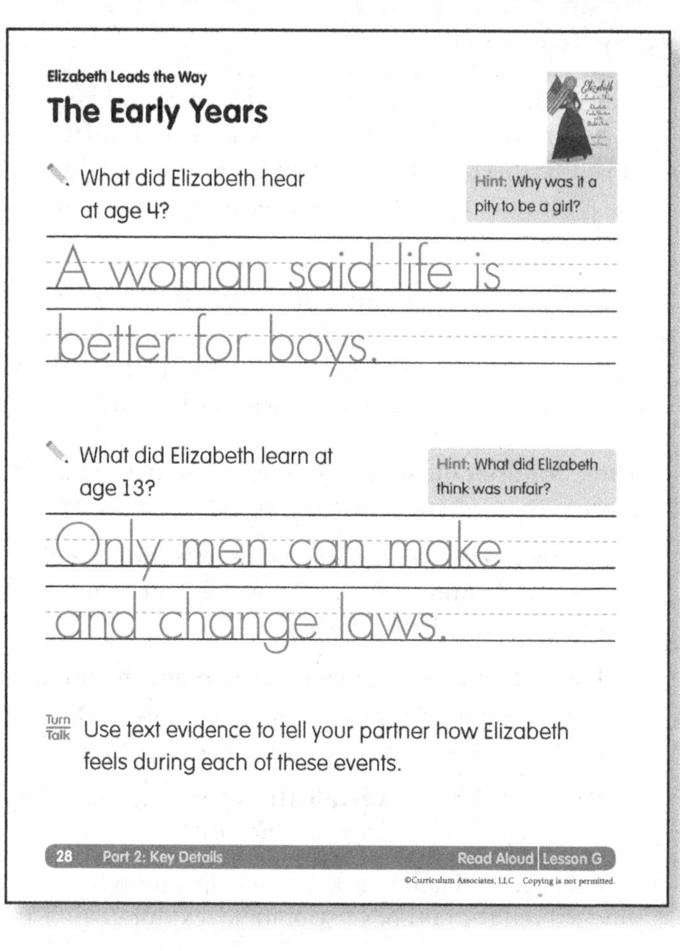
Elizabeth Leads the Way

The Early Years

What did Elizabeth hear at age 4?

Hint: Why was it a pity to be a girl?

A woman said life is better for boys.

What did Elizabeth learn at age 13?

Hint: What did Elizabeth think was unfair?

Only men can make and change laws.

Turn Talk Use text evidence to tell your partner how Elizabeth feels during each of these events.

28 Part 2: Key Details Read Aloud | Lesson G

©Curriculum Associates, LLC Copying is not permitted.

- **Have children discuss text evidence.** Read aloud the Turn and Talk activity. Suggest that children look at the illustrations and think about how they would feel if they were Elizabeth. Invite volunteers to share their ideas. *(SL.1.4)*

Tier Two Vocabulary: *matter*

- Display the second sentence on page 5. Underline the word *matter* and read it aloud. Have children repeat it after you.
- Ask children if they have ever heard this word used in a different way, such as *It doesn't matter if I wear my blue or black shorts today.* Have them tell what they think it means.
- Together, discuss that *matter* means "being important; to have meaning." Use it in a sentence, such as, *Being kind to others matters to me.*
- Have children tell about what matters to Elizabeth. Then have them share things that matter to each of them. *(L.1.4.a; L.1.5.c)*

Close Reading

- Help children use text features and illustrations to discuss Elizabeth's feelings. Display and read aloud page 9, including the word "Preposterous!" Then prompt:

  Who is saying the word *Preposterous!* and how do you know? *(Elizabeth. The word looks like it is coming out of her mouth)*

  How does the author describe Elizabeth's feelings? *(She says Elizabeth is "horrified.")*

  What do both of these details help you understand about Elizabeth? *(that Elizabeth is very upset; They tell why she decided she could do anything a boy could do.) (RI.1.7)*

PART 3: Reread for Meaning

Step by Step

- **Reread to learn about Elizabeth's idea.** Explain that children will listen and look for details about how Elizabeth begins her fight for women's right to vote. Instruct them to listen closely as you reread pages 14–23.

Tip: Provide background knowledge on slavery in the United States. Help children connect women's rights with the idea of rights for all people in order to help them understand why Elizabeth admired Henry.

- **Have children identify key details.** Use questions such as these to guide discussion. *(RI.1.1; SL.1.1; SL.1.2)*

  Pages 18–19: What does Elizabeth find out at Lucretia's lunch? *(Other women feel the same way that she does about women's rights.)*

  Pages 21-22: How does Elizabeth get the idea that women should vote? *(She remembers that you need to be able to vote to change laws.)*

  Page 23: Why do Elizabeth's friends gasp? *(They are shocked by her huge, daring idea.)*

- Use the Close Reading activity to help children understand the author's use of italic text for emphasis.
- **Guide children to demonstrate understanding.** Direct children to turn to Student Book page 29. Read each item and Hint aloud. Help children respond with complete sentences. *(L.1.1; L.1.2)*

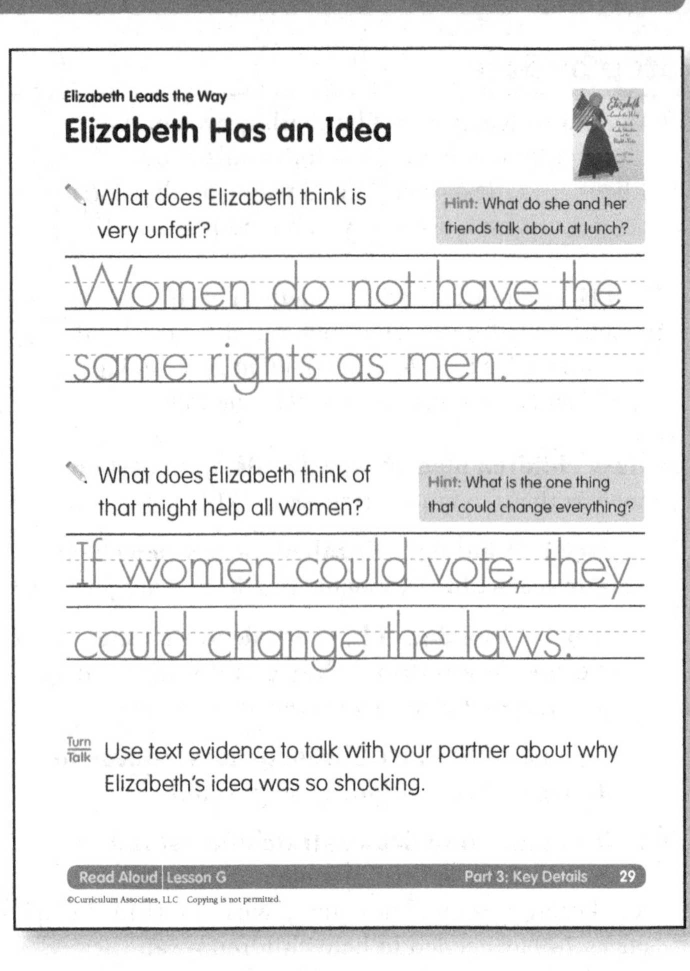
Elizabeth Leads the Way

Elizabeth Has an Idea

What does Elizabeth think is very unfair?

Hint: What do she and her friends talk about at lunch?

Women do not have the same rights as men.

What does Elizabeth think of that might help all women?

Hint: What is the one thing that could change everything?

If women could vote, they could change the laws.

Turn Talk Use text evidence to talk with your partner about why Elizabeth's idea was so shocking.

Read Aloud | Lesson G Part 3: Key Details 29

- **Have children discuss text evidence.** Read aloud the Turn and Talk activity. Help children recall details about women's rights from the first part of the book to support their ideas. Invite volunteers to share their ideas. *(SL.1.4)*

Tier Two Vocabulary: *proposed*

- Display the second sentence on page 19. Underline the word *proposed* and read it aloud. Have children repeat it after you.
- Ask children if they have ever heard *propose* used in another way, such as *I propose that we have pizza for dinner*, or *I propose going to the park instead of the pool.* Have children tell what they think it means.
- Together, discuss that *propose* means "to tell an idea." Use it in a sentence, such as, *I propose that we have three-day weekends.*
- Have children propose things they would like to do during or after school. *(L.1.4.a; L.1.5.c)*

Close Reading

- Help children understand how italic words, or words with letters that lean forward, can help readers notice something important.
- Circulate and show page 22. Point to the italic words as you walk around. Then read the first sentence, emphasizing *one* and *every*. Prompt:

  Why did I read *one* and *every* a little louder, with more emphasis? *(they look different)*

  What do these words help us understand? *(They show how important her idea is; They show how big of a difference her idea could make.)*

- Repeat for the italic words on pages 15, 17, and 20.

 PART 4: Reread for Meaning

Step by Step

- **Reread to learn how Elizabeth changes America.** Tell children to listen closely and look for details about Elizabeth's speech and the fight for women's right to vote. Reread pages 24–31 aloud.
- **Have children identify key details.** Use questions such as these to guide discussion. *(RI.1.1; SL.1.1; SL.1.2)*

  Page 27: What idea does the Declaration of Rights and Sentiments challenge? *(that only men are created equal)*

  Pages 28–29: Why are people arguing after the speech? *(They do not all agree with Elizabeth.)*

  Pages 30–31: How do we know Elizabeth changed America? *(She was the first to argue that women should have the right to vote. They do now.)*

Tip: Display the map on pages 30–31. Discuss the image of a stone tossed in water and how it helps readers understand how Elizabeth's idea spread.

- **Guide children to demonstrate understanding.** Direct children to turn to Student Book page 30. Read aloud each prompt and the Hint. Remind children to write in complete sentences. *(L.1.1; L.1.2)*
- **Have children discuss text evidence.** Read aloud the Turn and Talk activity. Encourage children to explain why they chose each detail. Invite volunteers to share their drawings. *(SL.1.4, SL.1.5)*

Elizabeth Leads the Way

Elizabeth Makes a Change

Draw a picture of Elizabeth making her famous speech.

Children should draw Elizabeth reading a speech in front of many people.

Write what is happening in your picture.

Elizabeth is standing up for women's rights.

Turn Talk Describe your picture to your partner. Support the details with evidence from the book.

30 Part 4: Key Details Read Aloud | Lesson G

- **Review *Elizabeth Leads the Way.*** Use the prompts in the Book Review to revisit and record the topic and key details. Have children refer to their Student Book pages to recall ideas. *(RI.1.2)*

Integrating Foundational Skills

Use these activities to integrate foundational skills into your reading of *Elizabeth Leads the Way.*

1. Display and read these words together: *jump, work, learn, wash, cook.* Add *-s, -ing,* and *-ed* to each word, one at a time. Have children read each new word. Then display the words *talked, meeting, looks, filled, leads, gasped, mending, waited,* and *fills.* Have children identify each ending and read the word aloud, with and without the ending. *(RF.1.3.f)*
2. Display the irregularly spelled words *one, your, come, do, was, again, could, from, have, should, were,* and *would.* Have children read them aloud. Ask children to use each word in a sentence. *(RF.1.3.g)*

Book Review

- As children review key details from *Elizabeth Leads the Way,* record their answers on chart paper. Keep the chart on hand for revisiting later.

  What makes Elizabeth decide to show she can do anything a boy can do? *(She learns that many laws are unfair to women and that women cannot vote to change them.)*

  Why is Elizabeth's idea to have women vote so shocking? *(because people were used to women not making laws)*

  Why does Elizabeth give a speech at Seneca Falls? *(to tell others that women are equal to men and should have the same rights as men)*

Writing Activity

Write a Narrative *(W.1.3)*

- Have children write a narrative from the point of view of Elizabeth's father telling about some of the events of Elizabeth's life. Reread pages 8–13 as needed to help children recall details about Elizabeth's father and his feelings. Help children recall that Elizabeth's father was proud of her but that he also worried about her.
- Before children begin, explain that their narratives should include two or more events in correct order. Remind them to include important details about each event and to close their narratives with a final thought or idea. Have children work in pairs to brainstorm events such as the conversation about the woman who would lose her farm (pages 8–9) or Elizabeth going off to school instead of getting married (pages 12–13).
- List some words that children might use to describe the sequence of events, such as *then, next,* or *soon.*
- Invite children to share their narratives with the class.

Speaking and Listening Activity

Have a Discussion *(SL.1.1)*

- Have children take part in a collaborative discussion about classroom rules.
- Remind children that Elizabeth Cady Stanton and Henry Stanton wanted laws to be fair. Explain that children can think about how to make classroom rules fair for everyone, too.
- Form small groups of children. Help each group decide on three rules they think would make things fair. Provide an example such as this: *We will take turns in alphabetical order feeding the classroom fish.* Record ideas on chart paper to help children remember.
- Have children share their ideas with the group. Remind them to listen carefully, take turns to speak, and stay on topic.
- Have children ask questions if they do not understand something that is said. Also remind them not to simply recite their own points but to respond to the comments of others as well.
- After the discussion, have children take a vote on the three most important rules that help make things fair. Post the results of the vote in the classroom.

Language Activity

Determiners *(L.1.1.h)*

- Help children practice identifying and using determiners in sentences.
- Display these words, and help children read them: *the, a, an, this, that.* Explain that we use these words to tell "which one." Then display and read aloud this sentence: *Elizabeth read a speech.*
- Write *the, an, this,* and *that* on stick-on notes. Distribute the notes and have children use them to replace the word *a.*
- After each replacement, discuss how the meaning of the sentence changes. For example, explain: A speech *could be any speech Elizabeth read.* The speech *means I am telling about one special speech.*
- Display these words, and help children read them: *some, any.* Explain that we use these words to tell "how many." Then display and read aloud this sentence: *Some of Elizabeth's friends helped her write the speech.*
- Point to *Some.* Ask: *How many of Elizabeth's friends helped her?* Guide children to see that not all, but *some* of her friends helped. Then change *Some* to *Not any.* Discuss the change in meaning. *("Not any" means that none of her friends helped.)*

Lesson 8 (Student Book pages 73–76)

Describing Connections

CCSS

RI.1.3: Describe the connection between two individuals, events, ideas, or pieces of information in a text.

Required Read Alouds: F *(Butterflies and Moths)*; G *(Elizabeth Leads the Way)*

Lesson Objectives

- Identify text clues that signal sequence, cause and effect, and other types of connections.
- Explain how ideas and events in a text are connected.
- Recognize how describing connections between text events and ideas helps readers understand and remember key details.

The Learning Progression

- **Grade K:** CCSS RI.K.3 requires children, with prompting and support, to tell how two specific pieces of information are connected in a text.
- **Grade 1: CCSS RI.1.3 builds on the Grade K standard by having children work more independently to identify and describe the connections between two pieces of information in a text.**
- **Grade 2:** CCSS RI.2.3 expands the scope of the standard by expecting children to identify connections among a series of more complex ideas, such as historical events, scientific concepts, and steps in a procedure.

Prerequisite Skills

- Describe the connection between two individuals, events, ideas, or pieces of information, with prompting and support.
- Order events in the correct sequence.
- Identify cause and effect in pairs of events

Tap Children's Prior Knowledge

- Remind children that an event is something that happens. Display the heading *Events in Order,* along with the words *First, Next,* and *Last* on separate lines. Have children name events that happened at school today. Write an event beside each word.
- Explain that *first, next,* and *last* show that these events happened in a certain order. Ask: *Would this make sense if [event 3] happened before [event 1]? (no)* Explain that some events have to happen in a certain order to make sense; other events can happen in any order.
- Then tell children that some events happen in order because one event causes another event to occur. Display the chart headings *Cause* and *Effect.*
- Flip the light switch. Ask what happened. *(It got darker.)* Then ask why. *(You turned off the lights.)* Explain that what happened is the effect, and why it happened is the cause. Record the events beneath the appropriate headings.
- Point to the chart and describe what happened: *I turned off the lights, so it got darker. It got darker because I turned off the lights.* Explain that the words *so* and *because* signal a cause-and-effect connection.
- Tell children that in this lesson, they will look for time-order and cause-and-effect connections between the events and ideas in texts they have read.

Ready Teacher Toolbox Teacher-Toolbox.com

	Prerequisite Skills	*RI.1.3*
Ready Lessons	✓	✓
Tools for Instruction		✓✓
Interactive Tutorials		✓✓

Additional CCSS

RI.1.1; RI.1.2; RI.1.7; SL.1.1; SL.1.2; L.1.1; L.1.2 (See page A38 for full text.)

Part 1: Introduction

Step by Step

- **Introduce the standard.** Have children turn to page 73 in their Student Books. Read aloud the speech bubble. Remind children that they already know about two kinds of connections: time-order and cause-and-effect.
- **Explore types of connections.** Read the line below the speech bubble. Point out that each red arrow points to a kind of connection, and that there are examples in the yellow boxes below.
- Read aloud the first description. Have children underline the words *time order.* Then read aloud the examples and explain:

  This tells about changes in nature from one season to the next. Seasons happen in time order: *First, new leaves grow in spring. Next, flowers bloom in summer.*
- Discuss whether the order of these events can change and why. *(no, because the order of the seasons can't change)* Have children give examples of other things that happen in time order. For each example, discuss whether the order can change, and why or why not.
- Read aloud the second description, and have children underline *causes*. Review the terms *cause* and *effect*. Then read the examples and ask children to identify the cause and effect. Restate: *It rained a lot, so the rivers rose and flooded. The rivers rose and flooded because it rained a lot.*

Tip: Explain that some events can be connected by both time order *and* cause and effect. Reread the second example. Ask which event happened first and which happened next. Then ask which is the cause and which is the effect.

- Point out the clue words that signal connections:

  ***First* and *next* are clue words about time order. *So* and *because* are clue words about cause and effect. Authors sometimes use clue words to show how they connect events and ideas.**

  If there are no clue words, you have to think about the details provided to figure out the connections. Then you can use clue words on your own to describe the connection.

Listen and Learn

Describing Connections

To **connect** means to fit together. Events and ideas in informational text can connect in different ways.

Here are two kinds of connections:

- Events follow each other in time order:
  1. New leaves grow in spring.
  2. Flowers bloom in summer.
- One event or idea causes another:
  1. A lot of rain falls at once.
  2. Rivers rise and flood.

Describing connections between events and ideas helps you understand and remember key details.

Lesson 8 Part 1: Introduction 73

- Read aloud the following pairs of events and discuss time-order and cause-and-effect connections:

  On Monday, I went to music class. On Tuesday, I played outside. *(They are connected by time order, but one does not cause the other.)*

  I forgot to brush my hair. My hair was messy all day! *(They are in order and one causes the other. The cause-and-effect connection tells why it is messy.)*
- **Explain why readers describe connections.** Read aloud the bottom of the page. Explain that looking for and describing connections helps readers focus on key details and understand how they fit together.
- Share an example of how describing connections helped you understand the details of a text. You might talk about the order of events in a description of a game or causes and effects in a text about pollution.
- **Have children demonstrate understanding.** Call on individuals to share what they have learned so far about describing connections.

Part 2: Modeled Instruction

Step by Step

- **Review Part 1; preview Part 2.** Ask volunteers to share things they should think about in order to figure out connections between events and ideas. Then have children turn to Student Book page 74.
- **Revisit *Butterflies and Moths.*** Have children briefly recall the topic and key details, using the chart created for the Book Review on Teacher Resource Book page 71. *(RI.1.2)*
- **Model describing connections.** Read aloud the directions and events on Student Book page 74. Explain that you will model how to describe the connection between the events. Read aloud pages 10–11 of *Butterflies and Moths.* Then think aloud:

  Sometimes authors use clue words to show connections. I'm going to look for clue words that tell about the events described here.

  The words *begins* and *after* tell me that something happens at the start, and something else happens later. So, I think these events are connected by time-order. To check, I'll use time-order words: *First, an egg is laid. Next, a tiny dot moves inside the egg.* That makes sense!

Tip: Help children understand that sometimes readers must interpret the text to describe an event. Reread the first sentence on page 10 and model how to describe this event by saying "an egg is laid."

- Read aloud the prompt on Student Book page 74, as well as the Hint. Ask children what words you used to connect the events. *(first, next)* Discuss how to word the response to the question and model writing it in a complete sentence. Have children write their own responses. *(L.1.1; L.1.2)*
- Use the Close Reading activity to model describing different kinds of connections in the same text.
- **Have children demonstrate understanding.** Have partners complete the Turn and Talk activity. Encourage them to discuss how they know the events are not related by cause and effect, and which clues tell them this.
- Invite children to share their discussions with the class. *(SL.1.1)*

Practice Together

Describing Connections

in *Butterflies and Moths,* pages 10–11

Read about two events in this part of the book.

Event 1: The life of a butterfly or moth begins with an egg.

Event 2: The egg has a tiny moving dot inside of it.

What kind of connection links the two events?

Hint: Did one event cause the other to happen?

The events happen in time order.

Turn Talk: Describe the connection between the events. Use text evidence to support your thinking.

74 Part 2: Modeled Instruction Lesson 8

Close Reading

- Tell children that the same text can have events connected by time order and by cause and effect.
- Before re-reading page 11 of *Butterflies and Moths,* tell children to raise their hands when they hear a time-order word such as *when, first, then,* and *after.*
- After reading, have children use time-order words to tell about the events in order. *(First the caterpillar crawls out of the shell. Next it eats the shell. Last it eats the leaves it sees.)*
- Reread the page, having children identify the clue words *because* and *so.* Ask children to use both words to tell about the connection between the events. *(Caterpillar mothers lay eggs on leaves so their babies have food. Caterpillar babies have food because they are born on leaves.)*
- Discuss how being able to describe both types of connections helps children better understand the key details of the text.

Part 3: Guided Practice

Step by Step

- **Review Parts 1 and 2; preview Part 3.** Have children review the types of connections they can make in texts and the ways to describe them. Direct children to Student Book page 75. Explain that you will guide them through this page.
- **Revisit *Elizabeth Leads the Way.*** Have children recall the topic and key details, using the chart you created for the Book Review on Teacher Resource Book page 89. *(RI.1.2)*
- **Guide children to describe connections.** Read aloud the activity at the top of Student Book page 75. Remind children that when a text does not have clue words, readers need to listen carefully to figure out connections. Tell children to listen for connections as you read aloud pages 8–9. Then prompt:

  What does Elizabeth's father tell the woman? *(Her farm will be taken away from her.) (RI.1.1)*

  What is the idea that the law states, or says? *(Without a husband, nothing belongs to a woman.)*

  What does Elizabeth feel and say when she hears the law? *(She feels horrified. She says the law should be cut out of books.)*

Tip: Take a moment to define *horrified* so children truly understand the depth of Elizabeth's feelings. Tell them it means "shocked and upset," and give an example such as this: *I was horrified when I saw kids dropping trash in my favorite park.*

  How are the idea and Elizabeth's feelings connected? *(The idea causes her feelings.)*

- **Guide children to write responses.** Read aloud the question and the Hint. Help children use clue words to restate the idea and event. Then remind them that cause-and-effect connections tell why—they are not just in order. Discuss answers, and have children write them. *(L.1.1; L.1.2)*
- Use the Close Reading activity to give children additional opportunities to identify connections.
- **Have children demonstrate understanding.** Read aloud the Turn and Talk activity. Have children explain why Elizabeth was horrified. Invite partners to share their answers. *(SL.1.1)*

Practice Together

Describing Connections

***in Elizabeth Leads the Way*, pages 8–9**

Read about an idea and an event in this part of the book.

Idea: The law said that nothing could belong to a woman without a husband.

Event: Elizabeth was horrified by this unfairness.

What kind of connection links the idea and the event?

Hint: Did one event cause the other to happen?

The idea causes the event to happen.

Turn Talk Describe the connection between the idea and the event. Use text evidence to support your thinking.

Lesson 8 Part 3: Guided Practice 75

Close Reading

- Tell children to listen for another connection in *Elizabeth Leads the Way.* Read aloud page 9, then prompt:

  What does Judge Cady tell Elizabeth? *(He tells her it wouldn't matter if they cut the law out of books—it would still be the law. And only men are allowed to change laws.)*

  What details tell how Elizabeth feels about that idea? *(The expression on her face looks angry. She yells "preposterous" which means "ridiculous" or "outrageous.")*

  What causes Elizabeth to decide that she can do anything any boy can do? *(She is angry about the unfair law. She wants to prove that women can do things men can do.)*

- Guide children to use clue words to describe the connection between what Judge Cady says and what Elizabeth decides.

Part 4: Independent Practice

Step by Step

- **Review Parts 1–3; preview Part 4.** Invite a volunteer to tell why describing connections in a text helps readers. Then direct children to Student Book page 76. Explain that they will now describe connections by themselves, following the same pattern as on the previous two pages.
- **Have children describe connections independently.** Display *Elizabeth Leads the Way*, and tell children they will describe a connection in another part of the book.
- Read aloud the activity at the top of Student Book page 76. Then instruct children to touch their noses if they hear a clue word while you read aloud page 12 of *Elizabeth Leads the Way*.
- Ask students to think about the clue word they heard and what kind of connection it shows.

Tip: If children struggle to identify a clue word, explain that *since* means "because." Use it to replace the word *because* in a sentence to help illustrate its meaning and function.

- Read aloud the question and Hint. Have children write their answer in a complete sentence. Then discuss the answer. *(L.1.1; L.1.2)*
- Use the Close Reading activity to have children explore an additional type of connection.
- **Have children demonstrate understanding.** Read aloud the Turn and Talk activity. Have partners use clue words to tell about the connection. Then challenge them to tell what they learned about Elizabeth by describing this connection. Discuss children's answers. *(SL.1.1)*
- **Have children reflect on their learning.** Ask children to look back at Student Book pages 74–76 and tell what they learned about the subject of each book by describing connections between ideas and events. Then have them tell how describing connections can help them better understand informational texts. Chart their ideas.

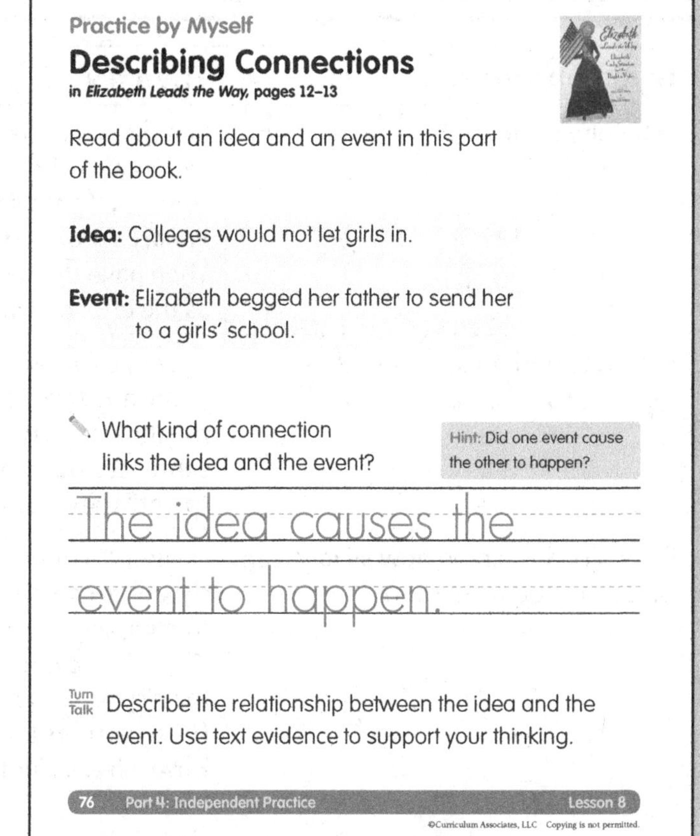

Practice by Myself

Describing Connections

in *Elizabeth Leads the Way*, pages 12–13

Read about an idea and an event in this part of the book.

Idea: Colleges would not let girls in.

Event: Elizabeth begged her father to send her to a girls' school.

What kind of connection links the idea and the event?

Hint: Did one event cause the other to happen?

The idea causes the event to happen.

Turn Talk Describe the relationship between the idea and the event. Use text evidence to support your thinking.

76 Part 4: Independent Practice Lesson 8

©Curriculum Associates, LLC Copying is not permitted.

Close Reading

- Tell children that compare and contrast is a different type of connection.
- Read aloud page 13 of *Elizabeth Leads the Way*. Then prompt:

  What two things happen on this page? *(Most young ladies get married, wash dishes, do laundry, and have babies. Elizabeth studies.)*

  What does the clue word *while* tell us about when these things happen? *(They happen at the same time.)*

  What do you notice about what Elizabeth was doing compared to the other young ladies? *(Elizabeth was doing something very different.)*

- Discuss how it must have seemed to others that Elizabeth did everything differently. Explain that describing this connection helps readers understand what kind of person Elizabeth was.

Assessment and Remediation

If you observe . . .	Then try . . .
Difficulty distinguishing causes from effects	Reminding students that a cause always happens before the effect. Write causes and effects on separate slips of paper; for example: *I forgot to use sunblock. I got a sunburn; I dropped an apple. The apple got bruised; I felt hungry. I ate a sandwich.* Have children put each pair of events in time order. Then have them identify the first event as the cause and the second event as the effect. Invite them to tell why the cause led to the effect.
Difficulty finding text clues to the types of connections	Having children make flash cards of common clue words, with *Time Order* or *Cause and Effect* as the heading on each card. Have partners use the cards to practice: one child holds up a card. Then the other says a sentence or sentences that go with the clue word(s). Children can keep the cards to refer to until they readily recognize the clue words in context.
Difficulty describing how an idea can be connected to an event	Having children complete sentence frames to tell how their own ideas or thoughts can cause events. Display these sentence frames and model how to complete them: *Because I think ______, I______. I believe______, so I ______. (Because I think it's important to stay safe, I wear a helmet when I ride my bicycle. I believe in being healthy, so I eat fruits and vegetables every day.)* Have partners take turns completing each frame with their own examples. Have a few volunteers share their sentences with the class.

Connect to the Anchor Standard

R3: *Analyze how and why individuals, events, and ideas develop and interact over the course of a text.*

In mastering Standard 3 throughout the grades, students evolve from describing the connections between discrete pieces of information in a text to explaining complex relationships among ideas presented in scientific, historical, and technical texts. In later grades, students also bring to bear their knowledge of a number of different text structures as part of their analyses, including chronology, cause/effect, problem/solution, and comparison. They learn to constantly ask questions focused on how and why authors choose to present information: *What is the first thing I notice? What is the next thing? How are the two things connected? What patterns develop across the book? Why did the author draw parallels between two individuals, events, or ideas?* Use the following activities to help your students begin the transition to these ways of thinking.

- Help children draw parallels between Henry Stanton and Elizabeth Cady Stanton. Read aloud pages 14–15 of *Elizabeth Leads the Way.* Use text evidence to discuss what kind of person Henry is. *(He is fair.)* Reread page 9, and discuss the connections between Henry's and Elizabeth's ideas about fairness and rights. Discuss why the connection between Henry's and Elizabeth's ideas is so important. *(It explains why Elizabeth married him.) (RI.1.1; SL.1.2)*

- Help children connect ideas from different parts of a book. Reread pages 17 and 39 of *Butterflies and Moths.* Guide children to compare and contrast the information on each page. Discuss the important idea that children learn by comparing the pages: a butterfly needs protection from predators throughout its whole life cycle. *(RI.1.7)*

Introduction

Before administering the Unit 2 Check, you may wish to review with children how to answer multiple-choice questions and offer some test-taking tips. Begin by writing the following sentences on the board, followed by the multiple-choice question:

Can you imagine going to sleep for the entire winter? That's what some animals, like bears, do because they cannot find enough food during the cold months. Animals like dogs and cats don't do this, though.

Which animal likes to sleep all winter?

A elephant

B bear

C dog

Guide children through the process of answering a multiple-choice question. Think aloud:

Today you will listen as I read aloud a book, and then you will answer some questions about details in the book. Remember, when you answer a multiple-choice question, only one of the answers is correct. To choose the correct answer, you draw a circle around the letter next to that answer. *(Read aloud the passage and the question.)*

First, try to rule out one of the wrong answers. For example, in this question, we can rule out choice A, "elephant." Choice A is a wrong answer because I didn't read the word *elephant*.

Next, decide which words in the question are the most important. Then look for those words in the sentences. The first sentence asks me about sleeping during the winter. The second one tells me that bears do this, and then tells why. I think "bear" is the right answer. (*Circle "B" on the board.*)

Now I need to check my work. The sentences say that bears sleep all winter. Is that the answer I circled? Yes it is!

Step by Step

- Revisit *Who Eats What?* Have children review the main topic and key details.
- Have children follow along as you read aloud the directions on page 77 of their Student Books.

Unit 2 Check

Listen closely as your teacher reads. Then answer the questions.

Where are humans in a food chain?

A at the bottom

B in the middle

(C) at the top

Why are green plants at the beginning of all food chains?

(A) Green plants make their own food.

B Green plants need water and air to live.

C Green plants grow and die.

What is the main topic of **Who Eats What?**

(A) how food chains and food webs work

B how fish are part of some food chains

C how plants only fit into one food chain

77

- Then read aloud one or more pages from the text, as specified below, before having children complete each item. Display the appropriate pages for children to view while they read and answer each question.
- For item 1, reread pages 8–10; display page 9.
- For item 2, reread pages 12–13; display page 12.
- For items 3 and 4, reread pages 14–21; display page 19.

Note: Read aloud each question, answer choice, and Hint before directing children to answer it.

- When children have finished, reread each question and discuss the correct answer. Point to evidence in the text and pictures. Then use the Answer Analysis to discuss the correct answer.

Answer Analysis

1 This item requires children to answer a question about a key detail from the text. (***RI.1.1***)

The best answer is choice C, "at the top." The words on page 9 say "you are the top of a slightly longer food chain," and that is what the pictures show. The food chain starts with grass, so it's at the bottom. Then the arrow shows energy moving to the cow who eats the grass. Finally, the energy in the cow's milk moves into you. Because humans are at the top of a food chain, choices A and B, "at the bottom" and "in the middle," are not correct answers.

2 This item draws children's attention to the connection between two ideas about the importance of green plants. ***(RI.1.3)***

The best answer is choice A, "Green plants make their own food." Here on page 12, it says plants can "make their own food" and goes on to say plants "do not need to eat something else." Even though both choices B and C tell facts about plants, they do not explain why green plants are at the beginning of all food chains.

3 This item asks children to identify the most important idea the text describes: its main topic. ***(RI.1.2)***

The best answer is choice A, "how food chains and food webs work." That's what most of the text tells about. Choice B, "how fish are part of some food chains," is a fact, but the book talks about other food chains and webs, too. That choice is not the best one. Choice C is not a good answer because it is not true. We learned from reading the book that plants are part of all food chains, not just one.

4 This item requires children to describe in writing how seeds, a mouse, and a snake are connected. ***(RI.1.3)***

Sample Response: They describe links in a food chain.

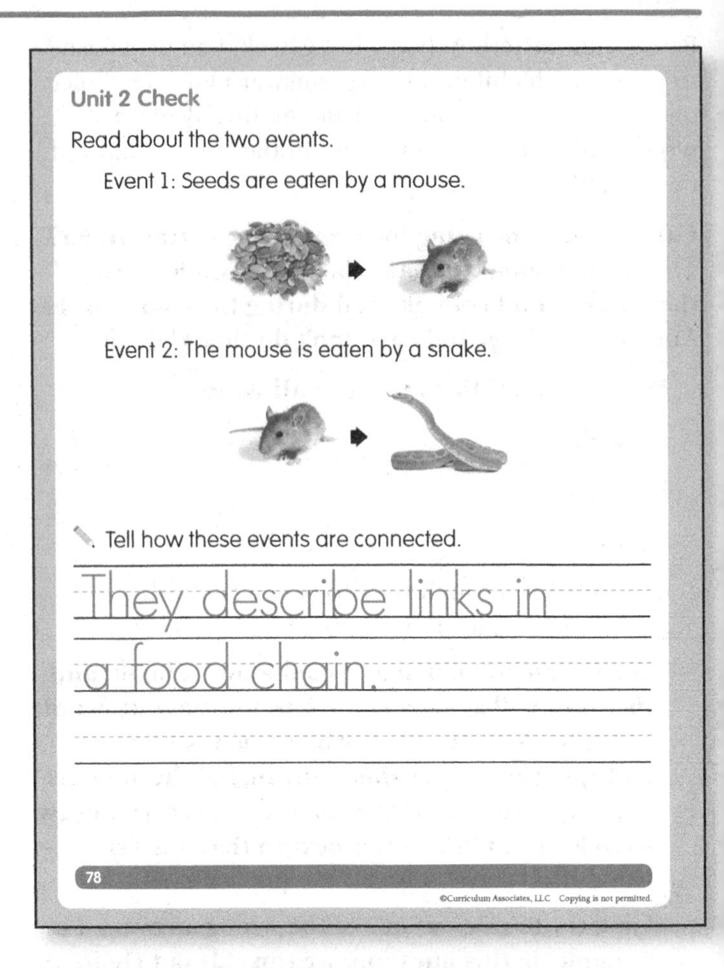

Your answer needs to tell why the events happen in this order, and what is being described. First, seeds are eaten by a mouse, and then the mouse is eaten by a snake. You must tell about the connection between the events: they are describing a food chain.

If necessary, illustrate the concept by drawing or writing, from bottom to top, seeds, a mouse, and a snake. Connect them with arrows in the order of a food chain.

Unit 3

Craft and Structure in Literature

The following pacing chart shows a recommended schedule for teaching the lessons in Unit 3. Each Read Aloud and Focus Lesson is taught over the course of three days. There is also time allotted in each Focus Lesson for teaching Tap Children's Prior Knowledge and Differentiated Instruction.

Day	Lesson/Activity	Time (minutes)
1	Unit 3 Opener (optional); Tap Children's Prior Knowledge; Lesson 9: Part 1	30
2	Lesson 9: Parts 2 and 3	30
3	Lesson 9: Part 4; Differentiated Instruction (optional)	30
4	Read Aloud Lesson H: Introduction; Part 1	30
5	Read Aloud Lesson H: Parts 2 and Part 3	30
6	Read Aloud Lesson H: Part 4; Additional Activities (optional)	30
7	Tap Children's Prior Knowledge; Lesson 10: Part 1	30
8	Lesson 10: Parts 2 and 3	30
9	Lesson 10: Part 4; Differentiated Instruction (optional)	30
10	Tap Children's Prior Knowledge; Lesson 11: Part 1	30
11	Lesson 11: Parts 2 and 3	30
12	Lesson 11: Part 4; Differentiated Instruction (optional)	30
13	Tap Children's Prior Knowledge; Lesson 12: Part 1	30
14	Lesson 12: Parts 2 and 3	30
15	Lesson 12: Part 4; Differentiated Instruction (optional)	30
16	Unit 3 Check	30

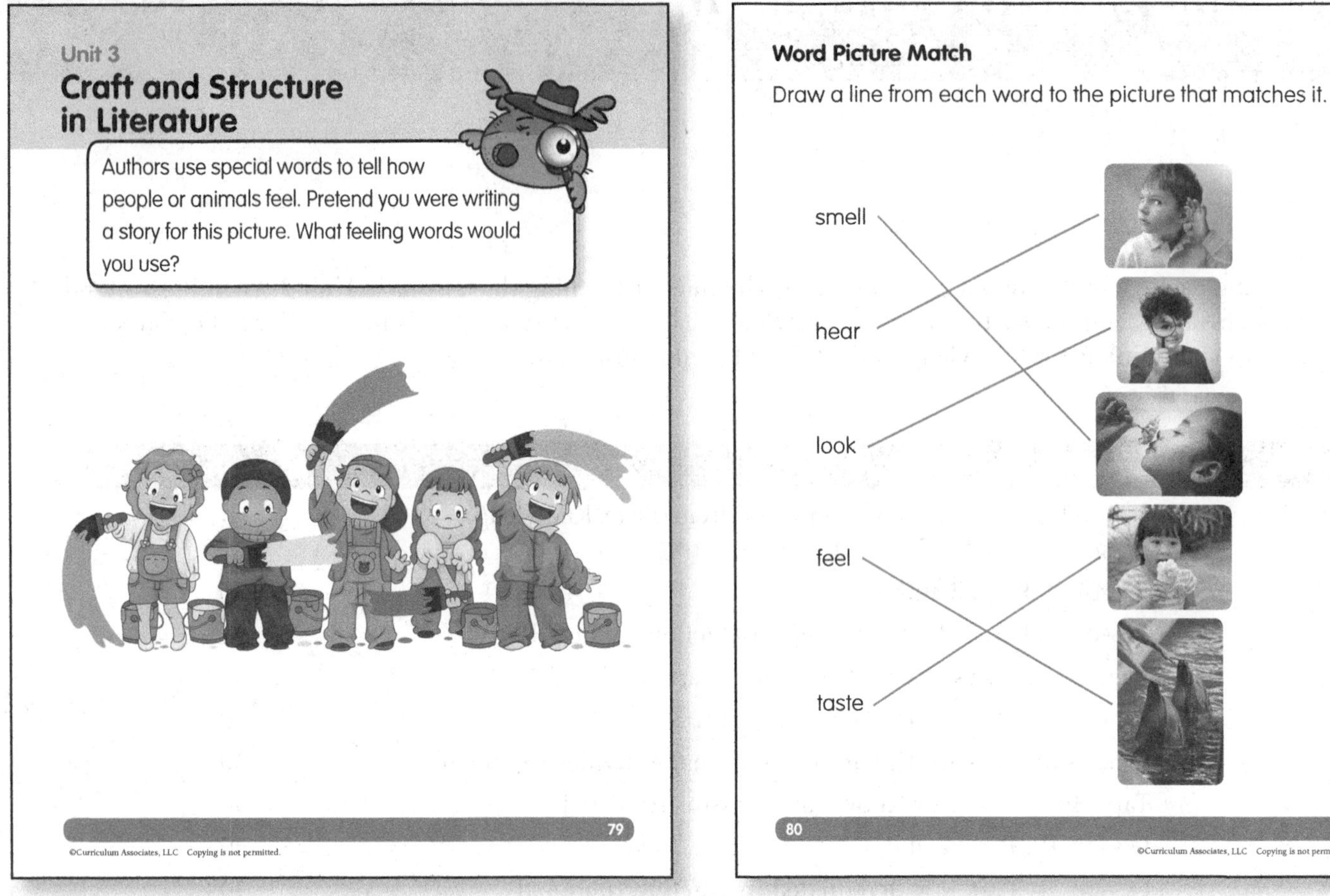

Step by Step

Explain that in this unit, children will read stories and poems that use special words to tell what things are like and how characters feel. They will look at different types of books. They will also learn about who is telling the stories they read.

- Have children turn to page 79. Read aloud the introductory sentences and question.
- Discuss the illustration and invite children to describe what they see. *(kids having fun painting)* As necessary, encourage children to ask and answer *who*, *what*, *where*, *when*, *why*, and *how* questions for further inspiration.

Encourage children to tell you what feeling words they would use if they were writing a story about this picture. Write their responses on chart paper and discuss each one.

- Then have children turn to page 80.
- Read aloud the directions at the top of the page.
- Read aloud the first word. Have children say it. Then have them put a finger on the picture that matches the word. Ask them to draw a line from the word to the picture.
- Repeat the procedure for the other words.
- When children have finished the word picture match, have volunteers show or tell you their answers.
- Have children tell you ways they can use their senses.

Lesson 9 (Student Book pages 81–84)

Feeling Words

CCSS

RL.1.4: Identify words and phrases in stories or poems that suggest feelings . . . .

Required Read Alouds: *Projectable 2 ("Sometimes"); B (The Polar Bear Son)*

Lesson Objectives

- Identify words and phrases that explicitly describe an author's or character's feelings.
- Identify words and phrases that imply an author's or character's feelings.
- Use text evidence to draw conclusions about an author's or character's feelings.

The Learning Progression

- **Grade K:** CCSS RL.K.4 requires children to ask and answer questions about unfamiliar words in a text, with prompting and support.
- **Grade 1: CCSS RL.1.4 focuses the Grade K standard by having children identify words and phrases in stories or poems that suggest feelings.**
- **Grade 2:** CCSS RL.2.4 further develops the standard by asking children to notice how words and phrases in stories and poems provide rhythm and meaning.

Prerequisite Skills

- Ask and answer questions about unknown words in a text.
- Identify story characters and events with prompting and support.
- Describe familiar feelings and emotions.

Tap Children's Prior Knowledge

- Tell children that people can have many different feelings, such as *happy, sad,* or *afraid.* Work together to brainstorm a list of words that tell feelings. Record the ideas on chart paper with the heading *Feeling Words.* Explain that the words all tell feelings, or emotions.
- Ask children to tell how they would feel in these situations: your class throws a party for you that you weren't expecting; you trip and fall in the lunch room; your friend goes away on a family trip for a week; you get a new puppy; you have to wait for a long time.
- Help children name a range of feelings such as *surprised, embarrassed, lonely, excited,* and *impatient.* Add the words to the list.
- Point to several different words on the list. For each word, have children pantomime what they look like or do when they feel that emotion. Invite volunteers to give examples of times they felt that way.
- Tell children that, just like them, characters in stories have feelings. Explain that they will learn how to find words in stories and poems that show and tell how characters feel. Explain that this will help them better understand story characters.

Ready *Teacher Toolbox* Teacher-Toolbox.com

	Prerequisite Skills	RL.1.4
Ready Lessons		✓
Tools for Instruction	✓✓	
Interactive Tutorials		

Additional CCSS

RL.1.2; SL.1.1; SL.1.4; L.1.1; L.1.2; L.1.5 (See page A38 for full text.)

Part 1: Introduction

Step by Step

- **Introduce the standard.** Have children turn to page 81 in their Student Books. Read aloud the speech bubble.
- **Review examples of feeling words.** Read aloud the line below the speech bubble. Explain that you are going to explore some words that tell feelings.
- Read aloud the first statement. Have children circle the word *tell*. Explain:

  Sometimes an author tells you exactly how a character feels. The words below are words an author could use to tell how a character feels.

- Read aloud the first example word in the yellow box, *glad*. Model how to demonstrate its meaning:

  I can show the feeling *glad*. I give a big smile. I clap my hands. These things show I feel glad.

- Read the next word, *sad*. Have children repeat the word and then demonstrate their understanding of it with a facial expression or gesture. Continue with the remaining words.
- Brainstorm additional feeling words with children. Add the words to the chart from the Tap Children's Prior Knowledge activity on page 101. Tell children that they can use these words in their own writing.
- **Guide children to identify feelings.** Read aloud the second statement. Have children circle the word *show*. Explain that sometime authors show readers how a character is feeling by describing the things the character says or does.
- Read aloud the first sentence in the yellow box. Explain to children:

  This sentence does not have a word that tells how Sami feels. But I can figure it out. I read the word *giggled*. I know that when people *giggle*, they feel happy. So I think that Sami feels happy.

- Read aloud the second sentence. Point to the words *looked down* and *blushed*. Explain that when you *blush*, your face turns red. Discuss with children the kinds of feelings or situations that could make someone lower their eyes and blush. Discuss how Will might feel. *(embarrassed, ashamed, confused, nervous)*

Listen and Learn

Feeling Words

Authors sometimes use **feeling words**. Some feeling words are happy, angry, and excited. These words show emotion.

Look carefully at these examples:

- Some words tell how a character feels.

glad	proud	silly	cozy
sad	lonely	hurt	sorry
grumpy	worried	shy	curious

- Some words show how a character feels. You have to figure out how they show feelings.
  - Sami giggled when the puppy licked her nose.
  - Will looked down and blushed.

Notice feeling words when you read. Authors use them to help you understand characters and their actions.

- **Explain why readers notice feeling words.** Read aloud the bottom of the page. Write the sentence: *Joe was at the party.* Ask: *How does Joe feel?* Elicit that we don't know. Then rewrite the sentence: *Joe was excited to be at the party.* Use the example to discuss why an author might include feeling words in writing.
- **Have children demonstrate understanding.** Call on volunteers to share what they have learned so far about feeling words. Encourage them to tell how understanding feeling words helps them know more about a how a character feels.

Part 2: Modeled Instruction

Step by Step

- **Review Part 1; preview Part 2.** Discuss what children have learned about how authors use feeling words. Direct children to Student Book page 82.
- **Revisit *The Polar Bear Son.*** Invite children to briefly retell the story, using pages 7–10 of their Student Books. *(RL.1.2)*
- **Model how to identify feeling words.** Explain that you will model how to find feeling words in a book. Read aloud page 24 of *The Polar Bear Son.* Think aloud:

  I will reread and look for words that tell how the old woman feels. (Read aloud the page.) **I did not find any words that tell exactly how she feels. I'll look again. This time I will look for words that *show* how she feels.**

- Read aloud each sentence. Point out that none of them have words like *sad* or *worried* to tell how the old woman feels.
- In the last sentence, point out the words *crying bitterly.* Pantomime what it means to cry bitterly. Discuss that the author chose these words to show how the old woman feels—she is not just a little sad, but extremely sad.

Tip: Help children understand the author's word choices by giving examples of other words the author might have written, such as, *The old woman sniffled a little.* Discuss how these words would change the reader's understanding of the old woman's feelings.

- **Model writing your responses.** Read aloud the first question and Hint on the Student Book page. Discuss the answer. Model how to write the words from the story that show how the old woman feels. Have children write their own responses. *(L.1.1)*
- Read aloud the second question and Hint. Discuss the clues—the words *crying bitterly* and the meaning of *bitterly.* Model writing the answer. Have children write their own. *(L.1.2)*
- **Have children demonstrate understanding.** Read aloud the Turn and Talk activity. Remind children to look for words that tell and show feelings. Invite them to share their evidence with the class. *(SL.1.1; SL.1.4)*
- Use the Close Reading activity to help children identify more words that show a character's feelings.

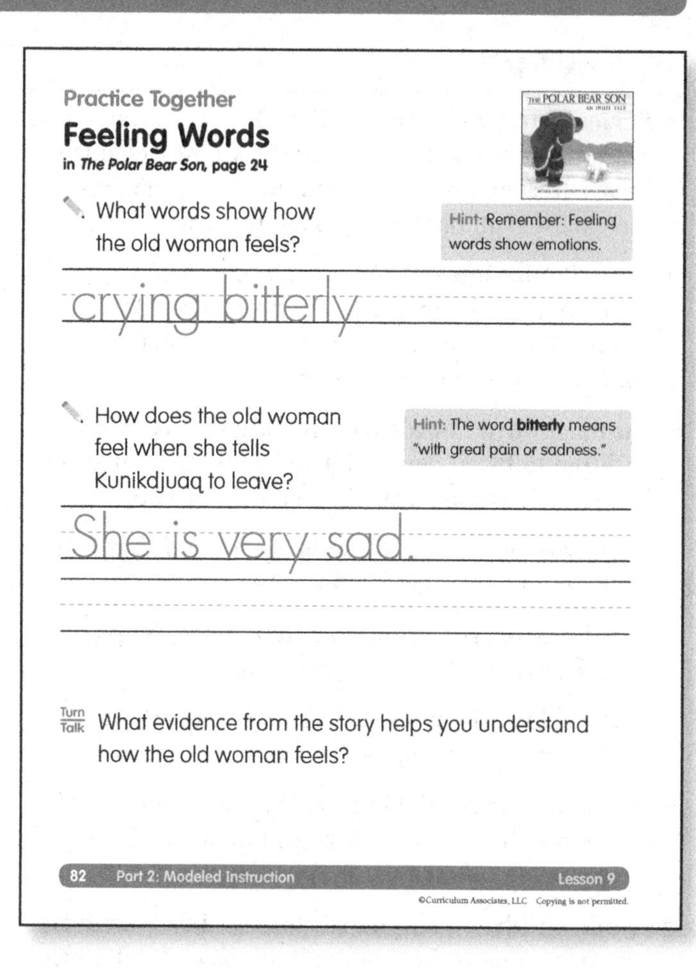

Practice Together

Feeling Words

in *The Polar Bear Son,* page 24

What words show how the old woman feels?

Hint: Remember: Feeling words show emotions.

crying bitterly

How does the old woman feel when she tells Kunikdjuaq to leave?

Hint: The word **bitterly** means "with great pain or sadness."

She is very sad.

Turn Talk What evidence from the story helps you understand how the old woman feels?

82 Part 2: Modeled Instruction Lesson 9

©Curriculum Associates, LLC Copying is not permitted.

Close Reading

- Remind children that some words tell feelings and other words show feelings. Read aloud page 27 of *The Polar Bear Son* and prompt:

  What word on this page tells how the old woman and the children feel? *(sadly)*

  How does this word tell a feeling? *(It says exactly how the old woman and the children feel. They feel sad.)*

  How do the words "disappear into the distance" help show that this is a sad moment? *(They make it seem like Kunikdjuaq will never come back.)*

- Point out that the author uses words that both tell and show that the old woman and children are sad. Explain that noticing evidence about feelings helps readers know how the author wants them to feel.

Part 3: Guided Practice

Step by Step

- **Review Parts 1–2; preview Part 3.** Have children give examples of words that tell and show how a character feels. Direct children to Student Book page 83. Explain that you will guide them through this page.
- **Read "Sometimes."** Invite children to listen as you read aloud the poem on Teacher Resource Book pages 207–208. Briefly discuss what the poem is about and who the poet might be.
- **Guide children to identify feeling words.** Ask children to listen closely for words that tell or show feelings. As you read the first stanza, prompt:

  Do you hear words like *happy* or *sad* that tell the poet's feelings? *(no)*

  What words do you hear that show the poet's feelings? *(smile, scream, shout, laugh)*

  How does the poet feel about going outside? *(happy and excited; having fun)*
- Repeat for the second stanza. Have children identify the words that show feelings and name the feelings. *(stomp my feet, frown, scowl, pout; mad, grumpy, upset)*
- **Guide children to write responses.** Read aloud the first question on the Student Book page. Explain that children should listen for the actions that show the poet's feelings. Read aloud the first stanza. Discuss responses and have children write the words. *(L.1.1)*
- Read aloud the second question and Hint. Prompt:

  How does the poet feel when she plays outside and smiles, screams, shouts, and laughs? *(happy and excited)*
- Have children act out the answer before they write it in a complete sentence. *(L.1.2)*

Tip: Help children realize that they must look at all of the words before deciding how a character feels. For example, if they only look at the word *scream*, they might think the poet feels afraid or hurt.

- Use the Close Reading activity to examine how an author chooses words carefully to express feelings.
- **Have children demonstrate understanding.** Have partners complete the Turn and Talk activity. Ask them to explain what words helped them understand how the poet is feeling. *(SL.1.1; SL.1.4)*

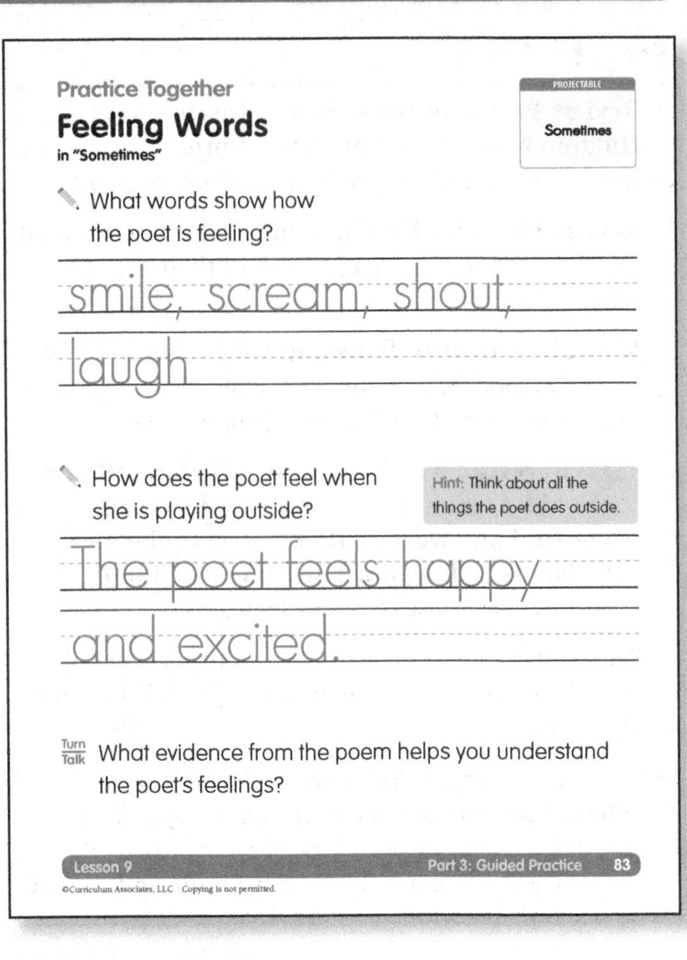

Close Reading

- Remind children that authors choose words that tell or show specific feelings. Reread the first stanza of "Sometimes." Then think aloud:

  I read that the poet goes out to play, and smiles, screams, shouts, and laughs.

  The poet's choice of words helps me figure out how she feels. They help me understand that she feels happy and excited.
- Write this alternate version of the stanza: *Sometimes I get a feeling. When I go out to play, I see no friends at all, And sit by myself all day.*
- Work with children to identify words that show the poet's actions *(see no friends, sit by myself)* and then describe how she might feel. *(lonely, bored)*
- Discuss how the choice of words changes the reader's understanding of the poet's feelings.

Part 4: Independent Practice

Step by Step

- **Review Parts 1–3; preview Part 4.** Invite a volunteer to tell how noticing feeling words helps readers understand characters. Then direct children to turn to Student Book page 84.
- **Have children identify feeling words independently.** Explain that now children will practice identifying a poet's feelings by themselves. Tell children that, as on previous pages, they will listen for words that tell or show feelings and use them to tell what the feeling is.
- Read aloud the first question on the Student Book page. Make sure children understand that they should be listening for words that show how the poet feels.
- Have children listen closely as you read aloud the third stanza of the poem. Prompt them to identify the feeling words:

  What words show how the poet feels? *(fight tears, whine, sigh, mope)*

- Have children write the words. Then read aloud the second question along with the Hint. Prompt:

  The poet can't get her own way so she fights tears, whines, sighs, and mopes. How do you think the poet feels? *(upset and frustrated)*

- Have children write a complete sentence to answer the question. *(L.1.1; L.1.2)*

Tip: If children are unsure how to infer the poet's feelings from her actions, review what she does. Say: *Imagine you don't get your way and you are crying and whining. Do you feel happy or upset?*

- Discuss answers to the first and second questions.
- **Have children demonstrate understanding.** Have partners complete the Turn and Talk activity by recalling evidence in the poem about the poet's feelings. Invite children to share their responses with the class. *(SL.1.1; SL.1.4)*
- Use the Close Reading activity to help children further explore the feeling words in the poem.
- **Have children reflect on their learning.** Guide children in a discussion about how identifying feeling words helps readers understand characters. Chart their ideas.

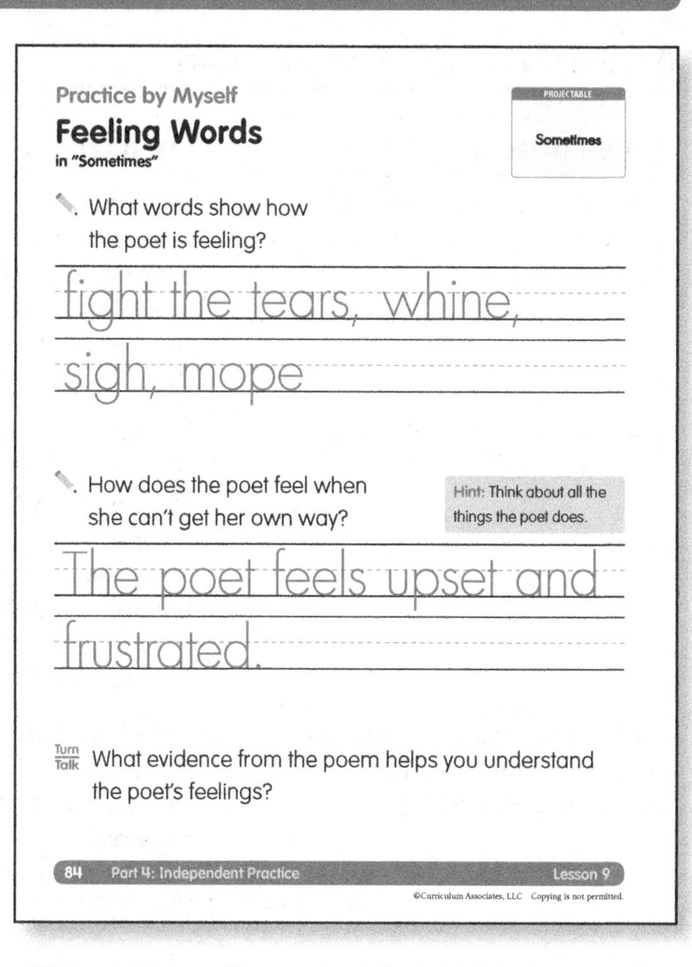
Practice by Myself

Feeling Words

in "Sometimes"

PROJECTABLE

Sometimes

What words show how the poet is feeling?

fight the tears, whine, sigh, mope

How does the poet feel when she can't get her own way?

Hint: Think about all the things the poet does.

The poet feels upset and frustrated.

Turn Talk What evidence from the poem helps you understand the poet's feelings?

84 Part 4: Independent Practice Lesson 9

©Curriculum Associates, LLC Copying is not permitted.

Close Reading

- Point out that feeling words help readers know how a character or author is feeling. Sometimes, readers need to think about the feeling words along with other words in the text to figure out exactly why a character feels the way they do.
- Tell children they will decide why the poet feels the way she does. Reread the last stanza of "Sometimes" and prompt:

  What words in the first two lines show feelings? *(scream, shout, stomp, pout, whine, frown, play)*

  What words in the last two lines show a feeling? *(YAWN)*

  What feeling is it? *(tired)*

  Think about the all these feeling words. Why does the poet feel tired at the end of every day? *(She is tired from all the activities she does and the feelings she experiences.)*

Differentiated Instruction

Assessment and Remediation

If you observe . . .	Then try . . .
Difficulty identifying explicit feeling words	Sorting words. Display two feelings words and one non-feeling word in random order, for example: *happy, short, excited.* Have children identify the words in each group that are feeling words. Continue with four or five other groups or until children can accurately identify the feeling words. Then have children use the feeling words in sentences. If needed, provide sentence starters such as *I feel happy when* ____________. *(L.1.5)*
Difficulty identifying implicit feeling words	Providing sample sentences and having children identify the words that show specific feelings. On chart paper, write: *The puppy wagged its tail and licked my face.* Ask children what words in the sentence show that the puppy is happy *(wagged its tail)* and happy to see you. *(licked my face)* Continue with additional examples. For instance, have children look for words that show Mike is tired: *Mike walked slowly to the bus stop, dragging his backpack behind him. (walked slowly, dragging)* Have children find words that show Gabby is nervous: *Gabby gnawed on her nails as she waited for the curtain to open.*
Difficulty drawing conclusions about a character's feelings based on text evidence	Retelling a familiar story such as, *The Boy Who Cried Wolf.* Write a sentence that includes words to show how the boy feels: *When the boy saw the wolf, he leaped up and shouted a loud warning.* Read the sentence and discuss how the words *leaped up* and *shouted a loud warning* lead readers to conclude that the boy is startled and afraid.

Connect to the Anchor Standard

R4: *Interpret words and phrases as they are used in a text, including determining technical, connotative, and figurative meanings, and analyze how specific word choices shape meaning or tone.*

Throughout the grades, Standard 4 follows a progression from the literal understanding of words and phrases to the recognition of connotative and figurative meanings in texts. In later grades, readers refine their ability to distinguish literal from nonliteral language with questions such as the following: *How does the author use language to make meaning? How do the author's word choices create tone? How does the author use allusions, metaphors, and similes? What effect do these word choices have on the text and on the reader?* Use the following activities to help your students begin this transition.

- Discuss how the poet uses repetition in the poem "Sometimes." Point out that the first line in the first four stanzas begins with the same words, "Sometimes I get a feeling." Ask: *Each time you read the words "Sometimes I get a feeling," what do you expect to read about next? (a different kind of feeling)* Point to the first line of the last stanza and discuss why the poet uses different words there. *(They show that something different is coming and that it is the end of the poem.)*
- Read aloud page 28 of *The Polar Bear Son.* Discuss the meanings of the words *alone* and *lonely. (To be alone means "to be by yourself;" to feel lonely means "to feel sad because you are by yourself.")* Prompt discussion: *The old woman still lived in the village with the other villagers, so why does the author say she was "alone again"? Do you think she always felt lonely, or just some of the time? What evidence tells you this?*

Read Aloud Lesson H (Student Book pages 31–34)

Mike Mulligan and His Steam Shovel

Lesson Objectives

You will read aloud *Mike Mulligan and His Steam Shovel*, which children will revisit in later lessons. Children will:

- Answer questions about key details in the story.
- Describe characters and major events, using key details.
- Retell the story, including key details.

About the Text

Summary

Mike Mulligan and his steam shovel, Mary Anne, had been digging together for years until new shovels came along and took away all their jobs. When Mike and his steam shovel get a chance to dig a cellar for a new town hall in the country, they prove that they can still be useful.

Genre: Fantasy

- *Mike Mulligan and His Steam Shovel* is a type of story called a fantasy. Remind children that in a fantasy, animals, or in this case machines, act like people.
- Use the cover illustration to point out that the steam shovel has eyes and a mouth, like a person.

Critical Vocabulary

- Prior to reading, briefly define the following words:

  steam shovel (p. 3) a machine that digs big holes

  cellar (p. 13) an underground room; a basement

  furnace (p. 39) a machine that heats a building

  janitor (p. 39) a person who cleans and takes care of a building
- As you read, pause to point to the words as you encounter them, and review their definitions.

Word Bank

- To support children in writing about the story, display a word bank containing the Critical Vocabulary and the characters' names (*Mike* and *Mary Anne*).
- Add other important story words, such as *Popperville* and *town hall*, on subsequent readings.

New Concepts: Energy Sources

- When first introducing the book, explain that some machines, such as refrigerators, get their power from electricity, while other machines, such as cars, get their power from gasoline.
- Explain that Mary Anne gets her power from steam, a form of power that isn't used much anymore.

Ready *Teacher Toolbox* Teacher-Toolbox.com

	Prerequisite Skills	RL.1.2
Ready Lessons		✓
Tools for Instruction	✓✓	✓
Interactive Tutorials	✓✓	

CCSS Focus

RL.1.2 *Retell stories, including key details. . .*

ADDITIONAL STANDARDS: **RL.1.1; RL.1.3; RL.1.7; RF.1.2.a, d; RF.1.3.f; W.1.1; SL.1.1.a, b, c; SL.1.2; SL.1.4; SL.1.5; L.1.1.b; L.1.2.a; L.1.4.a** *(See page A31 for full text.)*

PART 1: First Read (Characters)

Step by Step

- **Introduce *Mike Mulligan and His Steam Shovel.*** Display the book. Then read aloud the title and the name of the author, Virginia Lee Burton. Point out that she is also the illustrator.
- **Set the purpose for reading.** Tell children that readers make sense of a story by identifying the characters and then keeping track of what happens to them.
- Explain that as you read aloud, children should listen closely to identify the characters in this story.
- **Read aloud *Mike Mulligan and His Steam Shovel.*** Read the story all the way through, pausing only to briefly define challenging vocabulary.
- **Guide children to review the characters.** After reading, use questions such as these to discuss the characters. *(RL.1.1; SL.1.1; SL.1.2)*

  Who are the main characters? *(Mike, Mary Anne)*

  How can we tell they are the main characters? *(The story is about what happens to them.)*

  Who are some of the other characters? *(Henry B. Swap, the little boy)*

- Direct children to turn to Student Book page 31. Read aloud the first item, along with the Hint. Help children eliminate secondary characters such as Henry B. Swap and the little boy. *(RL.1.3)*

Tip: Display the book cover and reread the title. Point out that book titles often tell who one or more of the main characters are.

- Prompt children to write the names of the characters beneath their pictures.
- **Have children discuss story evidence.** Read aloud the Turn and Talk activity. Encourage children to connect details in their picture to details in the story, and remind them to think about some things that each character says and does during the story. *(SL.1.4; SL.1.5)*

Mike Mulligan and His Steam Shovel

The Main Characters

Draw the two main characters.

Hint: Who is the story mostly about?

Children should draw one picture each of Mike and Mary Anne.

Name each character.

Mike	Mary Anne

Turn Talk Use your pictures and story evidence to tell your partner what you know about each character.

Read Aloud | Lesson H   Part 1: Characters 31

ELL Support: Jobs People Do

- Explain that jobs are the types of work that people do. The people in a city or a town such as Popperville do many different jobs.
- Point to the words *postman*, *milkman*, and *doctor* on page 26.
- Explain that a postman's job is to deliver the mail. In the past, a milkman's job was to deliver bottles of milk to people's houses. A doctor's job is to take care of people's health.
- Have children find the milkman and the postman in the illustration on pages 26 and 27.
- Ask children to point to and say the words *postman*, *milkman*, and *doctor* aloud. Have volunteers explain each job.

Step by Step

- **Reread and discuss the beginning.** Read pages 3–17 aloud. Use questions such as these to guide discussion. *(RL.1.1; SL.1.1; SL.1.2)*

  Pages 5–13: What do Mike and Mary Anne help build? *(canals, railways, highways, landing fields)*

  Pages 14–15: Why are Mike and Mary Anne sad? *(New shovels came and took all the jobs.)*

  Page 17: What problem do Mike and Mary Anne have? *(No one wants steam shovels anymore.)*

- Use the Close Reading activity to help children look for evidence in the illustrations.
- **Focus on a key detail.** Direct children to turn to Student Book page 32. Read aloud the first item and the Hint. Recall when and why Mike and Mary Anne were happy, and help children understand why the new shovels change that. *(RL.1.3)*
- Prompt children to complete the second item.

Tip: Scaffold for emerging writers by providing a sentence starter: *Mike and Mary Anne feel_____.*

- **Have children discuss story evidence.** Read aloud the Turn and Talk activity. Encourage children to connect ideas in the beginning of the story in order to explain why Mike and Mary Anne are sad. *(SL.1.4)*

Mike Mulligan and His Steam Shovel

In the Beginning

Draw the way Mike and Mary Anne feel when the new shovels come.

Hint: They cannot do what they love most anymore.

Children might draw Mike and Mary Anne with sad faces, or they might recreate the picture on page 15.

Write what is happening in your picture.

Mike and Mary Anne feel sad.

Turn Talk Why do Mike and Mary Anne feel this way? What evidence in the story tells you this?

32 Part 2: Beginning Read Aloud | Lesson H

- Discuss the most important details from this part of the story. Encourage children to use their Student Book pages to recall details.

Tier Two Vocabulary: *Proud of*

- Have children recall who Mike Mulligan is proud of. *(Mary Anne)* Guide them to point to the phrase *proud of* in the story as they give their answers.
- Work with children to determine that the phrase *proud of* means "feeling very good about yourself or someone you know."
- Provide an example of a time when you were proud of the class. You may say *I was proud of our class when we won the Class of the Month award.*
- Then have volunteers name a time when they were proud of themselves. Discuss examples and non-examples, such as breaking a rule or not telling the truth. *(L.1.5.c)*

Close Reading

- Remind children that good readers look for evidence in the words and pictures.
- Display the illustration on page 15, and read the writing on the fence. Prompt:

  What details do you notice? *(Mary Anne is crying and Mike looks sad.)*

  How does this picture help you understand Mike and Mary Anne's problem? *(The writing on the fence tells what Mike and Mary Anne are sad about. No one wants steam shovels anymore.) (RL.1.7)*

Step by Step

- **Reread and discuss the middle.** Read pages 18–37 aloud. Then use questions such as these to guide discussion about this part of the story. *(RL.1.1; SL.1.1; SL.1.2)*

  Page 20: Why does Henry B. Swap give Mike the job? *(Mike promises to dig the cellar in one day.)*

  Pages 22–32: What makes Mike and Mary Anne work so fast? *(Lots of people come to watch them.)*

  Page 37: What do Mike and Mary Anne see once they are done digging? *(They are stuck in the cellar.)*

- Use the Close Reading activity to help children think more about what Mike does and why.
- **Focus on a key detail.** Direct children to turn to Student Book page 33, and read aloud the first item. Use the Hint to focus children's drawings on Mike and Mary Anne digging the cellar. *(RL.1.3)*

Tip: If children are struggling with what to draw, have them close their eyes and visualize as you reread page 35. Prompt them to draw what they imagine.

- Prompt children to complete the second item.
- **Have children discuss story evidence.** Read aloud the Turn and Talk activity, and circulate as children discuss the connections between details in their pictures and the story. *(SL.1.4; SL.1.5)*

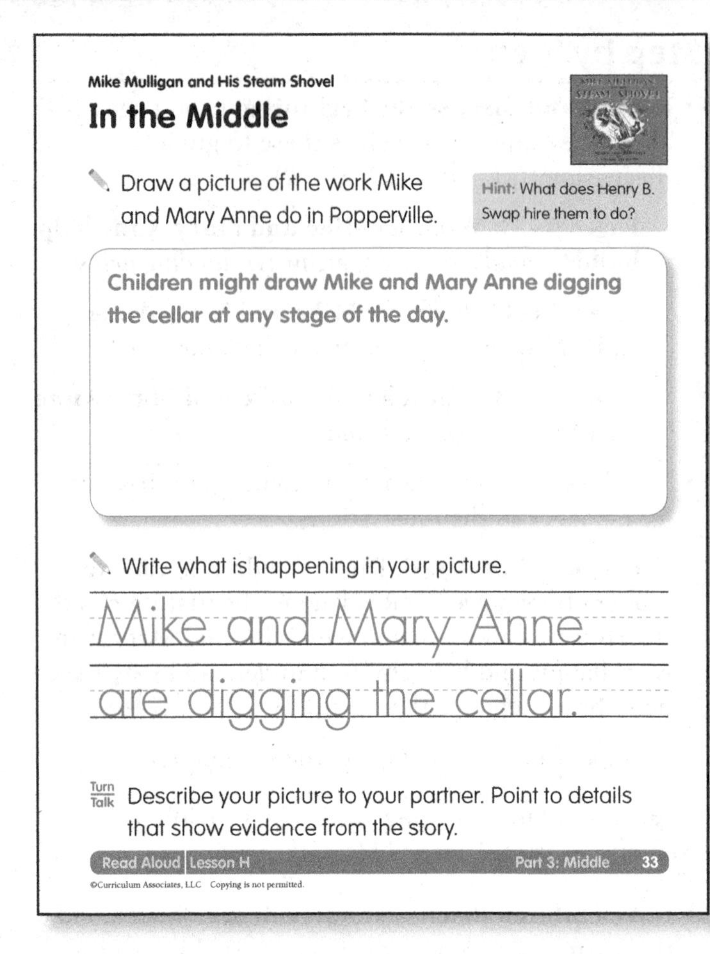
Mike Mulligan and His Steam Shovel

In the Middle

Draw a picture of the work Mike and Mary Anne do in Popperville.

Hint: What does Henry B. Swap hire them to do?

Children might draw Mike and Mary Anne digging the cellar at any stage of the day.

Write what is happening in your picture.

Mike and Mary Anne are digging the cellar.

Turn Talk Describe your picture to your partner. Point to details that show evidence from the story.

Read Aloud | Lesson H Part 3: Middle 33

©Curriculum Associates, LLC Copying is not permitted.

- Work with children to identify the most important ideas from this part of the story. Encourage them to use their Student Book pages to recall ideas.

Tier Two Vocabulary: *Decide*

- Ask children what Henry B. Swap decides on page 20. Invite a volunteer to point to *deciding.*
- Work with children to determine that the word *decide* means "to make up one's mind about," and it often involves choices.
- Provide an example of a time when you decide something. You may say *Every Monday I decide which student will be the line leader.*
- Then have children take turns naming a time when they decide or have decided something. Encourage them to practice using the word, and use their answers to familiarize them with other common forms such as *decided* and *deciding.*

Close Reading

- Reread page 20, and then use the following questions to help children examine Mike Mulligan:

  What does Mike promise to Henry B. Swap? *(Mary Anne can dig the cellar in one day.)*

  What evidence tells you that Mike's promise is risky? *("He had never been quite sure that this was true." Mike doesn't know for sure that Mary Anne can dig the cellar in a day.)*

  Why does Mike make this risky promise? Use evidence to support your answer. *(He is proud of Mary Anne. He took good care of her and wants to prove that she can still do a great job.)*

Step by Step

- **Reread and discuss the end.** Read pages 38–44 aloud. Discuss the way the story ends, using questions such as these. *(RL.1.1; SL.1.1; SL.1.2)*

  Page 39: What idea does the little boy have? *(He thinks Mary Anne should stay in the cellar to be the furnace and Mike should stay to be the janitor.)*

  Page 39: How does this idea solve Mike and Mary Anne's problem from earlier in the story? *(They have work to do now. People want them again.)*

  Page 44: How do Mike and Mary Anne feel now? *(They feel happy.)*

- Use the Close Reading activity to identify evidence that the problem is solved.
- **Focus on a key detail.** Direct children to turn to Student Book page 34, and read aloud the first item. Use the Hint to help children understand that Mike and Mary Anne are staying in the town hall. *(RL.1.3)*
- Prompt children to complete the second item.

Tip: Support developing writers by providing additional lined paper for children who wish to describe their pictures in more detail.

- **Have children discuss story evidence.** Read aloud the Turn and Talk activity. Encourage children to recall particular words and phrases from the text to explain their drawings. *(SL.1.4; SL.1.5)*

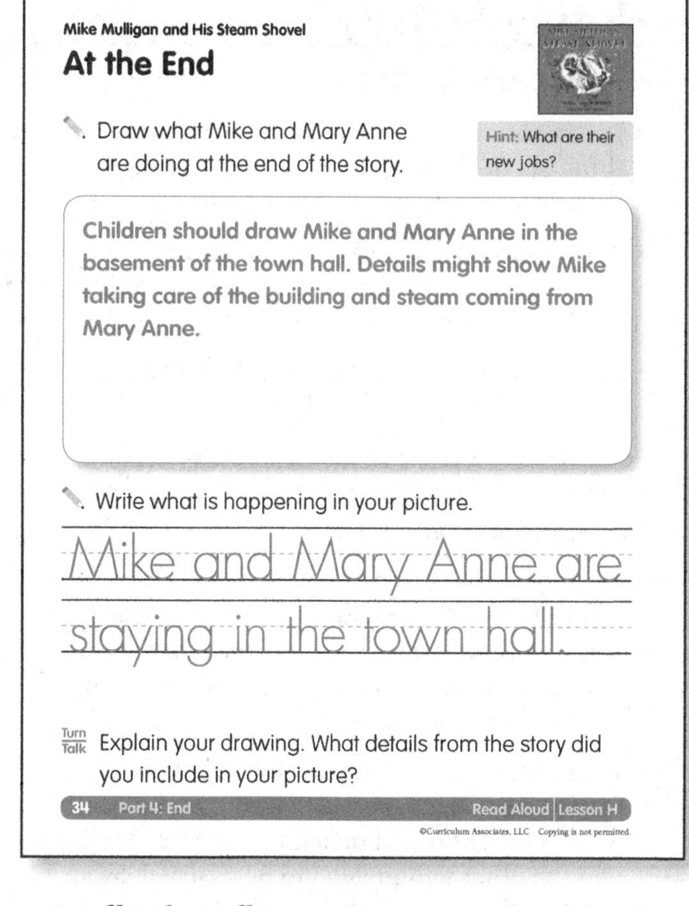

Mike Mulligan and His Steam Shovel

At the End

Draw what Mike and Mary Anne are doing at the end of the story.

Hint: What are their new jobs?

Children should draw Mike and Mary Anne in the basement of the town hall. Details might show Mike taking care of the building and steam coming from Mary Anne.

Write what is happening in your picture.

Mike and Mary Anne are staying in the town hall.

Turn Talk Explain your drawing. What details from the story did you include in your picture?

34 Part 4: End Read Aloud | Lesson H

©Curriculum Associates, LLC Copying is not permitted.

- **Retell *Mike Mulligan and His Steam Shovel.*** Guide a round-robin retelling of the entire story. Prompt children to refer to their Student Books as they take turns naming important ideas in sequence. Provide corrective feedback as needed. *(RL.1.2)*

Integrating Foundational Skills

Use these tasks as opportunities to integrate foundational skills into your reading of *Mike Mulligan and His Steam Shovel.*

1. Have children practice sounding out each sound in the following words: *had, get, dug, way, let, pay*. Help them to identify which words have a short vowel sound and which have a long vowel sound. *(Short vowel sound: had, get, dug, let; Long vowel sound: way, pay) (RF.1.2.a; RF.1.2.d)*
2. Reread and display the following words: *happened, everybody, talking, best, leave, keeping, smiled, quite*. Ask children to tell which words have an inflectional ending, such as *-ing, -ed,* or *-s*. *(happened, talking, keeping, smiled) (RF.1.3.f)*

Close Reading

- Explain that active readers draw conclusions from details in a story. Look for evidence that shows how Mike and Mary Anne's problem is solved.
- Point to and reread the little boy's idea on page 39 and the description on page 44. Then ask:

  Do any of these sentences say that Mike and Mary Anne's problem is solved? *(no)*

  How do these sentences help us to understand that the problem is solved? *(The sentences show how it was solved. The little boy explains the kind of work they will do, and the last page shows that Mike and Mary Anne are happy in the cellar. They are not sad anymore.)*

Writing Activity

Write an Opinion *(W.1.1)*

- Direct children to look back at the pictures they drew on page 34 of their Student Books and ask them to think about the way the story ends. Discuss children's opinions about the end of the story. Ask: *Do you like the way this story ends? Why or why not?*
- Ask children to write a sentence stating whether they liked or did not like the way the story ends. Encourage them to include the title of the book. Then ask children to write a sentence explaining why they did or did not like the way the story ends.
- Invite volunteers to read aloud their writing.

Speaking and Listening Activity

Get into Character *(SL.1.4)*

- Brainstorm with children what they know about Henry B. Swap. Encourage them to describe the way he thinks, feels, and acts. Then do the same with Mike Mulligan. Write children's ideas in two columns on chart paper.
- Have children work in pairs to act out a conversation between Mike Mulligan and Henry B. Swap. One child will pretend to be Mike Mulligan, and the other will pretend to be Henry B. Swap.
- Encourage children to use what they know from the conversation that takes place in the story, but also to add in observations that aren't written. For instance, Henry B. Swap might say, "Mike is never going to finish this job, and I will get it for free!"
- Invite volunteers to share their reenactments with the class.

Language Activity

Common and Proper Nouns *(L.1.1.b; L.1.2.a)*

- Remind children that a *noun* is a word that names a person, place, or thing. Explain that there are different kinds of nouns—common nouns and proper nouns.
- Turn to page 17 of *Mike Mulligan and His Steam Shovel*, and point out the words *shovels* and *town*. Explain that these are common nouns because they name general things. They could refer to any kind of shovel, or any town.
- Then point out the words *Mary Anne* and *Popperville* and say: *These are examples of proper nouns. A proper noun names a specific person, place, or thing. A proper noun begins with a capital letter, no matter where it is in a sentence. Names are examples of proper nouns.*
- Using examples from the story, work with children to pair proper nouns with their common nouns. *(Mary Anne/shovel; Popperville/town; Mike Mulligan/man)*

Lesson 10 (Student Book pages 85–88)

Sensory Words

CCSS

RL.1.4: Identify words and phrases in stories or poems that . . . appeal to the senses.

Required Read Alouds: *Projectable 3 ("I'm Staying Home From School Today"); H (Mike Mulligan and His Steam Shovel)*

Lesson Objectives

- Identify sensory words and phrases used to describe details in a poem.
- Identify sensory words and phrases used to describe details in a story.
- Understand how sensory words help readers picture what is happening in a text.

The Learning Progression

- **Grade K:** CCSS RL.K.4 requires children to ask and answer questions about unknown words in a text with prompting and support.
- **Grade 1: CCSS RL.1.4 focuses children's word-level analysis by having them identify the words and phrases in a poem or story that appeal to the senses.**
- **Grade 2:** CCSS RL.2.4 requires children to evaluate the expressive qualities of words by asking them to describe how words and phrases supply rhythm and meaning in a story, poem, or song.

Prerequisite Skills

- Know basic body parts associated with the five senses, and state their functions.
- Ask and answer questions about unfamiliar words in a text.
- Retell story details with prompting and support.

Tap Children's Prior Knowledge

- Tell children that they have five senses, and that we use our senses to find out about the world around us. Help children name the ways we use our senses and the body part we use for each sense. *(see or look with eyes, hear with ears, smell with nose, taste with tongue, and touch or feel with hands or skin)*
- Begin a chart with the headings *See/Look, Hear, Smell, Taste,* and *Touch/Feel.* Tell children that they will add words to the chart that tell about each sense.
- Point to the heading *See/Look.* Ask questions such as the following about what familiar objects look like: *What does the chalkboard look like? (dusty, dull) What does glitter look like? (shiny) What does the lost-and-found box look like? (messy)* Write children's responses below the heading.
- Continue for the remaining headings, using questions such as the following: *How does a whisper sound? (quiet) How does garbage smell? (stinky) How does candy taste? (sweet) How does a kitten's fur feel? (soft)*
- Read aloud the words in each column. Tell children that words that tell about the senses are called *sensory words.* Explain that they will learn how to identify sensory words and use them to picture what is happening in a story or poem.

Ready *Teacher Toolbox* — Teacher-Toolbox.com

	Prerequisite Skills	*RL.1.4*
Ready Lessons		✓
Tools for Instruction	✓ ✓	✓
Interactive Tutorials	✓	

Additional CCSS

RL.1.2; W.1.5; SL.1.1; SL.1.4; L.1.1; L.1.2; L.1.5 (See page A38 for full text.)

Step by Step

- **Introduce the standard.** Have children turn to page 85 in their Student Books. Read aloud the speech bubble.
- **Review questions about sensory words.** Read the line below the speech bubble, and point out that what follows are questions good readers can ask about sensory words.
- Read aloud the first question. Have children find and underline the word *describing*. Explain:

  ***Describing* means telling what something is like. Knowing what the author is describing will help you understand the words the author uses.**

- Read aloud the second question. Have children find and underline the word *senses*. Then read each sense word as children indicate the related body part by pointing to their eyes, ears, nose, or mouth, and wiggling their fingers. Explain:

  To answer this question, decide if the words tell about looking with your eyes, hearing with your ears, smelling with your nose, tasting with your mouth, or feeling with your hands.

- Read aloud the third question. Have children find and underline the word *picture*. Explain:

  Sensory words help you imagine what it would be like to be right there in the story. Making pictures in your mind as you read can help you understand the exact thing the author describes.

- Guide children to picture details when they hear sensory words. Tell children to close their eyes, listen, and picture in their minds what you are going to describe. Then describe being in a familiar place, such as a local swimming hole:

  I am sitting on a big, smooth rock. The rock is hot from the sun. I hear water rippling and splashing, and children laughing. I can hear leaves rustling. I feel cold water lapping at my toes.

- Have children open their eyes and discuss what place they pictured. Have them tell what words helped them picture it. *(big, smooth, hot, rippling, splashing, laughing, rustling, cold, lapping)* Discuss that both single words and groups of words, or phrases, can describe things you experience with your senses.

Listen and Learn

Sensory Words

Authors use **sensory words** to describe story details. Sensory words tell how things look, sound, smell, taste, or feel.

Here are some questions that you can ask about sensory words:

- What is the author describing?
- Which senses do the words tell about?

  look | hear  | smell
  taste | feel

- What do the words make you picture in your mind?

Notice sensory words when you read. An author uses these words to help you imagine exactly what something is like.

- **Explain why readers and writers use sensory words.** Read aloud the bottom of the page. Then share an example of a time when sensory words helped you understand a story. Explain:

  When I read *The Three Billy Goats Gruff*, the words said the first billy goat had a "tiny squeak of a voice" and his hooves went "trip trip trap" over the bridge. The sensory words *tiny squeak* and *trip trip trap* helped me understand that the first billy goat was small.

Tip: Explain that, like authors, children can use many different sensory words in their writing. Review some of the sensory words on the chart from the activity on page 113. Tell children they will have a chance to use words like these at the end of the lesson.

- **Have children demonstrate understanding.** Call on individuals to share what they have learned so far about identifying sensory words.

 Part 2: Modeled Instruction

Step by Step

- **Review Part 1; preview Part 2.** Ask volunteers to share questions they learned to ask about sensory words. Have children turn to Student Book page 86.
- **Read "I'm Staying Home From School Today."** Have children listen closely as you read pages 209–210. Discuss who is saying the words, whether or not children were surprised by this, and why.

Tip: Explain that this poem has rhythm, or beats, and rhymes, or words with the same ending sounds. Help children clap the beat and find rhymes to see how the language appeals to the sense of hearing.

- **Model identifying sensory words.** Think aloud:

  First, I'll think about what the poet is describing. He's pretending to be sick. He's telling how he feels. I'll look for the sensory words he uses to describe how he feels.

- Reread the poem aloud. Have children raise their hands when they hear words that tell how the poet says he feels. *(pain, pounding, ache, shiver, cold, sore)* Repeat for words that tell what the poet says he looks like *(blue)* and sounds like. *(cough, sneeze)*
- Read aloud the first activity on the Student Book page. Discuss which sense each picture on the right stands for. Then point to the words and the pictures opposite them as you model completing the first row. Explain:

  Can you hear or taste cold and sore? No! You *feel* cold and sore, so I'll circle the hand.

- **Model recording your response.** Show children how to circle the correct picture. Continue through the items, explaining answer choices and having children circle the correct sense for each item.
- Read aloud the second activity and the Hint. Ask children to think about the words in the Hint and picture how the poet feels. Model, and then have children write the answer. *(L.1.1; L.1.2)*
- Use the Close Reading activity to discuss the choices authors make when using sensory words to describe.
- **Have children demonstrate understanding.** Have partners complete the Turn and Talk activity by recalling words and phrases that show how the poet is pretending to feel. Share evidence. *(SL.1.1; SL.1.4)*

Practice Together

Sensory Words

in "I'm Staying Home From School Today"

PROJECTABLE
I'm Staying Home From School Today

Read the words from the poem.
Circle the sense they tell about.

1. cold, sore	ear, hand (circled), lips
2. blue	nose, eye (circled), ear
3. cough, sneeze	ear (circled), hand, lips

What do the words help you picture?

Hint: What would it feel like to be cold, sore, coughing, and sneezing?

I picture the poet feeling very sick.

Turn Talk What evidence from the poem tells how the poet is pretending to feel?

86 Part 2: Modeled Instruction Lesson 10

Close Reading

- Tell children that now they will look closely at some of the words the poet uses in "I'm Staying Home From School Today."
- Read the first stanza aloud. Prompt children:

  What does *pounding* mean? *(It means hitting hard or banging over and over.)*

  What do you imagine a pain pounding in someone's head would feel like? *(It would feel like someone is hitting your head over and over.)*

  Why does the author use the word *pounding* instead of *hurting*? (Hurting *doesn't help you imagine what the pain is like;* pounding *tells you more about the how the pain feels.)*

- Discuss that authors choose words carefully to help readers imagine exactly what an experience might sound or feel like. Tell children that they can do the same when they are writing.

Part 3: Guided Practice

Step by Step

- **Review Parts 1–2; preview Part 3.** Have children recall questions they can ask about sensory words. Direct them to turn to Student Book page 87. Explain that you will guide them through this page.
- **Revisit *Mike Mulligan and His Steam Shovel*.** Invite children to briefly retell the story, using pages 31–34 of their Student Books. *(RL.1.2)*
- **Guide children to identify sensory words.** Ask children to listen carefully as you read aloud page 32 of *Mike Mulligan and His Steam Shovel*. Have them listen for sensory words and phrases that help them picture the scene in their minds.

Tip: To help children picture page 32, read with dramatic expression. Wave your hands to show flying dirt. Squint your eyes and cough. Read the last four lines louder and louder, and faster and faster.

- Reread the page, having children close their eyes, listen, and touch their eyes, ears, nose, mouth, or hands when they hear a corresponding sensory word or phrase. Pause to discuss what the words help them picture.
- **Guide children to record their responses.** Read aloud the directions and Hint at the top of the Student Book page. Review the pictures that show each of the senses, having children name the sense each one stands for.
- Read each item in the activity and guide children to complete it, using prompts such as the following:

  Would you see, feel, or taste "dirt flying everywhere"? *(You could see it; you might feel it, too.)*

  Which picture should you circle to show that you see the dirt? *(the eye)* **Circle it now.**

- Read aloud the second activity. Discuss the answer before children write theirs in complete sentences. *(L.1.1; L.1.2)*
- Use the Close Reading activity to discuss what the sensory words show about the scene and Mary Anne.
- **Have children demonstrate understanding.** Have partners complete the Turn and Talk activity by recalling sensory words and phrases that helped them picture the sights and sounds. Invite children to share their evidence in class discussion. *(SL.1.1; SL.1.4)*

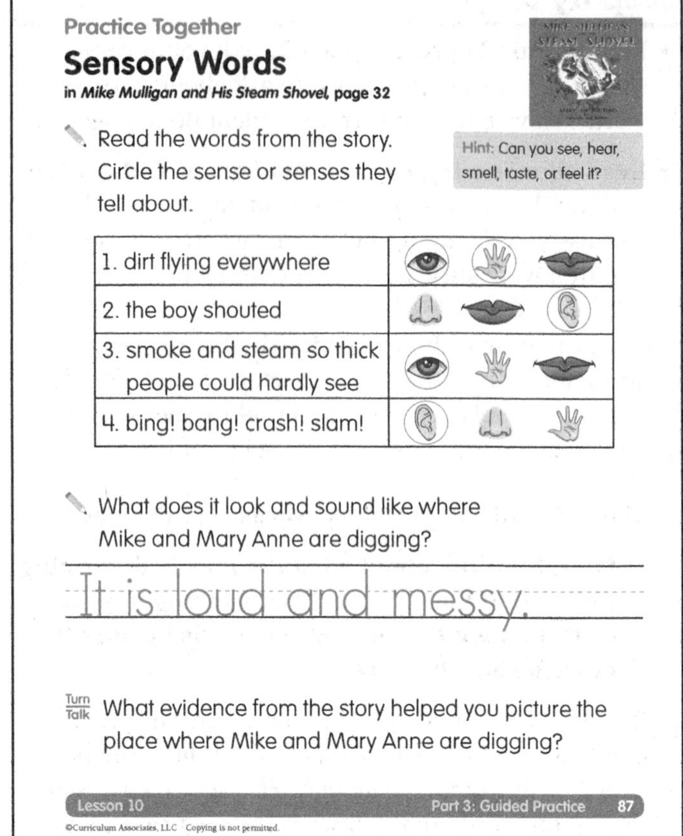

Practice Together

Sensory Words

in Mike Mulligan and His Steam Shovel, page 32

Read the words from the story. Circle the sense or senses they tell about.

Hint: Can you see, hear, smell, taste, or feel it?

1. dirt flying everywhere	
2. the boy shouted	
3. smoke and steam so thick people could hardly see	
4. bing! bang! crash! slam!	

What does it look and sound like where Mike and Mary Anne are digging?

It is loud and messy.

Turn Talk What evidence from the story helped you picture the place where Mike and Mary Anne are digging?

Lesson 10 Part 3: Guided Practice 87

Close Reading

- Tell children that now they will think about what sensory words show about the scene and about Mary Anne. Reread the fourth sentence on page 34. Then prompt:

  What do you picture about the dirt when you hear the word *flying*? *(that dirt is being tossed around in the air)*

  Look at the picture. Why do you think the dirt is flying? *(because Mary Anne is digging so fast)*

  What do the text and the picture show about how much smoke and steam there is? *(There is a lot. The picture shows the smoke blocking out the sun. The text says people could hardly see.)*

  Why was there so much smoke and steam? *(Mary Anne makes smoke and steam as she works. She is working hard, so she makes a lot.)*

- Discuss how the sensory words help bring the scene to life.

Part 4: Independent Practice

Step by Step

- **Review Parts 1–3; preview Part 4.** Ask volunteers to tell how identifying sensory words helps readers.
- Direct children to turn to Student Book page 88. Explain that they will work on their own to identify sensory words and use them to picture and describe a scene. Emphasize that, as on previous pages, they will read words, circle pictures to show senses, and answer a question.
- **Have children identify sensory words independently.** Display *Mike Mulligan and His Steam Shovel.* Tell children they will look for sensory words in another part of the book.
- Tell children to listen closely for sensory words that help them picture what is happening as you read aloud page 34.

Tip: Use a dramatic reading to help children picture this scene. Reread page 34 aloud slowly, using a hushed voice to indicate the calming scene. Use gestures to show that the air was clearing.

- Read aloud the directions and Hint for the first activity on the Student Book page. Then read each of the phrases in items 1–3, using prompts such as the following to help children complete each row:

  Think about what the words describe. Which sense would you use?

  Which picture should you circle?

- Read aloud the second activity. Have children write their answers in complete sentences. *(L.1.1; L.1.2)*
- Discuss answers to both activities.
- Use the Close Reading activity to examine how an author chooses words to create pictures and feelings.
- **Have children demonstrate understanding.** Have partners complete the Turn and Talk activity by recalling sensory words and phrases that helped them picture the sights and sounds in the text. Invite children to share their evidence in class discussion.
- **Have children reflect on their learning.** Guide children in a discussion about how recognizing sensory words helps them picture what is happening in poems and stories. Chart their ideas.

Practice by Myself

Sensory Words

in Mike Mulligan and His Steam Shovel, page 34

Read the words from the story. Circle the sense or senses they tell about.

Hint: Can you see, hear, smell, taste, or feel it?

1. suddenly it was quiet	nose	mouth	ear (circled)
2. dirt settled down	nose	eye (circled)	ear
3. smoke and steam cleared away	ear	mouth	eye (circled)

What does it look and sound like when Mike and Mary Anne are finished digging?

It becomes quiet and less messy.

Turn Talk What evidence from the story helped you picture what happens when Mike and Mary Anne finish digging?

88 Part 4: Independent Practice Lesson 10

Close Reading

- Remind children that authors use sensory words to help readers picture what something is like.
- Ask children to picture the scene as you reread pages 32–34 of *Mike Mulligan and His Steam Shovel* aloud. Then prompt:

  How are the scenes on these pages different from each other? *(The first scene is loud, noisy, and dirty; the second is calm and quiet.)*

  What words in the story signal the change between them? *("Then suddenly it was quiet.")*

  How does the sudden change from loud to quiet make you feel as a reader? *(excited or nervous about what might happen next)*

- Discuss how the author used sensory words to create two very different scenes, and that by changing from one to the other with the word *suddenly,* the author makes the story more exciting and dramatic.

Differentiated Instruction

Assessment and Remediation

If you observe . . .	Then try . . .
Difficulty remembering the five senses	Having children make a sense diagram to use as they identify sense words. Have children draw a face and hands. Guide them to label the body parts *(eyes, ear, nose, mouth, hands)* with the corresponding senses. *(see, hear, smell, taste, feel)* Children can use the diagram to help them remember the senses.
Difficulty identifying which sense a word or phrase tells about	Practicing with the following sensory words and phrases: *salty, rough, buzz, flash, spicy, damp, twinkling, perfumed, silky; the wind howled, the spoiled meat reeked, a peppery cracker.* Read aloud each word or phrase and discuss which sense it describes, using prompts such as the following: *Can you hear it or taste it when something is spicy? Do you feel it or smell it when something is rough?*
Difficulty making a mental picture of what is happening in a text	Inviting children to draw pictures of what is happening in the text. Encourage children to share their drawings and to explain them using sensory words.

Connect to the Anchor Standard

R4: *Interpret words and phrases as they are used in a text, including determining technical, connotative, and figurative meanings, and analyze how specific word choices shape meaning or tone.*

Throughout the grades, Standard 4 builds towards a more sophisticated analysis of word meaning and word choice. In later grades, students transition from recognizing sensory descriptions to asking higher-level questions about words, including examining allusions and figurative language. They analyze the effects of an author's deliberate choice of words by asking questions such as: *What words stand out? How does the author use language to make the reader feel a certain way? Which words are literal and which are nonliteral? How and why does the author use figurative language? How would the meaning of the text change if other words were used?* Use the following activities to help your students begin this transition.

- Help children understand that an author chooses words for effect. Reread pages 33–34 of *Mike Mulligan and His Steam Shovel.* Ask children why the author didn't just write "Mike Mulligan and Mary Anne dug fast and well. Dirt was everywhere. Then there was the cellar, all finished." Compare versions and discuss how the author's words make the reader feel like they are in the scene and make the story more exciting and dramatic. *(SL.1.1; SL.1.4; L.1.5)*
- Together, write a sensory description of a place. Have children choose a familiar place, such as the playground, a busy hallway, or the cafeteria. List words that tell what they see, hear, smell, taste, or feel there. (You may want to revisit the list of sensory words from the activity on page 113.) Together, use the words to write a description that makes readers feel as if they are surrounded by the sights and sounds of the scene. *(W.1.5)*

Lesson 11 (Student Book pages 89–92)

Types of Books

CCSS

RL.1.5: Explain major differences between books that tell stories and books that give information, drawing on a wide reading of a range of text types.

Required Read Alouds: A (*The Empty Pot*); B (*The Polar Bear Son*); F (*Butterflies and Moths*); G (*Elizabeth Leads the Way*); H (*Mike Mulligan and His Steam Shovel*); I (*Earthworms*)

Lesson Objectives

- Use the characteristics of a text to identify a fiction book and an informational book.
- Compare and contrast fiction and informational books.
- Understand purposes for reading fiction and informational books.

The Learning Progression

- **Grade K:** CCSS RL.K.5 introduces the idea that there are different types of texts, with the expectation that children can readily recognize familiar genres such as poems and storybooks.
- **Grade 1: CCSS RL.1.5 requires children to discriminate between different text types and describe specific differences between literary texts and informational texts.**
- **Grade 2:** CCSS RL.2.5 asks children to take a deeper look at the structure of a story, specifically calling for children to analyze a story's beginning and ending.

Prerequisite Skills

- Recognize common types of texts.
- Distinguish between fantasy and reality.
- Understand that a fact is a true statement.
- Identify major events in the beginning, middle, and end of a story with prompting and support.

Tap Children's Prior Knowledge

- Begin a chart with the headings *Made-up, Real,* and *Fact.* Tell children that they already know a lot about how to tell the difference between things that are made-up and things that are real.
- Explain that something is made-up if we create it from our imagination but it doesn't exist in real life. Give an example of something that is made-up, such as cartoon characters. Have children suggest other made-up things, and record them on the chart.
- Then explain that real things exist in real life—you can touch them, see them, or hear them. Give a few examples of things that are real, such as frogs, your principal, and the local library. Have children name some more examples, and add them to the chart.
- Finally, explain that a *fact* is something that is true. Give examples of simple classroom facts such as this: *There are 25 desks in this room.* Tell children that they probably know a lot of facts about things such as dinosaurs, bicycles, sports, or plants. Invite them to suggest some facts to add to the chart.
- Tell children that in this lesson, they will learn to tell the difference between books that have made-up stories and books that have facts.

Ready *Teacher Toolbox* Teacher-Toolbox.com

	Prerequisite Skills	RL.1.5
Ready Lessons	✓	✓
Tools for Instruction	✓✓	
Interactive Tutorials	✓✓	

Additional CCSS

RL.1.2; RL.1.7; RI.1.2; RI.1.7; SL.1.1; SL.1.2; SL.1.5 (See page A38 for full text.)

Step by Step

- **Introduce the standard.** Direct children to page 89 in their Student Books. Read aloud the speech bubble.
- **Review characteristics of fiction.** Read the sentence below the speech bubble, and explain that the chart describes different types of books.
- Read the *Fiction Books* column, and think aloud:

  Sometimes it's easy to tell that a story is made-up because things happen that couldn't happen in real life. Other times, a story is made-up, but it seems like it could really happen. All stories have a plot, which means that events happen in order from beginning to middle to end.

- Point out that fiction books usually have illustrations, or pictures that someone draws. Explain that they usually do not have photographs, because photographs show real things.
- Choose a few volunteers to look on classroom shelves for examples of fiction stories they have read. Together find characters and illustrations in a few books. If you have chapter books, point out the text features—the table of contents and chapter titles.
- **Review characteristics of informational text.** Read aloud the *Informational Books* column. Explain that informational books give facts or details about real things rather than made-up things.
- Choose a few volunteers to look on classroom shelves for examples of informational books they have read. Have children name the topic of each book. Then help them find examples of photographs, illustrations, and text features such as a table of contents, diagrams, headings, and captions.
- Explain that a biography is a special type of informational book that tells the story of a person's life. Say:

  A biography can seem like a fiction book because it is told about a person and it is organized by a plot with a beginning, middle, and end. However, it is an informational book because it is a true story, it has facts and dates, and it often has photographs.

- Choose a few volunteers to look on classroom shelves for examples of biographies they have read.

Listen and Learn

Types of Books

Some books tell stories. They are **fiction** books. Some books give information. They are **informational** books.

This chart helps you tell the difference between fiction books and informational books.

Fiction Books	Informational Books
• tell a made-up story	• tell facts or information
• organized by a plot with events that happen in order	• organized by topic and key details
• have illustrations, not photographs	• have photographs and/or illustrations
• sometimes have text features	• usually have text features

Before you read a book, think about what kind of book it is. This will help you know how to read it.

Tip: To further develop children's understanding of genre, have them sort all the books they have pulled from classroom shelves into smaller groups and tell what is similar about each group.

- **Explain why readers need to distinguish types of books.** Read aloud the bottom of the page, and share some examples of times you read books for different purposes. For instance, you wanted to find out what flowers would grow in your garden, so you read an informational book about plants; you wanted to read a suspenseful story, so you chose a mystery book.
- **Have children demonstrate understanding.** Call on individuals to share what they have learned so far about different types of texts. Invite them to share titles of favorite books and tell whether they are fiction or informational books.

Part 2: Modeled Instruction

Step by Step

- **Review Part 1; preview Part 2.** Ask volunteers to tell how to decide if a book is fiction or informational. Direct children to Student Book page 90.
- **Revisit *Mike Mulligan and His Steam Shovel*.** Have children briefly retell the story using Student Book pages 31–34. *(RL.1.2)*
- **Model identifying types of books.** Display *Mike Mulligan and His Steam Shovel.* Explain that you will model deciding what type of book it is. Think aloud:

  This book has characters named Mike and Mary Anne. It has a plot, or events that happen in order from beginning to end. It also has illustrations, but they show a steam shovel with eyes and a mouth. Real steam shovels don't have eyes or mouths! This book must be fiction.

- Display *Earthworms.* Page through the book and point out the table of contents, the photograph and caption on page 6, the illustrations and captions on page 7, and the diagram on page 10. Read aloud a few facts from pages 10–11.

Tip: Remind children that a *fact* is something that is true and real. Explain that we can check if the description of the earthworm's body is true by looking at a real earthworm.

- Ask children if *Earthworms* is a fiction book. *(no)* Together conclude that it is an informational book, and have children use the details in the chart on Student Book page 89 to tell why.
- **Model recording your responses.** Read aloud the directions and contents of the chart on Student Book page 90. Then model filling it in by looking through each book to verify that it has or does not have the characteristic described in each row.
- Continue modeling, having children record their answers. Then read the prompt and the Hint below the chart. Model how to respond by drawing a line from each book title to the correct book type.
- Use the Close Reading activity to discuss text features.
- **Have children demonstrate understanding.** Read the Turn and Talk activity. As a class, discuss which pieces of evidence were the most helpful and whether any of them were confusing. *(RL.1.7; SL.1.1; SL.1.2)*

Practice Together

Types of Books

in *Mike Mulligan and His Steam Shovel* and *Earthworms*

Complete the table to show what is in each book.

	Mike Mulligan and His Steam Shovel	Earthworms
illustrations	x	x
photographs		x
text features		x
a made-up story about characters	x	
facts about a topic		x

Draw a line to complete each sentence.

Hint: What kinds of pictures are usually in a fiction book?

1. Mike Mulligan and His Steam Shovel — is a fiction book.
2. Earthworms — is an informational book.

Turn Talk Tell your partner what evidence you used to decide the genre of each book.

90 Part 2: Modeled Instruction Lesson 11

Close Reading

- Explain that sometimes fiction and informational books borrow features from each other. Display the inside front cover of *Mike Mulligan and His Steam Shovel.* Prompt:

  Do you think this diagram is made-up or does it show the real parts of a steam shovel? *(It shows the real parts of a steam shovel, but the steam shovel has a made-up face.)*

- Read aloud page 14, and prompt:

  Do you think this is something made-up or something that really happened? *(This part of the story could have really happened.)*

- Help children understand that even though the book has some information that could be real, it is still a made-up story about characters.
- Point out that, for this reason, children should think about everything they know about a book to decide what type of book it is.

Part 3: Guided Practice

Step by Step

- **Review Parts 1–2; preview Part 3.** Have children tell what visual and text clues they can look for when deciding if a book is fiction or informational. Direct them to turn to Student Book page 91. Explain that you will guide them through this page.
- **Revisit *Elizabeth Leads the Way* and *The Polar Bear Son*.** Have children briefly retell each story. Encourage them to use the chart created for the Book Review on Teacher Resource Book page 89 and Student Book pages 7–10. *(RI.1.2; RL.1.2)*
- **Guide children to identify book types.** Page through *Elizabeth Leads the Way*, and prompt:

  What types of pictures do you see? *(illustrations)*

  Are there events that happen in order? *(yes)*

  Are the people in the story real people or made-up characters? How do you know? *(real people; There is a photograph of Elizabeth at the front, and there are facts about her life at the back.)*
- Use a show of hands to have children vote on whether *Elizabeth Leads the Way* is a fiction book or an informational book. Confirm that it is a true story about the life of a real person, called a *biography*, so it is an informational book.

Tip: Remind children that there are different types of informational books that are written for different purposes. If children wanted to do research on Stanton, they should use a reference book instead.

- Use the Close Reading activity to explore evidence that Elizabeth Cady Stanton was a real person.
- Repeat the prompts above for *The Polar Bear Son*. Children should point out that the polar bear does not behave like a real bear. Have children vote on the type of book it is, and confirm that it is fiction.
- **Guide children to write responses.** Read aloud each activity on Student Book page 91 and guide children to complete them, discussing responses as needed.
- **Have children demonstrate understanding.** Read aloud the Turn and Talk activity, and encourage children to name evidence that is not mentioned in the table. Invite children to share their answers with the whole class. *(RL.1.7; SL.1.1; SL.1.2)*

Practice Together

Types of Books

in *Elizabeth Leads the Way* and *The Polar Bear Son*

Complete the table to show what is in each book.

	Elizabeth Leads the Way	*The Polar Bear Son*
illustrations	x	x
plot with events	x	x
a made-up story about characters		x
a true story about real people	x	

Draw a line to complete each sentence.

Hint: Do polar bears really hug people?

1. Elizabeth Leads the Way —— is an informational book.
2. The Polar Bear Son —— is a fiction book.

Turn Talk Tell your partner what evidence you used to decide the genre of each book.

Lesson 11 Part 3: Guided Practice 91

Close Reading

- Tell children that sometimes it can be tricky to figure out if a book is about a real person or a made-up character.
- Display page 32 of *Elizabeth Leads the Way*, and read aloud the heading and the first paragraph. Then prompt:

  Do these words tell about a made-up character? *(No. They tell facts about the life of Elizabeth Cady Stanton.)*

  How can you tell? *(It contains dates.)*
- Explain that *sources* are books and articles in which authors find facts and information. Prompt:

  Why do you think the author used sources? *(to find facts about Elizabeth Cady Stanton)*
- Guide children to see that the evidence shows that Elizabeth Cady Stanton was real and that this book is informational.

Part 4: Independent Practice

Step by Step

- **Review Parts 1–3; preview Part 4.** Ask children to tell why they might read a fiction book or an informational book. Then direct them to turn to Student Book page 92. Explain that now they will work independently to decide if books are fiction or informational.
- **Revisit *Butterflies and Moths* and *The Empty Pot*.** Have children review each book, using the chart created for Book Review on Teacher Resource Book page 71 and Student Book pages 3–6. *(RI.1.2; RL.1.2)*
- **Have children identify book types independently.** Read aloud the directions and the content of the chart on Student Book page 92.
- Page through each book as you guide children to complete the corresponding column of the chart. Use prompts such as these:

  Are these illustrations or photographs? How do you know?

  Do you see any text features in this book? If yes, what do you see?

- Have children record their answers silently. Then read aloud the directions for the second activity. Have children draw a line to show whether each book is fiction or informational.
- Have children share their responses for each activity.

Tip: Review that *The Empty Pot* is a folktale, or a fiction story told for many years, and that *Butterflies and Moths* is a science book that gives information through photographs and text.

- Use the Close Reading activity to have children focus on specific evidence that supports their decision about *The Empty Pot*.
- **Have children demonstrate understanding.** Have partners do the Turn and Talk activity by describing the evidence they used to make their decisions. They should refer to the table and identify visual as well as text evidence. *(RL.1.7; SL.1.1; SL.1.2)*
- **Have children reflect on their learning.** Have children discuss what they learned about book types, and why they might read each type of book. Reinforce that informational texts can be read for pleasure, too.

Practice by Myself

Types of Books

in *Butterflies and Moths* and *The Empty Pot*

Complete the table to show what is in each book.

	Butterflies and Moths	*The Empty Pot*
illustrations		x
photographs	x	
text features	x	
a made-up story about characters		x
facts about a topic	x	

Draw a line to complete each sentence.

Hint: Which book has a beginning, middle, and end?

1. The Empty Pot — is a fiction book.
2. Butterflies and Moths — is an informational book.

Turn Talk Tell your partner what evidence you used to decide the genre of each book.

Close Reading

- Remind children that to decide whether a book is fiction or informational, they should look carefully at the pictures and think about what the words say.
- Display the final page of *The Empty Pot*, and read it aloud. Then prompt:

  How would you describe this picture? Does it show real things? *(It is an illustration. Some parts of it could be real, but others are not, like the birds carrying flowers and the horses smiling.)*

  Is Ping a real person or a character? *(a character)*

  If you had trouble deciding whether Ping is real, what else could you think about? *(I would notice that the book tells a story with the events happening in order. The book does not give main ideas and details or facts about a topic.)*

Differentiated Instruction

Assessment and Remediation

If you observe . . .	Then try . . .
Difficulty seeing that illustrations can show real things	Having children create their own realistic drawings. Display the food-chain drawings on pages 16–19 of *Who Eats What?* and point out that they show real plants and animals. Then have each child make a realistic drawing of a favorite animal. Have children add labels or a caption to tell facts about the animals. Discuss why their drawings could be in an informational text. *(SL.1.5)*
Difficulty deciding whether the people and events described in a book are real or made-up	Creating a checklist to decide. Display the headings *Real* and *Made-Up.* Together brainstorm and list clues that tell if a person in a book is real or made-up. *(Real: photograph, date of birth, date of important event, lives in real place; Made-Up: characters do things real people or animals can't do)* Give partners a biography or a story book from the classroom shelves, and have them use the checklist to determine if the people are real or made-up. Have children discuss their answers and evidence with the class.
Difficulty making a decision about genre	Having the class compare books from the same genre. Distribute different informational books to partners. Prompt partners to find and display book features, using questions such as the following: *Does your book have a table of contents? Are there words in dark print that divide the text into sections? Are there photographs or drawings of real things? Can you find a fact?* Discuss responses as a class. Repeat with fiction books, asking: *Who is in the story? What events happen? Does anything happen that can't happen in real life?*

Connect to the Anchor Standard

R5: *Analyze the structure of texts, including how specific sentences, paragraphs, and larger portions of the text (e.g., a section, chapter, scene, or stanza) relate to each other and the whole.*

In mastering Standard 5 throughout the grades, students begin by using structural differences to identify different types of texts. In later grades, students relate text structures to component parts at the sentence and word level in order to deepen their understanding of a text and increase their appreciation of an author's aesthetic decisions. They will ask questions such as the following: *How are the features of this text the same or different than other texts I have read? Why did the author choose to present them this way? How did the author organize the information, and why? How does this word/scene/information relate to the rest of the text? Why did the author write this text?* Use the following activities to help your students begin transitioning toward these ways of thinking.

- Have children identify purposes for reading different books. Display a variety of classroom books, one by one. Have children discuss what they can tell about the book by looking at the title and features. Ask: *Why would you read this book? Why do you think the author wrote this book?* Discuss how the features helped children decide the purpose for reading.
- Have students compare book formats. Display an informational text, a fiction book, and a poetry book. Prompt: *What do you notice about the writing on the pages? Which parts look the same or different than the other books? What does the writing sound like when you read it? How is the language the same or different than the other books? What are the illustrations for?* Help children see that an author's choices affect how readers understand and enjoy books. *(RL.1.7; RI.1.7; SL.1.2)*

Lesson 12 (Student Book pages 93–96)

Who Is Telling the Story?

CCSS

RL.1.6: Identify who is telling the story at various points in a text.

Required Read Alouds: A (*The Empty Pot*); C (*My Rotten Redheaded Older Brother*); H (*Mike Mulligan and His Steam Shovel*)

Lesson Objectives

- Recognize that stories are told by narrators.
- Understand that a narrator can be the author or a character in the story.
- Identify who is narrating a story.
- Use textual evidence to support conclusions about who is narrating the story.

The Learning Progression

- **Grade K:** CCSS RL.K.6 requires children to identify an author and illustrator and describe their roles in telling a story with prompting and support.
- **Grade 1: CCSS RL.1.6 builds on the Grade K standard by having children identify who is telling the story—the author or a character.**
- **Grade 2:** CCSS RL.2.6 expands upon the scope of the standard by having children acknowledge differences in the points of view of characters. Children are asked to demonstrate different points of view by speaking in different voices for each character when reading dialogue aloud.

Prerequisite Skills

- Identify the author of a story with prompting and support.
- Describe an author's role in telling a story with prompting and support.
- Identify characters in a story with prompting and support.

Tap Children's Prior Knowledge

- Remind children how to identify an author. Display *Mike Mulligan and His Steam Shovel* and read the title. Say: *The cover of a book shows the title. It also shows one or more names.* Point to the author's name and read it aloud. Ask: *Why is Virginia Lee Burton's name on the cover? (She is the author.)*
- Remind children that sometimes the word *by* gives a clue to who the author is. Point out that the author's name often appears on the title page as well as on the cover.
- Ask: *What does the author do? (The author writes the story.)* Explain that authors write stories about characters, or the people or animals the story is about. Have children recall some of the characters from *Mike Mulligan and His Steam Shovel. (Mike, Mary Anne)*
- Explain that when an author writes, he or she must decide who is going to tell the story. Sometimes the author tells the story. Other times, the author has one of the characters tell the story.
- Tell children that in this lesson, they will learn how to identify who is telling a story—the author or a character.

Ready Teacher Toolbox Teacher-Toolbox.com

	Prerequisite Skills	*RL.1.6*
Ready Lessons	✓	✓
Tools for Instruction		
Interactive Tutorials		

Additional CCSS

RL.1.2; RL.1.7; SL.1.1; SL.1.2; SL.1.4; SL.1.5; L.1.1; L.1.2 (*See page A38 for full text.*)

Part 1: Introduction

Step by Step

- **Introduce the standard.** Have children turn to page 93 in their Student Books. Read aloud the speech bubble.
- **Review how to identify a character-narrator.** Read the line below the speech bubble, and point out that the first example describes a character-narrator.
- Read aloud the first example. Have children underline the word *character*. Ask them to listen closely for the words *I*, *me*, *my*, and *we* as you read aloud the text in the yellow box. Then guide them to find and circle the words in the story.

Tip: To help emergent readers recognize the target words, read each sentence aloud, point to each target word, and use your voice to emphasize the word.

- Tell children that they can use other words in the text to figure out who the narrator is. Read the first example again. Explain:

  The words "my big sister" and "lets me play with her toys" show that the narrator is a character, who also happens to be a younger brother or sister.

- **Review how to identify an author-narrator.** Read aloud the second example. Have children underline the word *author*. Review that if the narrator is a character in the story, he or she uses the words *I*, *me*, *my*, or *we*. Read aloud the text in the yellow box, and prompt:

  Is the narrator a character in the story? *(no)*

  What evidence tells you this? *(The narrator does not use the words* I, me, my, *or* we.*)*

- Point out that Meghan and Ava are the characters' names. Then explain:

  An author-narrator does not tell what happens to himself or herself; he or she only tells about the characters.

- Guide children to find the words the author-narrator uses to tell about the characters in the story. *(Meghan, Ava, they, she)* Have them circle the words.
- Tell children that good readers look for clues in different parts of the story to be sure about who the narrator is. Explain that you will practice doing this together later in the lesson.

Listen and Learn

Who Is Telling the Story?

The **narrator** is the person telling a story. The narrator can be a character in the story or the author of the story.

Look carefully at these examples.

- A character is telling this story. The character uses the words I, me, my, and we.

  I love my big sister Ava. We do everything together. When Ava lets me play with her toys, I am always extra careful.

- The author is telling this story. The author does not use the words I, me, my, and we.

  Meghan and Ava are sisters. They do everything together. When Meghan plays with Ava's toys, she is always extra careful.

Identifying the narrator will help you think carefully about who is giving the details in a story.

- **Explain why readers identify the narrator.** Read aloud the bottom of the page. Explain that knowing who is telling the story helps you know more about characters and events.
- Share an example of a time when identifying the narrator helped you think carefully about the details in the story. For instance, knowing that the character Alexander was the narrator of *Alexander and the Terrible, Horrible, No Good, Very Bad Day* helped you understand more about his feelings.
- **Have children demonstrate understanding.** Call on individuals to share what they have learned so far about the narrator of a story. Encourage them to demonstrate how an author tells a story versus how a character tells a story.

Part 2: Modeled Instruction

Step by Step

- **Review Part 1; Preview Part 2.** Ask volunteers to share strategies they learned to identify who is telling a story. Have children turn to Student Book page 94.
- **Revisit *My Rotten Redheaded Older Brother.*** Invite children to briefly retell the story, using pages 11–14 of their Student Books. *(RL.1.2)*
- **Model identifying the narrator.** Read aloud pages 8–11. Then think aloud:

  I'm going to look for words that show who the narrator is. First I'll look for *I, me, my,* or *we.* "My brother and our mother and I all lived . . ." In this first sentence, I see the words *My* and *I.* (Point to the words.) **This tells me the narrator is one of the characters in the story.**

Tip: You may wish to explain that this does not apply to words in quotation marks, which indicate words that a character is speaking.

- Continue rereading each paragraph. Ask children to raise a hand when they hear *I, me, my* or *we*, and point to it in the text.
- Read aloud and explain the directions for the first activity on the Student Book page.
- Read the first set of choices. Have children listen for the words as you reread the first sentence on page 8 of *My Rotten Redheaded Older Brother.*
- Reread the sentence for the second set of choices. Then read the first sentence on page 11 and guide children through the third set of choices.
- Read aloud the second activity, along with the Hint. Have children look for the target words in the answers they circled to decide if the narrator is a character.
- **Model writing your response.** Model how to write the answer in a complete sentence. *(L.1.1; L.1.2)*
- Use the Close Reading activity to help children identify which character is the narrator.
- **Have children demonstrate understanding.** Have partners complete the Turn and Talk activity by recalling words, phrases, and other clues that helped them identify the narrator. Invite children to share their evidence in class discussion. *(SL.1.1; SL.1.2)*

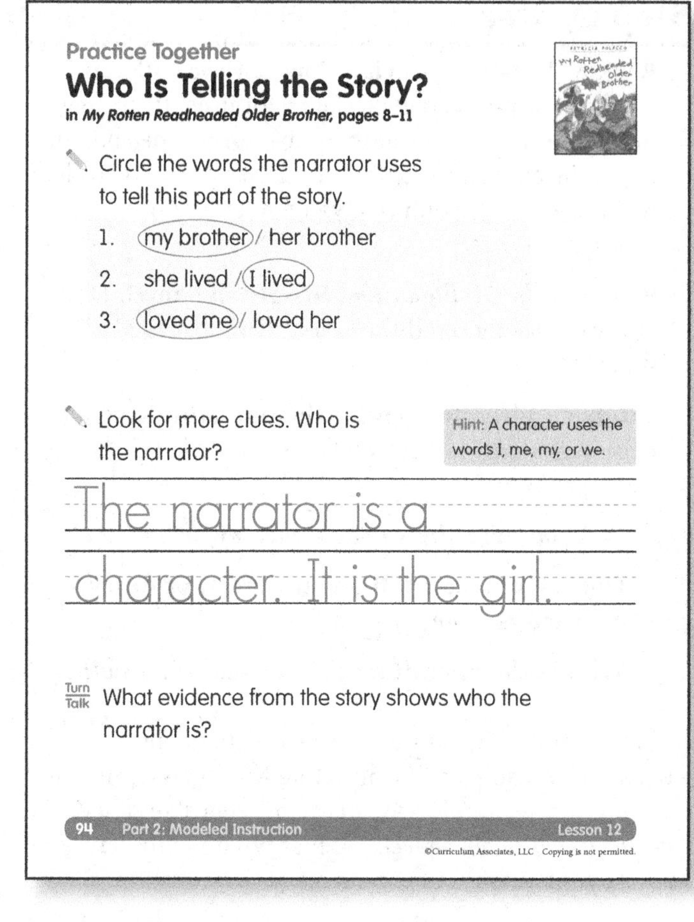

Practice Together

Who Is Telling the Story?

in *My Rotten Readheaded Older Brother,* pages 8–11

Circle the words the narrator uses to tell this part of the story.

1. my brother / her brother
2. she lived / I lived
3. loved me / loved her

Look for more clues. Who is the narrator?

Hint: A character uses the words I, me, my, or we.

The narrator is a character. It is the girl.

Turn Talk What evidence from the story shows who the narrator is?

94 Part 2: Modeled Instruction Lesson 12

©Curriculum Associates, LLC Copying is not permitted.

Close Reading

- Guide children to read closely for clues that tell which character is the narrator. Begin with the first page of the story. Think aloud:

  The story begins, "My brother and our mother and I all lived with my grandparents..." I see a grandmother and two children in the picture. I'm not sure which child is the narrator.

  On page 11 it says "my bubbie didn't seem to know...how perfectly awful my brother really was!" Look at the picture. Who do you think is saying those words? *(the girl) (RL.1.7)*

- Discuss how these examples are pieces of evidence that help you justify your answer about who the narrator is. Prompt children to add this evidence to their answer lines, using a complete sentence.

Part 3: Guided Practice

Step by Step

- **Review Parts 1–2; preview Part 3.** Have children recall the words a character-narrator uses. *(I, me, my, we)* Remind them that author-narrators name and tell about the characters. Direct children to turn to Student Book page 95. Explain that you will guide them through this page.
- **Revisit *Mike Mulligan and His Steam Shovel.*** Have children briefly retell the story, using pages 31–34 of their Student Books. *(RL.1.2)*
- **Guide children to identify the narrator.** Read aloud page 3 of *Mike Mulligan and His Steam Shovel.* Then prompt:

  Did you hear the words *I, me, my,* or *we*? *(no)*

  Did the narrator tell about herself or other characters? *(other characters)*

  Who is the narrator? *(The narrator is the author.)*

Tip: To reinforce children's decision about the narrator, reread page 3 from Mike Mulligan's point of view. For example, say: *I have a steam shovel, a beautiful red steam shovel.* Discuss what is different about your version of the story.

- Use the Close Reading activity to help children find additional evidence to identify the narrator.
- Tell children you will complete the Student Book page together.
- Review the directions and answer choices for the first activity. Reread page 3 of the story as needed.
- **Guide children to write responses.** Have children complete the second activity. Share the Hint and prompt them to identify the narrator. *(L.1.1; L.1.2)*
- **Have children demonstrate understanding.** Have children complete the Turn and Talk activity. Encourage them to use the choices they made in the first activity as evidence, in addition to other words and phrases they heard. Invite children to share their answers. *(SL.1.1; SL.1.2)*

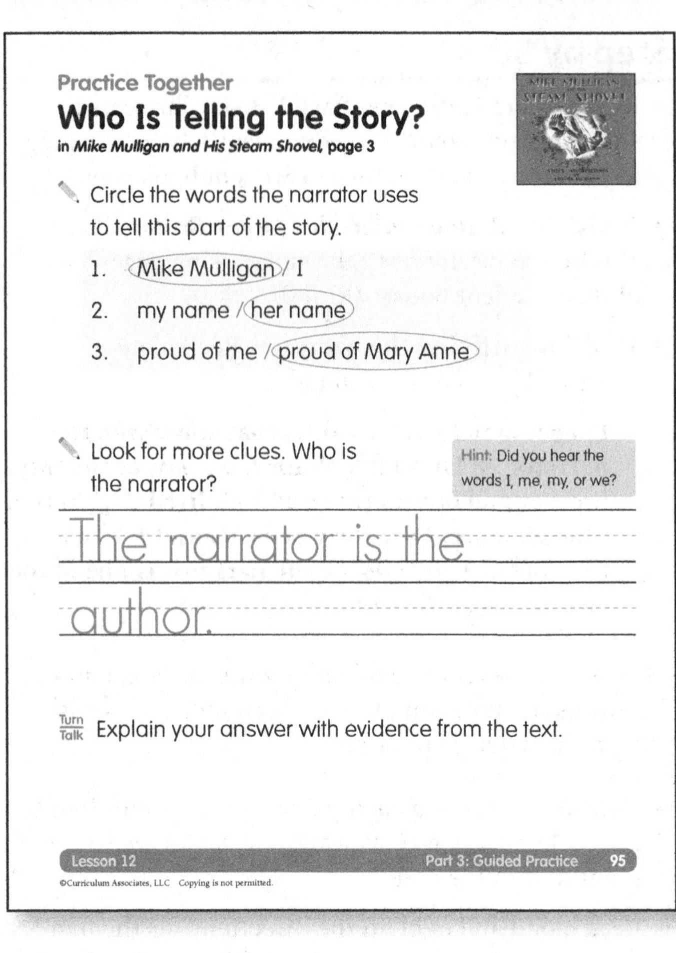
Practice Together

Who Is Telling the Story?

in *Mike Mulligan and His Steam Shovel,* page 3

Circle the words the narrator uses to tell this part of the story.

1. Mike Mulligan / I
2. my name / her name
3. proud of me / proud of Mary Anne

Look for more clues. Who is the narrator?

Hint: Did you hear the words I, me, my, or we?

The narrator is the author.

Turn Talk Explain your answer with evidence from the text.

Lesson 12 Part 3: Guided Practice 95

©Curriculum Associates, LLC Copying is not permitted.

Close Reading

- Tell children that a good strategy for identifying the narrator is to read ahead and look for more evidence. Read aloud pages 4 and 5, and ask:

  Did you hear the words *I, me, my,* or *we*? *(no)*
- Reread the beginning of each sentence, and ask:

  What do you hear many times? *(Mike Mulligan and Mary Anne)*

  Why is this evidence that the narrator is the author? *(It is evidence because the narrator is naming and telling about the characters and not telling about herself.)*

Part 4: Independent Practice

Step by Step

- **Review Parts 1–3; preview Part 4.** Ask children to explain how to identify a narrator. Direct them to turn to Student Book page 96.
- Tell children they will now practice identifying the narrator by themselves. Explain that, as on the previous pages, first they will do an activity about the narrator and then they will name the narrator.
- **Revisit *The Empty Pot*.** Have children briefly retell the story, using pages 3–6 of their Student Books. *(RL.1.2)*
- **Have children identify the narrator independently.** Have children listen closely as you read aloud pages 3–6 of *The Empty Pot*. Remind them to listen for evidence that tells who is narrating the story. Slowly read the pages again.
- Read aloud each answer choice in the first activity, and ask children to circle the words they heard in the story. Reread the story pages and answer choices as needed.
- Ask children to think about who the narrator might be, without telling the answer. Then tell them to check their answer by listening for more clues as you continue reading the story.
- Read aloud pages 9–11. Then read aloud the second activity and the Hint. Have children write their answers in complete sentences. *(L.1.1; L.1.2)*
- **Have children demonstrate understanding.** Have partners complete the Turn and Talk activity by recalling the clues they heard in the story. For additional guidance, prompt:

  What words would Ping use to tell about himself? *(I, me, my, we)*

  What words does the narrator use to tell about Ping? *(Ping, he, a boy)*

  Who is the narrator? *(the author)*
- Use the Close Reading activity to help children find additional evidence of the author-narrator in *The Empty Pot*.
- **Have children reflect on their learning.** Have children tell one way to distinguish between an author-narrator and a character-narrator. Invite them to share some ways to look for additional evidence to be sure of the narrator.

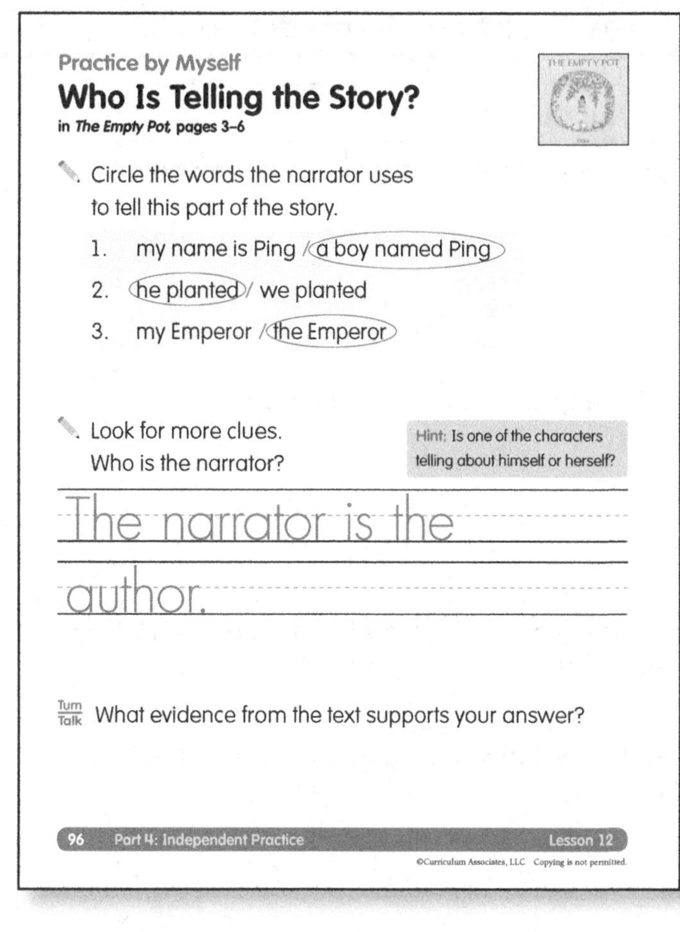
Practice by Myself

Who Is Telling the Story?

in *The Empty Pot* pages 3–6

Circle the words the narrator uses to tell this part of the story.

1. my name is Ping / (a boy named Ping)
2. (he planted) / we planted
3. my Emperor / (the Emperor)

Look for more clues. Who is the narrator?

Hint: Is one of the characters telling about himself or herself?

The narrator is the author.

Turn Talk What evidence from the text supports your answer?

96 Part 4: Independent Practice Lesson 12

©Curriculum Associates, LLC Copying is not permitted.

Close Reading

- Explain that readers need to look carefully at evidence when they decide who the narrator is.
- Read aloud pages 30–31 of *The Empty Pot*. Then prompt:

  I see the word *I* used many times. Does this mean that the narrator is a character? *(no)*

  Explain your answer. *(These words are in quotation marks. The Emperor is saying them, not the narrator.)*
- Work together to look for and discuss all of the evidence on these pages that shows who the narrator is. *(the names Emperor and Ping; the words "he exclaimed"; none of the words* I, me, my, *or* we *outside of quotation marks)*

Differentiated Instruction

Assessment and Remediation

If you observe . . .	Then try . . .
Difficulty understanding what a narrator does	Retelling a familiar story, such as the nursery rhyme "Jack and Jill," while two children act it out. Before you begin, introduce yourself as the narrator. Introduce the two actors as the characters Jack and Jill. After the story has been told, ask: *What was the narrator's job? (to tell about what was happening)*
Difficulty distinguishing pronouns	Practicing pronoun substitution in a concrete example. Hand a child (e.g., *Jake*) an eraser. Write *Jake holds the eraser.* on the board. Cross out the *s* in *holds,* and ask the child to subsitute the correct pronoun for *Jake* to describe what he is doing. *(I)* Continue with sentences such as *This is Jake's eraser (my)* and *The teacher gave Jake the eraser. (me)*
Difficulty distinguishing when a character is telling the story	Revisiting the two examples on Student Book page 93 and talking with children about how the stories are identical, except for the narrator.
Difficulty distinguishing when an author is telling the story	Inviting a child to briefly recount an event. Write three sentences from the recounting, from the third-person point of view. Point out how the child, as a character-narrator, told the events as he or she experienced them, while you, an author-narrator, told about the "character" and events without being involved in what happened.

Connect to the Anchor Standard

R6: *Assess how point of view or purpose shapes the content and style of a text.*

Throughout the grades, Standard 6 builds toward more sophisticated analysis of point of view—both the author's and the characters'. In later grades, students explore abstract concepts such as the style of a text and how it is affected by an author's deliberate choices. Readers transition from taking a story for granted as fixed and finite to asking high-level questions about the author's choices: *Why is a character telling this story instead of the author? How do I feel when I listen to the story? Would I feel differently if another character told it? What does the author want me to feel?* Use the following activities to help your students begin this transition.

- Reread page 11 of *My Rotten Redheaded Older Brother.* Discuss how Treesha feels about Richie. Point out the language she uses, including "hair that was like wire" and "looked like a weasel with glasses." Discuss whether Richie might describe himself this way if he were the narrator. Then have children offer descriptions of Treesha from Richie's point of view. Ask how these alternate descriptions change the story. *(SL.1.1; SL.1.2; SL.1.4)*
- Reread pages 42–44 of *Mike Mulligan and His Steam Shovel.* Discuss how Mike Mulligan might narrate this part of the story. What words would he use to tell about his feelings? Have children act out the scene, once with Mike Mulligan as the narrator and once with the author as narrator. Discuss the similarities and differences. *(SL.1.5)*

Introduction

Before administering the Unit 3 Check, you may wish to review how to answer multiple-choice questions and offer a new test-taking tip. Begin by writing the following sentence and question on the board:

Nabi's favorite part of gardening is digging in the soil.

What does the word soil mean?

A flower

B water

C dirt

Guide children through the process of answering a multiple-choice question:

Today you will listen as I read aloud a story, and then you will answer some questions about details in the story. Remember, when you answer a multiple-choice question, only one of the answers is correct. To choose the correct answer, draw a circle around the letter next to that answer.

Some questions may ask about the meaning of a word. One way to check your answer is to see if it makes sense in the sentence. Reread the sentence, and then plug in, or replace the underlined word with your answer. If the sentence does not make sense, the answer is probably not correct. Here, the unknown word is *soil*. Let's plug in choice A, "flower." *(Have a volunteer read the sentence.)* **That doesn't sound right, does it? The answer should be something that you can dig into. Which answer is something that you can dig into?** *(dirt)* **Let's try plugging *dirt* into the sentence.** *(Select another volunteer to read the sentence.)* **That sounds much better!** *(Circle "C" on the board.)*

Unit 3 Check

Listen closely as your teacher reads. Then answer the questions.

What words tell how Rosa María feels about the party after it ends?

A "I know I have forgotten something."

B "Heavens! Where is my mind?"

(C) "It was a wonderful day!"

Read this sentence about a mousetrap.

"When it was set and ready to snap, she turned off the light and went to bed."

What sense does the word **snap** tell about?

A smell

(B) hear

C taste

97

Step by Step

- Revisit *Mice and Beans* and invite children to retell important story details using the illustrations.
- Have children follow along as you read aloud the directions on page 97 of their Student Books.
- Then read aloud one or more pages from the text, as specified below, before having children complete each item. Display the appropriate pages for children to view while they read and answer each question.
- For item 1, reread page 27; display the illustration on page 25.
- For item 2, reread page 5; display the illustration on pages 4–5.
- For item 4, reread page 27; display the illustrations on pages 26–27.
- As needed for items 3 and 5, reread pages 24– 27. Display various illustrations of the mice, including pages 18–19 and 20–21.

Note: Read aloud each question, answer choice, and Hint before directing children to answer it.

- When children have finished, reread each question and discuss the correct answer. Point to evidence in the text and pictures. Then use the Answer Analysis to discuss the correct answer.

Answer Analysis

1 This item requires children to identify evidence from the story that suggests how Rosa María feels. **(*RL.1.4*)**

The best answer is choice C, "It was a wonderful day!" On page 27, the words tell how Rosa María thinks back on the party. She is contented, which means she is pleased and happy, and she pictures the happy look on Catalina's face at the party. Then she says those words in choice C. Choices A and B are other things that Rosa María says to herself on different pages, but they only tell details about her plans, not about how she feels once the party is over. They are not the best answer choices.

2 This item asks children to relate the author's word choice to the sense it describes. **(*RL.1.4*)**

The best answer is choice B, "hear." The word *snap* is the sound you hear when a mousetrap has something inside of it. *Snap* does not describe what you might smell or taste, so choices A and C are not good answers.

3 This item requires children to identify the narrator of the story. **(*RL.1.6*)**

The best answer is choice C, "the author." We know that the mice do not speak in the story; they only show up in the pictures, so choice B is not a good answer. And the text does not use *I*, *me* or *my* unless Rosa María actually talks to herself. This means someone who is not a character tells most of the story. So choice A, "Rosa María," is not a good answer, either, because she is a character.

4 Item 4 asks children to identify a character's feelings based on what she says. **(*RL.1.4*)**

The best answer is choice B, "upset." We find out on the first page of the story that Rosa María thinks there's room in the house for everyone, "except for a mouse." She also sets mousetraps each night to catch the mice she doesn't want in her house. For these reasons, we know she is not laughing, so choice A does not make sense. And the exclamation point tells me that Rosa María is speaking with excitement, so I don't think choice C makes sense, either.

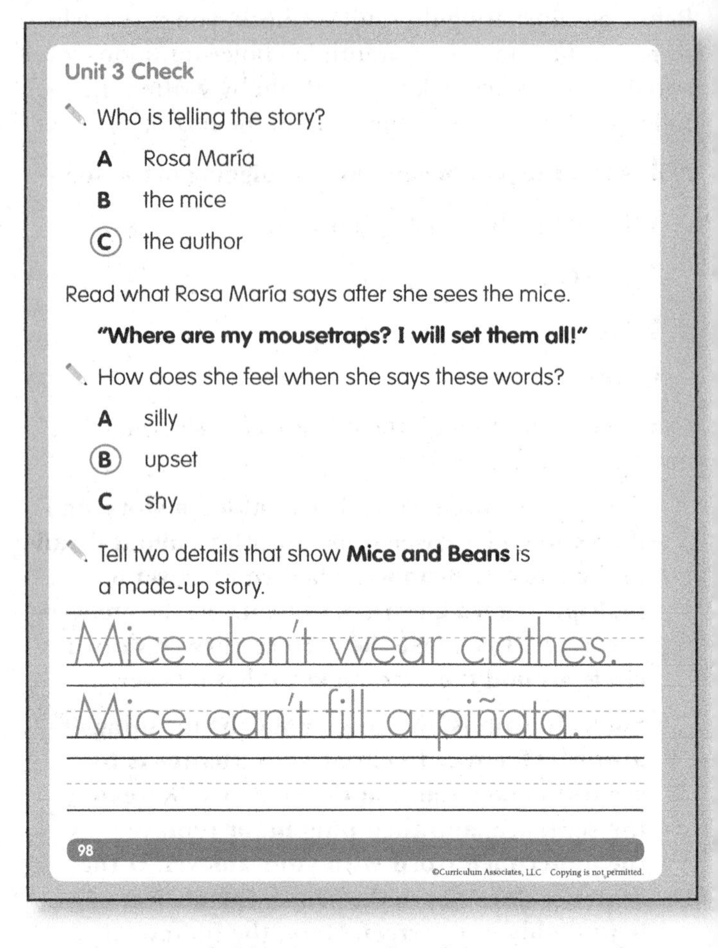
Unit 3 Check

Who is telling the story?

A Rosa María

B the mice

(C) the author

Read what Rosa María says after she sees the mice.

"Where are my mousetraps? I will set them all!"

How does she feel when she says these words?

A silly

(B) upset

C shy

Tell two details that show **Mice and Beans** is a made-up story.

Mice don't wear clothes.

Mice can't fill a piñata.

98

©Curriculum Associates, LLC Copying is not permitted.

5 In item 5, children must identify two pieces of evidence that signify the book is a work of fiction. **(*RL.1.5*)**

Accept responses that are supported by story details. Sample Response: Real mice do not wear clothes or read. Real mice cannot put candy in a piñata.

Remember, fiction books do not give facts. Instead, they give made-up details that tell a story. Now, think about a story detail—how the mice help Rosa María by filling the piñata, for example. Real mice can't do that, so that's a made-up detail. Also, the illustrations show the mice doing other things real mice can't do, like wearing clothes and glasses or reading notes. These details show that this is a fiction story.

Unit 4

Craft and Structure in Informational Text

The following pacing chart shows a recommended schedule for teaching the lessons in Unit 4. Each Read Aloud and Focus Lesson is taught over the course of three days. There is also time allotted in each Focus Lesson for teaching Tap Children's Prior Knowledge and Differentiated Instruction.

Day	Lesson/Activity	Time (minutes)
1	Unit 4 Opener (optional); Read Aloud Lesson I: Introduction; Part 1	30
2	Read Aloud Lesson I: Parts 2 and 3	30
3	Read Aloud Lesson I: Part 4; Additional Activities (optional)	30
4	Tap Children's Prior Knowledge; Lesson 13: Part 1	30
5	Lesson 13: Parts 2 and 3	30
6	Lesson 13: Part 4; Differentiated Instruction (optional)	30
7	Tap Children's Prior Knowledge; Lesson 14: Part 1	30
8	Lesson 14: Parts 2 and 3	30
9	Lesson 14: Part 4; Differentiated Instruction (optional)	30
10	Tap Children's Prior Knowledge; Lesson 15: Part 1	30
11	Lesson 15: Parts 2 and 3	30
12	Lesson 15: Part 4; Differentiated Instruction (optional)	30
13	Tap Children's Prior Knowledge; Lesson 16: Part 1	30
14	Lesson 16: Parts 2 and 3	30
15	Lesson 16: Part 4; Differentiated Instruction (optional)	30
16	Unit 4 Check	30

Step by Step

Explain that in this unit, children will learn ways that authors organize ideas and choose what to say and show about real-world topics. Children will also listen to an informational text about a living creature they may know.

- Have children turn to page 99. Point out that the photograph shows creatures living in the real world. Then read aloud the introductory sentence and questions.
- Encourage children to use full sentences to describe the two bears, where they are, and what they are doing. *(brown [grizzly] bears, standing in a stream by a waterfall; one is trying to catch a fish.)*
- Read aloud the caption. Then ask what facts children learn from the words in it. *(The bears live in Alaska and are skilled at fishing.)*
- Briefly discuss how the photograph matches the words. Then have children describe how the information in each differs.
- Have children turn to page 100. Read aloud the title and directions at the top of the page.
- Have children put their fingers on the earthworm at the top of the page. Ask how it can escape from the bird. *(by crawling down into the underground tunnel and through the maze)*
- Before children draw the path, suggest that they use the eraser end of their pencils or their fingers to find the way the worm must crawl through the tunnels.

Read Aloud Lesson 1 (Student Book pages 35–38)

Earthworms

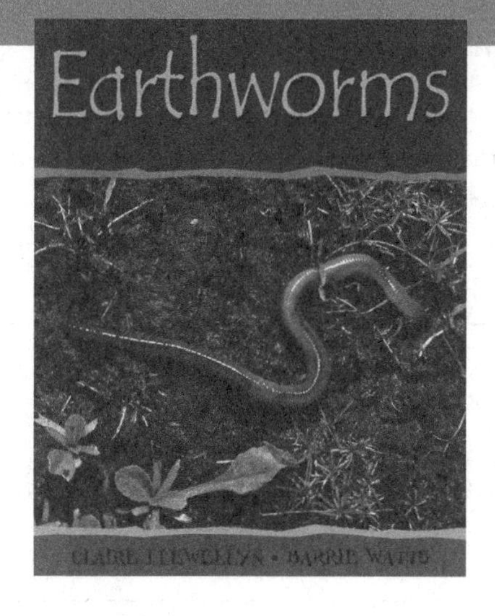

Lesson Objectives

You will read aloud *Earthworms*, which children will revisit in later lessons. Children will:

- Identify the main topic of a text and sections within it.
- Ask and answer questions about key details.
- Identify how the information in the text is organized.

About the Text

Summary

This book offers many important facts about earthworms, including what their bodies look like, where they live, what they eat, how they move, how they reproduce, and what preys on them.

Informational Text: Reference Book

- Explain that a reference book contains facts about a topic. These facts are organized in sections that tell more about one part of the main topic.
- Tell children that people often use reference books when they do research. Share an example of a time when you used a reference book similar to *Earthworms*.

Critical Vocabulary

- Prior to reading, briefly define the following words:

  soil (p. 6) dirt that a plant grows in

  segment (p. 10) a body part of a worm; one of many pieces that make up a worm

  bristle (p. 10) a short, hard hair

  cocoon (p. 19) the hard shell where worm eggs grow

- As you read, pause to point to the words as you encounter them, and review their definitions.

Word Bank

- To support children in writing about the text, display a word bank containing the Critical Vocabulary.
- Add other important words from the text, such as *compost*, *anchor*, and *pantry*, on subsequent readings.

New Concepts: Partners in Nature

- Explain that sometimes things in nature become partners and help each other in important ways. For example, trees give off the air humans breathe, and humans give off the air trees need to make food.
- As you read *Earthworms*, have children listen for ways that plants feed earthworms and earthworms help plants grow and stay healthy.

Ready *Teacher Toolbox* Teacher-Toolbox.com

	Prerequisite Skills	*RI.1.2*
Ready Lessons		✓
Tools for Instruction	✓✓	✓
Interactive Tutorials	✓	

CCSS Focus

RI.1.2 *. . . retell key details of a text.*

ADDITIONAL STANDARDS: ***RI.1.1; RF.1.3.a, c, g; W.1.2; SL.1.1.a, b; SL.1.2; SL.1.3; SL.1.5; L.1.1.f; L.1.2; L.1.4.a*** *(See page A38 for full text.)*

PART 1: First Read

Step by Step

- **Introduce and explore *Earthworms*.** Read aloud the title and point out the name of the authors, Claire Llewellyn and Barrie Watts.
- Display the front and back covers, and think aloud:

  The title tells me the topic of the book. I can see that this earthworm is in the dirt. I wonder if that's where it lives. Also, I notice a worm's body doesn't look the same all the way through. Since this is such an up-close picture, I wonder if this book will cover lots of details about a worm.

- Turn the pages of the book, and point out that each spread from page 6–25 has a similar organization. Ask children what they see repeated on each page including pictures, labels, and colored boxes. Discuss how this organization helps the reader. *(SL.1.1)*

Tip: Point out how the headings on each page are the same as the words on the Contents page. Discuss why this organization is helpful to readers.

- **Read aloud *Earthworms*.** Explain that usually, reference books are not read from start to finish but because this one is brief, you will read it aloud. As you read, pause to define challenging vocabulary.
- **Guide a review of the text.** Direct children to turn to Student Book page 35. Read aloud the first item, and invite volunteers to offer ways to complete the sentence, based on what they heard during reading. Have children record their answers. *(RI.1.2)*
- Read aloud the second item, and help children recall the features you found together. Display the book once more for review. Have children record their answers.
- Read aloud the Turn and Talk activity. Tell children the facts they choose can come from any part of the book. Encourage children to tell why they found a particular fact interesting. Invite children to share their ideas and discuss as a class.
- Ask children if they have any additional questions about earthworms after reading the text, such as *How much do earthworms eat?* or *How long do they live?* Discuss where you might look to find the answers to those questions.

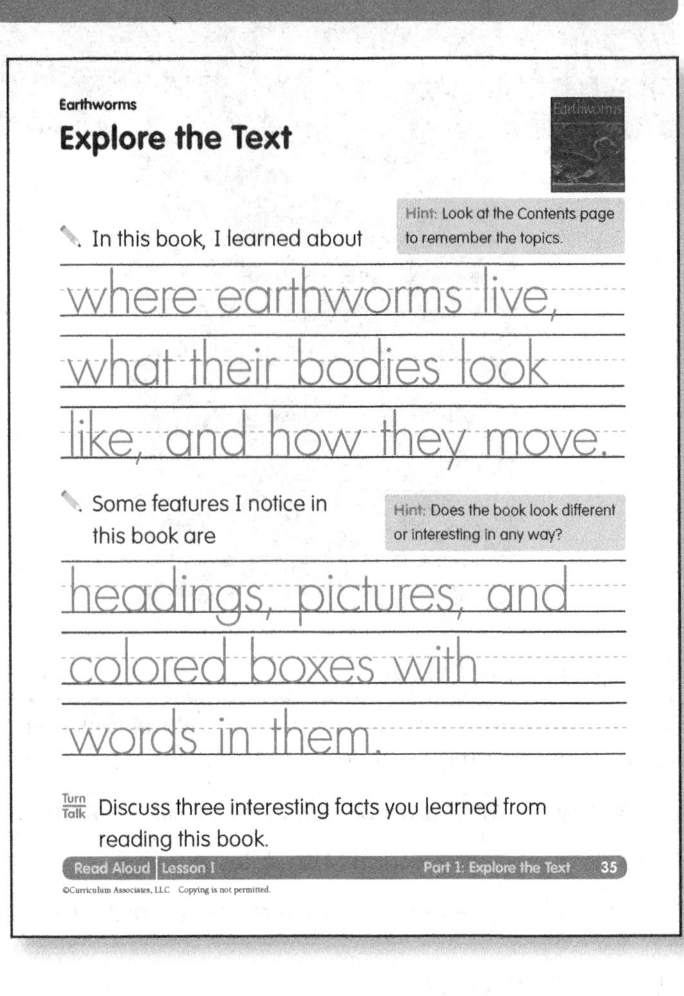

ELL Support: Words that Describe

- Explain that often the best way to learn about a topic is to pay close attention to the adjectives, or words that describe it.
- Point to the word *wriggly* on page 6. Read it, and have children repeat it after you. Explain that wriggling is a way of moving. Then demonstrate that *wriggle* means "to twist and turn your body."
- Ask children to show or tell how a wriggly worm would move.
- Repeat demonstrations with descriptive words throughout the book, such as *tiny* and *giant* (p. 7), *damp* (p. 8), *slimy* (p. 11), and *soft* (p. 12). Whenever possible, use tactile or visual aids to help children understand the word meaning.
- Ask children to point to each descriptive word and then tell how it describes an earthworm or something related to it.

PART 2: Reread for Meaning

Step by Step

- **Reread to learn basic facts about earthworms.** Explain that children will listen and look for details about where earthworms live and what their bodies look like. Use the Contents to find the pages that contain this information. Instruct children to listen closely as you reread pages 8–11.
- **Have children identify key details.** Use questions such as these to guide discussion. *(RI.1.1; SL.1.1; SL.1.2)*

  Pages 8–9: Where can you find earthworms? *(Earthworms live in soil, like the woods or a garden.)*

  Page 10: How is a worm's body different from yours? *(A worm has no skeleton, lungs, eyes, or ears. Its body is filled with liquid and it uses bristles to move.)*
- **Guide children to demonstrate understanding.** Direct children to turn to Student Book page 36. Guide them to complete the drawing. Then read the second item and have children write their answers.

Tip: Display the diagram on page 10 and allow children to use it for reference as they draw.

- **Have children discuss text evidence.** Read aloud the Turn and Talk activity. Encourage children to use words from the Word Bank to discuss their drawings. Invite children to share their drawings with the class. *(SL.1.5)*

Earthworms

Earthworm Basics

Draw an earthworm's body. Label its body parts.

Hint: How is a worm's body different from yours?

Children should draw the shape of a worm with visible segments, a saddle, and bristles.

List the names of some places you might find an earthworm.

soil, a garden, woods, a compost heap

Turn Talk Describe your picture to your partner. Point to details that show evidence from the text.

36 Part 2: Key Details Read Aloud | Lesson 1

©Curriculum Associates, LLC Copying is not permitted.

- **Reflect on text structure.** Use the Close Reading activity to help children think about how information in *Earthworms* is organized.

Tier Two Vocabulary: *Trapped*

- Display this sentence from page 11: "They take in air that is trapped in the soil."
- Ask children to brainstorm the meaning of *trapped*, based on word clues such as *in the soil* as well as prior knowledge about traps such as mousetraps. Help them determine that it means "stuck; caught; unable to escape." *(L.1.4.a)*
- Demonstrate the word's meaning by covering a small ball with a cup. Say: *The ball would move on its own, but it can't move because I trapped it.*
- Have volunteers tell why it helps a worm to have air trapped in the soil. Then invite them to give additional examples of things that can be trapped.

Close Reading

- Help children notice the way an author organizes information. Display the spread on pages 10–11. Prompt children:

  What do you notice about the words? Do they all look the same? *(Some words are in colored boxes, and some are not.)*
- On each page, point to and read the main text first, and then the colored box text below.
- Discuss how all the words relate to the heading, but the words in the colored box are bonus facts that are particularly interesting to know. Use the "Worm Wonders" spread on pages 26–27 to show how these "fun facts" are also set in colored boxes.

PART 3: Reread for Meaning

Step by Step

- **Reread to learn how an earthworm moves.** Explain that children will listen and look for details about earthworm movements. Use the Contents to find these pages. Instruct children to listen closely as you reread pages 14–17.
- **Have children identify key details.** Use questions such as these to guide discussion. *(RI.1.1; SL.1.1; SL.1.2)*

  Page 14: What do worms use to move? *(They use their muscles and their bristles.)*

  Page 16: How does a worm's body help it make tunnels? *(The slime makes the tunnels stay open.)*

  Page 17: Why can't you see earthworms on hot, sunny days? *(They go underground to stay cool.)*

- Use the Close Reading activity to help children think carefully about details in the text.
- **Guide children to demonstrate understanding.** Direct children to turn to Student Book page 37. Read aloud the writing prompt and the Hint.

Tip: Display the Word Bank to help children write challenging words. Offer correct spellings for words not in the bank once the activity is complete.

- As children write their answers, encourage them to think about how tunnels are made, how they stay open, how they help plants, and how worms use them in cold or dry weather. *(L.1.1; L.1.2)*

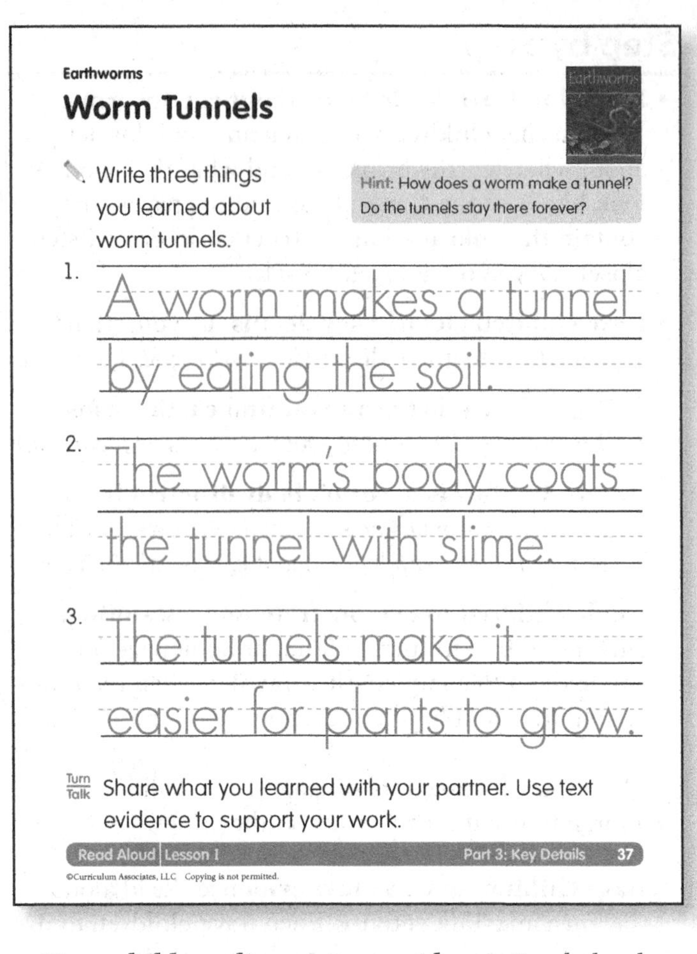

- **Have children discuss text evidence.** Read aloud the Turn and Talk activity. Encourage children to make the connection between the way a worm moves and the way tunnels are formed. Invite children to discuss their answers with the class.

Tier Two Vocabulary: *Anchor*

- Read the second sentence on page 15, and ask children to brainstorm the meaning of *anchor.* Help them determine that it means "to hold down firmly." Note that this word is an action, but an *anchor* is also an object that holds down a boat. *(L.1.4.a)*
- Provide an example of a time when you anchored something. You may say, *On a very windy day, I have to anchor the napkins on the picnic table so they don't all fly away.*
- Have volunteers tell more about how a worm anchors itself. Then invite them to give suggestions for other things that might need to be anchored and tell why.

Close Reading

- Help children practice asking and answering questions about details as they read. Read aloud page 16. Then prompt:

  How do you think the slime makes the tunnel stronger? *(It makes the dirt stick in place.)*

  Why does the worm need the tunnel to be strong? *(so it can move all the way through)*

- Explain that the answers are not on the page, but children can think about the details they've read so far in order to make educated guesses. As children discuss their answers, encourage them to build on each other's ideas. *(SL.1.1.b)*

Step by Step

- **Reread to learn about earthworm enemies.** Explain that children will listen and look for details about earthworm enemies. Use the Contents to find these pages. Instruct children to listen closely as you reread pages 22–25.
- **Have children identify key details.** Use questions such as these to guide discussion. *(RI.1.1; SL.1.1; SL.1.2)*

  Pages 22–25: Why are worms in danger during the day and night? *(During the day, birds pull them out of the ground. At night, hedgehogs, shrews, and moles hunt while the worms are looking for food.)*

  Page 25: Why are earthworms safer in the summer and fall? *(Birds go to eat plants and leave the earthworms alone.)*

- **Guide children to demonstrate understanding.** Direct children to turn to Student Book page 38. Review that a web shows how pieces of information are connected. Read aloud the prompt, and guide children to complete each circle in the web.

Tip: Offer emerging writers the option to draw the animal and tell what they drew or ask you to label it.

- **Have children discuss text evidence.** Read aloud the Turn and Talk activity, and invite children to elaborate on the prompt by drawing or acting it out. *(SL.1.5)*

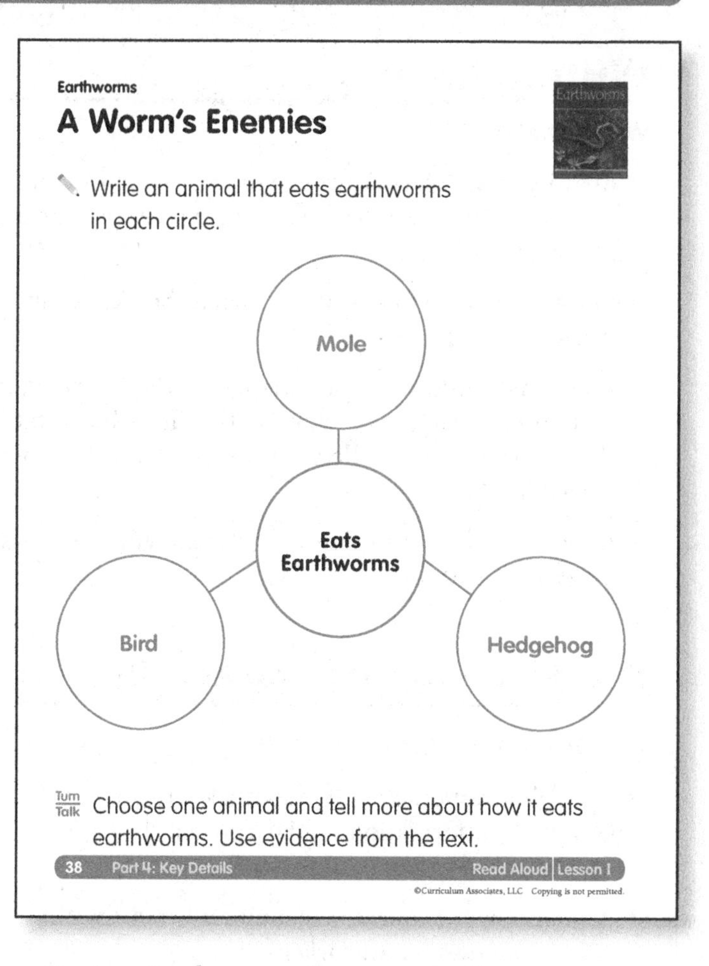

- **Review *Earthworms*.** Return to the Contents page to remind children of the topics covered in the book. Then use the prompts in the Book Review activity to guide a review of important concepts. *(RI.1.2)*

Integrating Foundational Skills

Use these tasks as opportunities to integrate foundational skills into your reading of *Earthworms*.

1. Read the following words, and have children identify the consonant digraph they share: *both, thirty. (/th/)* Ask which letters make the /th/ sound. *(t, h)* Repeat with the words *shrews (/sh/; s, h), when (/wh/; w, h)* and *such (/ch/; c, h). (RF.1.3.a)*
2. Display the words *come* and *mole*. Have children read them aloud and tell which word follows the rule for final *-e (mole)* and which has an irregular spelling *(come)*. Ask how they knew. *(*Mole *has a long vowel sound, but* come *does not.)* Repeat the exercise with *have (irregular spelling)* and *store (final -e). (RF.1.3.c; RF.1.3.g)*

Book Review

- As children review key details from *Earthworms*, record their answers on chart paper. Keep the chart on hand for later revisiting.

  Where do earthworms live? *(Earthworms live in soil in places like gardens, meadows, and woods.)*

  What do their bodies look like? *(Their bodies are a tube made of segments. They have a saddle in the middle and bristles on the outside.)*

  How do they move? *(They use their muscles to shrink or spread out and pull themselves forward.)*

  What do they eat? *(They eat dead plants.)*

  Which animals eat them? *(Hedgehogs, moles, and birds eat them.)*

Writing Activity

Write a Letter *(W.1.2)*

- Identify a local farm or community garden in your neighborhood, and have children craft letters to the gardners explaining what they have recently learned about earthworms, including why it would be helpful to have them in a garden.
- Prompt partners to brainstorm what they know about earthworms. Encourage them to make notes of their ideas as they discuss.
- Then have children work independently to write a letter that explains what they learned about earthworms, including where they live, what they look like, and how they help plants grow. Remind them to organize their writing in the following way: explain the reason for writing, give three facts, and then close the letter with a final thought.
- Invite volunteers to share their letters with the class. Then, if possible, help children send the letters to the local organization.

Speaking and Listening Activity

Ask Questions *(SL.1.1.a; SL.1.3)*

- Help children practice asking questions to gain more information or clarify what they don't understand.
- Ask what words questions commonly start with. *(who, what, where, why, when)*
- Organize children into small groups, and assign each group one question word. Have groups think of three questions they can ask about the book or about earthworms, beginning with their assigned word. Clarify that they can ask questions that may not be answered by the information in the book.
- Invite each group to ask their questions to the class. Prompt classmates to give answers that can be found in the text. For questions that cannot be answered with the text, brainstorm briefly about where you might look to find the answers.

Language Activity

Describe a Worm *(L.1.1.f)*

- Remind children that an *adjective* is a word that describes something. Find examples in the classroom, such as a yellow pencil or a hard desk, to illustrate its meaning.
- Tell children to pretend they are the only kids on Earth who know about earthworms, and they have to tell everyone else about them.
- Have partners make a list of adjectives they would use to describe earthworms. Remind them to think about what they heard in the text as well as what they saw in the pictures.
- Invite children to share their lists, and discuss which adjectives do the best job of helping someone picture an earthworm.

Lesson 13 (Student Book pages 101–104)

Finding Word Meanings

CCSS

RI.1.4: Ask and answer questions to help determine or clarify the meaning of words and phrases in a text.

Required Read Alouds: *G (Elizabeth Leads the Way); I (Earthworms)*

Lesson Objectives

- Locate text and picture evidence that helps determine or clarify the meaning of words and phrases.
- Ask and answer questions to determine or clarify the meaning of words and phrases in a text.
- Relate prior knowledge to text evidence in order to draw conclusions about word meaning.
- Explain the specific meanings of unfamiliar words as they are used in a text.

The Learning Progression

- **Grade K:** CCSS RI.K.4 expects children to ask and answer questions about unknown words in a text with prompting and support.
- **Grade 1: CCSS RI.1.4 advances the Grade K standard by having children work more independently to ask and answer questions that will help them determine or clarify the meaning of words and phrases in a text.**
- **Grade 2:** CCSS RI.2.4 furthers the standard by having children ask and answer questions to determine the meaning of words and phrases in subject-area texts about common Grade 2 topics.

Prerequisite Skills

- Understand the print concepts *word* and *picture*.
- Identify real-life connections between words and the different ways they can be used.
- Ask and answer questions about unknown words in a text with prompting and support.

Tap Children's Prior Knowledge

- Ask children to tell what they do when they hear a word they do not understand. Discuss the strategies they use to figure out the word's meaning. Then tell children they can ask questions and look for clues to figure out what an unfamiliar word means.
- Display a picture of an insect, such as a fly or a bee. Then write the following sentence on chart paper: *An insect's <u>thorax</u> holds its head, legs, wings, and abdomen.* Read the sentence aloud.
- Ask children what they think a *thorax* is. Prompt: *What do the words say the thorax does? Look at the picture. What part of the insect's body holds, or is attached to, the wings, legs, and head?*
- Discuss the clues, and have children point to the thorax in the picture. Then repeat the exercise, underlining *abdomen* and prompting children to look at word and picture clues to figure out its meaning.
- Explain that in this lesson, children will learn to ask and answer questions and look for clues that will help them understand the meanings of new words in texts.

Ready *Teacher Toolbox* — Teacher-Toolbox.com

	Prerequisite Skills	RI.1.4
Ready Lessons	✓	✓
Tools for Instruction	✓	✓
Interactive Tutorials	✓✓	

Additional CCSS

RI.1.1; RI.1.2; RI.1.7; SL.1.1; SL.1.4; L.1.1; L.1.2; L.1.4; L.1.5 *(See page A38 for full text.)*

Part 1: Introduction

Step by Step

- **Introduce the standard.** Have children turn to page 101 in their Student Books. Read aloud the speech bubble.
- **Review questions about unfamiliar words.** Read the line below the speech bubble. Then read the example sentence. Explain that you will use the questions below the example to model finding the meaning of the word *crops*.
- Read aloud the first question. Have children underline *the words around the new word*. Then think aloud:

  I'll look at the words around *crops*. The word *grow* gives me a big clue. I know plants grow in the ground. The words *such as* tell me that onions, lettuce, and carrots are examples of crops. And the words *in a garden* tell me where crops grow. I know what a garden is! It's a place where flowers or vegetables grow.

- Read aloud the second question. Have children underline the word *pictures*. Explain:

  Next I'll ask what the picture shows about the new word. I see onions, lettuce, and carrots growing in rows in the ground.

- Read aloud the third question. Have children underline the words *I already know*. Explain:

  Now I'll think about what I already know. I know onions, lettuce, and carrots are vegetables that we eat. I know a garden is a place to grow plants. Crops grow in a garden, so *crops* must mean "plants people grow for food."

- Read aloud the last question, and have children underline the words *make sense*. Explain:

  I think I know what *crops* means, so I'll say the meaning in the sentence to see if it makes sense: *You can grow plants for food, such as onions, lettuce, and carrots in a garden.* So yes, the meaning of *crops*, "plants we grow for food," makes sense here.

Tip: Explain that sometimes there aren't enough clues in a text and children may have to use a dictionary. Caution that dictionaries often show several meanings for a word, and children should find the meaning that makes sense in the text.

Listen and Learn

Finding Word Meanings

When you read a hard word, you can ask questions to figure out its **meaning**.

Read the example. Then ask the questions below:

You can grow **crops** such as onions, lettuce, and carrots in a garden.

- What clues can I find in the words around the new word?
- What do the pictures show about the word?
- What do I already know about the word or the topic?
- Does the meaning I find make sense in the sentence?

Finding the meanings of new words can help you understand what you read.

Lesson 13 Part 1: Introduction 101

- **Explain why readers ask and answer questions about unfamiliar words.** Read aloud the bottom of the page. Then explain:

  It is important to pause and try to figure out the meanings of unfamiliar words. If you do not understand the words in a book, it is hard to figure out other things like what the book is about or what the author wants you to know.

- Share an example of a time when finding the meaning of a word helped you better understand a text. For example, when you were reading a recipe for a cake, you figured out that *whisking* is a certain way of stirring that you needed to do in order to make the cake light and fluffy.
- **Have children demonstrate understanding.** Call on individuals to share what they have learned so far about figuring out the meanings of new words. Invite them to share times when they got stuck on hard words and had trouble understanding a text.

Part 2: Modeled Instruction

Step by Step

- **Review Part 1; preview Part 2.** Ask volunteers to share questions they can ask about unfamiliar words. Then have children turn to Student Book page 102.
- **Revisit *Elizabeth Leads the Way.*** Have children review the main topic and key details, using the chart created for the Book Review on Teacher Resource Book page 89. *(RI.1.2)*
- **Model figuring out a word's meaning.** Explain that you are going to model finding the meaning of an unfamiliar word. Read aloud pages 9–10 of *Elizabeth Leads the Way*. Copy the first sentence on page 10 onto chart paper. Then think aloud:

  I'm not sure what *hurdles* means. First I'll ask, *What do the words around* hurdles *tell us?*

- Have volunteers underline words in the sentence that tell about hurdles. *("high"; "jumped over")* Prompt:

  What does the picture show about *hurdles?* *(The picture shows something that looks like a fence. Elizabeth is jumping over it on a horse.) (RI.1.7)*

- Invite children to share what they already know about hurdles. Explain that in some races, runners jump over things called *hurdles*. Prompt children to use text evidence and this real-life connection to determine the word's meaning:

  What do you think the word *hurdle* means? *(a fence or bar that you jump over) (L.1.4; L.1.5)*

- Reread the sentence with the new meaning substituted for *hurdles*. Ask if it makes sense. *(yes)*

Tip: Discuss why Elizabeth jumps over hurdles. Explain that figuring out the word *hurdles* helps readers understand an important detail about her.

- **Model writing your responses.** Read aloud the Student Book questions. Discuss each question, Hint, and answer. Model how to write the answers, then have children write their own. *(L.1.1, L.1.2)*
- **Have children demonstrate understanding.** Read aloud the Turn and Talk activity. Challenge children to practice using the word in different sentences. *(SL.1.1)*
- Use the Close Reading activity to model asking and answering questions about another word on page 10.

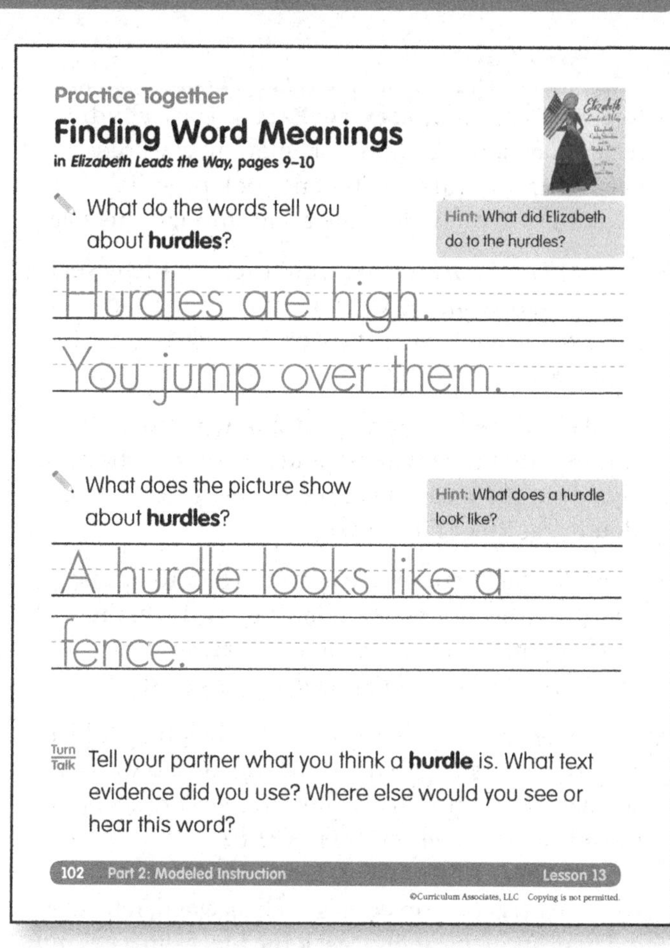

Practice Together

Finding Word Meanings

in Elizabeth Leads the Way, pages 9–10

What do the words tell you about **hurdles**?

Hint: What did Elizabeth do to the hurdles?

Hurdles are high.

You jump over them.

What does the picture show about **hurdles**?

Hint: What does a hurdle look like?

A hurdle looks like a fence.

Turn Talk Tell your partner what you think a **hurdle** is. What text evidence did you use? Where else would you see or hear this word?

102 Part 2: Modeled Instruction Lesson 13

©Curriculum Associates, LLC Copying is not permitted.

Close Reading

- Remind children that asking and answering questions can help them understand new words and important ideas in *Elizabeth Leads the Way.*
- Display the second sentence on page 10. Read it aloud and prompt:

  What do the words say is *raging?* *(the river)*

  What does the picture show about the river? *(The water is very wavy and swirling.)*

  Have you ever heard the word *rage* or *raging* before? Where did you hear it? *(If necessary, explain that* rage *means "anger," and* raging *means "acting in a very angry way.")*

  What do you think *raging* means in this sentence about a river? *(It means that the water is rushing fast with lots of waves.)*

- Discuss how the word *raging* helps children understand that Elizabeth is doing a daring thing.

Step by Step

- **Review Parts 1–2; preview Part 3.** Have children recall questions they can ask about new words. Direct them to turn to Student Book page 103. Explain that you will guide them through this page.
- **Revisit *Earthworms*.** Invite children to briefly review the main topic and key details, using the chart created for the Book Review on Teacher Resource Book page 139. *(RI.1.2)*
- **Guide children to figure out a new word.** Tell children that they will ask and answer questions to figure out the meaning of the word *segments*. Read aloud page 10 of *Earthworms*.
- Copy the last two sentences from page 10 on the board. Have volunteers underline words that tell about *segments*. *("Its body is a tube made of many tiny segments"; "is filled with liquid and has bristles")*
- Circulate and display the diagram, helping children read the labels. Ask what the diagram shows about segments. *(There are lots of them. They are small. A worm's body is made of them.) (RI.1.7)*

Tip: Use classroom materials such as wooden blocks to demonstrate meaning. Stack the blocks in a column. Explain that each individual piece is a *segment*.

- **Guide children to write responses.** Read aloud the Student Book questions and Hints. Discuss answers, and have children write their responses in complete sentences. *(L.1.1; L.1.2)*
- **Have children demonstrate understanding.** Read aloud the Turn and Talk activity. Prompt children to use evidence to understand the meaning of *segments:*

  Have you heard the words *segment* or *segments* before? Where? *(Children may name insects' bodies or parts of oranges.)*

  What do you think the word *segment* means? *(a piece of something) (SL.1.1; SL.1.4; L.1.4; L.1.5)*

- Together reread the sentences on the board, substituting the word *pieces* for *segments*. Discuss whether or not the sentences still makes sense.
- Use the Close Reading activity to guide children in asking and answering questions about another word on page 10.

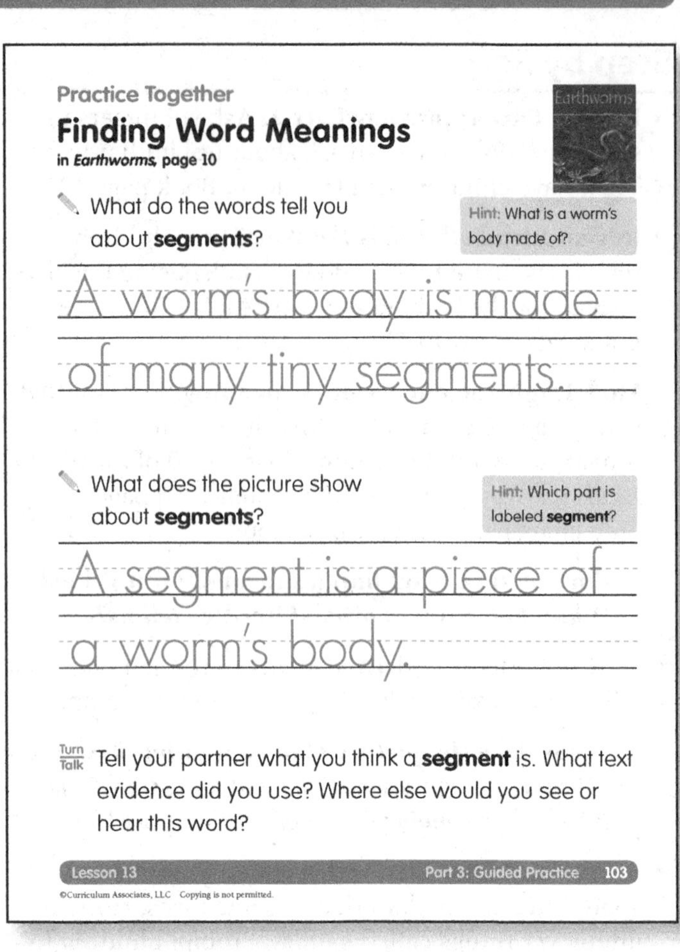

Close Reading

- Explain that when readers know something about a word, asking questions helps them clarify, or check, its meaning.
- Reread page 10 aloud, and direct children's attention to the second sentence you displayed earlier. Point to *bristles*, and think aloud:

  I think I know this word. My toothbrush and hairbrush both have bristles. I think bristles are the stiff hairs on a brush.

- Use the following prompts to check the meaning:

  What do the words tell about bristles? *(Bristles on the segments of the worm's body help it to move.) (RI.1.1)*

  What does the picture show about bristles? *(They look like hairs sticking up on the segments.)*

- Guide children to see that *bristles* does mean "stiff hairs," and that they can be found in other places than just toothbrushes and hairbrushes.

Part 4: Independent Practice

Step by Step

- **Review Parts 1–3; preview Part 4.** Have children share questions that readers can ask about new words. Direct them to Student Book page 104. Explain that they will now ask and answer questions about new words by themselves. Emphasize that the questions are the same as on the previous pages.
- **Have children figure out new words independently.** Display *Earthworms* and tell children that they will ask and answer questions about new words in another part of the book.
- Tell children to listen closely for the word *surface* and for evidence that tells what the word means. Read aloud page 11, omitting the caption at the bottom. Have children raise their hands when they hear the word *surface*. Then display the last two sentences.
- Reread the sentences, and ask children to think about what words tell more about *surface*. Then read aloud the first question and the Hint on the Student Book page. Have children write their answers. *(RI.1.1; L.1.1; L.1.2)*
- Read aloud the second question and the Hint. Circulate and display the pictures. Have children write their answers in complete sentences. Then discuss answers to both questions.
- **Have children demonstrate understanding.** Read aloud the Turn and Talk activity. Remind partners to use evidence they wrote about in their Student Books to help them decide on the meaning of *surface*. Invite children to share additional examples of the word in class discussion. *(SL.1.1; SL.1.4; L.1.5)*

Tip: Clarify the meaning of *surface* by using a non-example. Display page 17. Explain that the picture shows a worm underground, and that *underground* is the opposite of *on the surface*.

- Use the Close Reading activity to discuss what to do when word and picture evidence is not enough to determine meaning.
- **Have children reflect on their learning.** Have children review the questions they learned to ask about new words. Guide them to discuss how asking questions and thinking about where they have heard a word before can help them better understand words in new contexts. Chart their ideas.

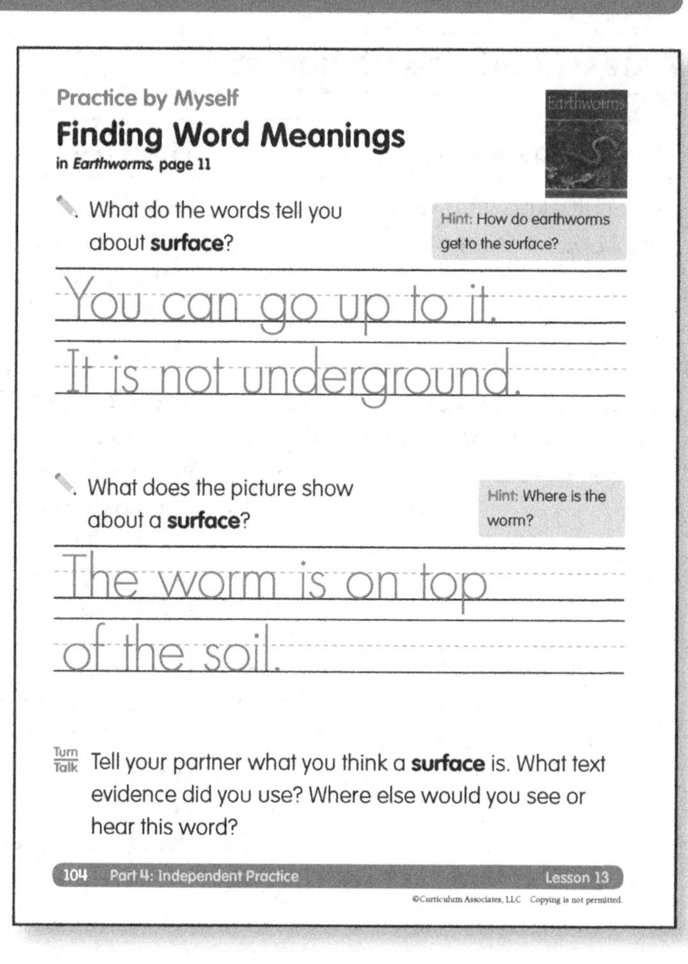
Practice by Myself

Finding Word Meanings

in *Earthworms*, page 11

What do the words tell you about **surface**?

Hint: How do earthworms get to the surface?

You can go up to it. It is not underground.

What does the picture show about a **surface**?

Hint: Where is the worm?

The worm is on top of the soil.

Turn Talk: Tell your partner what you think a **surface** is. What text evidence did you use? Where else would you see or hear this word?

104 Part 4: Independent Practice Lesson 13

©Curriculum Associates, LLC Copying is not permitted.

Close Reading

- Remind children that sometimes words and picture evidence do not give enough information about a word's meaning. Display page 11, and read aloud the caption at the bottom of the page.
- Write on the board "A worm's body is damp but not slimy." Read the sentence aloud, then prompt:

  What is this sentence about? *(a worm's body)*

  Which words describe a worm's body? *(damp, not slimy)*

  What does the picture show? *(The worm looks wet and shiny.) (RI.1.7)*

  What do you know about the word *slimy* from this evidence? *(It is not damp; it tells something about how a worm's body feels.)*

- Point out that readers might need to use other strategies to figure out the exact meaning. For instance, they can ask someone, or look it up in a dictionary and match the meaning to the picture.

Assessment and Remediation

If you observe . . .	Then try . . .
Difficulty knowing what questions to ask about word meanings	Providing practice with the questions on Student Book page 101. Have partners work together to ask and answer the questions about the following words in *Earthworms: giant* (p. 7), *rotting* (p. 12), *underground* (p. 17), and *enemy* (p. 23). Have the partners give a definition for each word and then explain their definitions based on the word and picture clues in the text.
Difficulty relating prior knowledge to a new word or to a known word in a new context	Scaffolding children. For example, on page 15 of *Earthworms,* read the sentence that contains the word *anchor.* Have children write or tell an example of the word in a context they recognize, such as a boat anchor. Then help them make connections in order to build understanding of the word in a new context. Ask a volunteer to use props to demonstrate how an anchor holds down a boat. Then discuss how an earthworm might use its bristles to anchor its body in the ground.
Difficulty locating text evidence that gives clues about unfamiliar words or phrases	Emphasizing that clues may be found before or after a word, and that readers may need to reread or read ahead, even on another page. Reread page 23 of *Elizabeth Leads the Way.* Draw a word web for *flabbergasted.* Guide children to identify the words *"shocking"* and *"gasped"* as evidence, and add these to the web. Repeat with the word *rumbling* on page 29, using the clues *"louder and louder and louder"* and *"argued."* Work with children to define each word, based on these related words.

Connect to the Anchor Standard

R4: *Interpret words and phrases as they are used in a text, including determining technical, connotative, and figurative meanings, and analyze how specific word choices shape meaning or tone.*

Throughout the grades, Standard 4 builds toward a more sophisticated analysis of vocabulary that students will encounter in both general and academic reading. In later grades, readers transition from looking for the basic definition of a word to interpreting its connotation and considering why the author chose it over alternative options. Students will independently analyze vocabulary as they question: *Is not knowing this word preventing me from understanding what I'm reading? Do I recognize this word but not the way it's being used here? Why did the author choose this particular word? Does this word make me feel a certain way?* Use the following activities to help your students begin this transition.

- Guide children to examine the impact of word meaning. Reread page 7 of *Elizabeth Leads the Way,* and discuss the word *pity.* Guide children to identify the words *sad* and *wrong* as clues that a *pity* is "a reason to feel sad or disappointed." Discuss how Elizabeth might have felt about hearing that being a girl is a pity. Talk about what actions those feelings inspired Elizabeth to take. *(L.1.5)*
- Help children consider the connotation of a word. Reread page 12 of *Elizabeth Leads the Way,* and ask children to tell what *begged* means. *(to ask for in a needy way)* Prompt: *Why didn't the author just write that Elizabeth asked her father to send her? Why did she choose the word* begged? Have children act out begging for a new pet. Discuss how the word *begged* helps the reader understand Elizabeth's feelings as stronger and more desperate than simply asking.

Lesson 14 (Student Book pages 105–108)

Text Features

CCSS

RI.1.5: Know and use various text features (e.g., headings, tables of contents, glossaries . . .) to locate key facts or information in a text.

Required Read Alouds: *I (Earthworms)*

Lesson Objectives

- Recognize that text features are parts of a book that guide readers in finding information.
- Use text features such as headings, tables of contents, and glossaries to find information in a book.
- Understand why authors include text features and how they help readers find information.

The Learning Progression

- **Grade K:** CCSS RI.K.5 expects children to identify the front and back cover and title page of a book.
- **Grade 1: CCSS RI.1.5 asks children to look beyond basic concepts of print to identify text features such as headings, tables of contents, and glossaries. Children are then asked to use these features to locate information in a text.**
- **Grade 2:** CCSS RI.2.5 expands the range of text features that children are expected to identify and use to locate information in a text; added features include captions, bold print, subheadings, and indexes.

Prerequisite Skills

- Identify the main topic of a text with prompting and support.
- Identify key details in a text with prompting and support.
- Describe the connection between two pieces of information in a text with prompting and support.

Tap Children's Prior Knowledge

- Explain that features are parts of something that are most noticeable. For example, the features of a bike might be its bright color, shiny wheels, a loud horn, or a license plate with the rider's name.
- Tell children that some features use words, such as the bike license plate with the rider's name. The words are usually different or noticeable in some way, such as being larger, bolder, or in color. This draws attention to them and lets the reader know that the information they give, such as the rider's name, is important.
- Point out examples of features that are noticeable in the classroom, such as a familiar poster or chart. Explain any elements, either visual or textual, that organize the information, such as a numbered list. Discuss the item with children and talk about what details make it noticeable or memorable for them.
- Go on a features hunt with children. Help them find examples of other features in the classroom, such as a sign, a class or bus schedule, or a word wall. As you identify each item together, discuss what elements, visual or textual, children notice about it.
- Explain that books can have features, too. Tell children that in this lesson, they will be learning how to use text features in books to find information.

Ready *Teacher Toolbox* Teacher-Toolbox.com

	Prerequisite Skills	*RI.1.5*
Ready Lessons	✓	✓
Tools for Instruction		✓
Interactive Tutorials		

Additional CCSS

RI.1.2; SL.1.1; SL.1.3; L.1.1; L.1.2 (See page A38 for full text.)

Step by Step

- **Introduce the standard.** Have children turn to page 105 in their Student Books. Read aloud the speech bubble.
- **Review descriptions of text features.** Read the line below the speech bubble. Tell children they will learn about three kinds of text features.
- Read aloud the first description. Have children underline the phrase *table of contents*. Display the table of contents in *Earthworms*. Explain:

  This page shows the topics that are in this book. (Point out the word *Contents*.) ***Contents* means "everything that is inside." This table of contents tells us that this book has different parts, or sections, inside.**

  (Move your finger down the left column.) **Each of these words is the title of a section.** (Point to the page numbers.) **These page numbers tell where each section begins and ends.**

Tip: Explain that one definition of a *table* is something we sit at. Another definition is a list that shows information in columns and rows. Explain that in many tables of contents, only the first page of a section is given.

- Read aloud the second description. Have children underline the word *heading*. Display page 8 in *Earthworms*. Point to and read the heading, *Finding Earthworms*. Explain that this is a title for the section of the book that describes where earthworms live.
- Read aloud the third description. Have children underline the word *glossary*. Explain that a glossary is like a dictionary—it shows words in alphabetical order and defines them. A glossary, however, gives definitions only for important words that are in the book.
- Tell children that if they do not understand a word in an informational book, they can see if the book has a glossary and try looking up the word there.
- Display the glossary on page 28 of *Earthworms*. Point out that the defined words are in bold print and appear in alphabetical order. Choose a word and read aloud its definition. Discuss with children why this word is important in the book.

Listen and Learn

Text Features

Text features are parts of a book that help readers locate important information.

Read about some text features:

- The **table of contents** shows what information is in a book. It also shows the page numbers where you can find the information.
- A **heading** is a short title for a section of the book. It shows what information is in that section.
- A **glossary** gives the meanings of important words that are used in the book.

Knowing how to use these text features will help you find information in a book.

Lesson 14 Part 1: Introduction 105

- Display examples of tables of contents, headings, and glossaries in other classroom books. Help children notice similarities and differences between each feature in the sample books and in *Earthworms*.
- **Explain why readers use text features.** Read aloud the bottom of the page. Explain that each text feature helps readers find different types of information in a book. Knowing what information each text feature gives can help readers find what they are looking for.
- Share an example of how you have used a text feature. For example, when reading a book about rattlesnakes, you may have wanted to learn more about where rattlesnakes live. Explain how you used the table of contents to find out what pages to read for that information.
- **Have children demonstrate understanding.** Call on individuals to share what they have learned so far about text features in books. Encourage them to give examples from the classroom books used for comparison above, as appropriate.

Part 2: Modeled Instruction

Step by Step

- **Review Part 1; preview Part 2.** Ask volunteers to share what they have learned about text features. Have children turn to Student Book page 106.
- **Revisit *Earthworms.*** Have children briefly recall the topic and key details, using the chart from the Book Review on Teacher Resource Book page 139. *(RI.1.2)*
- **Model how to use a table of contents.** Display the table of contents in *Earthworms.* Then think aloud:

  I want to find out what body parts a worm has. I look in the table of contents. Here is a section called *A Worm's Body* on pages 10–11. I'll read those pages to find out about a worm's body.

Tip: Help children understand how to read the table of contents. Point to and read a section title, then run your finger across the page to the corresponding page numbers.

- Use the same procedure to locate the pages for what worms eat *(Feeding,* pages 12–13) and how birds catch worms *(Food for Birds,* pages 24–25).
- Explain to children that if they don't have a specific question, they can still use the table of contents. Point to and read aloud the entry for pages 16–17, *Tunneling,* and ask what this section could be about. Turn to those pages and discuss how the information does or does not match children's ideas.
- Read aloud the directions and topics for the first Student Book activity. Point out that the words do not exactly match the titles in the table of contents. Explain that this is because readers' questions may be worded differently than the authors' topics.
- Model how to connect each topic on the Student Book page to a table-of-contents entry. Discuss.
- Read aloud the second activity and the Hint. Discuss the answer. *(SL.1.1)*
- **Model writing your responses.** Model how to write the answers for each activity. *(L.1.1; L.1.2)*
- Use the Close Reading activity to discuss why table-of-contents entries are useful for finding information.
- **Have children demonstrate understanding.** Assign the Turn and Talk activity. Review Student Book page 105 if needed. Share answers in discussion.

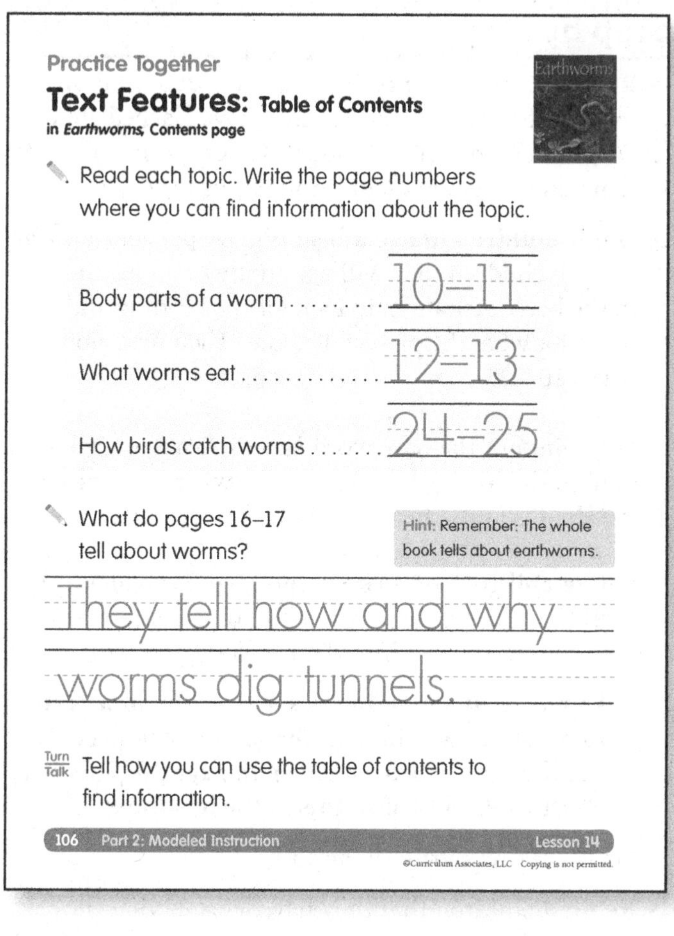
Practice Together

Text Features: Table of Contents
in *Earthworms,* Contents page

Read each topic. Write the page numbers where you can find information about the topic.

Body parts of a worm 10–11

What worms eat 12–13

How birds catch worms 24–25

What do pages 16–17 tell about worms?

Hint: Remember: The whole book tells about earthworms.

They tell how and why worms dig tunnels.

Turn Talk: Tell how you can use the table of contents to find information.

Close Reading

- Explain that authors use text features to help readers find information. Read aloud the first entry in the table of contents of *Earthworms.* Turn to page 6 and read the heading. Then prompt:

  What is the first section title in the table of contents? *(All Sorts of Worms)* **What is the heading on page 6?** *(All Sorts of Worms)*

  What do you notice about the section title and the heading? *(They are the same.)*

- Guide children to see that each section title in the table of contents is repeated as a heading on a page in the book. Discuss why the author does this. *(to help readers find information easily and quickly)*
- Discuss with children how the table of contents can help them understand what kinds of information are in a book. Guide them to see how using a table of contents can sometimes help them quickly find important details about a topic.

Part 3: Guided Practice

Step by Step

- **Review Parts 1–2; preview Part 3.** Have children recall different text features they have learned about. Direct them to turn to Student Book page 107. Explain that you will guide them through this page.
- **Guide children to use a heading.** Display *Earthworms* and tell children they will use another text feature in the book. Ask them to look for the heading and listen for what the pages tell about. Then read aloud pages 20–21.

Tip: Point out the base word *head* in *heading*. Tell children that one way to remember where to look for a heading is at the head, or top, of a section.

- **Guide children to write responses.** Read aloud the directions for the first Student Book question. Model how to find the heading. Think aloud:

  I know that a heading is a short title for a section of a book. I will look at the top of each page. I see the large word *Hatching* on page 20. This is a short title, so I think this is the heading.

- Have children write the heading.
- Remind children that they have learned that the main topic of a text is what the text is mostly about. Guide them to see how the heading *Hatching* tells the main topic of pages 20–21.
- Read aloud the second question and the Hint. Explain that a relationship is how two or more things, such as the heading and the text, are connected. Discuss the answer and have children write it in a complete sentence. *(L.1.1; L.1.2)*
- Use the Close Reading activity to help children relate a heading to its section of text.
- **Have children demonstrate understanding.** Have partners complete the Turn and Talk activity. If partners need support, prompt them:

  What is a heading? *(a short title at the beginning of a section)*

  What does a heading tell you? *(what the section is mostly about)*

- Invite volunteers to share their answers. Encourage children to discuss how headings and tables of contents are related to each other. *(SL.1.1)*

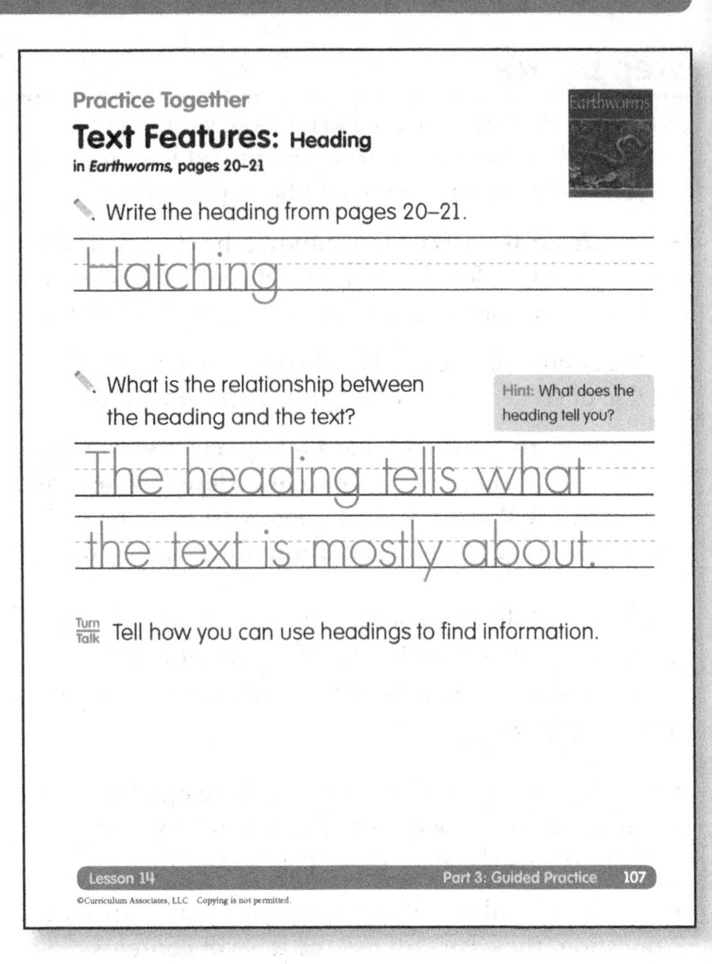
Practice Together

Text Features: Heading
in *Earthworms*, pages 20–21

Write the heading from pages 20–21.

Hatching

What is the relationship between the heading and the text?

Hint: What does the heading tell you?

The heading tells what the text is mostly about.

Turn Talk: Tell how you can use headings to find information.

Lesson 14 Part 3: Guided Practice 107

Close Reading

- Remind children that a heading is a short title that tells what a section is about. Read aloud pages 20–21 of *Earthworms*. Then think aloud:

  There is only one heading on these two pages, *Hatching*. When I read the text and look at the pictures, I find out that all the information is about how worms hatch.

- Point to the picture on page 20. Prompt children:

  What does this picture show? *(a cocoon)* **How is this picture related to the heading?** *(It shows where the worms are before they hatch.)*

- Point to the picture on page 21. Prompt children:

  What does this picture show? *(an adult worm with young worms)* **How is the picture related to the heading?** *(It shows what the young worms look like after they hatch.)*

- Discuss with children how readers can use headings to understand a section of a book.

Part 4: Independent Practice

Step by Step

- **Review Parts 1–3; preview Part 4.** Invite a volunteer to tell why it is important to know how to use text features. Then direct children to Student Book page 108. Explain that they will answer questions by themselves, using a glossary.
- Lead a brief discussion on glossaries. Prompt:

  Why does an author put a glossary in a book? *(The author wants to help readers understand the meanings of important words they may not know.)*

  How does the author decide which words to list? *(The author chooses important words readers need to know.)*
- Read page 22 of *Earthworms* aloud. Point out the word *shrews,* and ask children if they know what it means. Explain that if they do not know, they can try looking it up in the glossary.
- **Have children use a glossary independently.** Display the glossary on page 28 of *Earthworms.* Read aloud the first question on the Student Book page.
- Call on a volunteer to find the word *shrew* in the glossary. Tell children to listen closely as you read aloud the definition. Have children write the answer as a sentence in their own words. *(L.1.1; L.1.2)*
- Read aloud the second question and the Hint. Explain that a relationship is how two or more things, such as the glossary and the text, are connected. Have children write the answer in a complete sentence.
- Discuss answers to the first and second questions.
- Use the Close Reading activity to explain how glossary definitions give different information than the text describes.
- **Have children demonstrate understanding.** Have partners complete the Turn and Talk activity. Encourage them to refer to Student Book page 105 for support. Invite volunteers to share their answers. *(SL.1.1)*
- **Have children reflect on their learning.** Guide children in a discussion about how text features such as tables of contents, headings, and glossaries help readers find information. Chart their ideas.

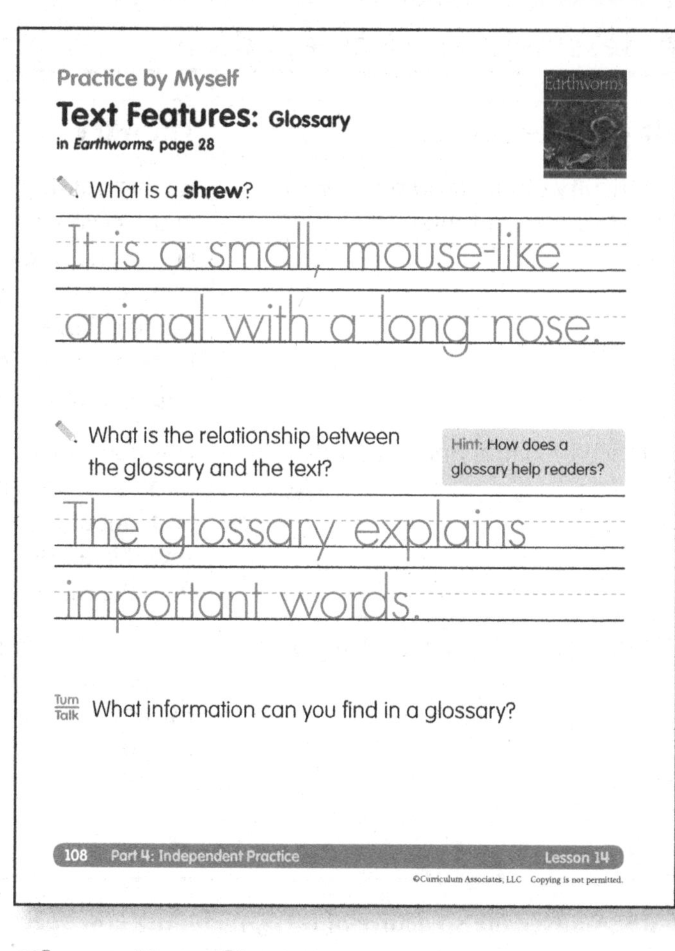

Practice by Myself

Text Features: Glossary

in *Earthworms,* page 28

What is a **shrew**?

It is a small, mouse-like animal with a long nose.

What is the relationship between the glossary and the text?

Hint: How does a glossary help readers?

The glossary explains important words.

Turn and Talk: What information can you find in a glossary?

108 Part 4: Independent Practice Lesson 14

©Curriculum Associates, LLC Copying is not permitted.

Close Reading

- Explain that a word's glossary definition will usually tell information that is different from the way the word is described in the text itself. Read aloud the information about an earthworm's bristles on pages 10, 15, and 25, and then read the definition of *bristle* on page 28. Prompt children:

  What do the sentences tell about bristles? *(Bristles help the worm move and anchor itself.)*

  What does the glossary definition tell about bristles? *(Bristles are "tiny, stiff hair[s].")*

  How are the details in each place different? *(The text tells what an earthworm's bristles help it to do. The glossary tells what bristles are in general.)*
- Discuss that the text and a glossary definition are meant to be used together to give the reader a more complete and specific understanding of a word. Guide children to understand that the author chooses the information and definition that will best help readers understand the topic.

Differentiated Instruction

Assessment and Remediation

If you observe . . .	Then try . . .
Difficulty understanding topics in the table of contents	Having children create a table of contents for a familiar informational book in the classroom (preferably a book without its own table of contents). Revisit the book together, looking for headings or for pages that present a clear idea or set of facts about the topic. Using *Earthworms* as a model, guide children to suggest headings for the classroom book and identify page numbers for each heading. Create the table of contents on chart paper, and then have children use it to locate information in the book.
Difficulty identifying headings	Using several nonfiction books with headings. Help children notice the location of each heading. Then discuss specific characteristics, such as the size and font of the letters, whether they are bold or italic, whether the heading is set off in a box, and so on. Point out that headings usually have a different style than the main text on pages.
Difficulty finding words in a glossary	Conducting a brief review of alphabetical order. Write several words on index cards, each beginning with a different letter, and distribute them to children. Read the words together and help children line them up in alphabetical order.

Connect to the Anchor Standard

R5: *Analyze the structure of texts, including how specific sentences, paragraphs, and larger portions of the text (e.g., a section, chapter, scene, or stanza) relate to each other and the whole.*

Throughout the grades, Standard 5 advances students' understanding of text structure. Students progress from recognizing and using text features to understanding the underlying structures of texts. Students will learn about the organization of a single text and about how information is related across texts. They will ask questions such as: *How has the author organized the information in the book? Why did the author choose to highlight certain information? How do text features help guide a reader through the book? How has the author moved from clear signposts, such as headings, to more subtle organizing principles, such as chronology, comparison, cause and effect, and problem/solution?* Use the following activities to help your students begin this transition.

- Examine why the author separated information on worms' predators into two sections. Read aloud pages 22–25 of *Earthworms.* Point out that both sections, *Enemies* and *Food for Birds,* tell about animals that eat worms. Discuss how the author covers a lot of information—four animals and the ways that each finds and captures worms. Guide children to see that having two sections organizes the information and helps readers make sense of it. *(SL.1.1; SL.1.3)*
- Relate text features to the structure of the book. Display the table of contents in *Earthworms.* Point out that it shows readers what they will read about. Page through and read headings, explaining that they tell what is coming next. Show the glossary at the end and explain that it tells readers where to look for definitions. Discuss how these text features are always found at the beginning, in the middle, and at the end to help readers find information.

Lesson 15 (Student Book pages 109–112)
More Text Features

CCSS

RI.1.5: Know and use various text features (e.g., . . . electronic menus, icons) to locate key facts or information in a text.

Required Read Alouds: *Projectable 4 (Famous Women: Susan B. Anthony)*

Lesson Objectives

- Recognize that digital text features guide readers in finding information.
- Use digital text features to find information.
- Understand how digital text features help readers find information.

The Learning Progression

- **Grade K:** CCSS RI.K.5 expects children to identify the front and back cover and title page of a book.
- **Grade 1: CCSS RI.1.5 asks children to look beyond basic concepts of print to identify digital text features such as electronic menus and icons. Children are then asked to use these features to locate information in a digital text.**
- **Grade 2:** CCSS RI.2.5 expands the range of text features that children are expected to identify and use to locate information in a text; added features include captions, bold print, subheadings, and indexes.

Prerequisite Skills

- Describe what a website is.
- Navigate successfully online by using the mouse, cursor, and clicks.
- Identify main topic and key details in a text with prompting and support.

Tap Children's Prior Knowledge

- Review that the purpose of text features is to help readers organize and find information in printed texts. Briefly discuss some examples of tables of contents, headings, and glossaries with children.
- Explain that readers use even more kinds of text features when they use a computer.
- Ask children to think about a grocery store and the signs that tell what foods are in each aisle. Discuss how these signs help you find things more easily. Explain that a text feature called a search field helps you do this on a computer; it helps you search for what you want so you can find it more quickly.
- Display a school lunch or restaurant menu. Ask children what it does. *(shows food choices)* Explain that a menu on a computer does something similar: it gives you choices about what to do next.
- Draw a smiley face and ask children what it means. Explain that a smiley face is an icon—a simple picture that gives information. Have children give examples of other icons *(recycling, wash hands)* and tell what they mean.
- Remind children that text features are good tools for finding information. Explain that in this lesson, they will learn about search fields, electronic menus, and icons.

Ready ***Teacher Toolbox*** *Teacher-Toolbox.com*

	Prerequisite Skills	RI.1.5
Ready Lessons		✓
Tools for Instruction		
Interactive Tutorials		

Additional CCSS

SL.1.1; SL.1.5; L.1.1; L.1.2 *(See page A38 for full text.)*

Part 1: Introduction

Step by Step

- **Introduce the standard.** Have children turn to page 109 in their Student Books. Read aloud the speech bubble.
- **Review descriptions of text features.** Read aloud the line below the speech bubble. Explain that each description that follows tells about a different digital text feature. Point out that *digital* refers to anything computerized. Digital devices include laptops, e-book readers, tablets, and smartphones.
- Read aloud the first description. Have children underline *search field*.
- Display the first page of *Famous Women* that shows screens from a website called Famous Women. Point out the search field in the top screen. Explain:

  When you want to find a name or a topic on a website, you can use a search field. You click in the box and type what you want to find.

  Then you either hit the Enter key or click on the word *GO* beside the search field to have the computer find what you want.
- Read aloud the second description. Have children underline *electronic menu*.
- Focus on the top screen, pointing out the menu and the cursor arrow that points to one item. Prompt:

  How is this menu like and not like a table of contents? *(It has topics, but no page numbers.)*
- Explain how to use this electronic menu:

  This menu has three topics to choose from. A person is choosing the middle topic, "Women in History." Once it is clicked on, the person will see information about that topic.
- Read aloud the third description. Have children underline *icon*. Explain that icons can be symbols, illustrations, or photographs. Have children recall icons they identified on page 153. Focus on the first screen of *Famous Women*. Prompt children:

  What is the icon for "Women in History"? *(a flag)*

Tip: Bookmark and share some age-appropriate websites with clear examples of the text features discussed here, such as www.funology.com or www.nationalgeographic.com/kids/littlekids/.

Listen and Learn

More Text Features

Text features help you find information. Websites have features that help you tell the computer what you want to see.

Read about some digital text features:

- You can use a **search field** to find information on a website or in an e-book. Type the topic you want to know about in the search field.
- An **electronic menu** is a list of topics. You choose a topic from the menu. Then you get information about that topic.
- An **icon** is a picture that stands for something. The choices in an electronic menu can be icons, words, or both.

Understanding how to use these text features will help you find information in a digital text.

- **Explain why text features are important.** Read aloud the bottom of Student Book page 109. Point out that these digital text features help readers understand what information is available and help them get to that information quickly, just as tables of contents and other text features in printed texts do.
- Share an example of a time when using these text features helped you quickly find information. For example, you might explain that you went to a site to find ideas for a costume. The site had hundreds of costumes, so you used the search field to type in the exact type of costume you wanted.
- **Have children demonstrate understanding.** Call on individuals to share what they have learned so far about the text features in digital texts. Encourage them to give examples of times they have used or worked with others to use these features and find information.

Part 2: Modeled Instruction

Step by Step

- **Review Part 1; preview Part 2.** Ask volunteers to share what they have learned about digital text features. Have children turn to Student Book page 110.
- **Model identifying a search field.** Display *Famous Women*. Help children focus on the magnifying glass, and the area beside it in the first screen. (You might want to cover up other parts of the screen.) Explain that together, these elements make up the search field on this website. Think aloud:

  I want to look up information on this website. I will look for a search field to help me. I see a field with the word *SEARCH* in it. This tells me where I can enter text about my topic. Clicking the button with the word *GO* on it will help me begin my search.

- Read aloud the first activity on the Student Book page. Point out the features, and read aloud the phrases that explain how each one might be used. Have children match each feature to its use.
- Read aloud the second activity and the Hint. Explain that Michelle Kwan is an ice-skater who won medals in two different Olympics. Model the steps you would take to search for her name using the search field.
- **Model writing your response.** Model writing the answer in a complete sentence. *(L.1.1; L.1.2)*
- **Discuss search fields.** Explain that when you use a search field, what you type as a topic is important. Point out that some topics are specific, like *Michelle Kwan*. Other topics, like *athletes,* will bring up much more information. Explain that you can make a big topic smaller, such as choosing one kind of athlete.
- Explain that some sites, like Famous Women, give information about a specific topic. Others, such as www.GoGooligans.com and wwww.KidRex.org, are sites you can use to search for information about any topic.
- Use the Close Reading activity to distinguish a general search site and searching within a website.
- **Have children demonstrate understanding.** Read aloud the Turn and Talk activity. Have volunteers share their process. *(SL.1.1)*

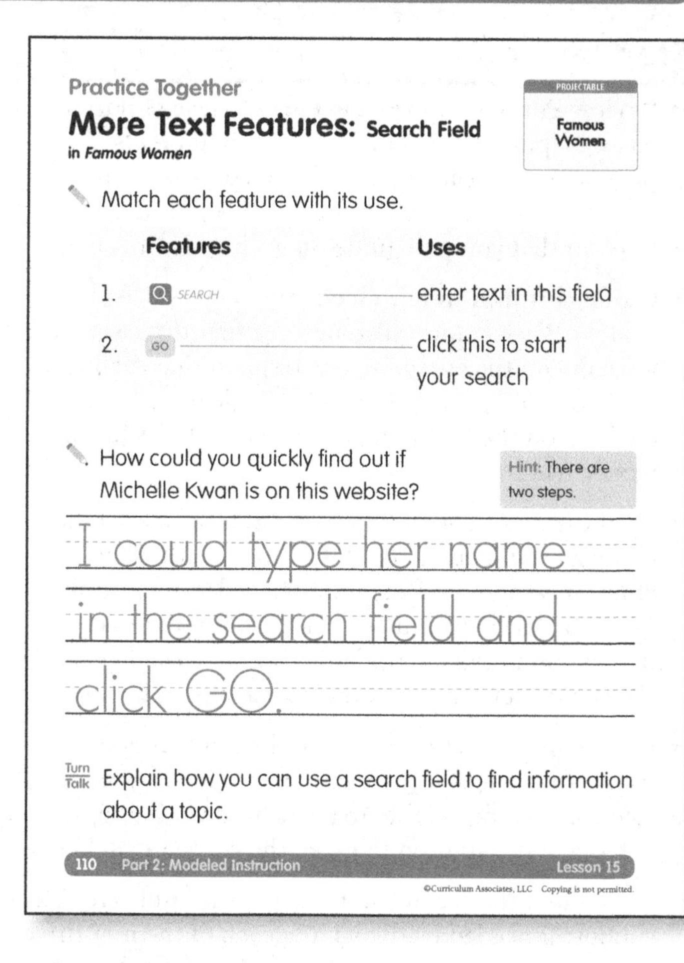
Practice Together

More Text Features: Search Field
in Famous Women

PROJECTABLE
Famous Women

Match each feature with its use.

Features	Uses
1. SEARCH	enter text in this field
2. GO	click this to start your search

How could you quickly find out if Michelle Kwan is on this website?

Hint: There are two steps.

I could type her name in the search field and click GO.

Turn Talk Explain how you can use a search field to find information about a topic.

110 Part 2: Modeled Instruction Lesson 15

©Curriculum Associates, LLC Copying is not permitted.

Close Reading

- Talk about what you might search for on different sites. Explain that you might look up a specific woman artist on Famous Women, while on a more general site, you might look for a list of all the women artists in the United States. Prompt:

  Tell why you would or would not search for information about George Washington on Famous Women. *(I wouldn't, because this site only has information about famous women, and George Washington was a man. I might search for him on a site about American presidents instead.)*

  Why does it make sense to search for Michelle Kwan on Famous Women? *(because she is a famous athlete and the site has a topic called "Women in Sports")*

- Guide children to see that using a search field well means thinking about what you want to find out and then deciding what kind of site will help you find the best information most quickly.

Part 3: Guided Practice

Step by Step

- **Review Parts 1–2; preview Part 3.** Have children recall helpful features included in digital texts. As they name the features, ask the purpose of each. Direct children to turn to Student Book page 111. Explain that you will guide them through this page.
- **Guide children to use electronic menus.** Display *Famous Women*. Move through the first three screens, focusing on the cursor arrow. Explain that each icon or set of words is part of an electronic menu, and clicking on the highlighted menu item leads to the next screen.
- Read the names of all four women in the electronic menu as you display the third screen. Ask what children would do if they wanted to learn more about Susan B. Anthony and how they would find that information. *(put the cursor on Susan's menu item and click on it)* Repeat for another name on the menu.
- Read aloud the first activity on the Student Book page. Point out that the menu items come from the electronic menu on the first screen. Read the topics aloud. Guide children to make the correct matches.
- Read aloud the second activity and the Hint. Provide support if needed by displaying each of the first three screens on *Famous Women* in turn, guiding children to correctly identify the menu items to use.
- **Guide children to write responses.** Have children write complete sentences. *(L.1.1; L.1.2)*

Tip: If children wonder how to move back to an earlier screen, point out the arrows at the top left that you can click to go back and forth between screens.

- Use the Close Reading activity to help children identify where they are within a website.
- **Have children demonstrate understanding.** Have partners complete the Turn and Talk activity. If they need support, prompt them:

  In a printed book, you use the table of contents to find what you want to read. Then you turn to the correct page. How do you get to the information you want to find in a digital text? *(click on the menu item)*

- Have volunteers share the procedures they have discussed. *(SL.1.1)*

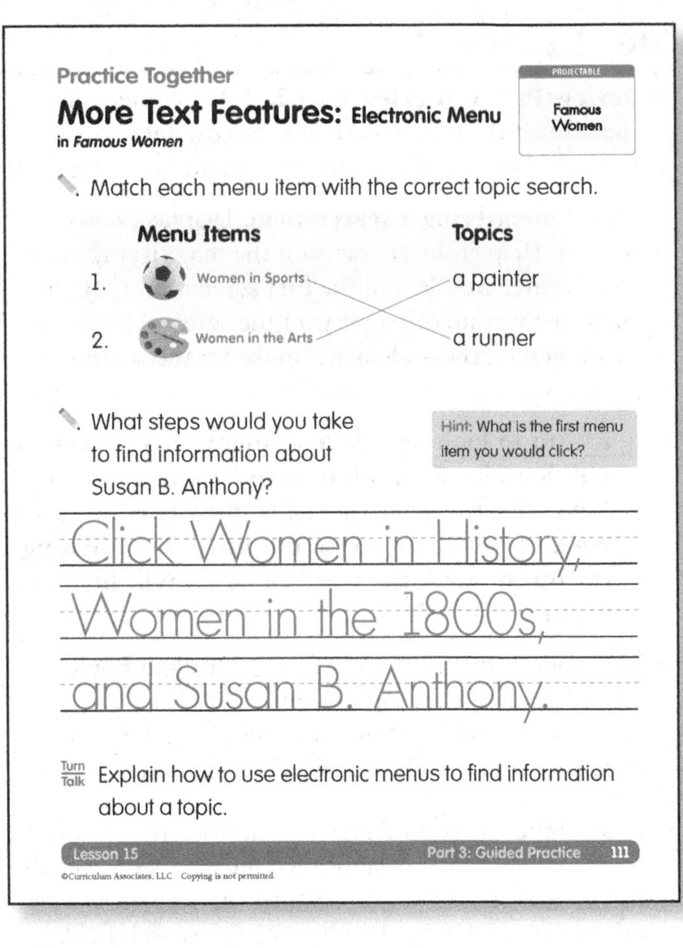
Practice Together

More Text Features: Electronic Menu in *Famous Women*

PROJECTABLE Famous Women

Match each menu item with the correct topic search.

Menu Items	Topics
1. Women in Sports	a painter
2. Women in the Arts	a runner

What steps would you take to find information about Susan B. Anthony?

Hint: What is the first menu item you would click?

Click Women in History, Women in the 1800s, and Susan B. Anthony.

Turn Talk Explain how to use electronic menus to find information about a topic.

Lesson 15 Part 3: Guided Practice 111

©Curriculum Associates, LLC Copying is not permitted.

Close Reading

- Display the third screen of *Famous Women.* Point out the title, Famous Women, and then draw attention to the "breadcrumb" line just below it. Tell children that this is one type of electronic menu that shows them the "trail" of screens they followed to get to the screen they are on. Explain:

  This line lists the different menu screens we have looked at to get to what is shown here. We began with the first screen, called the home screen. Then we clicked "Women in History." From that screen we clicked "Women in the 1800s," which is where we are now.

- Explain that when you click the menu item for "Susan B. Anthony," you will move to the next screen. Display the fourth screen. Prompt:

  Where do you look to see the screens you have clicked through to get to this one? *(They are listed in the line below the website's title.)*

Part 4: Independent Practice

Step by Step

- **Review Parts 1–3; preview Part 4.** Invite volunteers to name text features of digital texts and to tell why each one is useful. Then direct children to Student Book page 112. Explain that they will match items and then write an answer to a question, as on previous pages.
- **Have children identify icons independently.** Remind children that icons can be symbols, illustrations, or photographs. Icons can relate to the content of a digital text or they can be features that help the reader use the digital text in general.
- Display the second screen on *Famous Women.* Ask children what icons they see. *(printer, magnifier, soccer ball, flag, artist's palette)* Discuss what each one tells the reader.
- Repeat with the third screen, asking children what the icons are and what readers can do on this screen. *(pictures of four women; choose one of four women from the 1800s to learn about)*
- Explain that Elizabeth Cady Stanton and Susan B. Anthony were leaders in the movement for women's rights, Harriet Tubman helped to lead slaves to freedom, and Louisa May Alcott was a popular author who wrote the book *Little Women.*
- Read aloud the first activity on the Student Book page. Have children draw lines to make the matches.
- Read aloud the second activity and the Hint. Have children write their answers as complete sentences. *(L.1.1; L.1.2)*
- Use the Close Reading activity to help children think about what makes visual icons effective.
- Discuss answers to the first and second activities.
- **Have children demonstrate understanding.** Have partners complete the Turn and Talk activity. Point out that the question asks their opinion. To answer it, they need to give reasons why one way works better for them. Ask volunteers to share their ideas. *(SL.1.1)*
- **Have children reflect on their learning.** Guide children in a discussion about why learning to use text features will help them find the information they need in digital texts. Chart their ideas.

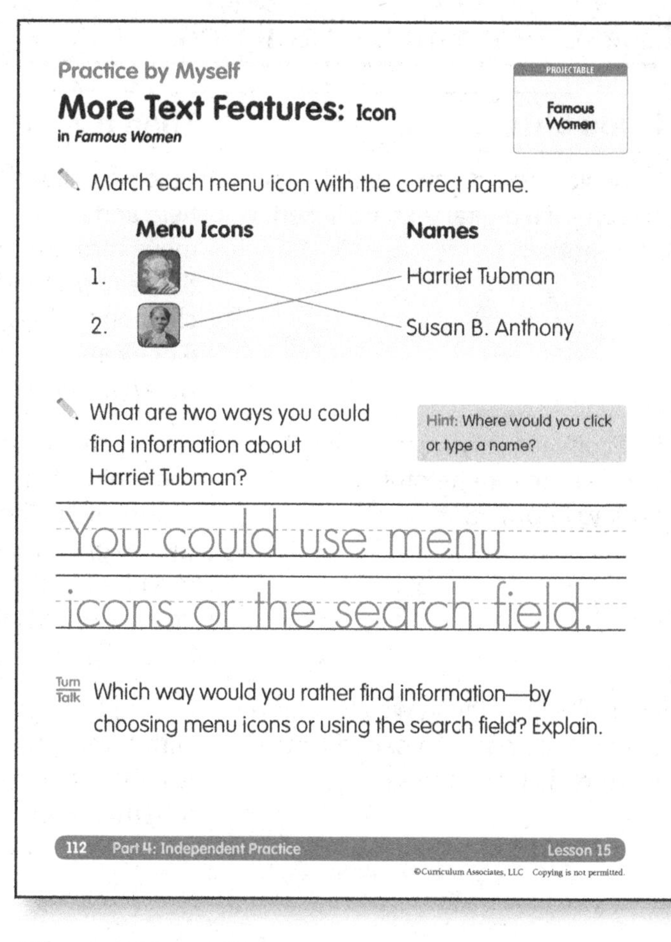
Practice by Myself

More Text Features: Icon
in *Famous Women*

PROJECTABLE
Famous Women

Match each menu icon with the correct name.

Menu Icons	Names
1.	Harriet Tubman
2.	Susan B. Anthony

What are two ways you could find information about Harriet Tubman?

Hint: Where would you click or type a name?

You could use menu icons or the search field.

Turn Talk Which way would you rather find information—by choosing menu icons or using the search field? Explain.

112 Part 4: Independent Practice Lesson 15

Close Reading

- Display the second screen on *Famous Women.* Discuss why it is helpful that the print and search icons look the same in most digital texts. Then discuss the menu icons. Prompt:

  Why is the icon for "Women in Sports" a soccer ball? *(Soccer is a sport all over the world.)*

  What other icons could have been used instead of a soccer ball? *(tennis ball, ice skate, basketball)*

- Hold a similar discussion about the other two menu icons. Then prompt:

  What is similar about these three icons? *(They are circles. They show just one item.)*

  Why are they similar? *(They belong together. They make up a menu.)*

- Look at the third screen together. Guide children to identify the icons on this screen and to discuss how they are similar and why.

Differentiated Instruction

Assessment and Remediation

If you observe . . .	Then try . . .
Difficulty seeing how the different screens of a digital text are linked to one another	Guiding children through an actual website. Direct children to use a search field and menu icons. If this is not possible, conduct a narrated simulation to move through the screens on *Famous Women*. Give children an object that they can pretend to use as a mouse. Then give a series of instructions for children to physically respond to as you display the corresponding screens. (For example: *Move the mouse until the arrow points at ______. Now click on it. Here is the next screen you see.)*
Difficulty identifying why digital text features are helpful in finding information	Having children think of real-world situations in which they need help finding something. For example, have them imagine that they have lost their favorite toy. To find it, they need to look in many different places where they think they might have left it. Point out how much easier it would be if they could go to a list of all their toys, click on the toy they want to find, and have it appear right away. Explain that this is how digital text features save time for readers—by letting them find what they want quickly, with just a little searching.
Difficulty identifying which items on a screen are part of a particular text feature, such as a menu	Having children practice sorting things into categories. Provide children with several objects that can be sorted by color, use, or some other feature. Ask them to create groups of objects and explain why those items go together. Then help children see how menu items on the projectable also go together in some way, such as by topic, similar wording, or icons.

Connect to the Anchor Standard

R5: *Analyze the structure of texts, including how specific sentences, paragraphs, and larger portions of the text (e.g., a section, chapter, scene, or stanza) relate to each other and the whole.*

In mastering Standard 5 throughout the grades, students move from using specific text features to identifying a text's structure, and finally to comparing and contrasting the structures of two different texts. Students gain an understanding of how working with a digital or print text's structure helps them navigate large amounts of information. In examining a text's structure, they might ask questions such as the following: *How do users move through web pages? How do digital text features help with this? How do parts of a digital or print text relate to each other? How will recognizing these relationships deepen my understanding of the text?* Use the following activities to help your students begin this transition.

- Have children design, draw, and label a new opening screen for *Famous Women*. Tell them to include these elements: print icon, search icon and search field, electronic menu for these three categories of women: Women in Music, Women in Science, Women in Politics. Invite children to add other elements to the screen, as long as they can explain why these would be useful. *(SL.1.5)*
- Read aloud the screens on *Famous Women* devoted to Susan B. Anthony. As you read, ask children to think of things that could be added to the screens to make them more interesting, or to allow readers to get to more information. For example, children might like to see more pictures; they might suggest that readers should be able to click on Elizabeth Cady Stanton's name within the text to go to the part of the site about her; or they might like to hear someone read one of Susan B. Anthony's speeches.

Lesson 16 (Student Book pages 113–116)

Words and Pictures

CCSS

RI.1.6: Distinguish between information provided by pictures or other illustrations and information provided by the words in a text.

Required Read Alouds: *Projectable 4 (Famous Women: Susan B. Anthony); E (Who Eats What?); I (Earthworms)*

Lesson Objectives

- Understand that both words and visuals provide information in books.
- Recognize that visuals often provide information beyond the words.
- Differentiate between information provided by words and information provided by visuals.
- Understand that using both words and visuals can help you learn more about a topic.

The Learning Progression

- **Grade K:** CCSS RI.K.6 requires children to name the author and illustrator of a text as well as the role of each.
- **Grade 1: CCSS RI.1.6 advances the Grade K standard by moving from identifying the roles of the author and illustrator to exploring the different products they create. Children locate and differentiate between information provided in the words and in the visuals in a text.**
- **Grade 2:** CCSS RI.2.6 moves back to the role of the author by going deeper into his or her role. Children determine the author's purpose for writing a text, such as to answer, explain, or describe.

Prerequisite Skills

- Name the author and illustrator of a text along with each one's roles.
- Identify the connections between words and pictures in a text with prompting and support.
- Answer questions about key details in a text with prompting and support.

Tap Children's Prior Knowledge

- Display a simple alphabet or number book in which the pictures clearly match the text. Read aloud a few pages, having children tell what the words say and what the picture shows on each page. Point out that on each of the pages, the words and the picture match closely.
- Ask children to tell what an author does and then what an illustrator does. *(An author writes the words; an illustrator draws the pictures.)* Discuss that often the author and the illustrator are two different people, and that each of them adds ideas to the book.
- Display a more complex text, such as a National Geographic, Penguin, or DK Reader. Read aloud a page or two and ask children to tell what the words say and what the pictures show.
- Discuss that books with more words often tell more complicated information, and the pictures do not always match every detail in the text.
- Explain that in this lesson, children will revisit familiar texts and look at the information provided in the words, then compare it to the information in the pictures or illustrations.

Ready *Teacher Toolbox* Teacher-Toolbox.com

	Prerequisite Skills	*RI.1.6*
Ready Lessons	✓	✓
Tools for Instruction	✓	
Interactive Tutorials		

Additional CCSS

RI.1.1; RI.1.2; SL.1.1; SL.1.2; SL.1.4; L.1.1; L.1.2 *(See page A38 for full text.)*

Part 1: Introduction

Step by Step

- **Introduce the standard.** Have children turn to page 113 in their Student Books. Read aloud the speech bubble.
- Explain that *information* means facts and knowledge about a subject. Remind children that earlier they learned about the difference between books that give information and books that tell stories. Review the chart on Student Book page 89.
- Explain that informational books provide information in two places—in words and pictures, which could be photographs, drawings, or diagrams. Refer to the discussion you led in the Tap Children's Prior Knowledge activity on page 159. Remind children that in some books, the information in words and pictures is the same.
- **Review questions to ask about words and pictures.** Read the line below the speech bubble, and point out that what follows are questions good readers ask themselves about information in words and pictures.
- Read aloud the first question. Have children circle the word *words*. Explain that the words in a book give details or descriptions that tell information.
- Read aloud the second question. Have children circle the word *pictures*. Point out that the pictures show information in a book. Then explain:

  Pictures, photographs, and diagrams are all ways to show information. A *picture* is a drawing made by an illustrator. A *photograph* is a picture made with a camera. A *diagram* is a drawing or photograph that shows the parts of something or how something works.

Tip: Support children's understanding of a diagram by displaying a concrete example, such as the diagram on page 10 of *Earthworms*. Read the labels and explain the purpose of this diagram.

- Read aloud the third and fourth questions. Have children circle the words *match* and *different*. Explain:

  Sometimes the words and the pictures in a book give the same information. But sometimes the pictures help you learn more than just what the words say.

Listen and Learn

Words and Pictures

Words in books give you **information**. Pictures, photographs, drawings, and diagrams also give you information.

Here are questions you can ask about the information in words and pictures:

- What information is in the words?
- What information is in the pictures? Look carefully.
- Does the information in the pictures match the information in the words?
- Do the pictures give different information than the words? What is different?

Pay attention to information in words and in pictures. Noticing both kinds of information will help you learn more about what you are reading.

- **Explain why readers need to use words and pictures.** Read aloud the bottom of the page. Explain how using words and pictures helps readers learn the information the author wants them to know.
- Share an example of a time when looking at both words and pictures helped you better understand information.
- For instance, in *Butterflies and Moths* the words tell about a caterpillar turning into a pupa, but the words do not describe the pupa. Instead, the pictures show what a pupa looks like. The pictures give more information than the words.
- Tell children about the expression "a picture is worth a thousand words." Explore what this expression means. Explain why children should remember it when reading a book with pictures.
- **Have children demonstrate understanding.** Call on individuals to share what they have learned so far about looking for information in words and pictures.

Part 2: Modeled Instruction

Step by Step

- **Review Part 1; preview Part 2.** Ask volunteers to share questions they can ask about words and pictures. Direct children to Student Book page 114.
- **Revisit *Earthworms*.** Have children briefly summarize the book, using the chart created for the Book Review on Teacher Resource Book page 139. *(RI.1.2)*
- **Model using words and pictures to get information.** Explain that you will model getting information from words and pictures. Reread page 15 of *Earthworms*. Point out that the pictures and captions show the steps of how a worm moves. Think aloud:

  First, I'll read the words to find the information they give. I learn from the words that a worm digs its bristles into the soil to help it move.

  Next, I'll look at the pictures. I notice that in the first picture, the worm is thick. In the second picture, the worm gets long and thin. I learn that the worm's body changes as it moves.

Tip: Help children distinguish the main text from the captions. Point out the different sizes and styles of the letters. Draw attention to the numbers and arrows connecting captions to pictures.

- Read aloud each question and Hint on the Student Book page. Discuss the answers.
- **Model writing your responses.** Model how to write the answers to the first and second questions in complete sentences. Have children write their responses. *(L.1.1; L.1.2)*
- Use the Close Reading activity to help children distinguish between the information in the words compared to the information in the pictures.
- **Have children demonstrate understanding.** Have children complete the Turn and Talk activity. Prompt:

  What do you learn from the words and pictures on this page? *(A worm moves by stretching its head forward, anchoring it, and then pulling up its body.)*

  Could you take away the words or the pictures and still understand how a worm moves? Explain. *(No. Having just one wouldn't give a complete picture.)*

- Invite volunteers to share their evidence in class discussion. *(SL.1.1; SL.1.2; SL.1.4)*

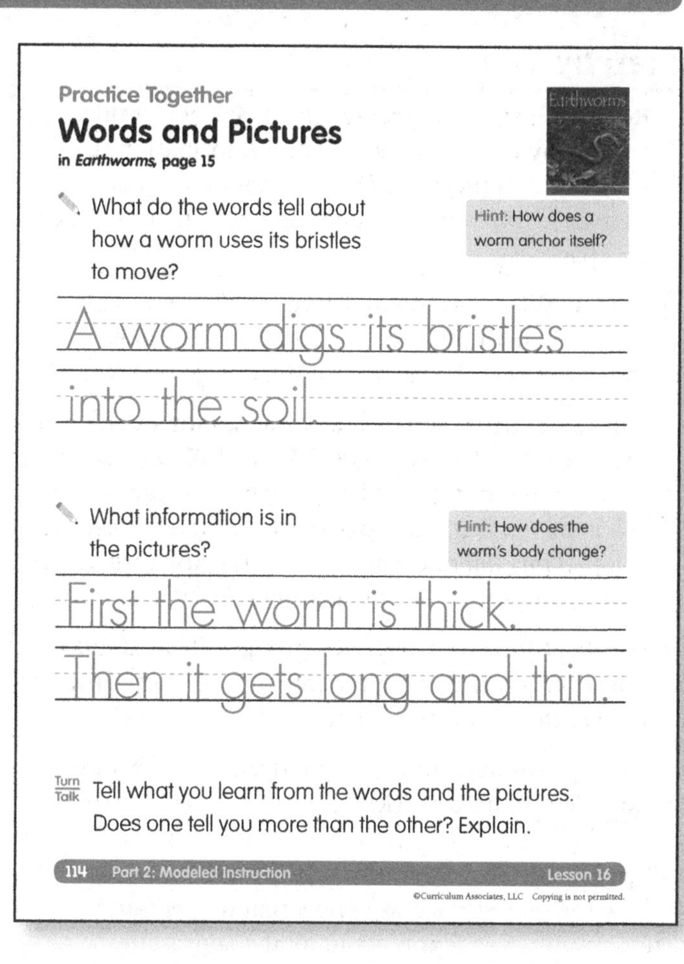

Practice Together

Words and Pictures

in *Earthworms*, page 15

What do the words tell about how a worm uses its bristles to move?

Hint: How does a worm anchor itself?

A worm digs its bristles into the soil.

What information is in the pictures?

Hint: How does the worm's body change?

First the worm is thick. Then it gets long and thin.

Turn Talk: Tell what you learn from the words and the pictures. Does one tell you more than the other? Explain.

114 Part 2: Modeled Instruction Lesson 16

©Curriculum Associates, LLC Copying is not permitted.

Close Reading

- Explain that good readers compare information in words and pictures to better understand ideas.
- Read aloud the captions on page 15 of *Earthworms* as children look at each picture. Then prompt:

  What do the pictures show about a worm's body when it moves? *(First the worm is thick. Then it stretches out and gets long and thin.)*

  What information about how a worm moves is in the words? *(It points its head where it wants to go, it uses its bristles to anchor first the back and then the front of its body; its head end gets thick and then thin.)*

  What information is in the words *and* the pictures? *(The worm gets thick and thin.)*

  How do the words give more information than the pictures do? *(The words explain how the worm uses its bristles; the picture only shows the worm stretching out.)*

Part 3: Guided Practice

Step by Step

- **Review Parts 1–2; preview Part 3.** Have children recall why it is important to find information in words and in pictures. Direct them to Student Book page 115. Explain that you will guide them through this page.
- **Revisit *Who Eats What?*** Have children summarize the book, using the chart created for the Book Review on Teacher Resource Book page 65. *(RI.1.2)*
- **Guide children to ask questions about words and pictures.** Read aloud pages 20–21 of *Who Eats What?* As you read, guide children to ask questions such as: *What animal is at the top of this food chain? Where did you find this information?* Discuss the answers, having children use text and picture evidence.
- **Guide children to write responses.** Read aloud the questions on the Student Book page. Use the Hints to help children answer them.
- Discuss answers and have children write them in complete sentences. *(RI.1.1; L.1.1; L.1.2)*

Tip: Explain that even though the picture does not show the sea's surface, we know that the picture is underwater. The text is about food chains in the sea and says that the plants and animals live underwater.

- Use the Close Reading activity to focus on information provided in the diagram and to prepare children for the Turn and Talk activity.
- **Have children demonstrate understanding.** Have children complete the Turn and Talk activity. Tell children that they may draw on ideas from the Student Book page or the Close Reading discussion. If children need support distinguishing information in words and pictures, prompt them:

  What do the words tell you that the picture does not show? *(Food chains in the sea are hard to study. They are underwater.)*

  What does the picture show that the words do not tell about? *(It shows plants and animals that are in one food chain in the sea.)*

- Invite volunteers to share their ideas with the class. *(SL.1.1; SL.1.2; SL.1.4)*

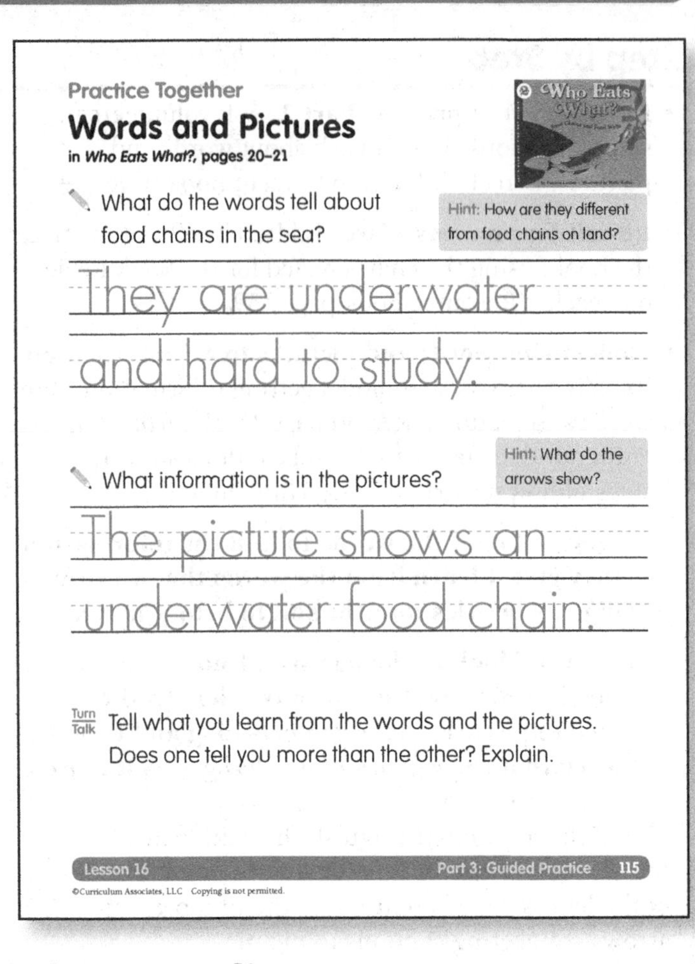

Close Reading

- Remind children that looking closely at pictures is one way to learn information. Display pages 20–21 of *Who Eats What?* Read the labels on the diagram. Then prompt children:

  What plants and animals does the picture show? *(tiny plants, striped anchovy, Atlantic mackerel, dog snapper, great barracuda)*

  Is this information in the words? *(no)*

  How does the picture give more information than the words do? *(It shows the plants and animals in one food chain.)*

  The words say that food chains in the sea are long. How does the picture show this? *(It shows five living things in a food chain.)*

- Ask what information matches in the words and picture. *(Food chains in the sea are long.)* Discuss what extra information is in the picture. *(It shows specific plants and animals in a food chain.)*

Step by Step

- **Review Parts 1–3; preview Part 4.** Invite a volunteer to tell why it is important to compare the information in words and pictures. Then direct children to Student Book page 116.
- Point out how this page is similar to the previous pages. The first question asks about information in the words and the second question asks about information in a visual element—a time line.
- **Read *Famous Women*.** Display and read aloud the web article on Teacher Resource Book pages 213–214. Briefly review the main topic and key details. *(RI.1.2)*
- **Have children find information independently.** Tell children they will answer questions about information in the words and in the time line. Tell children to listen for years the words tell about as you reread the text aloud.
- Read aloud the first question on the Student Book page. Have children write the answer in a complete sentence. *(RI.1.1; L.1.1; L.1.2)*
- Tell children to listen for the years the time line tells about. Then read aloud the words on the time line. Read aloud the second question, along with the Hint. Have children write the answer.
- Discuss responses to the first and second questions.
- Use the Close Reading activity to match and compare information in the words and in the time line.
- **Have children demonstrate understanding.** Have partners complete the Turn and Talk activity. If children need support finding information, prompt:

  What is one thing the words tell about a year that the time line does not? *(Elizabeth Cady Stanton gave a famous speech in 1848.)*

  What is one thing the time line tells about a year that the words do not? *(Susan B. Anthony was born in 1820.)*
- Invite children to share their ideas with the class. *(SL.1.1; SL.1.2; SL.1.4)*
- **Have children reflect on their learning.** Guide children in a discussion about why paying attention to words and pictures helps them better understand what they read. Chart their ideas.

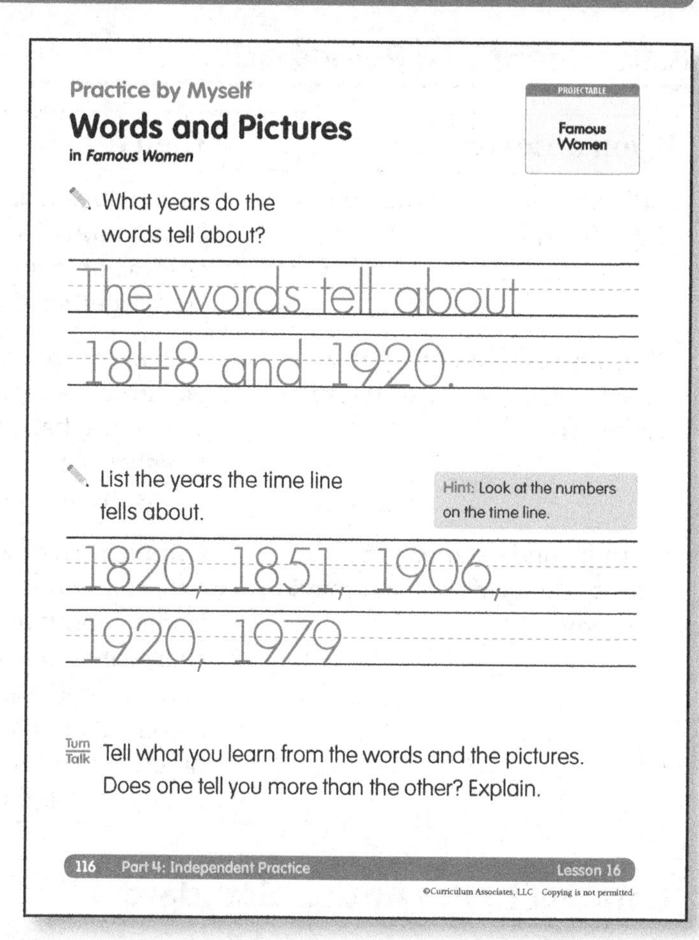
Practice by Myself

Words and Pictures

in *Famous Women*

PROJECTABLE

Famous Women

What years do the words tell about?

The words tell about 1848 and 1920.

List the years the time line tells about.

Hint: Look at the numbers on the time line.

1820, 1851, 1906, 1920, 1979

Turn Talk Tell what you learn from the words and the pictures. Does one tell you more than the other? Explain.

116 Part 4: Independent Practice Lesson 16

©Curriculum Associates, LLC Copying is not permitted.

Close Reading

- Guide children to locate the additional events in the time line. Reread the web article. Prompt:

  The first time line event tells that Susan B. Anthony was born in 1820. Do the words tell this information? *(no)* **What is the first date the words mention?** *(1848)*

  The second event in the time line tells that Susan met Elizabeth Cady Stanton in 1851. Let's see if the words give the same information. Listen closely as I reread.
- Reread the first paragraph, then prompt:

  What do the words say about when Susan met Elizabeth? *(three years after 1848)*
- Guide children to count three years from 1848 and match the date 1851 with the time line. Continue to compare the time line and the words.
- Explain that it is important to look carefully at visuals to learn all the information in a text.

Differentiated Instruction

Assessment and Remediation

If you observe . . .	Then try . . .
Difficulty getting information from pictures	Asking questions about a picture or photograph. Display a drawing or a photograph of an animal. Ask: *How big is the animal? What color is it? How does this animal move?* Invite children to ask questions of their own, and work together to answer each question using details in the picture.
Difficulty understanding how information in words and pictures can match	Having children make pairs of flashcards for practice matching words and pictures. Have each child draw or paste a picture on one index card, and write a sentence that tells about the picture on another index card. Mix the cards together and have small groups or partners work together to match the words and pictures.
Difficulty understanding how pictures can give more information than words	Comparing a description and a photograph of the same animal. Read aloud a short description of an animal. Ask children to name the information they learned about the animal from the description. Record this information on chart paper in a column with the heading *Words*. Then show a photograph of the animal, and have children tell what they see. Record these details in a second column with the heading *Picture*. Discuss what details are similar and different in each column. Point to places where details in the picture were not present in the words.

Connect to the Anchor Standard

R6: *Assess how point of view or purpose shapes the content and style of a text.*

Throughout the grades, Standard 6 progresses from having students use both text and pictures to gather information to identifying an author's purpose for writing a text. In later grades, students will learn to ask higher-level questions about the balance of text and pictures and also about the author's perspective: *Why did the author choose to put some information in the text and some information in the pictures? How is it helpful for readers to have some information presented visually? How would a book be different if all the information was presented in the text? What is the author's point of view? How does the author's perspective shape the text?* Use the following activities to help your students begin this transition.

- Help children understand how a book with only text is different from a book with text and pictures. Read aloud the main text on pages 22–23 of *Earthworms*, without displaying the pictures. Discuss that without pictures, readers don't know what a hedgehog or a mole looks like, how big either animal is in relationship to worms, or what the mole's special pantry for storing worms looks like. Display the pages and discuss the additional information in the pictures. *(SL.1.1; SL.1.4)*
- Guide children to identify an author's point of view. Read aloud pages 28–31 of *Who Eats What?* Discuss why the author wrote about hunters killing the sea otters. Guide children to see that the author is giving an example of how humans can change food chains and webs. Ask what the author thinks about people and food chains. *(People must be careful not to damage food chains and webs.)*

Introduction

Before administering the Unit 4 Check, you may wish to review with children how to answer multiple-choice questions and offer a new test-taking tip. Begin by writing the following question on the board:

Which of these events happens first?

A Molly eats breakfast.

B Molly wakes up.

C Molly goes to school.

Guide children through the process of answering a multiple-choice question:

Today you will listen as I read aloud a book, and then you will answer some questions about details in the book. Remember, when you answer a multiple-choice question, only one of the answers is correct. To choose the correct answer, you draw a circle around the letter next to that answer.

Some questions may ask you about the order of steps or events. If many things happen, it can be hard to remember what order they happened in. Here's a way to help you figure out the order:

Think about what makes the most sense. Picture your own morning routine. Ask yourself: *Can I eat breakfast before I wake up?* That isn't possible, so choice A cannot be correct. Now ask: *Can I wake up before I eat breakfast and go to school?* Yes, that makes sense. Finally, ask: *Can I go to school before I wake up or eat breakfast?* No, you cannot do choices A or C without first waking up. So choice B is correct. *(Circle "B" on the board.)*

When we answer questions about what we read, we always check our answers in the text. If these events happened in a book, we would look back at the pages where they took place and notice what order they happened in.

Step by Step

- Revisit *Earthworms* and invite children to retell important text details using the photographs and illustrations.
- Have children follow along as you read aloud the directions on page 117 of their Student Books.

Unit 4 Check

Listen closely as your teacher reads. Then answer the questions.

Read these sentences from **Earthworms**.

"A mole is an earthworm's greatest enemy. Moles sometimes eat thirty worms a day as they tunnel under the ground."

1. What do the words tell you about a worm's **enemy**?

A It is afraid of worms.

(B) It likes to feed on worms.

C It likes to hide next to worms.

2. Where can you look to find out when worms come out to eat?

A under the heading "A Worm's Body"

(B) under the heading "Feeding"

C under the heading "Hatching"

117

- Then read aloud one or more pages from the text, as specified below, before having children complete each item. Display the appropriate pages for children to view while they read and answer each question.
- For item 1, read the first two sentences on page 23; display the illustration.
- For item 2, display the table of contents on page 5.
- For item 4, display the glossary on page 28.
- For item 5, reread page 17; display the illustration.

Note: Read aloud each question, answer choice, and Hint before directing children to answer it.

- When children have finished, reread each question and discuss the correct answer. Point to evidence in the text and pictures. Then use the Answer Analysis to discuss the correct answer.

Answer Analysis

1 This item requires children to identify the meaning of a word using context. ***(RI.1.4)***

The best answer is choice B, "It likes to feed on worms." The words "eat thirty worms a day" are clues that moles kill earthworms for food. The text does not say that moles are afraid of worms or that they hide next to worms, so choices A and C are not good answer choices.

2 This item asks children to use the table of contents to determine where they can find information about a key detail. ***(RI.1.5)***

The best answer is choice B, "under the heading 'Feeding.'" The text given under choice A, "A Worm's Body," only describes its body parts, so that answer is not a good one. Choice C, the text about "Hatching," tells facts about worm eggs and baby worms. It probably would not tell anything about when worms come out to eat.

If necessary, reread the text in each of those sections, and discuss why certain facts are included in each section and how they relate to the heading.

3 This item asks children to select a topic from an electronic menu to identify where they might find information on a website. ***(RI.1.5)***

Remember, *Earthworms* tells ways that worms make the soil looser and finer. That makes it easier for plants to grow, especially in a garden. So the best answer is choice A, "Worms Help Plants." Choice B, "Fishing with Worms," is not a good choice. This link probably would not tell anything about how worms work in gardens. Choice C, "Different Kinds of Worms," might give a fact or two that answers the question, but it is not the best answer.

4 For this item, children must determine which information they could find in a glossary. ***(RI.1.5)***

A glossary is a list of challenging words that appear in a book, along with their meanings. So the correct answer is choice A, "what the word *cocoon* means." Choice B, "why worms eat dead leaves," is not correct because a glossary does not explain events or reasons. Choice C, "what baby worms look like," is not correct because a glossary does not give this type of descriptive information outside of a definition.

Unit 4 Check

Which topic on a website menu would tell how worms work in the garden?

- Ⓐ Worms Help Plants
- B Fishing with Worms
- C Different Kinds of Worms

Which of these would you find in a glossary?

- Ⓐ what the word **cocoon** means
- B why worms eat dead leaves
- C what baby worms look like

What does page 17 tell you about worms? Write one thing you learn from the picture. Then write one thing you learn from the text.

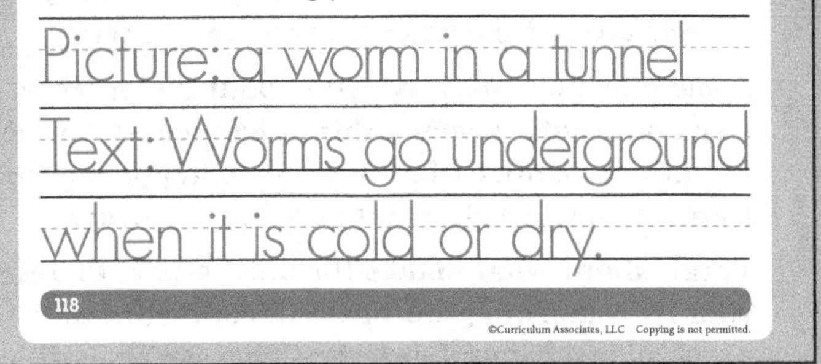
Picture: a worm in a tunnel
Text: Worms go underground
when it is cold or dry.

118

©Curriculum Associates, LLC Copying is not permitted.

5 For this item, children must distinguish between information they gain from the text and information they gain from an illustration. ***(RI.1.6)***

Sample Response: The picture shows a worm curled up at the bottom of a tunnel. The text tells how worms sleep underground when it is too cold or too dry.

This page gives lots of facts about worms. The picture helps us understand what the text is saying. It shows a worm curled up underground at the bottom of a tunnel. The text says that "worms push down a few feet below the surface, then coil up and go to sleep" when the weather gets too cold or dry. It also talks about the worm's burrow. Those details tell when, where, and why the worm in the picture is coiled up underground.

Unit 5

Integration of Knowledge and Ideas in Literature

The following pacing chart shows a recommended schedule for teaching the lessons in Unit 5. Each Read Aloud and Focus Lesson is taught over the course of three days. There is also time allotted in each Focus Lesson for teaching Tap Children's Prior Knowledge and Differentiated Instruction.

Day	Lesson/Activity	Time (minutes)
1	Unit 5 Opener (optional); Tap Children's Prior Knowledge; Lesson 17: Part 1	30
2	Lesson 17: Parts 2 and 3	30
3	Lesson 17: Part 4; Differentiated Instruction (optional)	30
4	Tap Children's Prior Knowledge; Lesson 18: Part 1	30
5	Lesson 18: Parts 2 and 3	30
6	Lesson 18: Part 4; Differentiated Instruction (optional)	30
7	Unit 5 Check	30

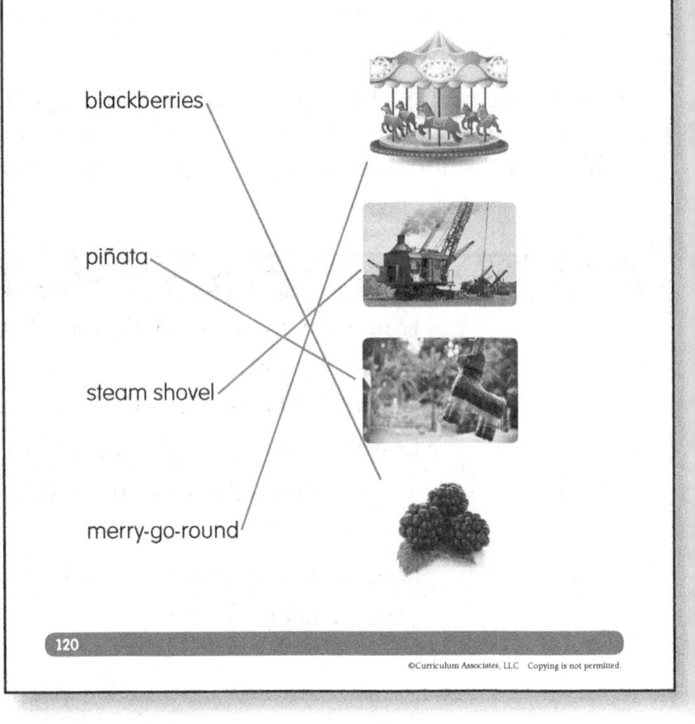

Step by Step

Explain that in this unit, children will learn how to compare and contrast details in different make-believe stories. Additionally, they will use word and picture details to draw conclusions about story characters and their experiences.

- Have children turn to page 119. Read aloud the introductory sentences. Invite a volunteer to explain what a story setting is. *(where and when a story takes place)*
- Allow children time to study the illustration to find details that will help them determine the setting.
- Point out that if this picture were to appear in a book, children might be able to predict some story details before they even start reading. They should, however, use the story words to confirm or change their predictions.
- Have children turn to page 120. Read aloud the title and directions at the top of the page.
- Read aloud the first word, *blackberries*. Have children repeat it. Then have them find the picture that matches the word. Ask children to draw a line from the word to the picture. Remind children that they learned about blackberry picking in the story *My Rotten Redheaded Older Brother.*
- Repeat the procedure for the other words.
- As time permits, have partners take turns using each word in an oral sentence.

Lesson 17 (Student Book pages 121–124)

Story Words and Pictures

CCSS

RL.1.7: Use illustrations and details in a story to describe its characters, setting, or events.

Required Read Alouds: C *(My Rotten Redheaded Older Brother)*; D *(Mice and Beans)*

Lesson Objectives

- Use story details to tell about characters, setting, or events.
- Use pictures to tell about characters, setting, or events.
- Use pictures to find more evidence about story details than the words tell.
- Understand how words and pictures help readers describe characters, setting, or events.

The Learning Progression

- **Grade K:** CCSS RL.K.7 requires children to tell, with prompting and support, how illustrations connect to the story in which they appear.
- **Grade 1: CCSS RL.1.7 builds on the Grade K standard by having children use illustrations and story details to tell about characters, setting, or events.**
- **Grade 2:** CCSS RL.2.7 further develops the standard by having children use information gathered from illustrations and words in a text to better understand its characters, setting, or plot.

Prerequisite Skills

- Recognize the difference between words and pictures in a story with prompting and support.
- Identify characters, settings, and events in a story with prompting and support.
- Ask and answer questions about key details in a story with prompting and support.

Tap Children's Prior Knowledge

- Remind children that details are small pieces of information. Ask children to look around the classroom and identify some details about it.
- Ask them to tell whether the details they are identifying are in words or in pictures. As needed, point out the distinction for children.
- Tell children that their classroom is like a story: all of them are the characters, the room and the school are the setting, and the things that happen each day are the events.
- Ask volunteers to each name a character and an event from the classroom. Record their responses in a three-column chart with these heads: *Characters; Setting; Event.* Model responses as needed, such as *Yesterday, Henry drew a giraffe in the classroom.*
- Have volunteers draw a picture to go with each event. Ask them to tell about the details in the picture and how it connects to the event.
- Explain that a story has details in its words and illustrations, too. Tell children that in this lesson, they will learn how words and illustrations work together to tell readers about the story's characters, setting, and events.

Ready *Teacher Toolbox* Teacher-Toolbox.com

	Prerequisite Skills	RL.1.7
Ready Lessons	✓	✓
Tools for Instruction	✓	
Interactive Tutorials		✓

Additional CCSS

RL.1.1; RL.1.2; RL.1.3; RL.1.4; SL.1.1; SL.1.2; SL.1.4; L.1.1; L.1.2 *(See page A38 for full text.)*

Part 1: Introduction

Step by Step

- **Introduce the standard.** Have children turn to page 121 in their Student Books. Read aloud the speech bubble.
- **Review questions about story words and pictures.** Read the line below the speech bubble, and point out that what follows are questions good readers can ask about story words and pictures.
- Read aloud the first question. Have children find and underline the phrase *words say*. Explain:

  The word *say* here means "tell about." The words in a story say, or tell, details about the story's characters, setting, and events. You must read or listen to the words to find out these details.

- Have children use the chart from the activity on page 169 to point out the words that tell about events in the classroom.
- Read aloud the second question. Have children find and underline the phrase *pictures show*. Explain that to answer this question, children must look carefully for details in the pictures. Have children point out picture details on the chart.
- Read aloud the third question. Explain:

  To answer this question, you need to compare the words and pictures. Look carefully. Decide if the pictures add details to what the words say or if the pictures do not show more.

Tip: If children have difficulty with the concept *more*, add a picture detail to the chart that is not described in the words. Discuss that the picture tells more than the words.

- **Explain why readers ask questions about words and pictures.** Read aloud the bottom of the page. Explain that good readers use story words and pictures to help them figure out the story details about characters, setting, and events.

Listen and Learn

Story Words and Pictures

Many stories have **words** and **pictures**. Both words and pictures can include details about characters, setting, or events.

Here are questions you can ask about words and pictures:

- What do the words say?
- What do the pictures show? Look carefully.
- Do the pictures show more than the words tell?

Noticing details in words and pictures will help you understand more about the characters, setting, and events in a story.

Lesson 17 Part 1: Introduction 121

- Share an example of a time when using story words and pictures helped you understand story details. For example, you might share how the words and pictures helped you find details about a character:

  When I read *The Ugly Duckling*, the words said that the ugly duckling looked "different" than the other ducklings. I looked at the picture to see how it looked different from the other ducks, both as a baby and as an adult.

- Point out that noticing words and pictures helped you understand that the character of the ugly duckling was really a swan.
- **Have children demonstrate understanding.** Ask children to share what they have learned so far about how story words and pictures give important details. Encourage children to give brief examples of details that words and pictures tell using classroom stories.

Part 2: Modeled Instruction

Step by Step

- **Review Part 1; preview Part 2.** Ask volunteers to share questions they can ask about story words and pictures. Direct them to Student Book page 122.
- **Revisit *My Rotten Redheaded Older Brother.*** Invite children to briefly retell the story, using pages 11–14 of their Student Books. *(RL.1.2)*
- **Model using words and pictures.** Explain that you are going to model using story words and pictures to find important details. Read aloud pages 18–19 of *My Rotten Redheaded Older Brother.* Then think aloud:

    I need to understand what rhubarb is. First, I think about the words that say rhubarb is a bush. Then Richie says, "It's the sourest stuff on this planet!" It probably doesn't taste good.

    Next, I look at the picture. Richie and the animals are making horrible sour faces, so I can see that they think rhubarb tastes bad. I think rhubarb is a plant that tastes sour.

Tip: If needed, help children identify the rhubarb bushes by connecting the stalk that Treesha is holding to what Richie is pointing at and sitting in.

- Read aloud the first Student Book page question and Hint. Discuss the answer to this question.
- Read aloud the second question and Hint. Ask children to describe how Richie and the animals look in the picture. Discuss the answer to this question.
- **Model writing your responses.** Model how to write the answers to both questions in complete sentences. Have children write their own responses. *(L.1.1; L.1.2)*
- Use the Close Reading activity to model using story words and pictures to find details about an important story event.
- **Have children demonstrate understanding.** Have partners complete the Turn and Talk activity. If children need support getting started, remind them of the details you talked about during the Close Reading discussion. *(SL.1.1; SL.1.2; SL.1.4)*
- Have children share what evidence they used and where they found it in the words and picture.

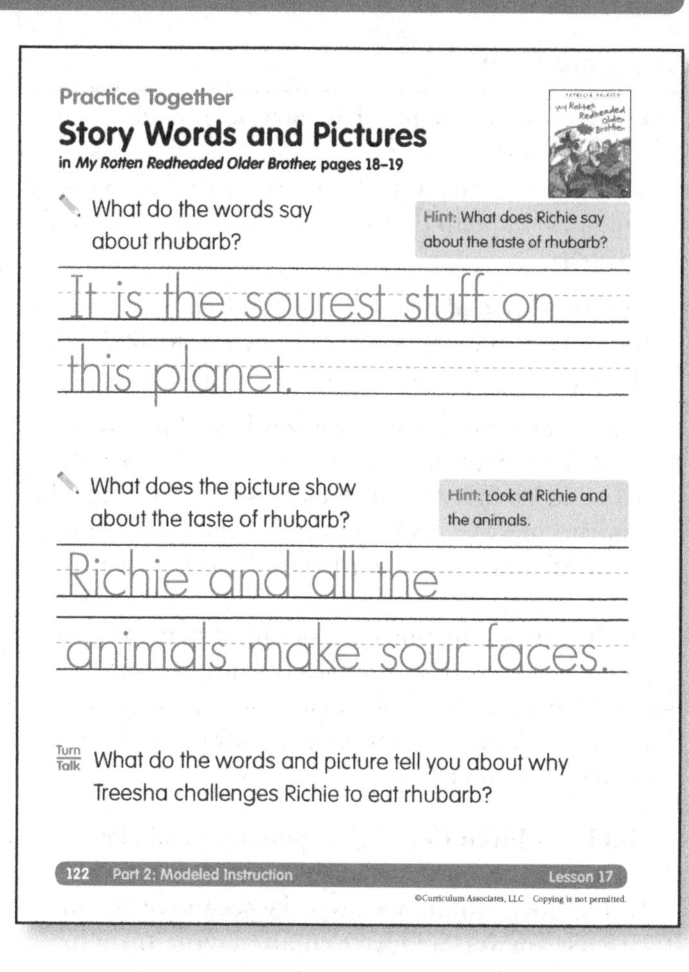

Practice Together

Story Words and Pictures

in *My Rotten Redheaded Older Brother,* pages 18–19

What do the words say about rhubarb?

Hint: What does Richie say about the taste of rhubarb?

It is the sourest stuff on this planet.

What does the picture show about the taste of rhubarb?

Hint: Look at Richie and the animals.

Richie and all the animals make sour faces.

Turn Talk What do the words and picture tell you about why Treesha challenges Richie to eat rhubarb?

122 Part 2: Modeled Instruction Lesson 17

Close Reading

- Remind children that both story words and pictures can include details about an event. Reread pages 18–19. Prompt children to explore this story event:

    What do the words say about Treesha's challenge to Richie? *(She challenges him to eat rhubarb "without getting the puckers.") (RL.1.4)*

    What word and picture evidence shows that Treesha thinks she can win? *(Richie says rhubarb is "the sourest stuff on this planet"; his face shows that he doesn't like it.)*

    How does the picture show more about Richie than the words tell? *(Richie says he won't get "the puckers" eating rhubarb, but the picture shows that he makes a face just thinking about it.)*

- Ask children to discuss additional details that the story words and picture tell about this event.

Step by Step

- **Review Parts 1–2; preview Part 3.** Have children recall questions they can ask about story words and pictures. Direct them to turn to Student Book page 123. Explain that you will guide them through this page.
- **Revisit *Mice and Beans*.** Have children briefly retell the story, using pages 15–18 of their Student Books. *(RL.1.2)*
- **Guide children to use story words and pictures.** Read aloud pages 6–7 of *Mice and Beans*. As you read, tell children to listen and look closely to find out what happens to Rosa María's napkins. Guide them to use the words and picture together to find evidence.

Tip: If children are unsure about how many napkins Rosa María should have versus the number she actually has, reread the first paragraph on page 6, having children listen for number words, or words that tell "how many."

- **Guide children to write responses.** Read aloud each question on the Student Book page. Use the Hint to help children answer the second question. Discuss answers and have children write them in complete sentences. *(L.1.1; L.1.2)*
- Use the Close Reading activity to help children understand how to examine words and pictures to learn about characters and events, and to help prepare them for the Turn and Talk activity.
- **Have children demonstrate understanding.** Have partners complete the Turn and Talk activity. If children need support, suggest that one partner describe what the words say and the other partner describe what the picture shows. Then have them combine these details. *(SL.1.1; SL.1.2; SL.1.4)*
- Have volunteers share evidence they found in the story words and the picture. Discuss how the words and picture give details about what happened to the missing napkin. *(RL.1.3)*

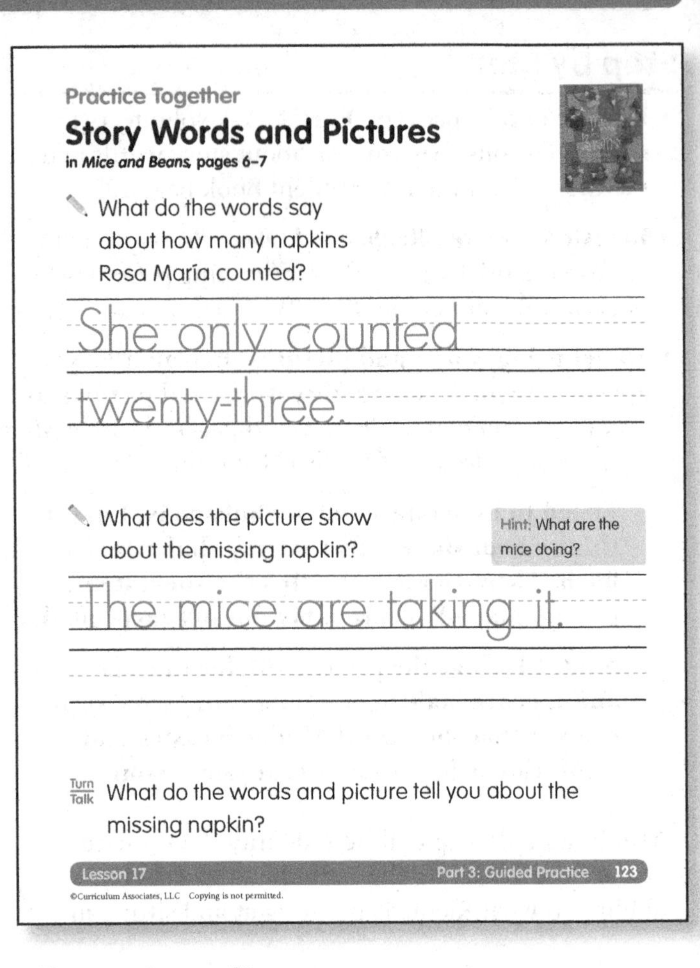

Practice Together

Story Words and Pictures

in *Mice and Beans*, pages 6–7

What do the words say about how many napkins Rosa María counted?

She only counted twenty-three.

What does the picture show about the missing napkin?

Hint: What are the mice doing?

The mice are taking it.

Turn Talk What do the words and picture tell you about the missing napkin?

Lesson 17 Part 3: Guided Practice 123

©Curriculum Associates, LLC Copying is not permitted.

Close Reading

- Guide children to use story words and pictures to understand details about the characters and story events. Reread pages 6–7. Think aloud about the details in the words and the picture:

  I will read the words to find details about the missing napkin. I read that Rosa María started off with twenty-four napkins, but then "she only counted twenty-three." I wonder if she knows what happened to the missing one?

  I will look for details in the picture. I see that Rosa María is looking down at her ironing while the mice are taking a napkin! I don't think she notices what the mice are doing. The words and picture help me understand more about the missing napkin.

- Have children describe what they would not know about the characters and events if they had not paid attention to the pictures in this story.

Part 4: Independent Practice

Step by Step

- **Review Parts 1–3; preview Part 4.** Invite a volunteer to tell how you can use story words and pictures to describe details. Then direct children to Student Book page 124.
- Tell children that they will be practicing how to use story words and pictures to describe details by themselves. Explain that the first question asks about the words in the story and the second question asks about the pictures, just as on the other pages they have done.
- **Have children use story words and pictures independently.** Display *Mice and Beans* and tell children they will look at words and pictures from another part of the book.
- Ask children to listen and look closely to find out something important about Rosa María's party. Read aloud pages 18–21. Circulate, and show the pictures.
- Read aloud the first question on the Student Book page. Explain that *party plans* means "all of the things you do to get ready for a party." Have children write the answer. *(L.1.1; L.1.2)*
- Read aloud the next question and the Hint. Have children look closely at the pictures on pages 18–21 before responding. Have children write their answer in a complete sentence.

Tip: Emphasize that the mice communicate with each other without words. Ask children whether they think having more words on these pages would be helpful or not and tell why.

- Use the Close Reading activity to help children identify story details on pages 20–21.
- Discuss answers to the first and second questions.
- **Have children demonstrate understanding.** Have partners complete the Turn and Talk activity. For a challenge, have them discuss ideas about why the word *WAS* is in all capital letters on page 19. Explain that the capital letters stress that not everything was ready. *(SL.1.1; SL.1.2; SL.1.4)*
- **Have children reflect on their learning.** Guide children in a discussion about how looking closely at story words and pictures helps them describe details. Chart their ideas.

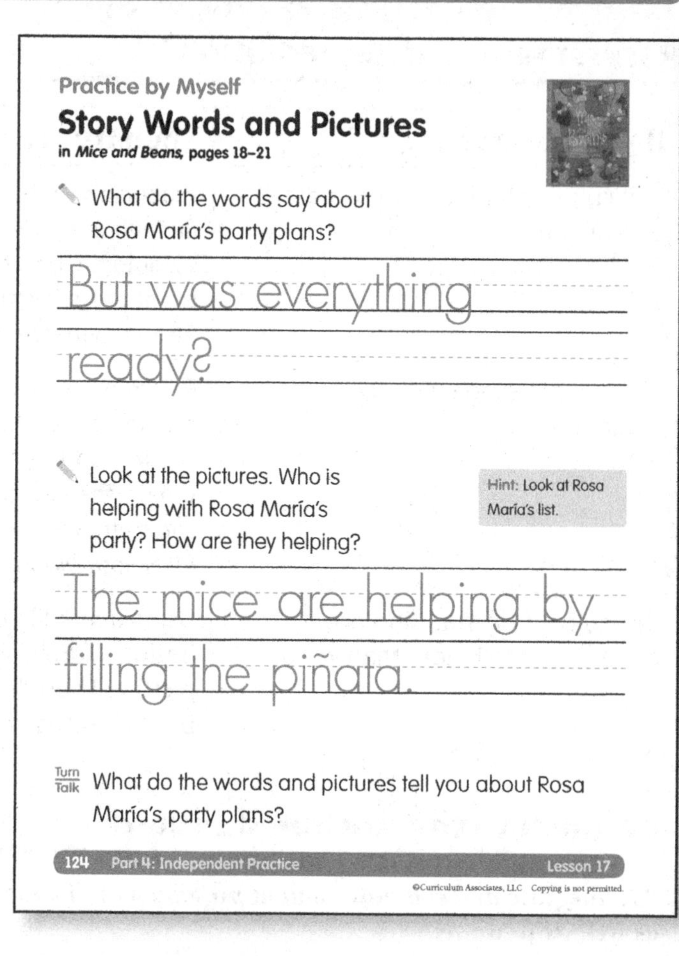
Practice by Myself

Story Words and Pictures
in *Mice and Beans*, pages 18–21

What do the words say about Rosa María's party plans?

But was everything ready?

Look at the pictures. Who is helping with Rosa María's party? How are they helping?

Hint: Look at Rosa María's list.

The mice are helping by filling the piñata.

Turn Talk What do the words and pictures tell you about Rosa María's party plans?

124 Part 4: Independent Practice Lesson 17

Close Reading

- Remind children that good readers use pictures to identify details about characters, setting, and events. Display pages 20–21. Prompt children:

  What does the picture show about the setting? *(This part of the story takes place in Rosa María's house.)*

  What story event does the picture show? *(The mice are filling the piñata with candy for the party.)*

  Look closely at the details in the picture. Use these details to describe this event. *(The mice have built a tower up to the piñata; they are passing candy pieces to the mouse at the top; that mouse is putting the pieces in the piñata.) (RL.1.3)*

- Discuss with children how the evidence from the picture helps them better understand how clever and helpful the mice are. Explain that the picture also show how the mice feel about Rosa María's party.

Assessment and Remediation

If you observe . . .	Then try . . .
Difficulty matching story words and pictures	Practicing with simpler examples. Display pages 16–17 of *My Rotten Redheaded Older Brother.* Read aloud the first sentence and phrase: "I guess I would have to face it. He could run the fastest . . ." Call on a volunteer to point to the picture that matches the words "He could run the fastest . . ." Repeat with the phrases in the rest of the sentence.
Difficulty finding evidence in pictures	Revisiting pages 30–31 of *Mice and Beans*. Read aloud the text. Explain that the picture shows more than the words tell. Work with children to find details that show what the mice have done with the mousetraps, the feathers from the piñata, the wooden spoon, the *bolsa,* and the candle. Discuss what the picture shows that the words in the story do not tell. *(the mice were the ones who took all of Rosa María's missing objects)*
Difficulty understanding how pictures can tell more than words	Using a real-life example. On the board, write, *I got a present for my birthday.* Beside it, draw a gift box with a bow. Discuss whether the words match the picture. Then draw a present you might have received, such as a watch or a book. Discuss how the second picture shows more than the words tell.

Connect to the Anchor Standard

R7: *Integrate and evaluate content presented in diverse media and formats, including visually and quantitatively, as well as in words.*

Throughout the grades, Standard 7 builds complexity through the use of many types of visuals, including illustrations and multimedia elements. Initially, students are expected to recognize how illustrations support and add to what the words in a story express, such as mood or character details. In later grades, students progress to comparing and contrasting a written story or drama with a visual or oral presentation of the text. They might consider the following questions: *What do the words say about character, setting, and events? How does this picture set the mood? How does the art contribute to the meaning of the text? How does the art add beauty? What information does the art give that the text does not?* Use the following activities to begin this transition.

- Explore how pictures help readers understand setting and character. Reread pages 2–3 of *Mice and Beans.* Ask children what the words say about Rosa María's house. *(It is "a tiny house with a tiny yard.")* Show the picture and ask what it shows about the house. *(It is bright pink with red curtains; it has flowers around it and is bright inside.)* Discuss what the picture details help readers understand about Rosa María. *(She works to make her house bright and cheerful.) (RL.1.3; SL.1.1; SL.1.2; SL.1.4)*
- Explore how authors and illustrators use words and pictures to create a feeling for the reader. Display and read aloud pages 34–35 of *My Rotten Redheaded Older Brother.* Ask children how Bubbie feels about Treesha and Richie. Have them justify their response with text evidence, and also describe the picture. Discuss how the words and the picture show the reader that the feeling of this moment is loving and caring.

Lesson 18 (Student Book pages 125–128)
Comparing Characters

CCSS

RL.1.9: Compare and contrast the adventures and experiences of characters in stories.

Required Read Alouds: *Projectable 1 (Happy Birthday Surprise!); B (The Polar Bear Son); D (Mice and Beans); H (Mike Mulligan and His Steam Shovel)*

Lesson Objectives

- Identify the similarities between the experiences of the main characters in two different stories.
- Identify the differences between the experiences of the main characters in two different stories.
- Understand how comparing and contrasting the experiences of characters helps you better understand the characters.

The Learning Progression

- **Grade K:** CCSS RL.K.9 expects children to compare and contrast characters' adventures and experiences in familiar stories, with prompting and support.
- **Grade 1: CCSS RL.1.9 asks that children begin to work more independently to compare and contrast characters' experiences when reading stories.**
- **Grade 2:** CCSS RL.2.9 requires that children move beyond characters to compare and contrast stories in general, specifically two versions of the same story.

Prerequisite Skills

- Ask and answer questions about characters and their experiences.
- Describe characters using evidence about their feelings and actions.
- Compare and contrast characters' experiences with prompting and support.

Tap Children's Prior Knowledge

- Have children think of something fun or interesting they did during the past weekend. Ask a volunteer to briefly describe his or her experience.
- After the description, ask children to raise a hand if they have ever had a similar experience. Invite a few children with raised hands to briefly share their related experiences.
- Point out that some children share common experiences and like to do the same sorts of things. However, note that there are also differences between what the children have experienced and like to do.
- Discuss how comparing the experiences people have had helps us learn about those people. For example, say: *Josh, you love being outside but Sam, you like being indoors practicing martial arts. Now I see why Josh is more excited when we read books about nature.*
- Tell children that in this lesson, they will compare and contrast the experiences of characters from different stories in order to get to know the characters better.

Ready *Teacher Toolbox* — Teacher-Toolbox.com

	Prerequisite Skills	RL.1.9
Ready Lessons	✓	✓
Tools for Instruction		✓✓
Interactive Tutorials		✓✓

Additional CCSS

RL.1.1; RL.1.2; RL.1.3; RL.1.7; SL.1.1; SL.1.4; L.1.1; L.1.2 *(See page A38 for full text.)*

Part 1: Introduction

Step by Step

- **Introduce the standard.** Have children turn to page 125 in their Student Books. Read aloud the speech bubble.
- Explain that an experience can be something you do in daily life. Give examples, such as going to school or playing soccer. Point out that an adventure is an experience that is exciting, daring, or unusual, such as going far away on a trip or riding on an elephant.
- Remind children that they already know how to ask questions about characters. Have them recall the questions. *(What does the character say, do, feel, and learn?)* Point out that they can ask these questions to find out about characters' experiences.
- **Review examples of characters' experiences.** Explain that you are going to read about the experiences of characters from the fairy tales *Beauty and the Beast* and *The Frog Prince.*
- Have children follow along as you read the first example. Guide them to circle the words that name the characters. *(A girl, an ugly beast, a handsome prince)* Then prompt:

  What does the girl say and do? *(She agrees to live with the beast, and she ends up marrying him.)*

Tip: Remind children that sometimes they must interpret words to learn what a character says or does. When the girl "agrees to marry the beast," they should understand that she says she will marry him.

- Discuss how asking and answering these questions helps readers identify and understand the character's experience. Then repeat with the second example.
- After reviewing each example, read aloud the first question at the bottom of the page. Support children by offering one similarity: both girls live with an ugly creature who then turns into a handsome prince. Have them suggest another similarity. *(Both girls live with the creatures because they need something.)*
- Read aloud the second question, and offer one difference: the beauty thinks the beast is kind and thoughtful, but the princess thinks the frog is disgusting. Have children suggest another. *(The beast changes after the beauty agrees to marry him; the frog changes because the princess keeps her promise.)*

Listen and Learn

Comparing Characters

An **experience** is something a character does or learns. A very exciting experience is called an **adventure**.

Read about the experiences of two characters:

A girl agrees to live with an ugly beast to save her father. She finds out that the beast is kind and thoughtful. When she agrees to marry the beast, he turns into a handsome prince.

A princess needs a frog's help. She promises to let the frog live with her and share her food. The princess thinks the frog is disgusting, but she keeps her promise. After three days, the frog turns into a handsome prince.

How are the experiences of these characters alike? How are they different? Comparing and contrasting can help you understand the characters better.

- **Explain why readers compare characters' experiences.** Explain that seeing how a character in one story is similar to or different from a character in another story helps you better understand both characters. Think aloud as you apply it to the examples on the page:

  I can see that the girl in the first example treats others much better than the princess does. That helps me understand how truly kind she is.

- Invite children to tell other things they see from comparing the girl with the princess.
- **Have children demonstrate understanding.** Call on individuals to share what they have learned so far about comparing characters. Encourage them to tell how comparing and contrasting characters' experiences helps them better understand the characters.

Part 2: Modeled Instruction

Step by Step

- **Review Part 1; preview Part 2.** Review how to compare the experiences of characters from different stories. Direct children to Student Book page 126.
- **Revisit *The Polar Bear Son* and *Mike Mulligan and His Steam Shovel*.** Invite volunteers to briefly retell both stories, using pages 7–10 and 31–34 of their Student Books. *(RL.1.2)*
- **Model comparing characters' experiences.** Explain that you will demonstrate comparing and contrasting two characters' experiences. Read aloud pages 28–33 of *The Polar Bear Son*. Then think aloud:

  First I'll think about the old woman's experience. She feels lonely and hungry. To help herself feel better, she goes to see Kunikdjuaq.

- Then read aloud pages 39–41 of *Mike Mulligan and His Steam Shovel*, again pausing to think aloud:

  Now I'll think about Mike Mulligan. He gets stuck in the cellar without a way out. But they solve the problem, and he feels happy because he gets to work in the cellar with Mary Ann.

- Use the Close Reading activity to model using picture details to describe characters' experiences.
- Think aloud to compare and contrast the old woman's and Mike Mulligan's experiences:

  Both characters go from feeling bad to feeling happy. They feel happy to be with their friends. The old woman has to walk a long way to see her friend, but Mike gets to stay where he is.

Tip: Use a Venn diagram to record similarities and differences. Explain that this kind of diagram is a helpful way to compare and contrast.

- **Model writing your responses.** Read aloud the first prompt on Student Book page 126. Discuss and record the answers. Then read aloud the second prompt and Hint below. Model how to write responses as children write in their books. *(RL.1.1; L.1.1; L.1.2)*
- **Have children demonstrate understanding.** Read aloud the Turn and Talk activity. Encourage children to discuss how the old woman and Mike Mulligan are different in other ways by recalling additional details from each story.

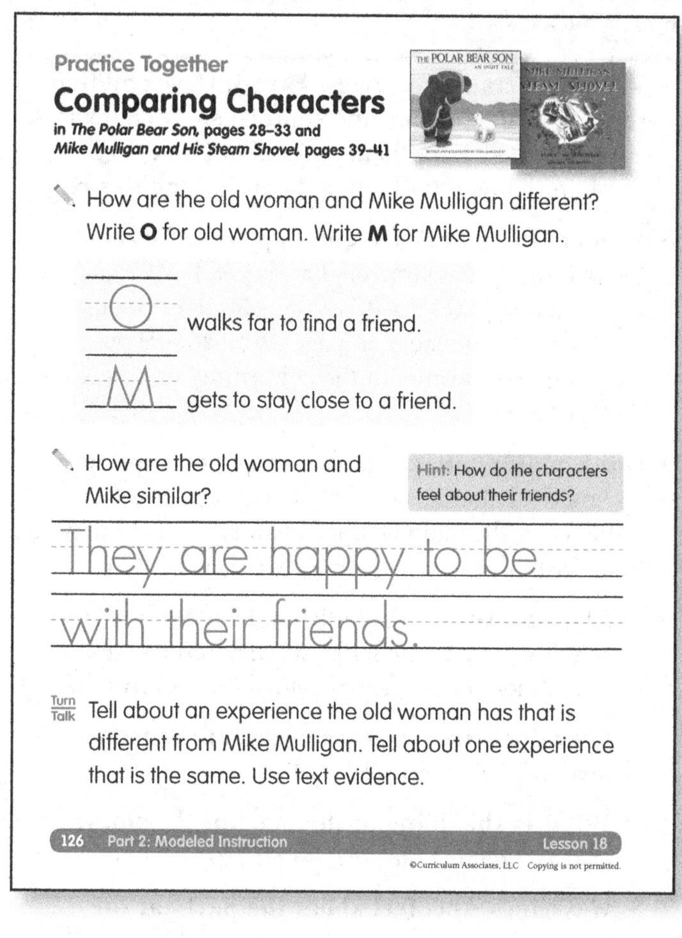

Practice Together

Comparing Characters

in *The Polar Bear Son*, pages 28–33 and *Mike Mulligan and His Steam Shovel*, pages 39–41

How are the old woman and Mike Mulligan different? Write **O** for old woman. Write **M** for Mike Mulligan.

O walks far to find a friend.

M gets to stay close to a friend.

How are the old woman and Mike similar?

Hint: How do the characters feel about their friends?

They are happy to be with their friends.

Turn Talk Tell about an experience the old woman has that is different from Mike Mulligan. Tell about one experience that is the same. Use text evidence.

126 Part 2: Modeled Instruction Lesson 18

©Curriculum Associates, LLC Copying is not permitted.

Close Reading

- Remind children that they can use picture details to help them describe characters' experiences.
- Display and reread pages 30–33 of *The Polar Bear Son*. Have children look carefully. Then prompt:

  What do the pictures show about how the characters feel? *(They are happy to be together; they run to see each other; they hug; they are smiling.) (RL.1.3; RL.1.7)*

- Point out that the pictures, not the text, show the old woman's feelings. Then display page 41 of *Mike Mulligan and His Steam Shovel*. Prompt:

  What does the picture show about how the characters feel? *(They are happy; everyone is smiling and some people are shaking hands.)*

- Have children tell how the old woman and Mike are the same. *(They are happy to be with friends.)* Point out that looking carefully at picture details helps readers make this comparison.

Step by Step

- **Review Parts 1–2; preview Part 3.** Have children recall how to compare and contrast story characters' experiences. Direct them to Student Book page 127. Explain that you will guide them through this page.
- **Revisit *Mice and Beans* and *Happy Birthday Surprise!*.** Have volunteers briefly retell *Mice and Beans,* using pages 15–18 of their Student Books. Then project the fable on pages 205–206. Help children retell events in the beginning, middle, and end. *(RL.1.2)*
- **Guide children to compare characters' experiences.** As you read aloud pages from both stories, ask children to focus on the main characters and their experiences in order to think about what is alike and different.
- Read aloud pages 2–5 of *Mice and Beans* and reread *Happy Birthday Surprise!* Have children use text and picture evidence in their responses as you prompt:

  How does Rosa María feel about the party? *(excited and happy) (RL.1.1)*

  What is she doing in this part of the story? *(She is planning the party.) (RL.1.3)*

  How does Abel feel about the party at the beginning of the story? *(excited and happy)*

  How does Abel feel by the time Chester arrives? *(nervous and upset)*

  What is Abel doing that makes him feel this way? *(He is trying to get everything ready for the party.)*
- **Guide children to write responses.** Read aloud the first two prompts on Student Book page 127. Discuss responses, and have children record answers in their books. *(L.1.1; L.1.2)*
- Use the Close Reading activity to learn more about the characters by comparing the way they each plan for their parties.
- **Have children demonstrate understanding.** Read aloud the Turn and Talk activity. Prompt children to think about how the characters feel and what experiences cause those feelings. Invite them to share the similarities and differences they identify. Discuss what they show about Rosa María and Abel. *(SL.1.1; SL.1.4)*

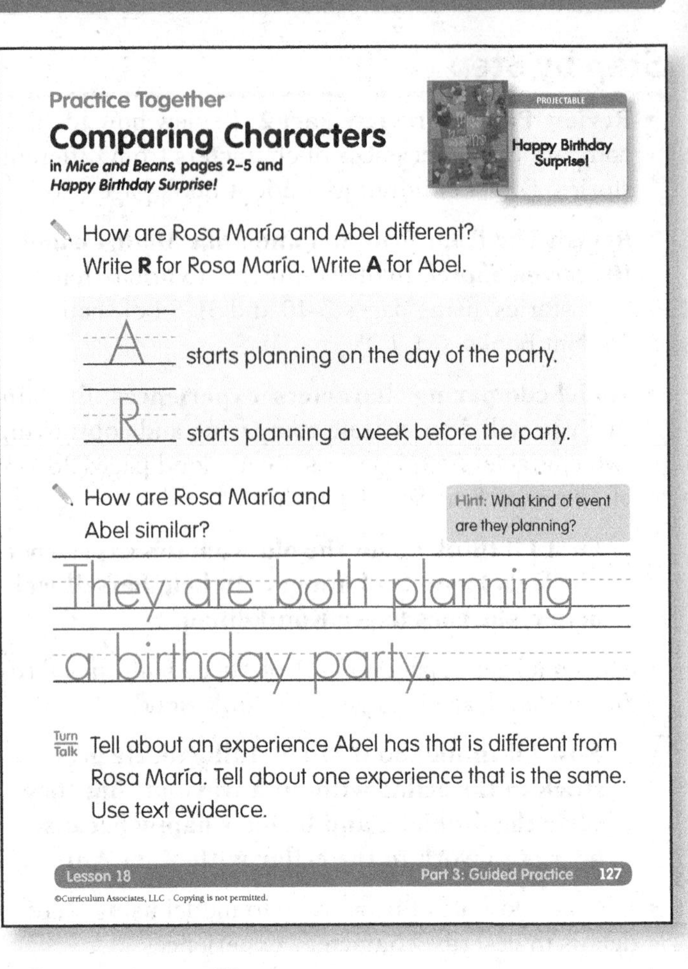

Close Reading

- Remind children that when they compare and contrast characters' experiences, they learn more about each character. Help them compare how Rosa María and Abel plan for their parties. Reread page 2 of *Mice and Beans* and prompt:

  Do you think Rosa María has given big parties before? *(yes)* **What evidence makes you think that?** *(The words say that she has a big family and loves to cook big meals for them.)*

  Do you think Abel has given a surprise party before? *(no)* **Why?** *(He is far behind. He doesn't know how long things will take to get done.)*

  Why does Rosa María prepare for her party so differently than Abel? *(She knows it takes time. She plans time to do all of the things she needs to do.)*
- Point out that comparing evidence about the characters' party planning help readers understand why they do things in certain ways.

Part 4: Independent Practice

Step by Step

- **Review Parts 1–3; preview Part 4.** Invite a volunteer to tell why it is important to compare the experiences of characters from different stories. Then direct children to Student Book page 128.
- Tell children they will now compare and contrast the experiences of characters by themselves. Explain that, as on the previous pages, first they will identify differences between the characters, then similarities.
- **Have children compare characters' experiences.** Display *Mice and Beans,* and tell children they will compare more of Rosa María's experiences to Abel's experiences in *Happy Birthday Surprise!*
- Read aloud pages 26–29 of *Mice and Beans,* having children listen for Rosa María's experiences. Then revisit *Happy Birthday Surprise!* Children may need to hear the entire story again. Alternatively, you can begin reading when Chester arrives at Abel's house.
- Read aloud the first prompt on Student Book page 128. Have children record answers. Then read aloud the second prompt and Hint. Have children write their answers in complete sentences. *(RL.1.1; L.1.1; L.1.2)*

Tip: If children struggle with the first activity, point to the words *finds out,* and ask which character did not know he or she had help until after the party.

- Use the Close Reading activity to have children focus on comparing the changes in both characters.
- **Have children demonstrate understanding.** Have partners complete the Turn and Talk activity. To help them begin, prompt:

  Do you think Rosa María's way of preparing for a party is better or worse than Abel's after reading about his experience? Explain your answer.

  Think about Rosa María's careful plans. Yet, she still forgets about the piñata. How does that help you understand the stress Abel feels?

- Have volunteers share ideas. *(RL.1.3; SL.1.1; SL.1.4)*
- **Have children reflect on their learning.** Guide children in a discussion about how comparing characters from different stories helps them understand both characters better. Chart their ideas.

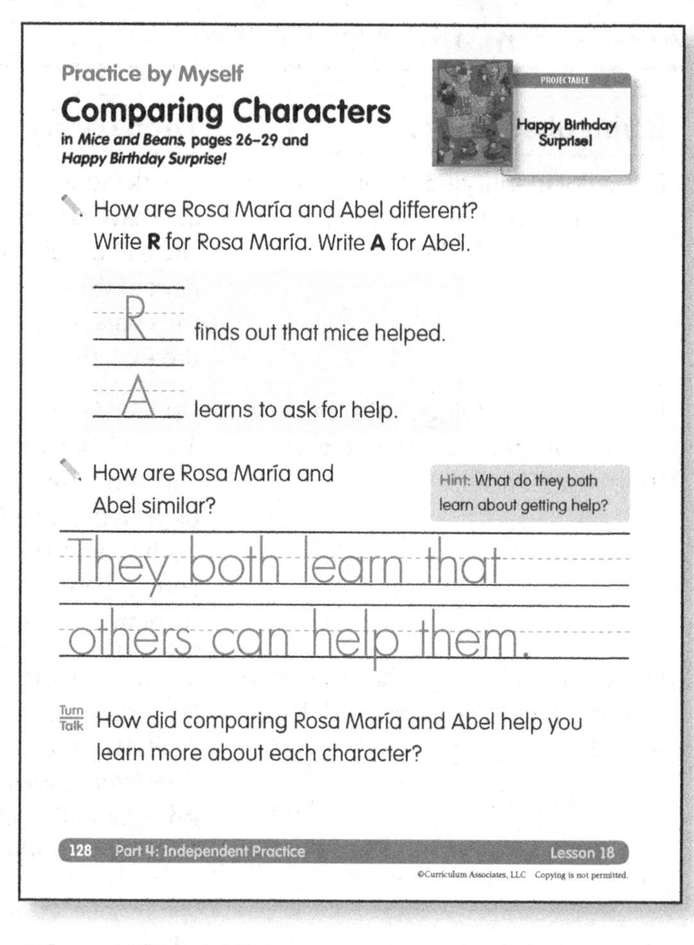

Practice by Myself

Comparing Characters

in Mice and Beans, pages 26–29 and *Happy Birthday Surprise!*

How are Rosa María and Abel different? Write **R** for Rosa María. Write **A** for Abel.

R finds out that mice helped.

A learns to ask for help.

How are Rosa María and Abel similar?

Hint: What do they both learn about getting help?

They both learn that others can help them.

Turn Talk How did comparing Rosa María and Abel help you learn more about each character?

128 Part 4: Independent Practice — Lesson 18

Close Reading

- Explain that sometimes characters change or learn from their experiences. Prompt children to compare how Rosa María and Abel change:

  Why does Rosa María change her mother's saying? *(She decides she has room for mice in her house, especially since they helped her.)*

  What does Abel say he will do the next time he has a party? *(He will ask for help.)*

  How is Rosa María's change similar to Abel's change? *(They both learn that getting help is a good thing.)*

  How are the changes different? Think about how the characters decide to change. *(Chester helps Abel see that he needs to change. Rosa María figures it out on her own.)*

- Explain that by comparing how characters change, readers learn more about the characters and can even learn a lesson about life.

Differentiated Instruction

Assessment and Remediation

If you observe . . .	Then try . . .
Difficulty identifying details about characters and their experiences	Practicing with familiar stories. Choose a fairy tale or familiar classroom story, and have children name a main character. Write it on the board inside of a circle. Prompt children to tell what the character does, says, feels, and learns. Record these ideas in circles connected to the center to form a web. Discuss the character's experiences and whether they are similar to or different from the experiences of characters in stories children have read recently.
Difficulty identifying similarities and differences between characters and their experiences	Using a Venn diagram to sort the details about characters' experiences. Revisit *Mice and Beans* and *Happy Birthday Surprise!* or two other familiar stories. Have children recall details about the experiences of Rosa María and Abel. As each detail is identified, write it on a stick-on note. Ask children if the detail is true of both characters or of just one character. Have volunteers place the detail in the correct part of the Venn diagram. (Write duplicate notes as needed.) After the diagram is complete, use it to restate similarities and differences.
Difficulty expressing what is learned by comparing characters and their experiences	Guiding children to notice what is significant about characters' differences. For example, begin by asking, *What is something Rosa María does better than Abel? Why is that?* Then build on children's responses by asking: *What could Abel learn from Rosa María?* Finally, discuss how the story might change if one character acted like another. Ask: *How would* Happy Birthday Surprise! *be different if Abel acted like Rosa María?*

Connect to the Anchor Standard

R9: *Analyze how two or more texts address similar themes or topics in order to build knowledge or to compare the approaches the authors take.*

In mastering Standard 9 throughout the grades, students move from comparing and contrasting specific elements of fiction within a single text to looking at how entire works are alike and different. As they evolve through the grades, students are expected to think more broadly about characters, settings, and events and analyze more subtle similarities and differences. Students will think about how a story's characters, theme, setting, plot, or topic reminds them of another story and ask questions such as these: *What other character has trouble expressing feelings, and why? How was a similar problem solved in another story? Why are two cultures' stories about this subject so similar, and yet what makes them different?* Use the following activities to help your students begin transitioning toward these ways of thinking.

- Point out that all four stories in this lesson are about helping others. Discuss what readers learn from each story. (The Polar Bear Son: *Loyal friends will always find a way to help each other;* Mike Mulligan and His Steam Shovel: *Friends are happiest when they work together;* Mice and Beans: *Sometimes help comes from surprising sources;* Happy Birthday Surprise!: *A true friend will always be there to help.)* Discuss how thinking about stories in this way deepens readers' understanding of each story.
- Have children think about the friendships that characters have in *Happy Birthday Surprise!*, *The Polar Bear Son*, and *Mike Mulligan and His Steam Shovel*. Discuss the ways in which each friendship has qualities that readers can relate to, even though one pair of friends is a woman and a bear, another is a man and his steam shovel, and yet another is a pair of mice.

Introduction

Before administering the Unit 5 Check, you may wish to review with children how to answer multiple-choice questions and offer a new test-taking tip. Begin by writing the following question on the board:

How is a character who blows down a pig's house like a character who tries to eat a little girl?

A They are both friendly.

B They are both hungry.

C They are both mean.

Guide children through the process of answering a multiple-choice question:

Today you will listen as I read from two stories, and then you will answer questions about details in each story. Remember, when you answer a multiple-choice question, only one of the answers is correct. To choose the correct answer, you draw a circle around the letter next to that answer.

Some questions may ask you to tell how details are alike or different. To answer these questions, you go back to the text and look for key details. The question on the board asks you to tell how two characters are alike. Let's go back and reread details about how the characters behave. Now let's think about each answer choice. Are these two characters friendly? (*No, they try to hurt others.*) **Are the characters hungry?** (*No, the story does not say they are hungry.*) **Are the characters mean?** (*Yes, they both do something to try to hurt someone.*) **So the correct choice is C.**

Unit 5 Check

Listen closely as your teacher reads. Then answer the questions.

Read what Treesha's brother Richard says in **My Rotten Redheaded Older Brother**.

"Bet I can pick more blackberries than you can."

. Why does Treesha look upset after she picks the berries?

A Her brother talks so low she can't hear him.

(B) Her brother is better at picking berries than she is.

C Her brother does not leave any berries for her to pick.

. Why do Mike and Mary Anne like to have people watch them work?

A They want someone to give them a job.

B They like to talk to new people.

(C) They dig faster and better.

129

Step by Step

- Revisit *My Rotten Redheaded Older Brother* and *Mike Mulligan and His Steam Shovel*. Invite children to retell important story details from each book.
- Have children follow along as you read aloud the directions on page 129 of their Student Books.
- Then read aloud one or more pages from the text, as specified below, before having children complete each item. Display the appropriate pages for children to view while they read and answer each question.
- For item 1, read pages 12–15 of *My Rotten Redheaded Older Brother*; display the illustration on page 15.
- For item 2, reread pages 22–32 of *Mike Mulligan and His Steam Shovel*; display the illustrations on pages 27 and 33.
- For item 3, read page 3 of *Mike Mulligan and His Steam Shovel*; display the illustration.
- For item 4, read page 28 of *My Rotten Redheaded Older Brother* and page 35 of *Mike Mulligan and His Steam Shovel*.
- For item 5, read pages 38 and 43 of *Mike Mulligan and His Steam Shovel* and pages 21 and 31–32 of *My Rotten Redheaded Older Brother*.

Note: Read aloud each question, answer choice, and Hint before directing children to answer it.

- When children have finished, reread each question and discuss the correct answer. Point to evidence in the text and pictures. Then use the Answer Analysis to discuss the correct answer.

Answer Analysis

1 This item requires children to use story details to describe why Treesha feels the way she does. ***(RL.1.7)***

The best answer is Choice B, "Her brother is better at picking berries than she is." Once again, Richard shows his little sister that he can do something better than she can. Choice A is not a good answer because Treesha's brother doesn't whisper to her. Choice C is not a good answer. The text says they both picked berries, so we know there were berries left for Treesha to pick.

2 This item asks children to use details in the words and pictures to describe Mike Mulligan's and Mary Anne's actions. ***(RL.1.7)***

The best answer is choice C, "They dig faster and better." Mike tells the little boy that he and Mary Anne always work faster and better when someone is watching them, and that's just what happens. The illustrations show this, too. Even though choices A and B seem like possible answers, they are not the best choice because the details support choice C as the best answer.

3 This item asks children to look at a picture and read the words on the page to answer an item about the way Mike Mulligan feels about Mary Anne. ***(RL.1.7)***

The best answer is choice A, "Mike is very proud of Mary Anne." The text says these words. The picture shows Mike smiling and pointing up to Mary Anne. Choice B is not correct because the picture doesn't show that "Mary Anne can dig more than anyone." Choice C is not correct because Mary Anne *is* smiling in this picture.

4 This item asks children to identify how two characters, Mike Mulligan and Treesha, are alike. This higher-level item asks children to make an inference based on story details and what they may already know. ***(RL.1.9)***

The best answer is choice A, "Both never stop trying." After newer shovels take all the jobs, Mike Mulligan doesn't give up. Instead, he works hard and digs the cellar with Mary Anne. Treesha stays on the merry-go-round longer than her brother, even though it makes her dizzy and she faints. Both Mike and Treesha are very determined. They never stop trying. Choice B is incorrect because it is the oppposite of what

Unit 5 Check

. What do the words and the picture help you know about **Mike Mulligan and His Steam Shovel**?

(A) Mike is very proud of Mary Anne.

B Mary Anne can dig more than anyone.

C Mary Anne can't smile.

. How are Mike Mulligan and Treesha the same?

(A) Both never stop trying.

B Both always give up.

C Both make others angry.

. How are Henry B. Swap in **Mike Mulligan and His Steam Shovel** and Richard in **My Rotten Redheaded Older Brother** alike at the end of the stories?

They are both nicer to others.

130

©Curriculum Associates, LLC Copying is not permitted.

Mike and Treesha do. Choice C is incorrect because the stories don't tell that either Mike or Treesha make others angry.

5 This item asks children to tell how two characters, Henry B. Swap and Richard, are alike at the end of the stories. ***(RL.1.9)***

Sample response: They are both nicer to others.

First, Henry B. Swap smiles "in rather a mean way" when he thinks he'll get the cellar dug for free. And he tells Mike he won't pay him when Mary Anne is stuck. But at the end of the story, Henry enjoys listening to Mike's stories, and smiles "in a way that isn't mean at all."

Although Richie teases Treesha a lot, he shows that he cares about his sister when he carries her home after she faints and runs to get a doctor. When Treesha thanks him, he blushes and says, "What's a big brother for, anyway." This shows that he can be a nice brother, too.

Unit 6

Integration of Knowledge and Ideas in Informational Text

The following pacing chart shows a recommended schedule for teaching the lessons in Unit 6. Each Read Aloud and Focus Lesson is taught over the course of three days. There is also time allotted in each Focus Lesson for teaching Tap Children's Prior Knowledge and Differentiated Instruction.

Day	Lesson/Activity	Time (minutes)
1	Unit 6 Opener (optional); Tap Children's Prior Knowledge; Lesson 19: Part 1	30
2	Lesson 19: Parts 2 and 3	30
3	Lesson 19: Part 4; Differentiated Instruction (optional)	30
4	Tap Children's Prior Knowledge; Lesson 20: Part 1	30
5	Lesson 20: Parts 2 and 3	30
6	Lesson 20: Part 4; Differentiated Instruction (optional)	30
7	Tap Children's Prior Knowledge; Lesson 21: Part 1	30
8	Lesson 21: Parts 2 and 3	30
9	Lesson 21: Part 4; Differentiated Instruction (optional)	30
10	Unit 6 Check	30

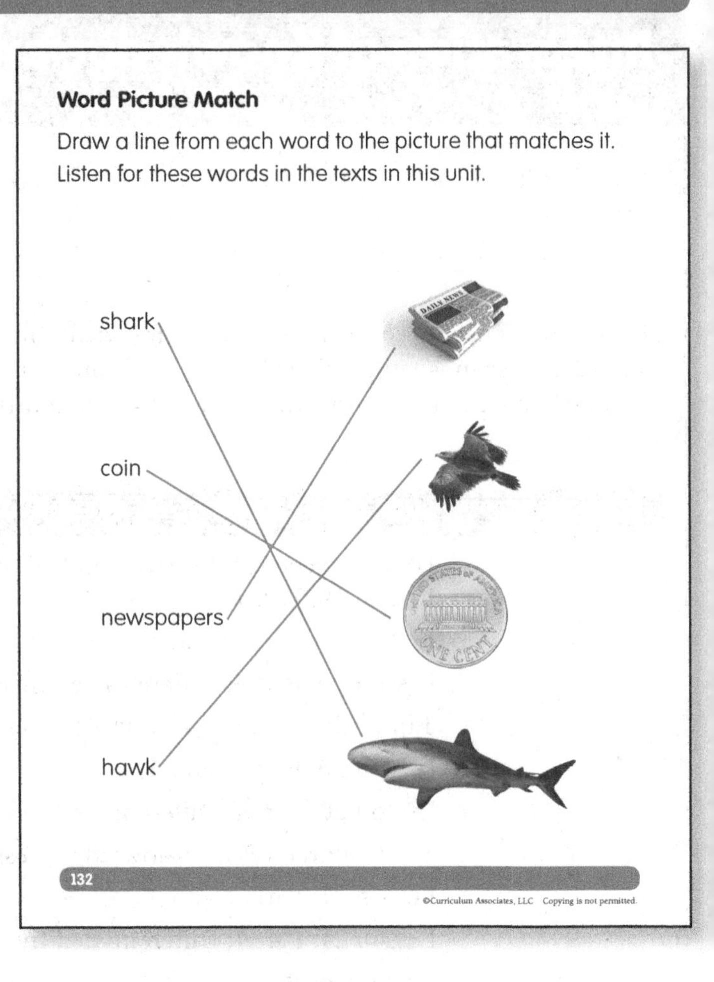

Step by Step

Explain that in this unit, children will learn more about how authors present information on real-world topics. As children compare different texts, they'll discover that some ideas are alike, some are different, and many are new and amazing!

- Have children turn to page 131. Read aloud the introductory sentence and questions.
- Help children compare and contrast details in the photographs. Begin by asking children to find how both pictures are alike. *(Both show lions in the wild; the animals have two ears, two eyes, and four legs.)*
- Then have children note details that are different. *(One photo shows adult lions, while the other shows lion cubs; the adults are resting on rocks, while the lion cubs are drinking at a water hole.)*
- Have children turn to page 132. Read aloud the title and directions at the top of the page.
- Read aloud the first word, *shark*. Have children repeat it. Then have them find the picture that matches the word. Ask children to draw a line from the word to the picture.
- Repeat the procedure for the other words.
- As time permits, have partners take turns telling a fact by using each word in a sentence.

Lesson 19 (Student Book pages 133–136)

Words with Pictures

CCSS

RI.1.7: Use the illustrations and details in a text to describe its key ideas.

Required Read Alouds: F *(Butterflies and Moths)*; G *(Elizabeth Leads the Way)*; I *(Earthworms)*

Lesson Objectives

- Use details from the words in a text to tell about its key ideas.
- Use details from the illustrations in a text to tell about its key ideas.
- Understand how words and illustrations in a text work together to help readers describe its key ideas.

The Learning Progression

- **Grade K:** CCSS RI.K.7 expects children to describe how the illustrations and words in a text are connected, with prompting and support. The focus is at the literal level, asking what person, place, thing or idea an illustration depicts.
- **Grade 1: CCSS RI.1.7 advances the Grade K standard by having children move beyond identifying what is depicted in an illustration to using the illustrations and words in a text to describe its key ideas.**
- **Grade 2:** CCSS RI.2.7 is narrower in focus than Grade K and Grade 1. In this grade, children describe how particular images contribute to and clarify the words in a text.

Prerequisite Skills

- Identify stated details in a text with prompting and support.
- Identify details in illustrations with prompting and support.
- Describe the relationship between illustrations and words with prompting and support.

Tap Children's Prior Knowledge

- Review with children what they have learned about finding picture and word details in stories. Help them recall questions they can ask to find details. *(What do the words say? What do the pictures show?)* List them in columns on chart paper. Then explain that children can ask these questions about other kinds of texts.
- Point to a classroom poster that includes words and one or more visual elements such as a diagram, photograph, or illustration.
- Ask children to name the details they find in the words. Add the details to the chart beneath the question *What do the words say?*
- Ask children to name the details they find in the pictures. Add the details to the chart beneath the question *What do the pictures show?*
- Discuss what children can learn from details in the words and image(s), and what they can learn when they put all this information together.
- Explain that in this lesson, children will use words and pictures to learn about key ideas in informational texts.

Ready *Teacher Toolbox* Teacher-Toolbox.com

	Prerequisite Skills	RI.1.7
Ready Lessons	✓	✓
Tools for Instruction	✓	
Interactive Tutorials		

Additional CCSS

RI.1.2; RI.1.6; SL.1.1; SL.1.4; L.1.1; L.1.2 (See page A38 for full text.)

Part 1: Introduction

Step by Step

- **Introduce the standard.** Have children turn to page 133 in their Student Books. Read aloud the speech bubble, and remind children that key ideas are the important ideas.
- **Review questions about details in words and pictures.** Read the line below the speech bubble. Point out that what follows are questions good readers ask about words and pictures so they can describe key ideas in a text.
- Read aloud the first question. Have children underline *words*. Then refer to the poster and the chart paper from the activity on page 185. Prompt:

  What details did you learn from the words on the poster?

- Help children pay particular attention to words that describe or answer the questions *who, what, when, where,* or *why.*
- Read aloud the second question. Have children underline the word *pictures.* Prompt:

  What details did you learn from the pictures on the poster?

Tip: Remind children that pictures in informational texts can be illustrations or photographs. Both include details, so readers should study them carefully.

- Discuss what children see, and support their observations as needed with prompts that draw attention to particular details.
- **Review using details to describe key ideas.** Read aloud the third question. Have children underline the phrase *words and pictures.* Prompt children to discuss how words and pictures both contribute to key ideas:

  Think about the word and picture details in the poster. What key, or important, ideas does the poster tell us?

  What details in the words tell about the key idea?

  What details in the pictures tell about the key idea?

Listen and Learn

Words with Pictures

You can find details in the **words** and **pictures** of a text. Putting together these details helps you describe **key ideas**.

Here are questions you can ask about words and pictures in a text:

- What do I learn from the details in the words?
- What do I learn from the details in the pictures?
- How do the details in the words and pictures fit together?

Asking questions about details in words and pictures will help you understand and describe the key ideas in a text.

Lesson 19 Part 1: Introduction 133

- **Explain why readers use words and pictures to describe key ideas.** Read aloud the bottom of the page. Explain that thinking about how the details in the words and pictures fit together gives readers a better understanding of key ideas than if they only read the words or only looked at the pictures.
- Share an example of a time when using word and picture details together helped you better understand key ideas. For example, reading the instructions and looking at the pictures in a cupcake recipe helped you know how much batter to put in each cup in the muffin tin.
- **Have children demonstrate understanding.** Call on individuals to share what they have learned so far about using the details in words and pictures to describe the key ideas in a text.

Step by Step

- **Review Part 1; preview Part 2.** Have children share questions they can ask to find details in words and pictures. Ask how the details help them describe key ideas. Then direct children to Student Book page 134.
- **Revisit *Elizabeth Leads the Way.*** Have children briefly recall the topic and key details, using the chart they created for the Book Review on Teacher Resource Book page 89. *(RI.1.2)*
- **Model asking questions about word and picture details.** Explain that you are going to ask yourself what you learn from the words and pictures in a text. Read aloud page 22 of *Elizabeth Leads the Way* and display the illustration. Then think aloud:

  The words say, "That was it! . . . If women could vote, they could help change . . . laws!" The words seem to say that this is a new idea. The picture shows Elizabeth holding up her arms, and her mouth is open. It looks like she's talking.

- **Model describing a key idea.** Explain that now you will use the word and picture details to describe a key idea. Think aloud:

  The words tell about a new idea—that women could vote and change laws. The picture shows Elizabeth talking excitedly, so I think this is Elizabeth's idea. The words and picture together tell me that Elizabeth has an exciting new idea—that women should vote!

Tip: Point to the large red letters and help children notice that they seem to be coming from Elizabeth. This is another clue that the big idea was hers.

- Read aloud each Student Book question. Use the Hints to discuss each answer with children.
- **Model writing your responses.** Model writing the answers to each question. Have children write their own complete sentences. *(L.1.1; L.1.2)*
- Use the Close Reading activity to help children use word and picture details to describe another key idea.
- **Have children demonstrate understanding.** Read aloud the Turn and Talk activity. Prompt partners to identify Elizabeth's big idea and recall evidence that helped them describe it. *(SL.1.1; SL.1.4)*

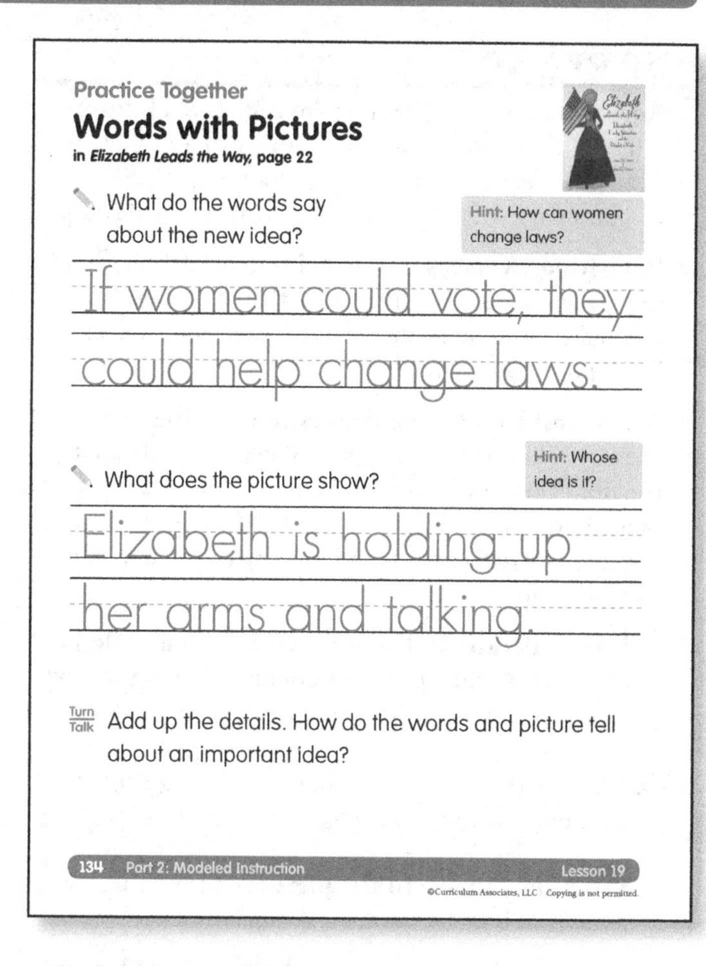

Practice Together

Words with Pictures

in *Elizabeth Leads the Way*, page 22

What do the words say about the new idea?

Hint: How can women change laws?

If women could vote, they could help change laws.

What does the picture show?

Hint: Whose idea is it?

Elizabeth is holding up her arms and talking.

Turn Talk Add up the details. How do the words and picture tell about an important idea?

134 Part 2: Modeled Instruction Lesson 19

©Curriculum Associates, LLC Copying is not permitted.

Close Reading

- Remind children that asking questions about word and picture details can help them describe key ideas.
- Read page 23 of *Elizabeth Leads the Way.* Prompt:

  What do the words say about Elizabeth's idea? *(The idea is shocking, huge, and daring. Elizabeth's friends gasp.)*

  What do the pictures show you about Elizabeth's friends? *(Their faces and hands show that they look surprised.)*

  What do the words and picture together tell you about Elizabeth's idea? *(The idea that women could vote is so surprising, even her friends can't imagine it happening.)*

- Discuss how understanding the reaction of Elizabeth's own friends helps readers understand why she might have to change a lot of people's minds about women being able to vote.

Part 3: Guided Practice

Step by Step

- **Review Parts 1–2; preview Part 3.** Have children tell why they ask questions about word and picture details. Direct them to Student Book page 135. Explain that you will guide them through this page.
- **Revisit *Earthworms*.** Have children briefly recall the topic and key details, using the chart they created for the Book Review on Teacher Resource Book page 139. *(RI.1.2)*
- **Guide children to use details to describe key ideas.** Tell children that as they listen to this part of the text, they will use details in the words and the picture to tell about a key idea. Read aloud the top of page 23 in *Earthworms*, and display the illustration. Then prompt:

  Which details in the words tell why a mole is an earthworm's greatest enemy? *(Moles eat thirty earthworms a day; they store worms in a pantry.)*

Tip: Be sure that children understand that a *pantry* is a cupboard or room used to store extra food.

  What do you see in the picture? *(A mole is looking at a lot of worms in a tunnel.)*

  Can the worms get out of the tunnel? Why or why not? *(No; the mole is blocking the tunnel.)*

  What do the picture details show about why a mole is an earthworm's greatest enemy? *(A mole traps lots of worms in a tunnel.)*

  What do you think the mole is going to do with the worms? *(eat them)* **How do you know?** *(The words say that moles store extra worms in a pantry, which is a place for extra food.)*

- **Guide children to write responses.** Read aloud each question and Hint on the Student Book page. Discuss answers and have children write them in complete sentences. *(SL.1.1; L.1.1; L.1.2)*
- Use the Close Reading activity to help children describe a key idea found in the text features.
- **Have children demonstrate understanding.** Assign the Turn and Talk activity. Ask partners to use evidence to describe key ideas about why moles are earthworm's greatest enemies. Have children share their evidence in class discussion. *(SL.1.4)*

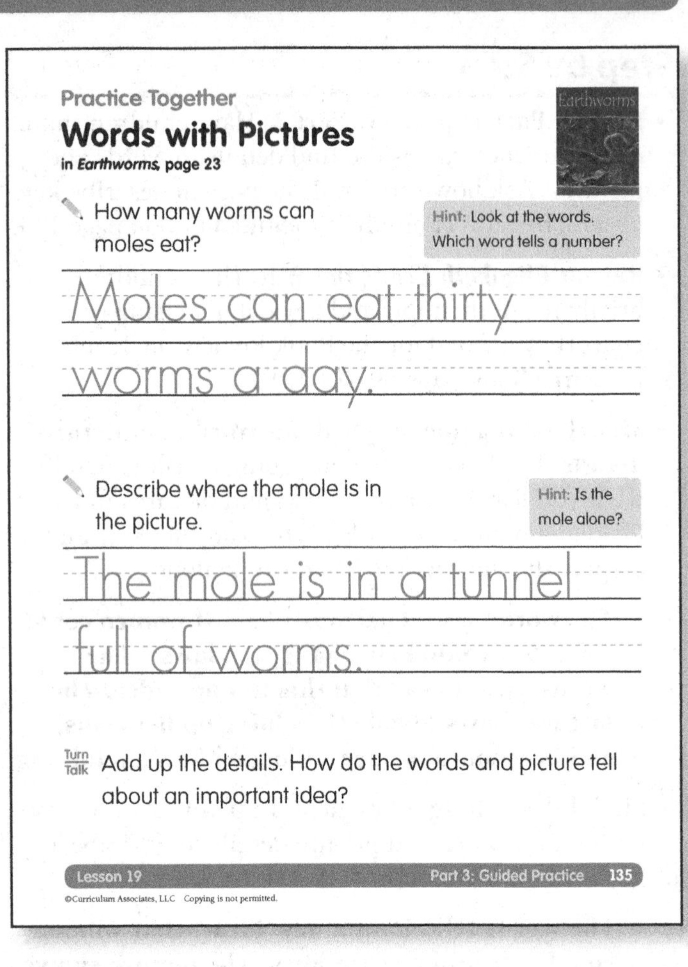

Close Reading

- Remind children that they can look for key ideas in captions and other text features.
- Display the picture on page 23. Then read aloud the caption and the text in the yellow box below. Help children use the words and picture to describe a key idea:

  What details do the words tell about a mole's pantry? *(Moles bite off the worms' heads to keep them from escaping from the pantry.)*

  What does the picture show about a mole's pantry? *(It is a space at the end of a tunnel where the mole piles up headless worms.)*

  What do you think the mole does with the worms in the pantry? *(It eats them later.)*

  What do the word and picture details tell about why a mole is an earthworm's greatest enemy? *(A mole eats so many earthworms, it has to save extra worms to eat later.)*

Step by Step

- **Review Parts 1–3; preview Part 4.** Have children tell why it is important to use details to describe key ideas.
- Direct children to Student Book page 136. Explain that they will work on their own to describe key ideas. Emphasize that they will answer questions about words and pictures as they did on previous pages.
- **Revisit *Butterflies and Moths*.** Have children briefly recall the topic and key details, using the chart they created for the Book Review on Teacher Resource Book page 71. *(RI.1.2)*
- **Have children use details to describe key ideas independently.** Read aloud the first question on the Student Book page. Tell children to listen for details about types of moths as you read aloud the first paragraph and the caption on page 9 of *Butterflies and Moths.*
- Reread the first question, and use the Hint to help children think about the answer. Reread the text as needed. Have children write their answers in complete sentences. *(L.1.1; L.1.2)*
- Read aloud the second question and the Hint. Display the photograph on page 8, rereading the caption as needed. Have children write their answers in complete sentences.
- Discuss the answers to both questions. Have children use their responses to describe the key ideas they learned about. *(There are many different types of moths; there are more types of moths than types of butterflies; some moth caterpillars sting.) (SL.1.1; SL.1.4)*

Tip: Use concept webs to help children see the connections between key ideas and details.

- Use the Close Reading activity to model finding additional details and key ideas.
- **Have children demonstrate understanding.** Have partners complete the Turn and Talk activity. Encourage them to use evidence from their Student Book page and from the Close Reading activity. Have children share their evidence in class discussion.
- **Have children reflect on their learning.** Have children discuss how asking questions and finding details in words and pictures can help them understand important ideas. Chart their ideas.

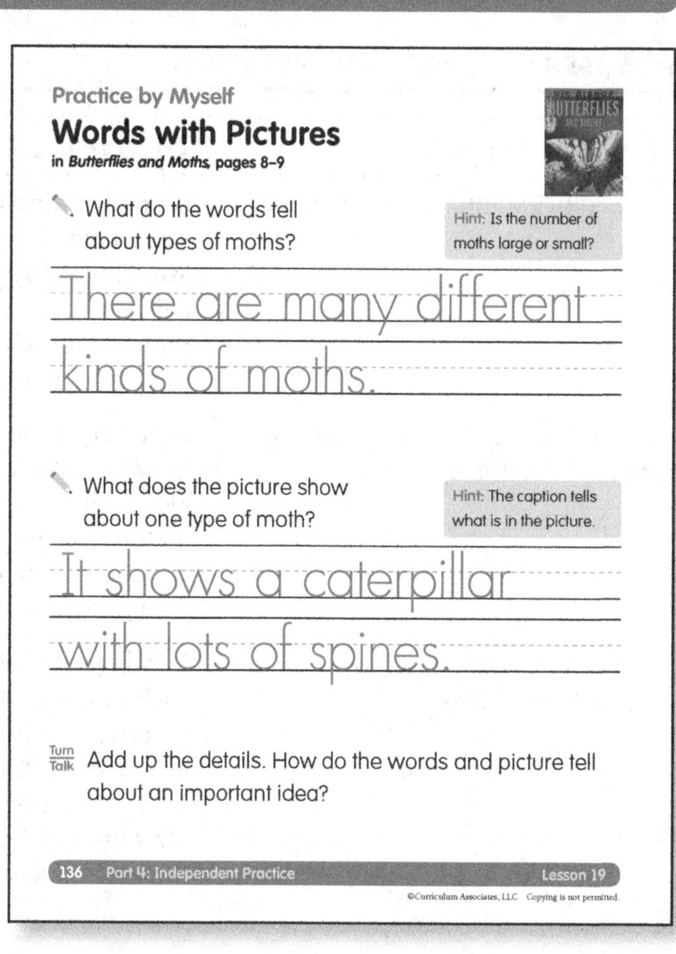

Practice by Myself

Words with Pictures

in *Butterflies and Moths,* pages 8–9

What do the words tell about types of moths?

Hint: Is the number of moths large or small?

There are many different kinds of moths.

What does the picture show about one type of moth?

Hint: The caption tells what is in the picture.

It shows a caterpillar with lots of spines.

Turn Talk Add up the details. How do the words and picture tell about an important idea?

136 Part 4: Independent Practice Lesson 19

©Curriculum Associates, LLC Copying is not permitted.

Close Reading

- Explain that sometimes a page can have many details and more than one key idea. Read the first two paragraphs on page 9. Prompt:

  What details do the words tell about butterflies and moths? *(There are thousands of different types; they live everywhere there are plants for them to eat; most live in the rain forest, including the largest moths.)*

  What key idea do we learn about where butterflies and moths live? *(They live in many places, but especially in the rainforest.)*

- Reread the final paragraph. Prompt:

  What do the details tell about? *(Moths can be tiny; some are weird; some feed on tears; others drink blood; the way they grow up is amazing.)*

  What is the key idea of this paragraph? *(Moths and butterflies are amazing in many different ways.)*

Differentiated Instruction

Assessment and Remediation

If you observe . . .	Then try . . .
Difficulty identifying details in text	Demonstrating how to separate the details in a text. Choose an informational text, and copy a paragraph onto chart paper. Ask children to listen for each separate idea, or detail, as you read aloud the text. Work with children to identify each detail, pointing out when a sentence has more than one, or when a detail is described by more than one sentence. Use different colored markers to underline the details as children identify them.
Limited vocabulary for describing details in pictures	Revisiting familiar books and describing picture details. Using *Elizabeth Leads the Way,* discuss with children what the pictures show about Elizabeth's feelings. Incorporate names for feelings into the discussion of the pictures; for example, *angry* for pages 6 and 9, *happy* for page 14, and *sad, unhappy* for page 17. Revisit the photographs in *Butterflies and Moths,* using color, size, and shape words to describe the details.
Difficulty fitting details together to describe key ideas	Matching details to key ideas. Display two key ideas about your classroom, such as *There are many different things to read* and *Our classroom is well organized.* Write details that tell about each idea on stick-on notes. For instance, *We have nature magazines.* or *Crayons are stored in a blue container.* Read aloud each detail and have a volunteer match it to the appropriate key idea. Reread the key idea and details, asking children to decide whether or not each detail tells about the key idea.

Connect to the Anchor Standard

R7: Integrate and evaluate content presented in diverse media and formats, including visually and quantitatively, as well as in words.

Throughout the grades, Standard 7 teaches students to integrate information presented through various media. In examining illustrations, photographs, maps, diagrams, and animations, students explain how the information these media present contributes to their overall understanding of the text. Students also learn to navigate formats to find information quickly and efficiently. As they integrate and seek information, they will ask questions such as these: *What details are in the text and illustrations? How do the text and illustrations work together to express key ideas? How do details in the visuals contribute to understanding of the text? Where will I find the information I am looking for?* Use the following activities to help your students begin this transition.

- Display the spreads from pages 27–31 of *Butterflies and Moths.* Circulate as needed so that each child gets a close look at the pictures. Invite children to write a caption for the pictures, based on what they see. Have volunteers read their captions aloud. Then read aloud the caption on page 31, and compare it to those that children wrote. Discuss how listening to the details in the real caption helps readers better understand the picture and the key idea that butterflies and moths are great fliers.
- Remind children that sometimes the pictures in a text add information that is not told in the words. Reread pages 30–31 of *Elizabeth Leads the Way.* Discuss how the illustration of the United States map helps readers understand how Elizabeth's idea spread. Note details that do not appear in the text, such as the major cities across the country where women were fighting for the right to vote. *(RI.1.6)*

Lesson 20 (Student Book pages 137–140)

Identifying Reasons

CCSS

RI.1.8: Identify the reasons an author gives to support points in a text.

Required Read Alouds: *Projectable 5 (Upsetting the Balance)*

Lesson Objectives

- Identify key points in a text.
- Identify reasons that support key points.
- Understand how identifying reasons can help you better understand a key point.

The Learning Progression

- **Grade K:** CCSS RI.K.8 expects children to identify reasons that support points in a text with prompting and support.
- **Grade 1: CCSS RI.1.8 builds on the Grade K standard by having children work more independently to identify reasons that support points in a text.**
- **Grade 2:** CCSS RI.2.8 expands upon the scope of the standard by having children consider and describe how reasons support specific points in a text.

Prerequisite Skills

- Understand that a key point is an important idea.
- Identify reasons that support points in a text with prompting and support.

Tap Children's Prior Knowledge

- Propose a topic about which children would likely have a strong opinion, such as getting a class pet. Invite children to state their opinions about it. Write one of the opinions on the board; for example, *It would be good for us to have a class pet.*
- Review that a key point is an important idea. Explain that the sentence on the board is a key point because it tells an idea that children think is important for others to understand.
- Prompt children to give reasons for the opinion. Ask, *What could you learn by having a class pet? Why would a class pet be helpful?*
- Review children's responses. Then explain that when they gave reasons for having a class pet, they were supporting, or explaining, their key point. Mention that a reason may be a fact, such as *A hamster is a small pet,* or an example, such as *Last year's class learned a lot about science by having a class pet.*
- Explain that when you want to convince someone about a key point, you give reasons to support it. Point out that authors do this, too. Tell children that in this lesson, they will learn how to find reasons that support, or explain, an author's key point.

Ready *Teacher Toolbox* Teacher-Toolbox.com

	Prerequisite Skills	*RI.1.8*
Ready Lessons	✓	✓
Tools for Instruction		✓
Interactive Tutorials	✓	

Additional CCSS

RI.1.2; SL.1.1; SL.1.2; L.1.1; L.1.2 *(See page A38 for full text.)*

Step by Step

- **Introduce the standard.** Have children turn to page 137 in their Student Books. Read aloud the speech bubble. Then read aloud the sentence beneath the speech bubble and tell children that the yellow boxes are examples of an author's key point and reasons.
- **Guide children to identify a key point.** Read aloud the first bullet. Have children underline the words *key point.* Then read the example. Emphasize that this is the key point, or important idea, that the author wants readers to understand.
- Point out that in this case, the key point is the author's opinion, or what she thinks or feels about the topic. Remind children of their opinion from the activity on page 191, and explain that an author's key point is often an opinion.
- **Guide children to identify reasons.** Read aloud the second bullet. Have children underline *Reasons*, and explain that a reason explains, or gives more information about, the author's key point. Review with children the reasons they provided to support their opinion in the activity on page 191.
- Tell children that once they identify the author's key point, they can identify supporting reasons by asking themselves whether each detail tells more about the key point. Read aloud the example. Then model:

  The first sentence says that bees can sting. I'll ask, *Does this reason tell why bees are helpful?* No, it tells how bees are harmful! So this reason does not support the point that bees are helpful.

- Work with children to ask questions about the remaining sentences:

  The next sentence says that bees help people. Does this reason tell why bees help more than they harm? *(Yes, it tells that they help people.)*

  The next sentence tells about how bees help plants make fruit. What clue word do you hear? *(help)* **How does this reason support the author's key point?** *(It tells one way that bees help plants.)*

Tip: Provide academic language by explaining that this sentence gives an *example* of a way that bees are helpful. Encourage children to practice using this language throughout the lesson.

Listen and Learn

Identifying Reasons

A **key point** is an important idea an author wants you to understand. Authors give **reasons** to support key points.

Look carefully at these examples:

- A key point tells an author's important idea.

  Bees help more than they harm.

- Reasons are facts or examples that support, or explain, why the author has that idea.

  You might be afraid of bees because they can sting. But bees do a lot to help people. Bees help plants make fruit by spreading pollen from flower to flower. A lot of the food you eat is thanks to bees!

Identifying the reasons an author gives will help you understand the key point.

Lesson 20 Part 1: Introduction 137

Does the last sentence explain how bees can help? *(yes)* **What clue words tell you this?** *(The words "thanks to bees" are a clue that the bees are helping, not harming.)*

- **Explain why readers identify reasons.** Read aloud the bottom of the page. Explain that reasons help readers understand what an author wants them to know, and why the author's point is important.
- Share an example of a time when a reason helped you understand an author's key point. For example, you were confused when an author wrote that chocolate lovers should protect the rain forest. Then you read the reason—chocolate is made from the seeds of cacao trees, and cacao trees grow in the rain forest.
- **Have children demonstrate understanding.** Call on individuals to share what they have learned so far about key points and supporting reasons. Have children give examples of things they have argued for, and the reasons they have provided, to reinforce their understanding.

Part 2: Modeled Instruction

Step by Step

- **Review Part 1; preview Part 2.** Ask children what they have learned about key points and supporting reasons. Have them turn to Student Book page 138.
- **Read *Upsetting the Balance.*** Display Projectable 5 on pages 215–216. Read it aloud. Work with children to briefly review key details. *(RI.1.2)*
- **Model identifying a key point and a reason.** Reread the first two paragraphs, then explain that you will think about what the details have in common in order to find the key point. Think aloud:

    (First paragraph) **In these sentences, the author tells about living things, such as squirrels, cows, and grass. The author tells that they are links in the food chain, and that food chains are important to all living things.**

    (Second paragraph) **In these sentences, the author gives details about food chains, such as what a link is and what it means for animals to be linked.**

    (First paragraph, last sentence) **This sentence tells about food chains *and* living things. I think this is the key point, or most important idea that the author wants me to know.**

- Use the Close Reading activity to model looking for a reason that supports the key point.
- Direct children to Student Book page 138, and read aloud the first activity, along with the Hint. Discuss the answer, including why the second option is incorrect, and circle the key point. Have children circle the key point on their own pages.
- **Model writing your response.** Read aloud the second prompt and the Hint. Discuss the answer, and model writing in a complete sentence. Have children write their own answers. *(L.1.1; L.1.2)*
- **Have children demonstrate understanding.** Read aloud the Turn and Talk activity. Prompt partners to evaluate the author's reason:

    Do you agree with the reason? Why or why not?

    Does the reason give enough information to explain the key point? Why or why not?

- Discuss responses. Have children use text evidence to explain their ideas. *(SL.1.1; SL.1.2)*

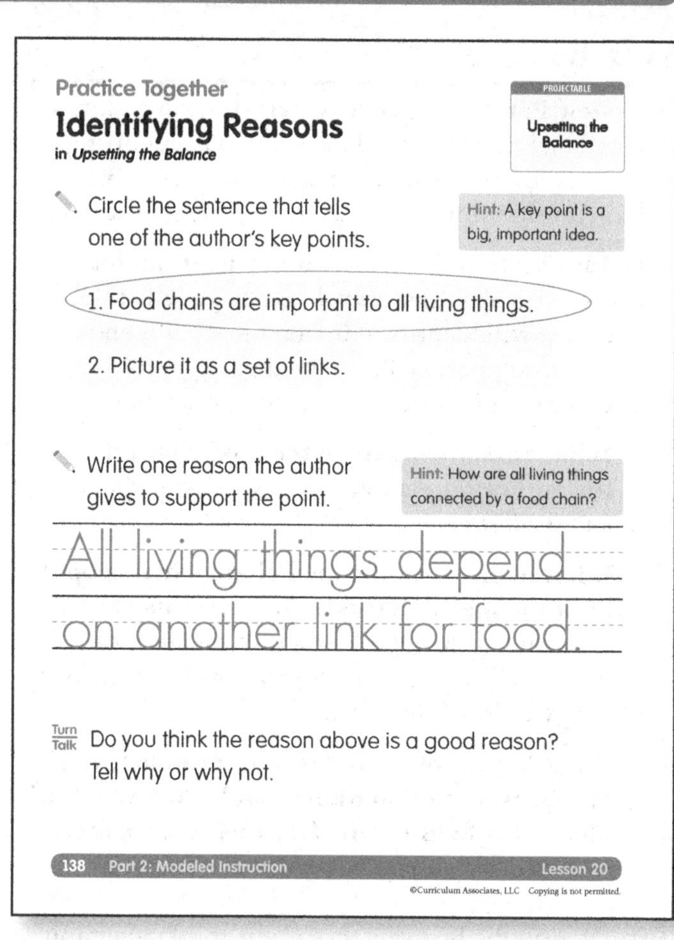

Practice Together

Identifying Reasons

in *Upsetting the Balance*

PROJECTABLE
Upsetting the Balance

Circle the sentence that tells one of the author's key points.

Hint: A key point is a big, important idea.

1. Food chains are important to all living things.

2. Picture it as a set of links.

Write one reason the author gives to support the point.

Hint: How are all living things connected by a food chain?

All living things depend on another link for food.

Turn Talk Do you think the reason above is a good reason? Tell why or why not.

138 Part 2: Modeled Instruction Lesson 20

Close Reading

- Explain to children that one way to look for reasons that support a key point is to turn the key point into a question. Display *Upsetting the Balance*, and think aloud:

    I know one key point: "Food chains are important to all living things." So I'll ask: *Why are food chains important to all living things?*

- Have children listen closely for the answer as you reread the second paragraph. Then prompt:

    Which sentence tells why food chains are important to all living things? *(the last one)* **How do you know?** *(It tells how all living things in a food chain depend on another "link" for food.)*

    Why didn't you choose any of the first three sentences? *(They only tell what a food chain is. They don't answer the question about why food chains are important to all living things.)*

Step by Step

- **Review Parts 1–2; preview Part 3.** Have children recall how to identify a key point and supporting reasons. Direct them to Student Book page 139. Explain that you will guide them through this page.
- **Guide children to identify a key point and a reason.** Display *Upsetting the Balance.* Tell children that they will identify a different key point and a reason to support it. Read aloud paragraphs 3–6. Then prompt children to identify the key point:

  What animals make up the food chain that the author tells about? *(sharks, cownose rays, and shellfish)*

  What happens to the food chain when people hunt too many sharks? *(The food chain breaks. There are too many cownose rays, and they eat too many shellfish. This causes problems for other living things and for fishermen.)*

  What key point, or important idea, does the author want you to understand when you read about this food chain? *(The choices we make can cause trouble for plants, animals, and people.)*

Tip: Reread the first sentence of the third paragraph. Guide children to see that this sentence is the key point because it tells why the story about the sharks in paragraphs 4–6 is important.

- Use the Close Reading activity to identify the reasons that support the key point.
- **Guide children to write responses.** Read aloud the first activity, along with the Hint. Discuss the answer, and have children circle it.
- Read aloud the second prompt and Hint. Discuss the answer, and have children write it in a complete sentence. *(L.1.1; L.1.2)*
- **Have children demonstrate understanding.** Read aloud the Turn and Talk activity. Ask whether or not children agree with the reason, and whether it gives enough information to explain the point. Encourage children to recall an additional example of a broken food chain from *Who Eats What?*
- Circulate and check that children give reasons for their thinking. Invite volunteers to share their answers. *(SL.1.1; SL.1.2)*

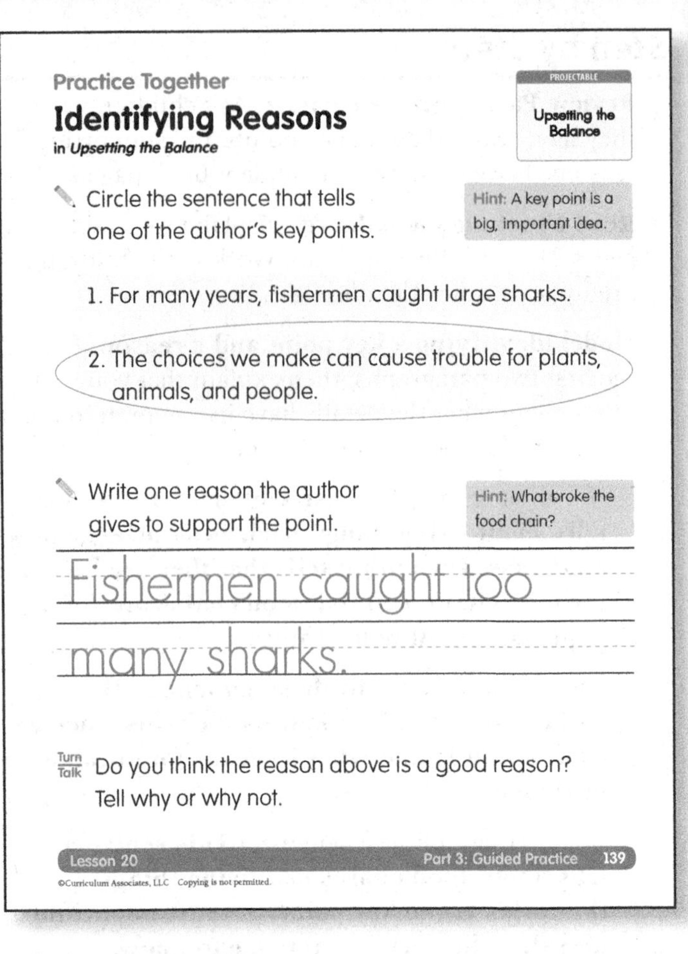

Close Reading

- Explain that an author usually includes more than one reason to support a key point. Review the key point. *(The choices we make can cause trouble for plants, animals, and people.)*
- Have children listen closely for reasons that support this key point as you reread paragraphs 4–5 of *Upsetting the Balance.* Prompt:

  What happened when there were fewer sharks? *(The number of cownose rays grew.)*

  What happened when there were more rays? *(More rays ate more shellfish.)*

  What happened when there were fewer shellfish? *(Fishermen couldn't make enough money. Creatures that ate shellfish went hungry.)*
- Record these events in a simple flow chart, and discuss the connection from one event to the next. Guide children to see how the whole sequence of events provides reasons that support the key point.

Part 4: Independent Practice

Step by Step

- **Review Parts 1–3; preview Part 4.** Invite a volunteer to tell why it is important to identify key points and supporting reasons. Then direct children to Student Book page 140.
- Tell children they will now find a key point and supporting reason by themselves. Point out that the activities on this page are similar to those on the previous pages: first children will circle a key point and then they will write one reason that supports it.
- **Have children identify a key point and reason independently.** Display *Upsetting the Balance,* and have children listen for a key point and supporting reason as you read aloud the last paragraph.
- Read aloud the first Student Book page activity, along with the Hint. Have children silently circle the key point. Reread as needed.

Tip: Tell children they can check their answer by making sure the sentence they chose as the key point answers the question in the Hint.

- Read aloud the second prompt, along with the Hint. Have children write the answer in a complete sentence. *(L.1.1; L.1.2)*
- Discuss answers for the first and second activities. Encourage children to explain why the sentence they did not circle is not a key point. *(SL.1.1; SL.1.2)*
- Use the Close Reading activity to identify additional supporting reasons.
- **Have children demonstrate understanding.** Have partners complete the Turn and Talk activity. Remind children to tell whether the reason gives enough information to explain the point. Encourage them to give some examples of wise choices people can make to protect living things.
- **Have children reflect on their learning.** Guide children in a discussion about how identifying an author's key points and reasons helps them better understand what they read. Invite them to give examples. Chart their ideas.

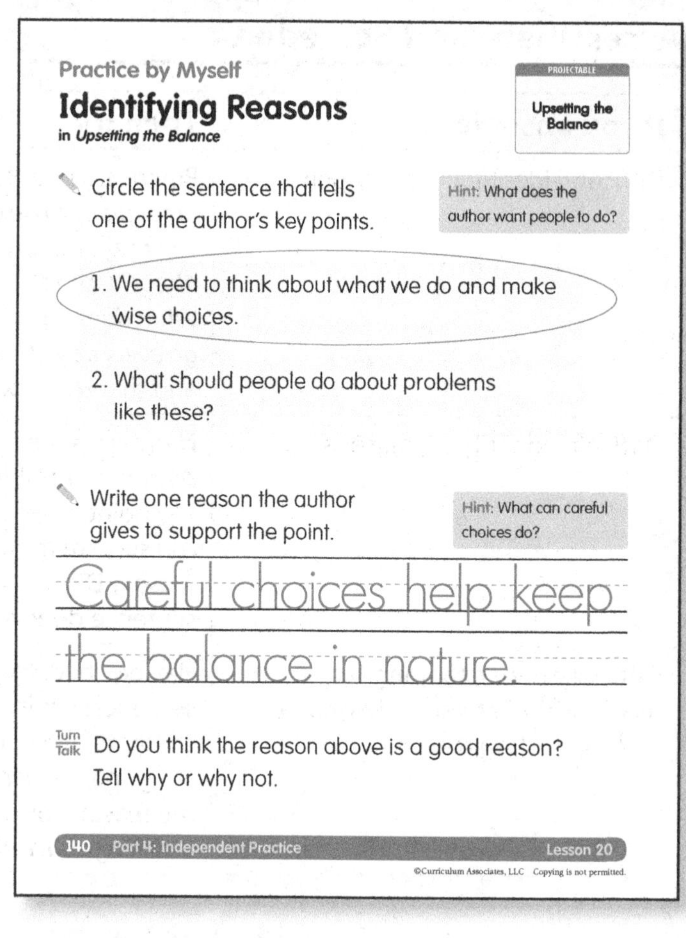
Practice by Myself

Identifying Reasons
in *Upsetting the Balance*

PROJECTABLE
Upsetting the Balance

Circle the sentence that tells one of the author's key points.

Hint: What does the author want people to do?

1. We need to think about what we do and make wise choices.
2. What should people do about problems like these?

Write one reason the author gives to support the point.

Hint: What can careful choices do?

Careful choices help keep the balance in nature.

Turn Talk Do you think the reason above is a good reason? Tell why or why not.

140 Part 4: Independent Practice Lesson 20

©Curriculum Associates, LLC Copying is not permitted.

Close Reading

- Remind children that authors often include more than one reason to support a key point. Explain that identifying all of the reasons helps readers better understand the author's point.
- Reread the last paragraph of *Upsetting the Balance.* Review the key point: *We need to think about what we do and make wise choices.* Then prompt:

  Why does the author think people should make wise choices? *(Careful choices keep the balance in nature.)*

  Why does the author think keeping the balance is important? *(It helps all the living things that share our planet.)*

  Think about the questions the author asks. What else does the author think making wise choices can do? *(solve problems and help living creatures instead of harming them)*

Assessment and Remediation

If you observe . . .	Then try . . .
Difficulty identifying a key point	Practicing with simple text. Write these sentences on the board: *School is a great place to go every day. You can read books. You can learn new things. You can make friends.* Read the sentences. Ask: *What are all of these sentences about? (school) What things can you do at school? (read, learn, make friends) What does the author want you to think about school? (That it is a great place to go every day.)* Guide children to see that the first sentence is the key point and that the next three sentences tell more about the key point.
Difficulty identifying reasons	Narrowing down options. State a key point, such as *Summer is the best season.* Tell children you will say two sentences, but only one supports the key point. Have them listen carefully as you say: *Fall comes after summer. You can swim at the beach.* Ask: *Which sentence tells why summer is the best season?* Discuss the answer and why it is correct. Then discuss how the first sentence does not tell more about why summer is the best season.
Difficulty understanding the relationship between a key point and supporting reasons	Having children provide reasons for a key point. Write and read aloud this sentence: *It is important to put things back where they belong.* Then have children give reasons that answer this question: *Why is it important to put things back where they belong?* Record their responses. Have children review the reasons by orally completing the following sentence: *It is important to put things back where they belong because* __________.

Connect to the Anchor Standard

R8: *Delineate and evaluate the argument and specific claims in a text, including the validity of the reasoning as well as the relevance and sufficiency of the evidence.*

Throughout the grades, Standard 8 teaches students not only to identify and describe how authors use reasons to support their points, but also to think about how an author structures an argument by using cause and effect, compare and contrast, or sequential text structures. In later grades, students learn to ask questions about an author's viewpoint, the method used to communicate it, and whether the argument is successfully made. These questions include the following: *What argument is the author making? How does the author support the argument? Is the evidence reliable and sufficient? What text structures help the author build the argument? Does the author's argument convince me to feel the same way?* Use the following activities to help your students begin this transition.

- Help children learn to evaluate an argument. State a key point and supporting reasons such as these: *Everyone should have a bike. You can get exercise riding a bike. Riding a bike is easy to learn. You can ride anywhere on a bike.* Identify the key point. Then prompt children to decide if each reason supports it with questions such as the following: *Is it true that you can get exercise riding a bike? Is getting exercise a good reason to have a bike?*
- Help children learn to identify a faulty reason. Have them listen carefully to a key point and supporting reasons; for example: *Grapes are a great snack. They come in different colors. They taste good. They are easy to carry.* Guide children to name the reason that does not support the key point. Discuss that even though it is true that grapes come in different colors, this fact does not tell more about why grapes are a great snack.

Lesson 21 (Student Book pages 141–144)

Comparing Two Texts

CCSS

RI.1.9: Identify basic similarities in and differences between two texts on the same topic (e.g., in illustrations, descriptions, or procedures).

Required Read Alouds: *Projectable 4 (Famous Women: Susan B. Anthony); F (Butterflies and Moths); G (Elizabeth Leads the Way); I (Earthworms)*

Lesson Objectives

- Identify basic similarities and differences between the illustrations in two texts.
- Identify basic similarities and differences between the words in two texts.
- Understand that comparing texts on the same topic can help readers better understand that topic.
- Understand that comparing texts on the same topic can help readers better understand each text.

The Learning Progression

- **Grade K:** CCSS RI.K.9 requires that children identify basic similarities and differences between two texts on the same topic with prompting and support.
- **Grade 1: CCSS RI.1.9 asks that children begin to independently identify basic similarities and differences between two texts on the same topic.**
- **Grade 2:** CCSS RI.2.9 requires that children first identify the most important ideas in two texts on the same topic, and then compare and contrast those ideas.

Prerequisite Skills

- Identify the topic of a text with prompting and support.
- Describe the relationship between illustrations and the text with prompting and support.
- Identify the roles of the author and illustrator.

Additional CCSS

RI.1.2; SL.1.1; SL.1.2; L.1.1; L.1.2 (See page A38 for full text.)

Tap Children's Prior Knowledge

- Hold up a pen and a pencil. Ask children to think about how they are the same and how they are different. Discuss the ideas together. *(Same: size, shape, used for writing; Different: ink vs. lead, color, eraseable vs. permanent)*
- Record each similarity and difference in a Venn diagram or a simple three-column chart. Guide children to see how the details are grouped as ways the pen and pencil are the same and ways the pen and pencil are different.
- Work with children to compare other items, such as crayons and paintbrushes, the sun and the moon, or windows and doors. Guide them to help you complete a Venn diagram or chart for the new items. Together, review the details for each pair of objects.
- Remind children that they have also practiced identifying things that are the same and different about fiction books and informational books. Invite volunteers to review some of these ideas.
- Explain that in this lesson, children will look for things that are the same and different in two texts that are about the same topic.

Ready *Teacher Toolbox* Teacher-Toolbox.com

	Prerequisite Skills	RI.1.9
Ready Lessons	✓	✓
Tools for Instruction	✓✓	✓
Interactive Tutorials		

Part 1: Introduction

Step by Step

- **Introduce the standard.** Have children turn to page 141 in their Student Books. Read aloud the speech bubble.

Tip: Review the lesson title, and explain that the word *compare* is often used to mean both compare and contrast, as children will be doing in this lesson.

- Display pages 38–39 of *Butterflies and Moths*. Read aloud the first paragraph. Discuss with children that these pages tell about predators, or enemies that eat butterflies and moths.
- Then display and read aloud page 22 of *Earthworms*. Ask children what this page is mostly about. *(enemies of earthworms)* Guide them to see that the pages in both texts tell about predators, or enemies.
- **Review questions to use when comparing texts.** Read aloud the line below the speech bubble on Student Book page 141. Point out that what follows are good questions readers ask themselves when they compare and contrast two texts on the same topic.
- Read aloud the first two questions, and think aloud:

  I see that both pictures show an animal being eaten; that is one way the pictures are the same. But one is a photograph and one is a drawing, so that is one way they are different.

- Have children point to and discuss other similarities and differences they notice in the pictures.
- Read aloud the next two questions, and think aloud:

  Both texts tell how some predators are active at night. This is one way the texts are the same. Each page tells about different animals that are predators. This is a way the texts are different.

- Invite children to tell specific details they hear in each text that show how they are different.
- **Explain why readers compare and contrast texts.** Read aloud the bottom of the page. Explain how comparing and contrasting texts helps you learn more about a topic:

  In these two texts, both authors wrote about predators, but each one told about different animals. When you compare the texts, you learn more about what different predators do.

Listen and Learn

Comparing Two Texts

When you **compare** two texts, you tell how they are alike. When you **contrast** texts, you tell how they are different.

You can ask these questions to compare and contrast two texts about the same topic.

- What is the same about the pictures?
- What is different about the pictures?
- In what ways are the words the same?
- In what ways are the words different?

When you compare and contrast texts about the same topic, you learn more about the topic. You also notice different ways that two authors can describe the same topic.

- Explain how comparing and contrasting texts helps you think about authors' choices:

  Comparing texts on the same topic makes me think about both authors' choices: why did one use photographs and the other use illustrations? Why did one tell just a few details and the other tell more? Asking and answering these questions makes me a good, active reader.

- Share an example of a time when comparing two texts helped you better understand a topic. For instance:

  I read one book about how to buy a bike that fits me. I read another book about bicycle safety. Both texts told me about riding a bicycle, but only the book about bicycle safety told me that I needed to buy a helmet, too.

- **Have children demonstrate understanding.** Call on individuals to share what they have learned so far about comparing two texts on the same topic, and how it helps them better understand the topic.

Part 2: Modeled Instruction

Step by Step

- **Review Part 1; preview Part 2.** Invite children to tell what questions they can ask when they compare two texts. Direct them to Student Book page 142.
- **Revisit *Elizabeth Leads the Way* and *Famous Women*.** Have children recall *Elizabeth Leads the Way,* using the chart from the Book Review on Teacher Resource Book page 89. Then reread *Famous Women: Susan B. Anthony* on pages 213–214. *(RI.1.2)*
- **Model comparing two texts.** Display the cover of *Elizabeth Leads the Way* and the photograph of Susan B. Anthony on page 214. Explain that you will model comparing and contrasting the pictures in each text. Then think aloud:

  First I will think of ways these pictures are the same. Both pictures show women, and I know from reading that both women are famous.

  Now I will think about how the pictures are different. This picture shows Elizabeth Cady Stanton and that one shows Susan B. Anthony. Plus, someone drew the the picture of Elizabeth, but Susan's picture is real.

- Discuss the images in more detail. Prompt:

  Would we know that Elizabeth is a real person if we only saw this picture? Why or why not? *(No, because made-up stories also have illustrations.)*

  Why is it helpful to see Susan's photograph instead of an illustration? *(We can see real details in a photograph that tell us more about her.)*

- Use the Close Reading activity to have children examine similarities and differences between photographs and illustrations in more detail.
- Read aloud each question and Hint on Student Book page 142. Discuss the answers. *(SL.1.1; SL.1.2)*
- **Model writing your responses.** Write sample answers to each question in complete sentences. Have children write their own responses. *(L.1.1; L.1.2)*
- **Have children demonstrate understanding.** Read aloud the Turn and Talk activity. Encourage children to use evidence from the Close Reading discussion to support their ideas. Invite volunteers to share.

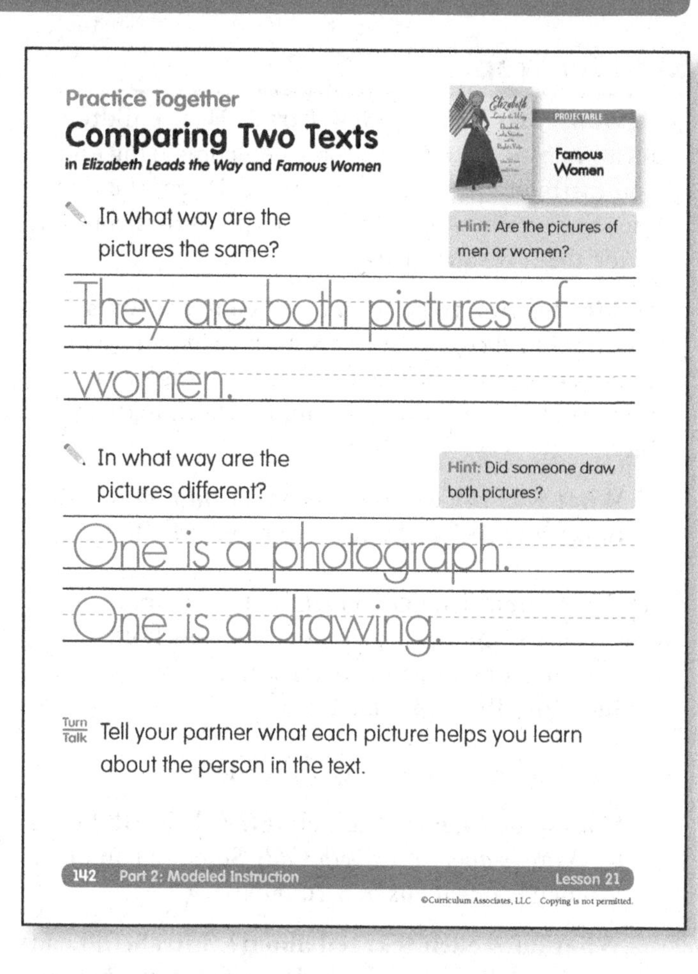

Close Reading

- Circulate and display the photograph of Elizabeth on page 3 of *Elizabeth Leads the Way.* Read aloud the writing on the bottom. Then prompt:

  What can we learn from this photograph? *(This is what Elizabeth looked like when she was 20 years old.)*

- Display the book cover once more. Prompt:

  How is this picture different? *(It is a drawing.)*

  What details do the drawing show that the photograph does not? *(Elizabeth is holding an American flag and wearing a sash that says "Vote for Women.")*

  How does the drawing help readers? *(It gives details about Elizabeth that are not in the photo.)*

- Discuss with children that photographs show true details, but illustrators can add key details to drawings that were not captured in any real photos.

Part 3: Guided Practice

Step by Step

- **Review Parts 1–2; preview Part 3.** Have children recall questions they can ask when comparing and contrasting texts on the same topic. Direct them to turn to Student Book page 143. Explain that you will guide them through this page.
- **Guide children to compare and contrast texts.** Display *Elizabeth Leads the Way* and *Famous Women.* Invite children to briefly recall key details in each text. Then prompt them to compare both texts in a big-picture way. *(RI.1.2)*

  What was the key idea, or most important idea, in both texts? *(fighting for women's right to vote)*

Tip: If children struggle to identify the common topic, use a Venn diagram to briefly review both texts. Then summarize the details they have in common into the topic statement.

- Prompt children to contrast the texts.

  Who does each text tell about? (Elizabeth Leads the Way *is about Elizabeth Cady Stanton;* Famous Women *is about Susan B. Anthony.)*

  What does each text tell about? (Elizabeth Leads the Way *tells about Elizabeth's early life and how she got the idea to help women vote;* Famous Women *tells about Susan B. Anthony as an adult and how she fought for women's right to vote.)*

- **Guide children to write responses.** Read aloud each question on Student Book page 143, along with the Hints. Have children write their answers in complete sentences. Answers may vary. *(L.1.1; L.1.2)*
- Use the Close Reading activity to compare and contrast information about the women in each text.
- **Have children demonstrate understanding.** Read aloud the Turn and Talk activity. Focus children's discussion with questions such as these:

  What did reading about Elizabeth help you understand about Susan?

  What did reading about Susan help you understand about Elizabeth?

- Invite children to share their responses in class discussion. *(SL.1.1; SL.1.2)*

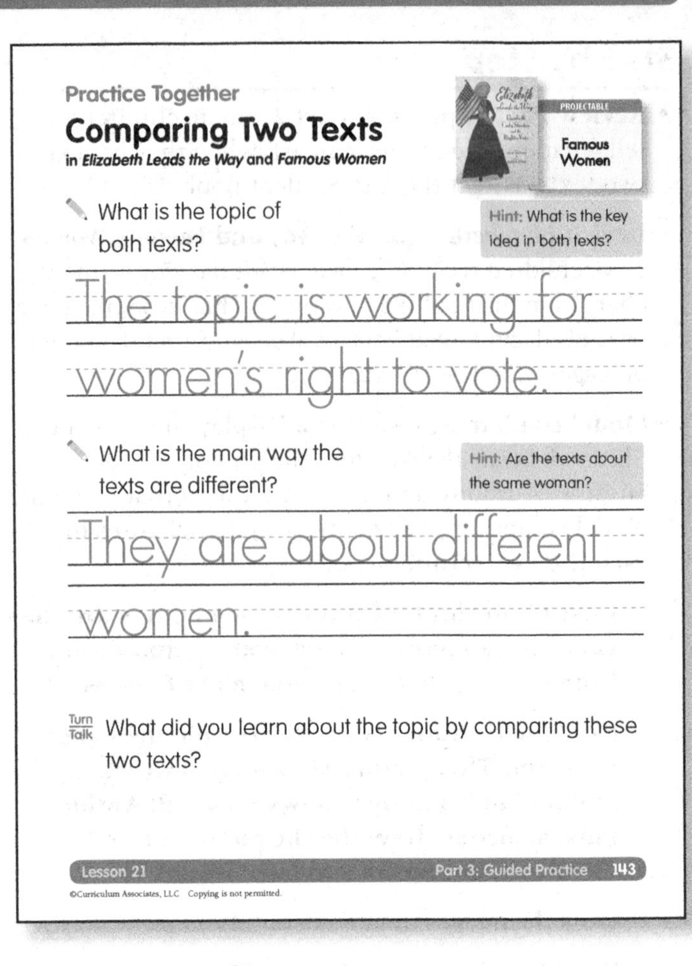

Close Reading

- Review the second paragraph of *Famous Women* on page 213. Then prompt:

  What words do you hear over and over? (both *and* agreed)

  What key idea do these repeating words tell about Susan and Elizabeth? *(They felt the same way about many things: women were not being treated fairly; the laws should be changed; and women should have the right to vote.)*

  Compare and contrast the information in this paragraph to *Elizabeth Leads the Way.* *(Both texts tell about how Elizabeth feels about women's rights, but* Elizabeth Leads the Way *does not tell about Susan B. Anthony at all.)*

- Point out that reading about Susan helps children understand that other women believed the same things as Elizabeth did, and that it took a lot of people a long time to change women's rights.

Part 4: Independent Practice

Step by Step

- **Review Parts 1–3; preview Part 4.** Invite a volunteer to tell why it is helpful to compare and contrast two texts on the same topic. Then direct children to Student Book page 144.
- Display *Elizabeth Leads the Way* and *Famous Women*. Explain that children will now compare the texts independently. Point out that the questions on this page are like those on the previous pages—the first asks about one way the texts are alike; the second asks about one way they are different.
- **Have children compare texts independently.** Read aloud the first question on Student Book page 144. Then have children listen for the answer as you reread "The Right to Vote" on page 214 of *Famous Women* and the Author's Note on page 32 of *Elizabeth Leads the Way*.
- Use the Close Reading activity to find specific text evidence that will help children answer the question.
- Have children write their answers in complete sentences. *(L.1.1; L.1.2)*
- Read aloud the second question. Then have children listen for the answer as you reread "A Special Coin" on page 214 of *Famous Women* and the third paragraph of the Author's Note on page 32 of *Elizabeth Leads the Way*.
- Reread the question, and read the Hint. Have children write their answers in complete sentences.

Tip: Consider providing additional paper for children who want to describe how Elizabeth was honored.

- **Have children demonstrate understanding.** Read aloud the Turn and Talk activity. Encourage children to look back at their Student Book pages for help in recalling details they compared in both texts. Then ask volunteers to share their ideas. *(SL.1.1; SL.1.2)*
- **Have children reflect on their learning.** Guide children in a discussion about how comparing two texts on the same topic helps them better understand the topic. Encourage them to use specific examples from this lesson. Chart their ideas.

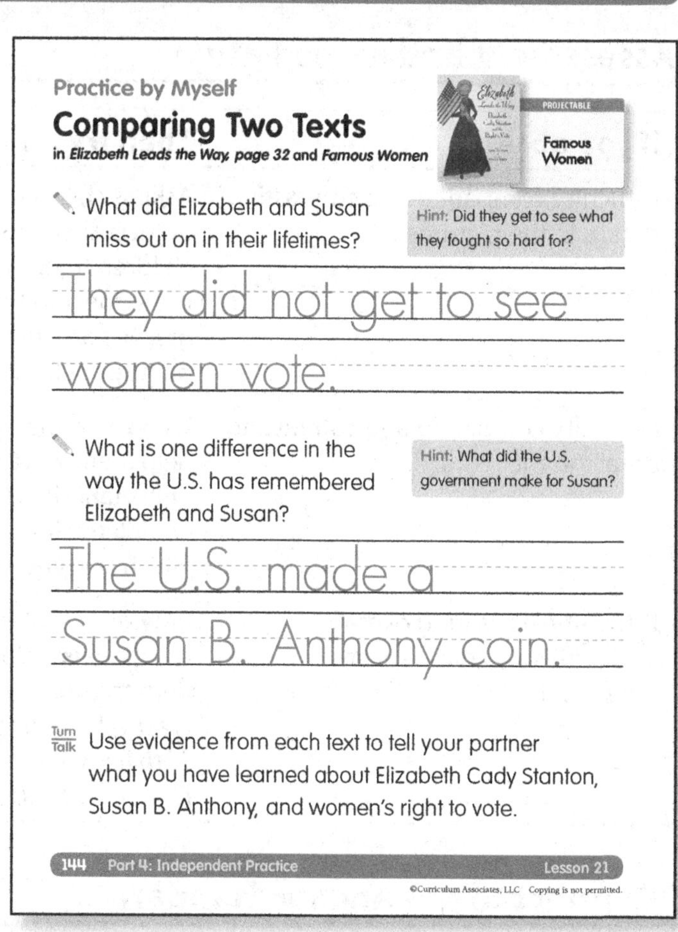

Close Reading

- Remind children that readers need to use text evidence to support their ideas.
- Reread "The Right to Vote" from page 214 of *Famous Women*. Then display the time line and ask:

  What details tell us that Susan died before women had the right to vote? *(The words tell us, and the time line shows that she died in 1906 and women got the right to vote in 1920.)*

- Then revisit the last paragraph on page 32 of *Elizabeth Leads the Way*. Ask:

  What details tell us that Elizabeth died before women had the right to vote? *(She died in 1902 and women got the right to vote in 1920.)*

- Discuss how focusing on and comparing these details in both texts helps children understand a key idea about the fight for women's right to vote.

Differentiated Instruction

Assessment and Remediation

If you observe . . .	Then try . . .
Difficulty comparing and contrasting details in the pictures	Asking children to compare and contrast two familiar objects. Choose objects such as a clock and a watch or a sweater and a jacket. Encourage children to name specific details in order to describe how the objects are the same and how they are different. Help them record their ideas in a graphic organizer such as a Venn diagram. Then begin practicing on simple pictures of familiar scenes, such as farms or playgrounds.
Difficulty comparing and contrasting details in the words	Using a simple diagram. Show children how to trace around one hand. Then help them write the topic of the text in the palm of the hand, and the five most important details on each finger and the thumb. After a diagram has been completed for each text, ask them which ideas are presented in both texts and which are presented in only one.
Difficulty expressing overall similarities and differences between texts	Providing sentence frames such as the following that children can use to compare and contrast: *Both texts have pictures that______.* *[Text 1] has a picture of______, but [Text 2] doesn't.* *Both texts tell about______.* *[Text 1] text tells about______, but [Text 2] doesn't.*

Connect to the Anchor Standard

R9: *Analyze how two or more texts address similar themes or topics in order to build knowledge or to compare the approaches the authors take.*

In mastering Standard 9 throughout the grades, students move from comparing and contrasting specific elements within two texts on the same topic to integrating different types of information from several texts in order to write or speak knowledgeably about a topic. As they move up the grades, students are expected not just to notice similarities and differences between texts but to evaluate how the differences make one text stronger than another. As they learn the importance of seeking out more than one source of information about a topic, they will ask questions about the texts such as these: *How does each author present the topic? How are the illustrations or descriptions similar or different? Which text is clearer? What makes it clearer?* Use the following activities to help your students begin transitioning toward these ways of thinking.

- Point out that two purposes of *Elizabeth Leads the Way* and *Famous Women* are to help readers get to know a person and to tell facts about women who worked for all women's right to vote. Ask: *Which purpose was more important to the author of* Elizabeth Leads the Way? *How do you know?* Repeat the questions for *Famous Women*. Discuss how the different purposes help to explain some of the differences between the details included in the texts.
- Explain that texts about events that happened long ago often feature illustrations because photographs did not exist before 1816. Show an example of more realistic illustrations than those in *Elizabeth Leads the Way*. Ask children which images—cartoonish, realistic, or photographic—they would find more useful in different situations, and why. Ask: *Which might be more helpful for finding facts? Which might help you understand an author's point of view?*

Introduction

Before administering the Unit 6 Check, you may wish to briefly review with children the multiple-choice test-taking tips they have learned in Units 1–5.

Guide children through the strategies they have learned to answer multiple-choice questions:

> **If you are not sure about an answer, remember that one of the choices is always correct. You can also look back at the text to help you decide. Look for words from the question that are also in the text.**
>
> **Be sure to read the whole question and all of the answer choices before you select an answer.**
>
> **Decide which words in the question are the most important. Underline those key words in the question.**
>
> **When answering a question about the meaning of a word, check your answer by plugging it into the sentence. Reread the sentence with your answer choice in place of the word. If the answer does not seem to make sense in the sentence, then it is probably not correct. Then reread the sentence with another answer choice plugged in. If the sentence makes sense, then your answer is possibly correct.**
>
> **To remember the order of events in a text, first think about whether the events only make sense in one order. Think about whether it is possible to have one thing happen before another. Then go back to the text and find the events. Notice what order they happen in.**
>
> **Sometimes, you'll be asked to find what is the same or different between two texts. To find the right answer, it's always a good idea to look back at both texts. You can use your fingers to skim, or run quickly over the text, until you find key words from the question. Then reread the whole paragraph where you found the key words to get all the important details.**

Step by Step

- Revisit Projectable 4, *Famous Women: Susan B. Anthony.* Invite children to retell important facts about Susan B. Anthony.
- Review key details in *Elizabeth Leads the Way.* Encourage children to retell important details.

Unit 6 Check

Listen closely as your teacher reads. Then answer the questions.

Read this key point from **Famous Women: Susan B. Anthony**.

> **"Finally, in 1920, a new law was passed. Women had the right to vote! People knew Susan's work had made it possible."**

What reason does the author give to explain how Susan's work helped women win the right to vote?

A Susan listened to the famous speech at Seneca Falls, New York.

B Susan showed Elizabeth Cady Stanton that women must be treated fairly.

(C) Susan gave speeches to say that women should be able to vote.

What is special about the Susan B. Anthony coin?

(A) It is the first U.S. coin to have a woman's face on it.

B It can be used to pay for trips around the country.

C It shows that people still listen to her speeches.

145

- Have children follow along as you read aloud the directions on page 145 of their Student Books.
- Then read aloud one or more pages from the text, as specified below, before having children complete each item. Display the appropriate pages for children to view while they read and answer each question.
- For items 1 and 2, reread the last two paragraphs on page 213 and all of page 214 of *Famous Women: Susan B. Anthony;* display the photograph of the coin on page 214.
- For items 3 and 4, reread pages 20–31 of *Elizabeth Leads the Way*; display the illustration on pages 30–31.

Note: Read aloud each question, answer choice, and Hint before directing children to answer it.

- When children have finished, reread each question and discuss the correct answer. Point to evidence in the text and pictures. Then use the Answer Analysis to discuss the correct answer.

Answer Analysis

1 This item requires children to identify a reason the author gives to support an important point made about Susan B. Anthony. ***(RI.1.8)***

The best answer is choice C, "Susan gave speeches to say that women should be able to vote." This is the only detail that we read about Susan's work. Neither choice A nor choice B is an accurate fact from the text. Susan did not attend the speech at Seneca Falls, New York, and the text said that she and Elizabeth Cady Stanton already agreed about how women should be treated.

2 This item asks children to describe a key idea using text details and a photograph. ***(RI.1.7)***

The best answer is choice A, "It is the first coin to have a woman's face on it." The text says that Susan was the first woman to receive this honor. Choice B might seem possible but the coin is not special for this reason, so choice B is incorrect. Choice C is incorrect because there is no connection between using the coin and listening to Susan's speeches. Susan's coin is special because it honored her work and was an important "first" for women.

3 This item requires children to interpret an important point the author makes about Elizabeth Cady Stanton and then identify a reason given to support it. (***RI.1.8***)

The best answer is choice C, "She changed people's ideas about women having the right to vote." The text explains many of Elizabeth's ideas about how women were not treated fairly and the need to change the laws. It also tells how she figures out the best way to do this—by working to get women the right to vote. Neither choice A nor choice B is a detail that is described in the text, so neither can be a description of the way Elizabeth changed America.

Unit 6 Check

Read one key point the author makes in **Elizabeth Leads the Way**.

Elizabeth changed America forever.

What reason does the author give to explain how Elizabeth changed America?

A She changed people's ideas about cooking, mending, and doing dishes.

B She changed people's ideas about the best way to hold a meeting.

Ⓒ She changed people's ideas about women having the right to vote.

Write one way that Susan B. Anthony and Elizabeth Cady Stanton were alike.

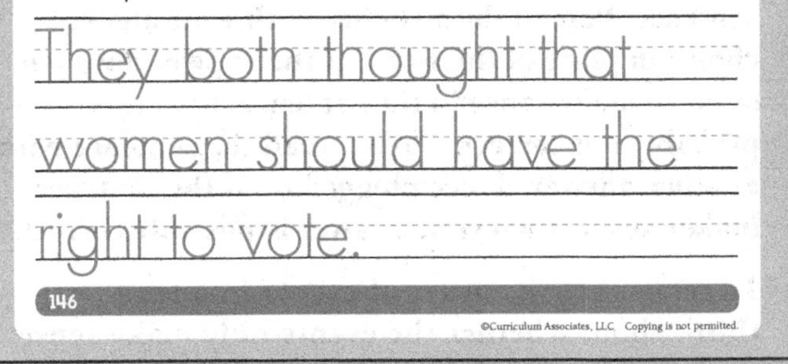

146

4 This item asks children to explain in writing an important similarity between two famous women, as described in texts on the same topic. ***(RI.1.9)***

Sample Response: They both thought that women shoud have the right to vote.

The two texts tell about two different women who made history: Elizabeth Cady Stanton and Susan B. Anthony. Both texts describe how each woman worked hard to change people's ideas about women's rights. Both Elizabeth and Susan fought to get women the right to vote.

Happy Birthday Surprise!

by Stephen Krensky

Abel was a very excited mouse. Today was his friend Daisy's birthday. And he was giving her a surprise party.

Abel started to clean his house. He wiped and cleaned and wiped again. A small cloud of dust followed him around.

"Achoooo!" sneezed Abel. "Achooo! Achooo!"

It was already past noon. "Oh, dear!" said Abel. He still had to bake the cake. He quickly mixed the eggs, flour, and sugar in a bowl.

"Sweet," said Abel, tasting the batter.

Once the cake was in the oven, he started wrapping Daisy's present. The paper went on easily. But the bow wouldn't stay tied.

Abel kept trying. His face got hot. His whiskers twitched.

"Hello? Is anyone home?"

Abel's friend Chester had arrived.

"What are you doing here so early?" asked Abel.

"I came to help you get ready."

"What makes you think I need help?" asked Abel. He felt a little embarrassed that he was so far behind.

Chester looked around. The house was still a mess.

"Just a wild guess," he said. "What's that burning smell?"

"Oh, no!" cried Abel.

He rushed into the kitchen. Smoke was pouring from the oven.

"This is terrible! The cake is ruined!"

"Don't worry," said Chester. "We still have time to make another. Why didn't you ask me for help earlier?"

"I thought I could do everything myself."

"Well," said Chester, "I hope you know better now."

Abel nodded. "From now on, I'll always ask for help when I need it."

"Surprise birthday parties are a lot of work," said Chester.

Abel smiled. "And that was the real surprise for me!"

Sometimes

by Laura Hidalgo

Sometimes I get a feeling.
When I go out to play,
I smile a lot and scream and shout
And laugh the day away.

5 Sometimes I get a feeling.
When I'm stuck inside all day,
I stomp my feet and frown and scowl
And pout the day away.

Sometimes I get a feeling.
10 When I can't get my way,
I fight the tears and whine and sigh
And mope the day away.

Sometimes I get a feeling.
When my birthday comes in May,
15 I wake up early and wait and wait
And watch the clock all day.

If I scream or shout or stomp or pout,
or whine or frown or play,
I still get the same feeling (YAWN)
20 At the end of every day.

I'm Staying Home From School Today

by Kenn Nesbitt, Revenge of the Lunch Ladies

I'm staying home from school today.
I'd rather be in bed
pretending that I have a pain
that's pounding in my head.

5 I'll say I have a stomach ache.
I'll claim I've got the flu.
I'll shiver like I'm cold
and hold my breath until I'm blue.

I'll fake a cough. I'll fake a sneeze.
10 I'll say my throat is sore.
If necessary I can throw
a tantrum on the floor.

I'm sure I'll get away with it.
Of that, there's little doubt.
15 But, even so, I really hope
my students don't find out.

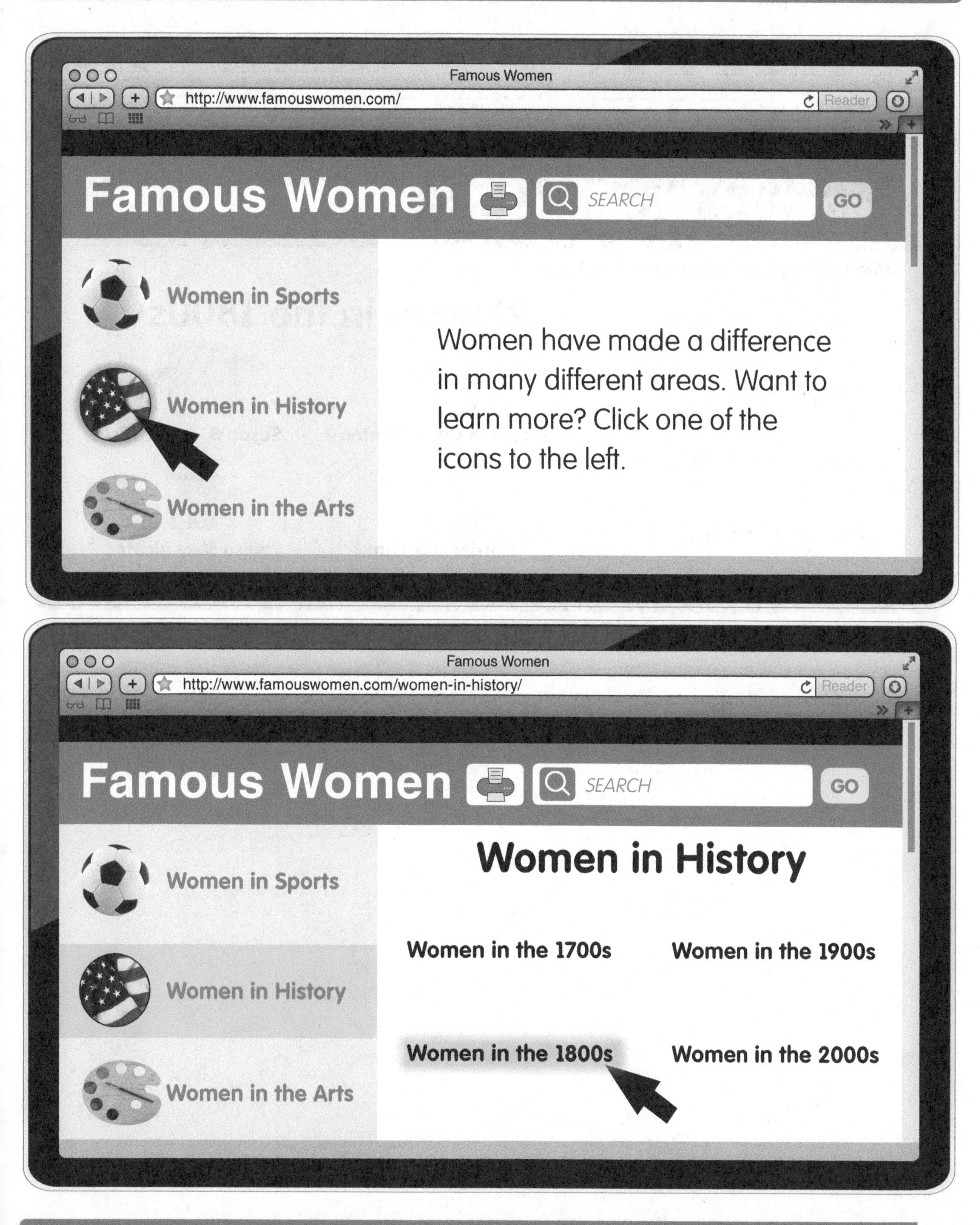
Famous Women
http://www.famouswomen.com/
Reader
Famous Women
SEARCH
GO
Women in Sports
Women in History
Women in the Arts
Women have made a difference in many different areas. Want to learn more? Click one of the icons to the left.
Famous Women
http://www.famouswomen.com/women-in-history/
Reader
Famous Women
SEARCH
GO
Women in Sports
Women in History
Women in the Arts
Women in History
Women in the 1700s
Women in the 1900s
Women in the 1800s
Women in the 2000s

Projectable 4

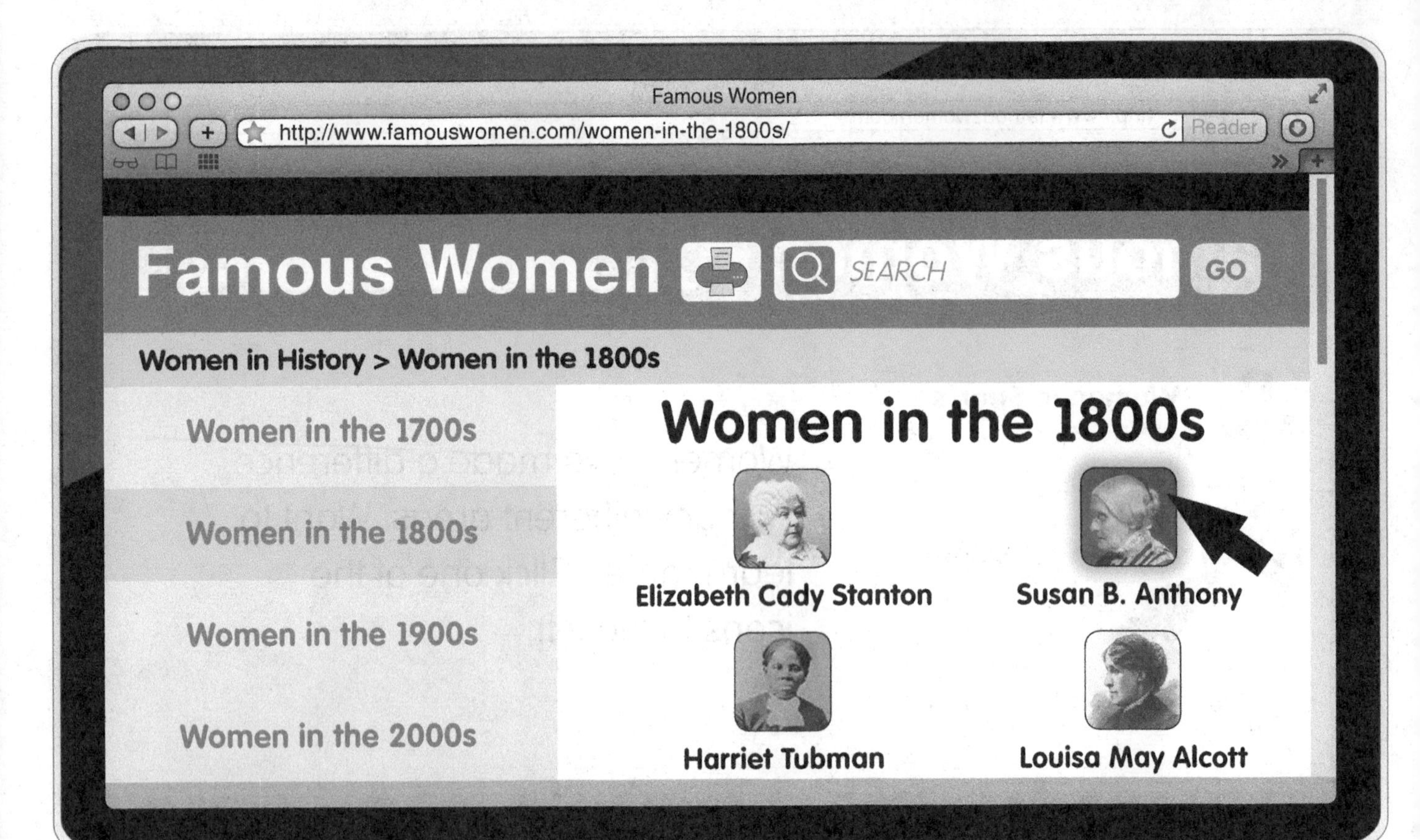

Susan B. Anthony

Susan B. Anthony was not at Seneca Falls, New York, in 1848. She did not hear Elizabeth Cady Stanton give her famous speech. But when Susan met Elizabeth three years later, she knew she had met a friend.

The two had so much in common! Both Susan and Elizabeth agreed that women were not being treated fairly. Both agreed that laws should be changed. And both agreed that, most definitely, women should have the right to vote.

Soon Susan added her voice to Elizabeth's. They worked hard to get everyone to understand their ideas. Susan traveled all around the country, giving speeches and writing about her feelings on women's rights.

Many men and women listened to what Susan had to say. But not everyone agreed with her. Some people yelled and threw things. Once, Susan was even arrested by the police. This did not stop her.

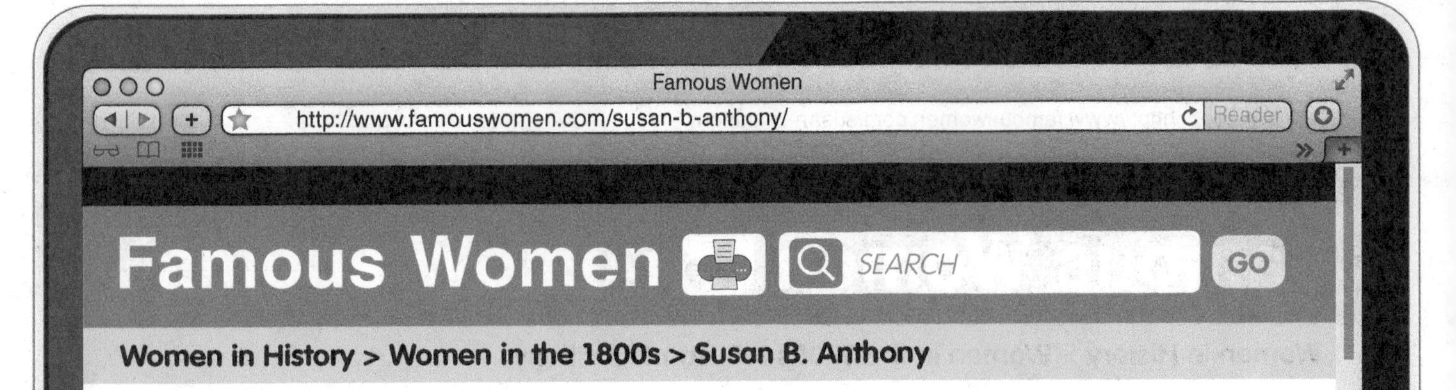

The Right to Vote

Year after year, Susan continued her work. And little by little, she convinced many people that women should be able to vote. But the lawmakers did not agree. When Susan died, women still did not have the right to vote. But her dream lived on. Other people worked to make it come true.

Finally, in 1920, a new law was passed. Women had the right to vote! People knew Susan's work had made it possible.

A Special Coin

Years later, the United States government made a coin with Susan's picture on it. She was the first woman to receive such an honor. And most likely, seeing this change in tradition would have made Susan quite proud.

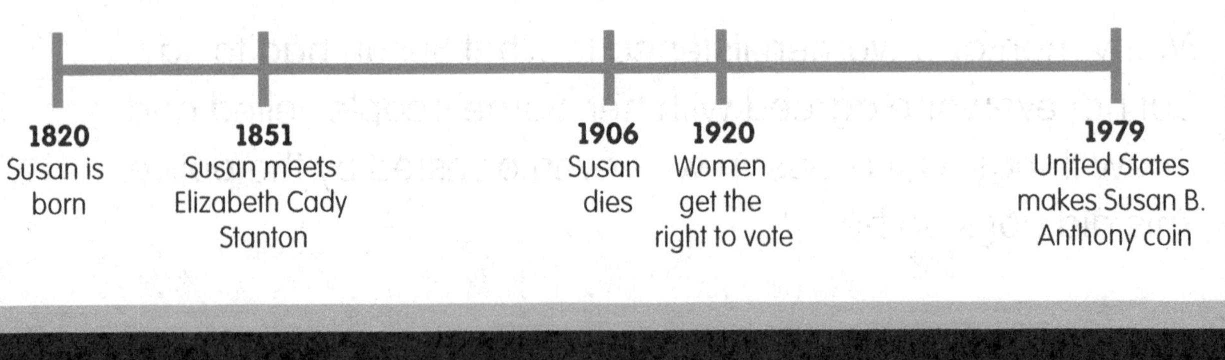

Upsetting the Balance

by David Fein

How are acorns, squirrels, and hawks connected? They are links in a food chain. How are grass, cows, and the cheese we eat connected? They, too, are links in a food chain. And food chains are important to all living things.

But, what's a food chain? Picture it as a set of links. Each link is a plant or animal that becomes a meal for the next. All living things in a food chain—even people—depend on another "link" for food.

Sometimes, though, the choices we make can cause trouble for plants, animals, and people, too. Sometimes we end up "breaking" the food chain, or at least changing it.

For many years, fishermen caught large sharks. They are at the top of a food chain and eat many things, including cownose rays. In turn, the cownose rays eat clams and other shellfish.

Once, this food chain was in balance, but then fishermen caught too many sharks. With fewer sharks hunting them, the number of cownose rays grew. And more rays ate more shellfish.

Soon shellfish became hard to find. Fishermen who caught shellfish began to suffer. There just weren't enough shellfish. Now the fishermen can't make enough money to live. And other creatures that eat shellfish may go hungry. That's a big problem!

What should people do to solve problems like these? How can we help and not harm other living creatures? We need to think about what we do and make wise choices. Careful choices can help keep the balance in nature. Keeping the balance helps all the living things that share our planet.

Cover Image Credits

p. 3: Demi, author and illustrator, THE EMPTY POT. Published by Henry Holt and Company, LLC., an imprint of Macmillan, 1990. Used by permission of Henry Holt and Company, LLC.

p. 9: Lydia Dabcovich, jacket illustrations, THE POLAR BEAR SON: AN INUIT TALE. Jacket illustration copyright © 1997 by Lydia Dabcovich. Used by permission of Houghton Mifflin Harcourt Publishing Company. All rights reserved.

p. 21: Patricia Polacco, author and illustrator, MY ROTTEN REDHEADED OLDER BROTHER. Copyright © 1994 by Patricia Polacco. Reprinted by permission of Simon & Schuster Books For Young Readers, an Imprint of Simon & Schuster Children's Publishing Division. All rights reserved.

p. 33: Cover of MICE AND BEANS by Pam Munoz Ryan, illustrated by Joe Cepeda. Illustrations copyright © 2001 by Joe Cepeda. Reprinted by permission of Scholastic Inc.

p. 61: Holly Keller, illustrator, WHO EATS WHAT? FOOD CHAINS AND FOOD WEBS. Published by HarperCollins, 1994. Used by permission of HarperCollins Publishers.

p. 67: Cover from BUTTERFLIES AND MOTHS by Nic Bishop. Copyright © 2009 by Nic Bishop. Reprinted by permission of Scholastic Inc.

p. 85: Rebecca Gibbon, illustrator, ELIZABETH LEADS THE WAY: ELIZABETH CADY STANTON AND THE RIGHT TO VOTE. Published by Henry Holt and Company, LLC., an imprint of Macmillan, 2010. Used by permission of Henry Holt and Company, LLC.

p. 107: Virginia Lee Burton, illustrator and author, MIKE MULLIGAN AND HIS STEAM SHOVEL. Copyright © 1939 by Virginia Lee Burton. Copyright © renewed 1967 by Virginia Lee Demetrios. Used by permission of Houghton Mifflin Harcourt Publishing Company. All rights reserved.

p. 135: Barrie Watts, photographs, EARTHWORMS. Photographs copyright © 2000 by Barrie Watts. All rights reserved. Reprinted by permission of Franklin Watts, an imprint of Scholastic Library Publishing, Inc.

Photo Credits

p. A11: Lisovskaya Natalia/Shutterstock

p. 211: Smileus/Fotolia.com

p. 211: Marius Graf/Fotolia.com

p. 211: klikk/Fotolia.com

pp. 211–214: Photo-K/Fotolia.com

p. 212: Library of Congress, Printers and Photographs Division LC-USZ62-28195

p. 212: Library of Congress, Printers and Photographs Division LC-USZ62-7816

p. 212: Library of Congress, Printers and Photographs Division LC-USZ61-452

pp. 212–213: Library of Congress, Printers and Photographs Division LC-USZ62-46713

p. 214: Scott Rothstein/Shutterstock